U. S. S. R.

an Bator

MANCHURIA

• Tsitsihar

• Harbin

LIA

(GOLIA)

CHAHAR

JEHOL

• Mukden

MONGOLIA

KOREA

SUIYUAN

THE GREAT WALL

Peking
Tientsin
Tsinghai
HOPEH

SHANSI

• Yenan

HWANG HO (YELLOW R.)

• Tsinan
SHANTUNG

Port Arthur
Weihaiwei

Inchon

Pusan

Tsingtao

YELLOW SEA

SHENSI

• Sian

Kaifeng
HONAN

KIANGSU

• Ankang

HUPEH

YANGTZE KIANG

Hankow

ANHWEI

Wuhu Nanking
Soochow Shanghai

Anking

Ningpo

EAST CHINA
SEA

nking

Yochow
Nanchang
Changsha
KIANGSI

Kukiang

CHEKIANG

HUNAN

Foochow

MATSU

AN

Kweilin

FUKIEN

KWANGSI

Yungnan

PEH R.

Amoy

QUEMOY

TAIWAN

SI R.

KWANGTUNG

Canton

Hong Kong

Macao

Kwang-chow-wan

SOUTH CHINA SEA

Miles
0   100   200   300

Books by Emily Hahn

Mainstream of the Modern World Series

EDITED BY JOHN GUNTHER

CHINA ONLY YESTERDAY: 1850–1950

The Mainstream of

DOUBLEDAY & COMPANY, INC.

he Modern World

CHINA
ONLY YESTERDAY:
1850-1950
A CENTURY OF CHANGE

by Emily Hahn

Garden City, New York

Library of Congress Catalog Card Number 62–11301
Copyright © 1963 by Emily Hahn Boxer
All Rights Reserved
Printed in the United States of America
First Edition

ACKNOWLEDGMENTS

I should like to thank those who helped me with this book, most particularly two former members of China's Customs Service. G. R. G. Worcester lent me books and suggested many sources. Rolla Rouse, who was a Commissioner of Customs from 1923 to 1950, not only gave me the run of his valuable collection of material dealing with Customs affairs, but read the manuscript carefully, pointing out errors and referring me to the proper authorities with which to check the facts. It was a time-consuming task, and I am very grateful to Mr. Rouse.

Mainstream of the Modern World Series

EDITED BY JOHN GUNTHER

CHINA ONLY YESTERDAY: 1850–1950

Chapter One

William Hickey was a very young man when he stopped off in China in 1769, coming home after his first voyage to India, but even then he was a good observer. The amiable chatterbox he became in his old age gave a vivid picture in his memoirs of the peculiar life he shared in Canton with his compatriots for those few weeks. To be sure, it wasn't the true China that he saw. The "factory" district, i.e., the place of foreign factors, or traders, was a fringe of flat land squeezed in between the city wall and the river, and this site, with the row of long narrow buildings that nearly filled it, was the only mainland ground on which the Red Hairs were permitted to set foot. Now and then they went to some island for a picnic; the sailors from their ships, in fact, *had* to take shore leave on certain islands. But the city of Canton, and the ordinary land of China, must not be entered. The country's rulers did not wish their people to be perverted by foreign devils. They trusted only a few merchants and a severely restricted number of domestic servants to have dealings with the dwellers in the factories. On one occasion the high-spirited Hickey broke the rules and went through a gate in the wall into the city. Children threw stones at him, and he was glad to get back to the East India Company territory where he lodged and had his meals with Company officers, ships' captains, and supercargoes, as the business managers of imports and exports were called. The East India Company held the monopoly of foreign trade in China. Hickey made no mention of what must have been a strange sight to his inexperienced eyes—the great walls of the City of Rams, the teeming narrow streets, the gaily painted boards or silk banners that advertised a shop's wares, and the pigtailed, shaven-pated men, clacking about the cobbled streets in clogs or moving softly in slippers.

He seems to have enjoyed his sojourn in the factory. He said that the Company people were hospitable and that he had luxurious, spacious quarters. He saw their warehouses, and the studios where they kept workmen busy preparing the articles that were to be shipped back to Europe. The British and other Europeans bought tea from the Chinese, and silk, china, nankeen (a kind of cotton cloth), and sago. In return they sold woolen cloth and metal, pepper and other spices from the isles of the Indies, and light cotton cloth and opium—though the East India Company never dealt in this commodity—from India, making up the difference with silver bullion and coins, usually Spanish dollars. They seem to have been blasé about the Chinese rarities they shipped home and sold so profitably, judging from one of William Hickey's anecdotes. He had made friends with a thirteen-year-old boy who was serving an apprenticeship in the factory.

"Bob Pott passed most of his time in our rooms, generally coming before I was up of a morning. He breakfasted with us, and if he took it into his head that McClintock was too long at a meal, or drank too much tea, he without the least ceremony overset the table. The first time he practiced this, I was very angry at such a quantity of handsome china being thus mischievously demolished, and expressed my displeasure thereat, which only excited the mirth of young pickle. 'Why, zounds!' said he, 'you surely forget where you are. I never suffer the servants to have the trouble of removing a tea equipage, always throwing the whole apparatus out of window or down stairs. They easily procure another batch from the steward's warehouse.'"

Hickey met and talked with only a very few Chinese—business acquaintances of his hosts—and decided that he liked none of the race. He took for gospel all he was told by the other foreigners, and naturally embraced their prejudices. He marveled at Chinese superstition, retailing several extraordinary anecdotes to illustrate their stupidity and ineptness. Though he was ill-informed and unfair in his judgment he was not high-handed in his attitude: like his friends he seems to have thought of these strange natives as unpleasant but not exactly inferior. The foreigners didn't look down on the Chinese. After all, they were scarcely in a position to do so. The boot was on the other foot; Chinese did look down on Westerners, as they did on all non-Chinese except the Manchus who were their overlords—and no doubt some high scholar-officials dared to do even that, in their

heart of hearts. In their estimation the Western traders were barbarians of low degree; they were traders, the lowest class of Chinese
civilization, where mankind was divided into four main groups—
scholars, then in descending quality farmers, workmen, and, last of
all, merchants. That the Emperor and government made much profit
from the taxes paid on barbarian trade had no softening effect whatever on their opinion of the barbarians. Of course the Chinese
merchants who did the actual bartering were in favor of the traders,
as far as they dared to show their feelings, but this was merely a
question of like understanding like, and they were not the lawmakers.

China, Chinese thought, the Chinese code of behavior, were conservative to a degree that the West could scarcely comprehend, let
alone appreciate. The officials who advised the Emperor realized
that their tight system would be pushed off balance if they permitted Western ideas to infiltrate. These tiresome, noisy, ill-bred
Europeans with their drunken sailors were not only offensive, but
representative of the danger of the unknown. For years they had
tried to get in, but the Chinese and Manchus still kept them mewed
up in one bit of land outside Canton's walls, over two thousand miles
from Peking. And however badly they were treated they never went
away altogether, which—though the Chinese and Manchus would
never have admitted it—was a good thing, since a total disappearance of Westerners would have embarrassed the administration
financially, and been the ruin of a great number of officials who
collected "squeeze" from the trade. Fortunately those peculiar Westerners had such an overpowering lust for trade that they seemed
capable of swallowing any amount of discouragement.

Of the Western nations who tried their hands at Far East trade,
Britain was the acknowledged leader. By means of the East India
Company it had held that position since 1715, the Company extending protective wings over the independent "country trade"—
plying between India, the East Indies, and China—as well. Certainly the British were kingpins when Hickey was there. They held
the biggest share of factory space, but there was little bad blood
between nationalities on that account, for they were banded together by necessity and their many common grievances. The restraint under which they lived was notorious. According to the Eight
Regulations imposed by the Chinese Viceroy (the Governor General of Kwangtung) and his colleagues, no foreign devil could stay

in Canton the year round, or any time except the season, from September to March, when tea and raw silk were brought down to the coast for sale. For the rest of the year the merchants must withdraw to Macao, which the Portuguese occupied not quite independently of Chinese supervision. In many ways, it must be admitted, the withdrawal was a good thing for the foreign devil's state of mind, for in the Canton factory he was practically in prison. He could not stray outside the factory limits, though on three days of the year, if properly chaperoned and in a party, he might visit one of the islands nearby. But even there he must not fraternize with the natives. Foreign devils could not keep arms, nor must their warships enter the Pearl River. Wives and families must not ever visit the factories. No women at all were permitted. While Hickey was there, all loading of foreign ships was suspended for a time because one of the captains was caught in the act of smuggling ashore "a smart little Madras girl" disguised as a boy. A Company man, on the subject of the best-known rule, observed to Hickey that the fact that no Europeans were ever allowed to pass the gates of the city was a circumstance "little to be regretted, because in fact there was nothing in Canton worth seeing." This sounds like sour grapes, but he was voicing an honest opinion held by most people in the Company.

      *   *   *

Though it is not strictly true, as the Chinese claim, that China always absorbs her conquerors, it is probably as accurate a statement as the other good old cliché, that history repeats itself. Both these slogans, like most of their kind, need qualifying. There is enough similarity between some of Cathay's cycles to give the aid and comfort of such thoughts to Chinese when they are in the process of being conquered, and are unhappy about it. The truth lies rather in a concept of China and her conquerors, like two noble metals lying close to each other, being miscible, silver soaking into gold for a slight depth at the surface, and vice versa. Since the dark, misty period when there was—perhaps—a state in China called the Hsia Kingdom, down to the Ch'ing Dynasty, there were periods when the Flowery Kingdom was subjected to such experience, when a strange race came in and took over the power. Five of these periods were lengthy. The T'o-pa, who were a Turkish people, moved from the north in the fourth century A.D., and imposed barbarian

rule until the middle of the sixth century, as the T'o-pa Wei Dynasty. In 907 the Tartar Ch'i-tan came—again from the north—and
stayed (the Liao Dynasty) more than two hundred years, holding
firmly to a large portion of the country, until they became civilized
and weakened. When they were overrun by another lot of barbarians called the Ju-chen, forerunners of the Manchus, the Ch'i-tan
could not defend themselves and went under. The Ju-chen (Chin
Dynasty) also took eagerly to Chinese ways and adapted themselves to civilization, but for some reason they were not so debilitated
as their predecessors, and put up a stout fight against Genghiz Khan
when he led his Mongols against them. However, Genghiz had his
way ultimately, and the Yuan Dynasty that he founded persisted
until well into the fourteenth century. Doubtless the Chinese told
themselves, all that time, that China always absorbs her conquerors,
but in 1368 the rule of the Mongol was at last thrown off. The Ming
Dynasty was Chinese, and it ruled—with considerable glory—until
invaders showed up in the seventeenth century: the Tartars, called
Manchus, who took over in 1644. They held on with tenacity. They
were still in power when the Red Hair barbarians from the West,
of whom some had already found foothold in Macao and Formosa,
began arriving in force from the sea, clamoring for permission to
trade in China without hindrance. By 1770 the Manchus, inevitably,
were much Sinicized, and had taken on certain Chinese ideas, particularly that one of holding all barbarians well away for as long as
possible. This Ch'ing Dynasty was no longer strong, but on the face
of it the structure still looked sound enough; certainly the Emperor
and his courtiers, both Manchu and Chinese, felt capable of living
in the traditional way, aloof from strangers. For their class, time was
standing still. They were not aware, or at least did not care, that
the world was shrinking. They must have known of British incur-
sions in India: though they disdained to show any concern of what
barbarians might be doing to each other out there, the knowledge
must have strengthened Imperial determination—if strengthening
were needed—never to run the risk of similar invasions at home.

After two hundred years of Manchu rule the Emperor's Chinese
were apparently loyal to him, and satisfied with the way things were.
Certainly those of high rank had reason to be. Within limits they
had power—only a few of the highest posts were reserved strictly
for Manchus—and they flourished. Nevertheless there were misgivings in the land, as there had been since the conquest. A Chinese

Emperor was the Son of Heaven and ruled by Heavenly Mandate. When, or if, it became apparent that the Mandate had expired, the Emperor had to be replaced, by what the Western world would call rebellion. But what of a Manchu Emperor? Had he ever really held the Mandate, barbarian as he was by ancestry? There were Chinese who felt that he could not, and so should not be on the throne. Some of them believed firmly in a prophecy that was going the rounds, that he would be removed two hundred years after his dynasty mounted the throne: that time was approaching.

All the while the British, far away in a mysterious country of which Peking knew nothing and cared less, went on developing plans in which China figured largely. The West had taken kindly to tea-drinking, even when a high tax made it a costly pleasure. The more tea that was brought out of Canton, the more other people smuggled it into England, until in self-defense the legitimate importers persuaded the government to lower the tax and put the smugglers out of business. The smuggling did stop as a result of this action, and though for a while it went hard with the revenuers when they lost a large part of the tax income, consumption of tea promptly increased. In Canton thousands of chests were bought and loaded and sent back to England, and thousands of taels of silver (a tael is a Chinese ounce, then worth six shillings eightpence) went to pay the exporters of China—and the Chinese customs officials—and the dozens of hangers-on, each of whom had a cut—and, ultimately, the Emperor in Peking, who, with his officers, got the residue. There was so much tea buying that the Western merchants found themselves in need of silver and coins with which to pay. The situation lent fresh vigor to their chronic complaints of restraint of trade. If only they could get into the country and stimulate public desire for the things they could supply from Britain! Nobody in Canton needed British wool, but up north it could be bitterly cold; the inhabitants of Chihli and Shensi and Shantung would love woolen cloth, once they'd tried it out, and there were other products as well that the Western merchants were sure they could sell, if only they could get a chance. They could not believe that the Emperor really understood what they were after. They thought he was insulated by his courtiers, deceived as to the true nature of foreign hopes and desires. After all, China had not always been sealed off from the great world. The pertinacity of the British was due in part to their hope, too, that history might repeat itself.

The door had been slammed in their faces, over and over again, whenever they prized it open. But in the past, through side doors, other traders had got into the country, by way of the overland Silk Routes; what had been done once could be done again, surely? And there had been many missionaries. It was a foreign faith, Buddhism, that took such a firm hold of the Chinese that it survived in its adopted home long after its roots died off in India. Nestorian Christianity, modern Christianity, Islam, Judaism—they had all got in. There were Jesuits at Court until the Society was disbanded. The first British Embassy that reached Peking, in 1793, found its footsteps impeded the whole way by European Catholic missionaries. If those white men could get in, why not the merchants?

The traders never realized the full extent of Chinese contempt for them as traders. Intellectuals like the Jesuits did: they understood the mentality of their hosts, yet even Jesuit understanding was not proof, ultimately, against banishment. The traders persisted in assuming that all mankind cared, just as they themselves did, for profit pure and simple: they overrated the simplicity of the problem, and when the Embassy failed, in spite of all Macartney's polish and intelligence, to get what they wanted, they were still unwilling to give up. Indeed, they could not give up. The investors at home kept pushing them, demanding that they expand: they were between a strong force and a blank wall. Something had to give. In the end, it was the wall that gave, pushed down by the Opium War.

This celebrated war was, from one point of view, the opening wedge to China's modernization. It was also, of course, a blatantly immoral settlement of a problem that should never have been posed. There were other contributions to the war, apart from the opium trade—which in any case had, under cover, a great number of Chinese and Manchu connivers in the game, as well as foreigners. There was the awkward fact of Peking's flat refusal ever to consider any foreign nation on an equal basis. According to Chinese tradition, China was the center of the world, the Middle Kingdom, The People. The Emperor was the Son of Heaven. Therefore, no envoy from any barbarian country must approach him, save as an inferior creature, on bended knee. Lord Macartney refused to perform the *k'ou-t'ou*, the ceremony of knocking the head on the ground in the presence of a superior person: he was pardoned this gross breach of manners because as a barbarian he didn't know any better, but the incident did not help his cause—namely, the furtherance of trade relations between the two countries. In fairness it must be said that it probably didn't harm it either—the project was doomed from the start. The gifts he had brought as a courtesy from the British King to China's ruler were referred to in all exchanges by two terms. Macartney called them "presents." The Chinese and Manchus called them "tribute." Neither side would give in on this point, and though it seems a small one, it indicated the root of the matter.

Then there was the fathomless abyss that lay between Western and Oriental concepts of justice. Chinese notions of proper trial and punishment scandalized the foreigners. They were based on the security-group system, by which any man in a group, especially the leader, might be called upon to suffer for the crime of another member. Whenever a foreign sailor broke the law, the Chinese would demand someone, anyone, from the same ship or even the same fleet, to punish whether or not he happened to be guilty. The whole idea was so abhorrent to the Western mind that Canton's foreigners did not take it quite seriously until fantasy merged with reality in the *Lady Hughes* affair of 1784. At that early date a gunner aboard a Company ship, the *Lady Hughes,* while firing a salute, accidentally sank a little boat and drowned two minor Chinese officials. The authorities demanded that the British hand over the gunner. As he was innocent of any wrong intent, the British refused. The Chinese promptly arrested another Englishman who had nothing whatever to do with the ship, and put a stop to all trade. At last, after the Chinese had promised to give the gunner a fair trial, the British did hand him over. Immediately, the Chinese put him to death by strangulation, and the horrified British never got over the shock. Then too, as was well known, the Chinese tortured their prisoners to obtain confessions. Appalled, yet fascinated, Europeans at home collected pictures of the different methods of Chinese torture. British justice was not always tempered with mercy in those days—very seldom, in fact—but even the hardest-hearted British magistrate felt that this was going too far. Many people in the West, when they thought of China, associated the word first of all with summary decapitations and torture.

The situation was made all the worse by a total absence of any proper means of communication. For one thing, no important Chinese official would let an Outer Barbarian hold audience with him: the merchants simply could not get *at* the people who mattered. Nor were they able to send letters, save on very infrequent occasions.

At any rate, they didn't often have the means to write in Chinese—Chinese scholars wouldn't do it for them, and they themselves could neither write nor speak the country's tongue. In such circumstances, intercourse could hardly be said to flourish, and one can understand why some of the simplest facts of China's government should have remained unknown to the foreigners—as, for example, the arrangement of the Imperial Court, by which the Emperor, far from being the secluded, indifferent monarch the barbarians thought he must be, was a hard-working, knowledgeable man, fully informed of his country's affairs. He was not being kept by his officials from the barbarians: he didn't want to see them. But he knew they were there.

Few foreigners could speak any Chinese at all, before the Opium War: the exceptions were some Catholic missionaries, whose legacy from bygone days of religious tolerance in Peking was a knowledge of Mandarin. What was needed in the south, of course, was someone who could speak Cantonese, and read and write Chinese characters. Westerners believed Chinese to be incredibly difficult, a language that could be acquired only by especially gifted people. (It is odd how that notion has persisted, despite much proof to the contrary, down to the present day.) Naturally no highly placed Chinese bothered to learn English, Latin, or French; they left the study of foreign languages to lowly clerks and Christian converts. In such circumstances, the already imperfect rapport between China and the West was sometimes almost imperceptible. When the first British Embassy was being formed—the one that set out from England in 1787, but never arrived in Peking—the administration was hard put to it even to find an interpreter. Finally they acquired the only European deemed capable of handling the post: he was a Frenchman named Galbert. The envoy, Colonel Cathcart, died on the way, so the project was abandoned and the other members of the party came back: Galbert too died during the return voyage. Five years later the Macartney Embassy was sent out. The business of finding a new interpreter was far more complicated and lengthy than the search for the ambassador himself. Lord Macartney's friend Sir George Staunton went to France on purpose to acquire a new Galbert, but he failed to discover one. He asked around in other countries; he asked in Gothenburg, Copenhagen, and Lisbon, all in vain. Ultimately an Italian cardinal directed him to a mission in Naples, where he found a number of young Chinese converts studying for the priesthood, and managed to obtain the services of two of these youths, who could write not only their native language but Latin and Italian as well. Nevertheless, when the Embassy arrived in China Macartney depended heavily on the accomplishments of Staunton's son, a twelve-year-old boy who, on the voyage out, had learned to write a number of characters. This child was called on, several times, to make fair copies of the party's diplomatic papers, since no Chinese would put himself on record as aiding the barbarians in such a way—his calligraphy would be recognized, and himself punished for presumption amounting to blasphemy. The little Staunton boy was held in considerable awe by the rest of the party, as one might well suppose. Macartney was frankly amazed by his genius.

It was a capital offense for a Chinese to teach Chinese to a foreigner, and so the only Chinese language school was in Singapore. Nevertheless as the years went by, the shortage of linguists was somewhat relieved. Young Staunton himself helped to alleviate it when he grew up and made his career in the East. But interpreters were still at a premium for half a century. In 1834 Dr. Robert Morrison, a Protestant missionary who deliberately learned Chinese so that he might the better compete with the Catholic Church, was the only one employed by the East India Company (which was being forced to wind up its affairs in Canton that year, and to relinquish its monopoly), and he nearly had a breakdown from overwork.

All the elements of an explosion were there, waiting—friction from misunderstanding, as well as friction from a certain understanding which did not make for peaceful relations, quarrels over the meting out of justice, crowded, frustrating conditions for the Western barbarians, bland contempt on the part of the Manchu-Chinese, and the opium trade. That troublesome commodity was first brought in in small quantities, and was used more as a medicine than for pleasure, but the traders found it a convenient medium of exchange, and exchange was something they badly needed. They wanted Chinese produce, but the Chinese appetite for foreign produce was far less keen: they could use hard cash and silver, but only just so much Indian muslin and Indonesian spice. World fluctuations made it inconvenient for the British to keep on shoveling silver into China: they would have preferred to barter, but how could they if the Chinese would not take what they offered? If only they could get into the country and open it up, they said repeatedly, things would be different. They could then create a demand for their products, but that way was barred. There remained opium. The Chinese appetite for that, at least, grew as fast as the stuff was supplied, until the situation was reversed—when the Chinese hadn't enough tea or silk to pay for it, they began handing out silver, and the Emperor's financial experts took alarm at the outflow of currency. They investigated. They discovered that not only was opium disrupting their economic system; it was a dangerous poison as well. It was outlawed, and its further import forbidden. Thereafter the drug had to be smuggled. Addiction spread, and with it came corruption. The Chinese at Canton as well as the foreign traders made fortunes from aiding and abetting the business. Finally, in 1838, the administration determined to root out the evil once and for all. Since the men on the spot had proved curiously ineffective, they selected a Viceroy, the famous Imperial Commissioner Lin, and sent him to Canton. Lin, a man of probity, was firm and abrupt in his methods. Deaf to temptation, he demanded from the British all the opium then waiting at Lintin—the offshore island where it was stored—or aboard their ships. He got, and burned forthwith, twenty thousand chests of the drug, which the merchants later valued at anything from two to five million pounds' worth. One thing led to another, and before he realized it the war was on. As history knows, the British won, with an ease shameful to Chinese patriots. The Ch'ing had never before fought a foreign war. Their army was out of date, their navy laughably inadequate, and those Chinese who understood what had happened felt bitter.

In the resulting Treaty of Nanking, signed on August 29, 1842, the Western nations got what they wanted at last—five open treaty ports (Canton, Amoy, Ningpo, Shanghai, Foochow) in which they might live and do business, and full ownership of the island called Victoria, Hong Kong, which had already for some time served, unofficially as it were, as headquarters for the British. Missionaries, too, were to be permitted access to the treaty ports, with freedom to build houses of worship. From the Chinese point of view it might have been worse. The Red Hairs did not demand more territory. They proved, in the end, to have been sincere in their claims that all they wanted was freedom for trade. The hated symbol, opium, was still legally forbidden, but the barbarians insisted that the Emperor pay a large indemnity to meet the expenses of the war, and this his representatives agreed to. The Americans, who until then had left Britain to take the land—as was natural, since Britain held by far the greater interest in the affair—followed suit by making a separate treaty of their own, embodying much the same principles, plus the famous "most-favored-nation" clause, which decreed similar treatment for all trading Western nations whenever any one should extract a new privilege. It was signed at Wang-hsia near Macao in 1844.

It looked as if a struggle of more than a century was over. The Outer Barbarians had a foothold—seven footholds, actually—in China, and were face to face at last with The People. It is not easy to tell, now, just what they expected to find behind the curtain. A hundred years earlier the Middle Kingdom had unwittingly enjoyed great popularity in the West, and was presumed to hold a wisdom unknown to Occidentals. Chinese culture, Chinese ethics, were mysterious and romantic. But things were different now. The ruffled captains and traders who had suffered in Canton's ghetto had no patience with the calm teachings of Confucius. For their part, from their experience, the country was populated by grabby merchants and ruffians of the worst description. Still, the first Europeans who came to settle in the treaty ports—the supercargoes, the ships' captains, the missionaries—must have felt curious and eager, and some genuine international friendships developed in spite of everything. The Manchus and Chinese were not eager at all. On the contrary. Nevertheless, they slowly realized that they would have to understand these intruders, if only the better to handle them, now that they were actually in the country.

*   *   *

The Ch'ing Dynasty at that time, poised though it was on the brink of a cliff, ruled an enormous territory, the greatest expansion ever achieved by the Manchus. From the Sakhalin River in the north to Burma and Annam in the south, with her western boundaries taking in Chinese Turkestan, Nepal, and Tibet, China was Asia's giant. Of necessity the system used to govern this huge territory was decentralized, allowing of elasticity, but in theory the administration in Peking was vigilant, keeping a sharp eye on the officials who managed the provinces and subject territories. There were in all twenty-one provincial governments—eighteen in China, and three more in Manchuria. Mongolia and Tibet were counted as subject territories. Burma, Korea, Annam, Siam, and Nepal were on a slightly different basis; they were tribute-paying nations. The officials in charge of these lands were given a good deal of leeway and for that reason had to be carefully chosen; even so, they had to report on their activities to the central government in Peking, which criticized or commended, and had absolute power to shift them, recall outright, punish, or reward them. A fundamental principle of the system, the wisdom of which is evident, was never to appoint any official to power in his own part of the country.

In the central government, the body with most power was the Grand Council. This was made up of a number of members which varied from time to time but was usually five or six. Some of them were Manchu, some Chinese—the Manchus had always realized that they must use native talent—but the proportion of nationals was not a fixed one. All members of the Council had to remain within call by His Majesty, day and night. Every day they had audience with him, usually between three and five in the morning, and held the exclusive privilege of sitting on mats in his presence. [Earl Swisher, *China's Management of the American Barbarians* (New Haven, 1951), p. 10.] They did not form an impenetrable hedge around the Emperor: officials outside were accustomed to "memorialize"— i.e., send a memorial, which was a letter in the form of an essay, combined with any papers appertaining to the matter—direct to His Majesty, who thus saw them before the Council did, and was able to bring them up for discussion thereafter. It was his custom to write marginal or interlinear notes on the paper; directions as to the edicts he wished issued, or merely words which mean "Known," or "Noted," but sometimes he made comments. During Commissioner Lin's difficulties with the Western barbarians, for example, the Tao-Kuang Emperor wrote opposite an item of information on these disagreeable people, "How abominable!" When the Emperor made these jottings he always used the Imperial Vermilion Pencil. In the period following the Opium War treaties, the Western barbarians corresponded with His Majesty indirectly by getting in touch with some official who would memorialize the Throne in the proper way. Usually the reply was quite prompt. The Emperor had his faults, but no one could accuse him of slacking his work.

Beneath the Council, the structure of administration widened out in time-honored pyramidal form. There were six Boards, nine Chief

Ministries of State, and the Hanlin Academy of literary dignitaries, which held a peculiar importance, since all new officials, in theory, were chosen through examinations imposed by these intellectuals. Beneath this level were a myriad smaller posts, in a pattern of great complexity which was dutifully followed. Every literate Chinese aspired to be a civil servant, unless he had warlike ambitions: in either case he must pass his literary examinations.

The eighteen Chinese provinces were administered by Governors General, sometimes called by the foreigners Viceroys: each province was subdivided into prefectures, then into independent sub-prefectures and so on, the smallest division being the district. The provinces of Manchuria were under military officers. The armed forces were organized in two parts, Manchu and Chinese, though segregation was not strictly enforced and the Manchu army contained Mongols and Chinese as well. These forces were the famous Bannermen, of whom most of the Western world had heard much and considered delightfully picturesque—an army of Eight Banners, each division marked by its colored standard: plain yellow, white, red, and blue, and the same colors again, bordered. The Chinese Provincial Forces, or Army of the Green Standard, consisted of both land and marine forces. At the end of the war, the Emperor and people felt that they had been badly let down by these unfortunate men, but the fact was that though some of them fought bravely, their equipment was hopelessly old-fashioned.

*   *   *

The system already mentioned, of selecting civil servants and other officials through examination, was centuries old. In theory it was perfectly logical, since the Chinese held that a grounding in the classics should supply wisdom to deal with any problem life offers. A child at school committed great masses of ancient teachings to memory—the Trimetrical Classic, the Thousand Character Classic, the Four Books, the Poetical Classic, the Book of History, the Book of Changes, and so on. If he was considered clever enough, and if his family or village could support him, he moved on to higher studies and, ultimately, to the examinations that were the gateway to office, and, through office, possible glory and certainly riches. A clan or village in supporting a local scholar was thus gambling on him.

If he made good, they got their investment back, with interest. If he didn't, well, that was that.

On the surface the method has advantages, because it opens a way to young aspirants who would otherwise be condemned to a life without opportunity, lost in the great masses of peasantry. In practice it did not necessarily work out well. Inevitably corruption crept into the examination procedure: the examiners themselves sometimes accepted bribes and awarded the hotly contested degrees accordingly, and some of the watchdogs who oversaw the scholars during examinations were willing to close their eyes to cheating if blindness were made worth their while. Every so often there was a grand exposure and clean-up, but sooner or later these things happened again. And sometimes cheating was not even necessary; it was not unheard-of for posts to be sold openly, when the administration needed funds. All this is not surprising, since for most of China's population existence was a struggle scarcely comprehensible to the Western barbarians, with their comparatively high material standards. The Chinese farmer faced cruel natural hazards of floods, drought, windstorms, and pestilence, and was further beset by the rules of inheritance. In this crowded agricultural land, a man's sons divided his property, so that a few generations might split up the original acres into very small plots, which led to less and less efficiency in production. It is no wonder that peasants should have sought a short cut to escape by bribing officials, nor that the officials, themselves often needy, should have fallen in with these schemes. It also follows, just as naturally, that the examination system didn't always select the fittest. Even at its best, without corruption, the method as a true gauge of intelligence is questionable. Certainly a Chinese student developed a phenomenal memory, but he was not encouraged to think for himself. Above all he was not to question the dictates of family and ancestor worship.

As for the position of women in nineteenth-century China, Western observers—missionaries in particular—were horrified at their degradation, or professed to be, but in many ways Chinese women were not all badly off. Females are never untrammeled in countries that practice polygamy, but in China they had more rights than they would have enjoyed in Japan or India. They were permitted to inherit, for example, and to own property. Perhaps the worst aspect of their life was foot-binding, though, after the extraordinary way of most human beings, most of them accepted it without question, let

alone rebellion, because it was the custom. (The Hakkas, in the
south, and the Manchus did not bind their girls' feet.) Also, poor
parents did not want many daughters, and sometimes abandoned
newborn girl-babies to die of exposure. Upper-class women were
kept in confinement like the Indian purdah; presumably the custom
was adopted from the Islamic tribes that made many converts in
China, and spread far beyond the confines of the religion it accompanied.

The Chinese unit of currency was the silver tael, or liang, roughly
an ounce in our weight. Its value fluctuated slightly according to
the purity of the silver. For poor people a more familiar medium
than the tael—which was sometimes known as the foot, because
the bullion was molded into a little stubby footlike ingot—was the
cash, a brass coin pierced with a square hole and strung with ninety-
nine brothers on a cord. Prices were quoted as so many strings of
cash. In 1842 ten strings added in value to one tael of silver; in
other words 1000 cash were worth a tael. That was the general rule,
but in times of economic upheaval cash could be devalued, and in
any case its worth was subject to countless little variations. In his
charming book *An Australian in China*, Dr. G. E. Morrison, who
wrote in 1894, describes this situation:

"Let me explain, in a few sentences, the 'cash' currency of the
Middle Kingdom. The current coin of China as everyone knows is
the brass cash, which is perforated so that it may be carried on a
string. Now, theoretically, a 'string of cash' contains 100 coins, and
in the Eastern provinces ten strings are the theoretical equivalent
of one Mexican dollar. But there are eighteen provinces in China,
and the number of brass cash passing for a string varies in each
province from the full 100, which I have never seen, to 83 in Taiyuen,
and down to 33 in the Eastern part of the province of Chihli. In
Peking I found the system charmingly simple. One thousand cash
are there represented by 100 coins, whereas 1000 'old cash' consist
of 1000 coins, though 1000 'capital cash' are only 500 coins. The
big cash are marked as 10 capital cash, but count the same as 5
old cash. Nowhere does a Chinaman mean 1000 cash when he speaks
of 1000 cash. In Tientsin 1000 cash means 500 cash—that is to say
5 times 100 cash, the 100 there being any number you can pass
except 100, though by agreement the 100 is usually estimated at
98. In Nanking I found a different system to prevail. There cash are
1075 the 1000, but of the 10 strings of 100 cash, 7 contain only 98

cash each, and 3 only 95, yet the surplus 75 cash—that is to say the number which for the time being is the Nanking equivalent of 75— are added all the same. At Lanchow in Chihli on the Imperial Chinese Railway near Shanhai-kwan, 16 old cash count as 100 cash, yet 33 are required to make up 200; in Tientsin from which point the railway starts, 1000 cash are really 500 cash and 98 count there as 100. Now 2000 Chihli cash are represented by 325 coins, and 1000 by 162 coins, and 6000 by 975 coins, which again count as 1000 large cash and equal on an average one Mexican dollar. Therefore to convert Lanchow cash into Tientsin cash you must divide the Lanchow cash by 3, count 975 as 1000, and consider this equal to a certain percentage of a theoretical amount of silver known as a tael, which is always varying of itself as well by the fluctuations in the market value of silver, and which is not alike in any two places, and may widely vary in different portions of the same place.

"Could anything be simpler? And yet there are those who say that the system of money exchange in China is both cumbrous and exasperating."

Chapter Two

Waiting on the step when the doors opened to the five ports, along with the merchants, were the foreign missionaries. They too had long been kept at bay, but now that treaties with Britain, America, and France had been signed, missionaries (like the merchants) were guaranteed right of entry to the Middle Kingdom in these nominated places: they too could build in the five ports and live there the year round, if they were so commanded by their societies at home. The feelings of the Western merchants for these men of God were mixed. Many of the hard-bitten mariners and traders didn't care for the idea of missionaries, but there was no denying that some of them, especially the medical ones, had proved very useful during the trying days of segregation. Their champions might further point out that missionaries were successful in penetrating China long before the door was slammed in barbarian faces. To be sure, those were Catholics, and the new flood of religious teachers was predominantly Protestant, but the principle was the same. Moreover, these people had lots of backing among the public at home, for the Western world was undergoing a great wave of evangelical fervor. Willy-nilly, trade and Christianity must move into China together.

Foreign missions were already well entrenched in India and Africa, and their patron societies had for years gazed yearningly toward China, as a natural field for the development of their aims. There may have been some jealousy in this desire, some wish to emulate the earlier Catholics, but there *was* a tradition of Protestant activity in the Far East, however small: the Dutch had occupied Formosa for a time in the seventeenth century, and introduced to the island a number of pastors and teachers of Christianity. But these men had met with little or no success among the Formosan

Chinese, and when the Dutch departed, all trace of their church died out. With the rise of nineteenth-century evangelism, the Protestants had to start again from scratch, like the Catholics. The British had nothing like as much access to Chinese literature as did the Catholic countries of France and Italy and Spain to help them in preparation for their work, but there was in the British Museum one document, a translation into Chinese of part of the New Testament, which was a legacy from the Jesuits in Peking. With this bit of material a young man named Robert Morrison started studying the language in 1804, because he was determined to go to China as a missionary. He found a literate Chinese in London to help him, but it must have been a staggering task even so. Morrison learned enough Chinese in three years to feel that he was prepared, and he then persuaded the London Missionary Society to send him out to Canton. They agreed, but his path wasn't clear even then: the East India Company, which didn't approve of missionaries, refused him passage in an Indiaman, and as their ships were the only ones that went all the way from England, Morrison had to go to New York and ship from there. Once he had arrived and found that he must regularize his position in the factory community (since the Chinese kept a sharp eye out for unauthorized barbarians), the same East India Company that had spurned him in England now took him onto their payroll as an interpreter. At that time, with his unusual knowledge, he was an immensely valuable acquisition, and the Company never had reason to regret changing its attitude. Later, he and some colleagues set up a printing press, and he also had a hand in founding the Anglo-Chinese School in Malacca.

An increasing number of missionaries followed in Morrison's trail, though most of them could not, like him, settle down in Canton, which was growing more and more crowded and uneasy as the century rolled on. They had to go to neighboring countries to found schools and build churches and institute hospitals—to Malaya and Macao and the East Indies and anywhere else that it was possible to live and work, as near as they could get to the forbidden country where they wished to go. Not all of them were British. Outstanding in their number was the Prussian Gützlaff, a brilliant linguist and no doubt a sincere man, though his morals seem to have been confused, for he worked with one of the biggest opium-importing companies in the business, and used to distribute tracts from opium-running ships offshore at coastal cities, at the same time the contraband chests were being unloaded. (Gützlaff's wife ran a mission school for convert girls.) All this time, from 1807 until 1842, the awkward fact was that no missionary was able to spread the Gospel in China itself, and this must have been very frustrating not only to them, but to the people at home who were contributing to the cause. Yet they did make headway, after a very slow start. The border countries where they worked had a high proportion of emigrant Chinese inhabitants, and among them Christianity made progress at a fair rate. Moreover, these converts had relatives inside China, and they were able to serve as deputy missionaries when they went home on visits. Within the barrier walls, therefore, some people became interested in the Western religion long before the missionaries arrived to teach them in person. Chinese peasants were not unalterably opposed to the new belief, like the governing classes, who were staunchly Confucianist by training and inclination, and intolerant of change. Humbler folk did not go very deeply into the intellectual aspects of it, but religion meant a good deal to them. Their beliefs were a mishmash derived from many sources, comprising worship of widely differing deities. They worshiped the ancient gods, and the Confucian "heaven" of which, or of whom, the Emperor was the Son. They worshiped the elements, which they thought of as guiding spirits. Though Confucius would not have approved, they prayed to Confucius. They had faith in the magical spells of Taoism, and ordered their lives by a fortune-telling apparatus worked for them by Buddhist priests. Buddhism had been taken up eagerly by the Chinese, who changed it around to suit themselves. And above all, they worshiped their ancestors. As to that, so did the aristocrats: so had Confucius himself. It was this facet of Confucianism that had brought down trouble on the heads of the Jesuits and got them expelled from Peking; the opposition of the Roman Church to "the Rites" turned the upper classes against Christianity from that time on. The peasants knew little of the Rites controversy. They knew Confucius had been a great man and was now a great spirit, but in their minds, the other world was full of great spirits. The governing classes were not so all-embracing: Confucius suited them.

This teacher and thinker who had such influence for centuries after his death—Kung Fu-tse, or Confucius—was born in the middle of the sixth century B.C., about a hundred years ahead of the Gautama Buddha. Throughout his life he was to deprecate modern innovations, and insist upon the relative excellence of the past, in which he believed there had been a golden age of perfection. He was no doubt influenced by the state of the country as he saw it, disorganized, in a phase of the Chou Dynasty when political control was at a low ebb, and the nation was merely a loosely held together congregation of states, each under its own prince. Confucius was born in Lu, now a part of Shantung. There are conflicting stories of his origin, which is not surprising considering when he lived: even in China where tradition preserves much, twenty-five hundred years is a long time for a people to remember everything. His mother may not have been his father's first wife: she may have been his concubine, but in China this does not make the child illegitimate, though some missionaries, writing of Confucius, seem to have thought it did. In any case his father was much older than his mother, and died when the boy was three. They were a poor family but they had influential connections, and Confucius was educated: in fact, he took to books so enthusiastically that before he was seventeen he was famous beyond the borders of his village. At seventeen he went to work—as a clerk in the government tax department—and he rose rapidly, within a few years becoming supervisor of the state fields and parks, and overseer of cattle breeding. It seems hardly a fitting job for an intellectual, but those were simpler times, and as we have already noted, a Chinese intellectual who passed the required examinations was deemed capable of filling any office in the civil service.

Confucius was already deeply preoccupied by his favorite study—tradition. He worried because he felt that many people had abandoned the old virtues like respect for law and order. In the ideal world of the past, things were arranged just as they should be, and everyone knew his place and stayed there. When he was twenty-four and his mother died, he put his principles into practice. According to the old customs, a son should mourn his parents for twenty-seven months after their death, and he should do it thoroughly, which meant retiring from his work and staying indoors to weep in seclusion. It was a well-known rule, but the people Confucius knew paid it lip service only; it was one of the many customs they had abandoned. Confucius revived it. Like a gentleman of old, he gave up his hard-won post and went into retirement. Everyone admired him for this extreme behavior, and a few bereaved sons even imitated him. Confucius's reputation was more than ever en-

hanced. Next, the sorrowing son gave orders to the local grave tenders that barrows should be erected over his parents' graves. It is not
clear now if he was again attempting to revive an ancient rite or if
the barrows were an invention of his own. Certainly the Chinese
of later ages did put up barrows over their dead. At any rate, there
too he seems to have done something that wasn't in the ordinary
run of life in Lu, but the workmen couldn't carry out his wishes,
because it was a very wet season and the barrows were washed
away as fast as they were erected. Informed of the failure, Confucius wept.

During his retirement he read intensively, and came to the conclusion that from then on his life ought to be devoted to teaching,
preaching, and generally saving his countrymen from looseness and
degeneration. He must stimulate interest in the old ways and tell
men about them: he must convince. When his mourning ended he
founded a school and gathered about him a number of disciples
through whom his philosophy and biography have been preserved.
(Perhaps none of his actual writing remains. When in the third
century B.C. the Emperor Shih-Huang-ti, in a burst of reforming
zeal, burned all books referring to China's past history, much of
Confucius's work was lost.) It was not an ordinary, stationary school,
but a peripatetic one. Confucius traveled a great deal, rebuking
princes and high officials when he thought rebuke was called for.
His own prince let him govern the state for a while. The nobles held
him in high esteem, and usually they listened courteously to his
advice, though they did not invariably follow it. Between journeys
the sage worked at books, annotating the classics, and thus became
a classic himself. He must have had an impressive yet lovable personality, because much oral testimony survives as to what he said
and did. His students recalled even the most trivial things about his
habits and tastes, including one anecdote that makes him seem very
human through inconsistency: when his wife died—he was sixty-six
at the time—Confucius's son began mourning her as his father had
mourned *his* mother, but only a year had passed when the young
man heard the old one mutter, "Ah, it has gone too far!" Upon which,
says the story, the son dried his tears and went back into the world.
But why should Confucius's followers have preserved another re-
mark of his—"If the meat is not cut into squares it should not be
eaten?" Has it some deep meaning? Did the sage wish to imply
that everything must be regular, or did he simply like his meat cut

into squares? Sometimes his parables are clearer. One day he was out walking in the country with his disciples, and they paused to watch a fowler at work. All the birds the man had caught in his snare were young ones. Confucius said:

"Where are the old birds?"

The man replied, "Oh, it's usually a young bird that gets caught, because older ones are experienced and know enough to avoid the snare. The only old birds who get caught in my net are foolish fowls that follow the young ones, and so come to grief."

This was the sort of thing Confucius liked to hear, and he seized the chance to expound a lesson. So it always is, he said; old heads are best. It would be a world full of pitfalls if the young did the leading.

He summed up the principles of virtue in the Five Relationships: between sovereign and subject, father and son, brother and brother, husband and wife, friend and friend, in that order. Incidentally, relationship between strangers was not mentioned, an omission that was to perplex the Chinese later when they had to grapple with just such a problem. Still, everything considered, it is not surprising that the ruling caste in China should have cherished Confucius's code of ethics, and continued to cherish it for twenty-four centuries.

Against such competition, how could the Johnny-come-lately Christians hope to conquer a nation's ideology? For competition it was: that question had been settled by the Chinese themselves in the Rites controversy, against the Jesuit contention that Confucianism was compatible with Christianity. The answer was that the uneducated were vulnerable to suggestion. They were kept in their place according to Confucian tenets, and it was not an attractive place, so they felt no gratitude to the pattern. It is doubtful if many of them thought this through, but the fact was there. In addition they had a natural longing for the emotional touch, if only as compensation for all the delights they couldn't enjoy: they wanted and needed some excitement, some promise. The austere, chilly ethics of Confucius did not satisfy this longing, for the Master's almighty power was impersonal. His "T'ien," or "Heaven," was in a sense the law of life and righteousness and power—though it was not alone in the constellation of powers—but it was not God as the Christians feel about God, a kind of super being with a benevolent interest in mankind. For such an interest the peasants sought in older or newer faiths than the code of Confucius, in their household gods and dead ancestors, the sorcery of Tao, or the beautiful statues of the Buddhists. The poor felt a response in these. Confucianism provided maxims, it is true, with excellent advice; a man could repeat these as incantations and acquire a sensation of being virtuous, but there was no emotional nourishment in it. In looking beyond Confucius, however, a man did not necessarily throw him away. On the contrary, he simply added to his body of beliefs. The Chinese were cheerfully capable of accommodating any number of religions, just as they would—if they could afford it—consult and retain a number of doctors, without relinquishing any one of them. If one religion or doctor was good, a number were so much the better. Even in the case of Christianity . . .

The purely Confucian temple, empty of graven images, full of immense spaces, dignified and quiet (unless it was used as an Examination Hall), was a place for meditation, for scholars. Nearer to the heart of the people were those other temples from which gods were not excluded. A vivid description of several "joss houses," as Westerners called Chinese temples—"joss" is from the Portuguese "dios"—is given by Lieutenant F. E. Forbes of Her Majesty's Navy, who was in China from 1842 to 1847, the first five years of peace after the Opium War. [Lieutenant F. E. Forbes, R.N., *Five Years in China*, London, 1848.] It was his good fortune to see the country untouched by Western influence: he enjoyed the experience, and recounted his explorations with happy zest. Of a Confucian temple he said:

"One establishment at Ningpo occupies about ten acres of land, laid out in ornamental temples of all sizes, triumphal entrances, fountains and tanks, and courts planted with trees, mostly yew. But, except on occasion of a festival, these are rarely or never visited, and the grass grows in abundance through the interstices of the pavement. The only ornaments are carved beams and huge frames, containing maxims and sayings of the patriarch." He said of the Taoist faith, "What few temples there are remaining are supported by a priesthood, dressed in flowing robes, and differing from every other class in China, except the Meaou-tse, in their mode of arranging the hair, which is collected into a knot on the crown of the head, and not plaited into a queue, or tail. Their tenets are visionary and mysterious. The earlier proselytes, like hermits, sought solitude in deserts and caverns, and were little more or less than maniacs, believing in all sorts of nonsense, good and evil spirits, earthly immortality, and terrestrial paradises, more especially Kwan-lin, the seat of everything that was delightful, situated somewhere in the west, with its groves, grottoes, delicious fruits, and warbling of birds. . . . (The temple) I entered, contains, amongst its godhead, the deities of the cycle, sixty in number, one for each year. . . . Besides these are the gods of fire, earth, and water, and the genii of the hills, rivers, thunder and lightning, etc. . . . There is also a representation of the Kwan-lin, richly gilt, covering a whole wall with its different gods and goddesses."

Best of all, Forbes liked the Buddhist temple and monastery of "Tien T'hung" in Chekiang, where he stayed for a time. He describes the beauty of the setting, "in a recess formed by two mountains at the close of the fertile valley," at the end of a mile-long avenue bordered with tall trees. High forest-covered hills rose behind, and a huge lotus-covered tank in front reflected the building. "The forest closes the area around an immense parallelogram . . . all traces of the road are lost, an extraordinary echo catches the veriest whisper. . . ." His detailed description gives a picture of a typical temple of its sort, though perhaps it is unusually fine; it was favored by an Emperor in the seventeenth century.

"On entering are the colossal statues of the four kings of heaven, about forty feet in height, of dried clay beautifully painted; . . . the two on each side are divided from each other by a stone pillar, round which a dragon is carved in high relief; . . . they are all in a sitting position on the right side; the first is black in the face, with chain-armour and a drawn sword in his right hand; opposite to him is one of a light complexion, also with chain-armour but no sword, . . . both the above wear belts clasped with a lion's head, and would appear to be gods of war. The attributes of the remaining two seem of more peaceable nature, both are of light complexion, and instead of chain-armour their breasts are gilt, . . . the one on the right side is playing on a musical instrument like a guitar, that on the left bears an umbrella in his right hand; at their feet are some figures the size of life, dressed as peasants, to show the contrast between the inhabitants of this and the other world. These occupy the two sides of the entrance, while in the centre is a small model temple, in which, facing the entrance, is a stout globular joss in a sedentary position, with a rosary of nine beads in his hand, whose jolly countenance and laughing open mouth give him a very Bacchanalian expression. Behind him, facing the other direction, is a warrior in gilt armour, supporting himself by a richly carved staff; his helmet is adorned with plumes. . . . A huge drum and moderately large bell finish the paraphernalia of the religious furniture of this temple. . . .

"A quadrangle ending in a flight of steps reaches the second temple, in which are the images of the San-paow-fuh, or three precious Buddhas, in colossal statues about fourteen feet high, each seated on a lotus flower. . . . These are highly gilt; at the back of each head is an enormous metal mirror to represent the halo of glory, while above a huge rich canopy, of magnificent carving and gilt, reaches the ceiling. These three figures are in the centre of the temple facing the door, paying homage to whom, and in attitude of prayer, in richly painted dresses, are, one on each side, two figures of men nine or ten feet high; they face a carved table, bearing a small model of a temple, an incense burner, two vases, and several candlesticks: above hangs a magnificent lantern; under the table are bronze vessels and small drums. . . . At the back of the San-paow-fuh, and facing the other entrance, is a highly executed image of the goddess Kwan-yin; she is represented seated on a lotus flower on the back of a horse with clawed feet; she is surrounded with angels in attitude of worship, floating about the azure heavens . . ." and so on, in rich profusion. This colorful collection of buildings is a good illustration of Chinese adaptability in religious affairs, for it had not always been a Buddhist place of worship: it was founded by a Taoist hermit who built his refuge on that spot. Because he had great powers of healing, the world soon beat a pathway to his door. As the years passed the hermit, being mortal though Taoist, disappeared, but by that time the valley river's waters had taken on his talents for healing and people continued to come to the place. At one time or another—the abbot who told all this to Forbes did not seem to know, or indeed to care, just when it happened—it became Buddhist, which seems to have mattered not a whit to the public.

During his visit the Lieutenant witnessed a procession in the vicinity, "in honour of Shin-nung, the divine husbandman and presiding deity of the mysteries of agriculture and medicine," who had no connection with Buddhism: the ceremony was Confucian, if anything. It was a very splendid procession, with a great lot of roast meat offerings to the god, and hundreds of worshipers, who were either sick or recently cured, doing homage in the form of kowtows. "The order . . . was as follows: first, the cards or boards, bearing the honorary titles of the god. . . . Bands of trumpets, gongs, drums, in sedans, highly ornamented, were here and there interspersed, and in the commencement, and near the end, was a huge lantern dragon, not less than forty feet long. . . . In a painted red car, filled with exotics, and carried by eight men, was seated a handsomely dressed youth; on his left hand, supported by a splint beneath the dress, stood a magnificently dressed young girl, balancing herself by two wands. . . . Great must have been the pain suffered by these two young people, for, immediately on halting, a man from the bystanders rushed in with long crutches and relieved the girl therewith, while another sprinkled their faces with water, to keep them from fainting. . . . Shopmen bearing teas and other dried herbs and fruits, as offerings; youths bearing banners, literati with tabards, inscribed with the wisdom of Kung-foo-tse; . . . while at the last came a large image of the god himself, dressed in the imperial (yellow) dress of satin, on its head a golden crown, the face of a high vermilion colour; it was borne in a sedan-chair, by twelve bearers, and attended by all the paraphernalia of a mandarin of the first rank. This procession was thoroughly of the Confucius school, and only gazed on by the priests of Fu (Buddha), in the precincts of whose domain it was enacted."

Nobody in his senses would try to disentangle thoroughly the bases of these various forms of worship that had grown up around a Chinese spa. But of one thing we may be sure. Any inhabitant of that valley, even if he were converted to Christianity, would put up a stout fight before he gave up surreptitious visits, when he happened not to be feeling well, to Kwan-ying, or the Laughing Buddha, or Shin-nung, or—which is most likely—all three of them simultaneously.

Clearly the missionaries had their work cut out for them, but thanks to the Chinese emigrés already encountered they did not approach it unprepared: they had considerable advance knowledge of national characteristics, and many of them knew the language. Indeed, this special talent held back the evangelical movement in a way, though it did draw together the two forces, commercial and evangelical, in their penetration of the Orient. The merchants and Western diplomats now living in the ports had immediate, urgent need of more and still more interpreters. The Queen's plenipotentiary, Sir Henry Pottinger, scoured the East for people to staff the new consulates, and though his was not the only claim, he had first priority. Missionaries had never been so much in demand. Though the Nanking Treaty was signed, it was not the end of negotiations for the plenipotentiary; sometimes he must have thought wearily that Nanking was only the beginning. Deeply involved in conversation and correspondence with mandarins, his dealings moved at a majestically slow pace, on which the difficulty of intercourse was only one drag among many. It took a year of hard work to hammer out a supplementary treaty on tariffs, a vitally important question for traders as well as for the Peking administration.

In these negotiations Sir Henry's opposite number was a Manchu, the Imperial Commissioner Ch'i-ying, a man well educated in Chinese style who was thus, in theory, fully equipped to deal with any diplomatic task that he might face. In actuality Ch'i-ying was as ignorant of Western barbarians as he was of the complexities of tariff questions. Sir Henry, no tariff expert himself, did at least have one advantage: he knew a little bit, though not much, about the Chinese. Until the shocking outcome of the war, Peking had never felt the need of a foreign affairs bureau; as for foreign policy, the Emperor had always maintained his famous one—arm's-length, no nonsense, and make them pay. Clearly this would no longer meet the requirements of the situation, and Ch'i-ying decided on a fresh approach. As we have seen, Confucius left no guide for him in how to deal with Western barbarians who had just won a war. Ch'i-ying decided to try behaving in the opposite manner to that of his predecessors. The barbarians must be soothed, and pleased, and disarmed by friendship. Though such behavior ran counter to all his instincts and training, Ch'i-ying adopted it, hoping that he would get better terms out of Pottinger if the Englishman thought of him as a friend.

> "There was an old man who said, 'How
> Shall I flee from this terrible cow?
> I shall sit on the stile
> And continue to smile,
> Which may soften the heart of the cow.'"

Ch'i-ying smiled, and entertained Sir Henry, and protested his love: he sent presents and asked for a picture of Lady Pottinger: he was nice to every Western barbarian he met. He did soften hearts, no doubt about it, but whether in the end the supplementary Treaty was any the better for that—from the Chinese point of view—is a moot point. At any rate, they were a long time coming to that end. The delay was very worrying for everyone connected with the chief cause of the war—trade. Such affairs couldn't wait beyond the Treaty of Nanking, and while Pottinger and Ch'i-ying corresponded, and waited for their letters to be interpreted; while Pottinger wrote dispatches to London and Ch'i-ying referred his moves to Peking and explained how crafty he was being, merchants were steadily bringing in cargo, either to the old stand at Canton or into the newly opened harbors to the north. For all this shipping, no working machinery now existed; former methods were outlawed. By the terms of the Nanking Treaty, the combination of Chinese merchants, nominally thirteen in number, called the Cohong, a name which had long been anathema to the Western traders, was disbanded. It should have been a relief that there was no more control, no more fixed prices; in theory the foreigners could now bargain and need not pay so much squeeze—but how were they to begin? Nothing had yet been arranged. Above all, there was no customs service. Ships kept coming until they were waiting in line, crowding the harbors, before the supplementary treaty was finished. After all that delay it was in the end rushed through, and suffered from being arranged under pressure. But at least for the moment a pattern of procedure was set up, the ships moved in and were unloaded, and goods changed hands. China's treaty ports were opened at last.

Sir Henry would have been surprised, even grieved, if he had known how unconvinced the Chinese and Manchus still were that the foreign incursion would be a good thing for them. He and the traders he represented were certain that their cause was just, and that circumstances would prove it to the most reluctant Chinese. Trade would grow as soon as their hands were untied; it would grow by leaps and bounds. Who on earth could question that growing trade was a good thing? Not the barbarians. The *Chinese Repository* [Editors, Bridgman and Williams], a quarterly which had been published since 1833 by missionaries in Canton for the benefit of the Western community, joyfully greeted the new life in its issue dated January 1843:

"Henceforth the Centre Kingdom—the celestial empire—ancient and long secluded China—takes rank among the nations of the earth, and becomes of one family with them. By the treaty, signed before

Nanking, August 29th, 1842, the spell which gave this government its fancied elevation was broken, its wall of seclusion breached, and a highway projected, whereupon the sons of Han may enjoy free intercourse with those of every race and in every clime. . . . Great allowances must be made for the ignorance and prejudices of the Chinese; and yet their ignorance and prejudices regarding foreigners are scarcely greater than ours are respecting them. . . . This empire is emphatically 'the great unknown.' With a few exceptions, foreigners know but little more of it than they do of the moon."

However, the foreigners now set to work busily to find out. For one thing, the Anglo-Chinese College was moved from Malacca to Hong Kong, ceded to Great Britain by the Treaty of Nanking, and its students were soon hard at work on English essays, in a contest sponsored by the Morrison Education Society. Some of these compositions are more truthful than flattering, giving as they do the Chinese view of the new order. (The original idea of the college, that there should be an equal number of English and Chinese students, had long since gone by the board, because there was a shortage of English boys in those parts.) The subject of the contest was Hong Kong.

"The island was covered with mat houses when the English first came here," wrote one boy. "But soon after all were nearly extirpated, market places were changed into good order, roads were constructed. . . . Now there are thousands of inhabitants English, Chinese, Hindus and others. The greater part of the Hindus are soldiers, but some of them are living in a bad manner. They take things without pay. . . . Before the English began this colony, it was a dwelling place of a great number of pirates. Many Chinese towns and villages have been ravaged by them, but they are now becoming less and less. Most of their wives are bad women. . . . There are a great number of police men in the town English and Chinese. The Chinese ones are very cruel, they go out seeking after money in a wrongful way all the day. The sailors on shore are also very bad; they are always drunken, and some of them strike the Chinese and trouble them. Hong-kong is now becoming more flourishing and famous, and a great point of union to the Chinese and English." Well, perhaps.

Chapter Three

Ch'i-ying had assumed an impossible task, of pleasing everybody, which in the end proved too much for him. But that end was a long way in the future. In the meantime his methods seemed to be successful in the extreme. The barbarians were behaving better than the administration had expected, and in Peking face was saved. The necessity of saving face and keeping the Emperor reassured was the greatest weakness of the Manchu Dynasty, and for that matter of other dynasties as well. It meant that the Emperor heard only watered down versions of events when his reign was in jeopardy. It may seem to foreign eyes, reading Ch'i-ying's memorials today, that the Imperial Commissioner was tactful with his sovereign to the degree of deceit, but as a matter of fact he was by far the most outspoken of the Emperor's officials. They were all victims of an occupational hazard: if they sent unfavorable reports they were likely to be reprimanded and degraded, if not put to death. Naturally, therefore, those men who had dealings with the British during the latter days of the war and in the postwar period of the discussions on the supplementary treaty were very careful indeed when writing memorials to the throne. The actual, bitter fact of defeat was played down, and the language of the Imperial edicts in reply continued in the old strain of hauteur: nothing had yet occurred, according to the Court's attitude, to change the basic situation. The Son of Heaven was still ruler of the world. Though China had surrendered, the British were still referred to as "rebel barbarians."

Nevertheless, the Chinese admitted that a thing or two might be learned from these despised outlanders. (This suppleness in Oriental mentality has always been the despair of Western logic-choppers.) An official who knew his facts might safely venture to criticize the prowess of Imperial troops if he made it clear that by so doing he was really affirming Chinese superiority: if the home forces had done badly, this proved that the barbarians weren't really so strong, after all. With proper precautions, there need be no next-time defeat. A week before the treaty was signed in Nanking, one of these officials was writing to the Throne:

"We consider that the ruthlessness of the rebel barbarians is entirely attributable to the weakness and unmanliness of (our) maritime forces, resulting in defeats." [Swisher, p. 82.] He described a piece of research that had just been done on an American-built ship, which his department had bought and taken apart to see why barbarian vessels gave such a good account of themselves in battle. He admitted that the thing was cleverly made—hard layers of leather, and copper and iron plates that even large cannon balls could hardly shatter. It was also fitted with cannons that could shoot to a great distance, "thus causing people to be very afraid of them." However, he continued stoutly, "I consider these to be by-products of China. Formerly when Sui attacked Ch'ien, they constructed a mast fifty feet high. . . . The barbarians have merely changed this device; their covering of ships with leather also to some extent follows the device of our war-junks, and is nothing to be marveled at." However, the writer recommended an ambitious program of shipbuilding along similar lines, as well as a revised system of tactics when next the Chinese had occasion to attack rebel ships. One thing to remember, for example: "Near the rebel ships, there is always noxious smoke. Licorice and brown sugar held in the mouth give instant relief."

In conclusion he spoke with proper anger against the erstwhile enemy: "Now the rebel barbarians, from the time they presented tribute in the Chia-ch'ing era,"—that is, the visit of Macartney's Embassy, when gifts were presented, and when, in fact, Chia-ch'ing's predecessor, the aging Ch'ien-Lung, was still Emperor—"have been arrogant in their language and draw maps everywhere they go. They have harbored mischief in their hearts for a long time. Having provocation, they rebel, and without provocation, they also rebel. Now their low and cowardly nature is worse than before. If we restrain them with temporary measures, how can it last for long?"

Spirited words indeed, which must never be expressed to the British themselves. Ch'i-ying had started the new fashion of soothing barbarians with courtesy, and he insisted that all his officials must follow his example. He selected assistants who were good at it, to help him with his delicate work. One such, General I-shan, actually bore as part of his title the adjective "Barbarian-pacifying," or "Rebel-pacifying." Some years later, the Westerners, discovering the true state of affairs from some state papers they turned up in Nanking, were indignant at what they considered China's two-faced policy, but by their own lights the officials were not being at all dishonorable; they were merely behaving in an adroit way. It must be remembered that rancor and vengefulness are perfectly normal emotions in a defeated people—something which conquerors, full of the joy of spring, are apt to overlook too quickly.

The British for the most part were genially disposed. Their struggle had not been arduous or costly; moreover, the war had taken place a long way from home. The public, cozy and good-tempered in England, were ready to ask the classic question, "Can't we be friends?" In Knightsbridge, an American entrepreneur with a shrewd eye for profit built a Chinese Museum, an enterprise generally welcomed. Queen Victoria herself visited the exhibition in June 1843, the day before the doors were opened, and according to the *Morning Post* was much struck with the display. At the entrance was a Chinese summer-house, "an exact copy of a summer residence made in China." Beyond was the great hall. "The appearance of the room is China in miniature; nothing is foreign to the subject; all is Chinese." It sounds rather crowded, but then, China *is* crowded. There were embroideries, lanterns, paintings, scrolls, samples of furniture both aristocratic and poor. The *Morning Herald* also described the show, with "evidences of idol worship of China, of her commerce, her manufactures, her paintings, her carvings." Among other things was a complete replica of a joss house. Life-size figures represented a "priest of Buddha and of the Tau set in full canonicals," as well as gentlemen, servants, soldiers, archers, shields, spears, and a party of literary men in summer costume, reading and reciting. Crowds flocked to the Museum. The mood in England was reminiscent of the eighteenth-century rage for *chinoiserie*. People thought once again with kindness of those quaint pigtailed Orientals, though their sentiments were not shared to any large extent by their compatriots in Canton. There, only a few months before, in November 1842, the old factory district had been attacked and burned down by a mob from the walled city. According to the angry foreigners, this mob had been incited by officials. This is not unlikely, but the Governor of Kwangtung, reporting on the incident to the Throne, abstained from any unseemly admission of such a thing and minimized the affair in time-honored fashion. He merely said that his people, in their natural indignation, had committed some excesses against the grasping barbarians.

The "natural indignation" of the people was often mentioned by Chinese officials when they were called on to explain to impatient barbarians why there was delay in implementing the terms of the Nanking Treaty, as for example that clause which gave barbarians the right to go into the cities. "The people are still indignant," the officials would say. "They are not yet accustomed to the new regime; they are not educated yet. It is not safe for you to go into the city. It is for your own sakes that we urge you not to go." They had another good excuse ready to give barbarian captains when these grasping creatures showed themselves in a hurry to start trading in the treaty ports. Some barbarian ships sailed to Shanghai and Ningpo before the tariff regulations had been settled (as they were, ultimately, in the supplementary treaty); this could not be permitted, and the Chinese found great satisfaction in turning them away. They were always directed to go back to Canton. As long as officialdom could get away with it, change was postponed. Every step was fought. Some of the officials no doubt entertained wild hopes that the whole Nanking settlement would turn out to be a temporary nuisance only. But they were mistaken. In its lumbering way, in spite of all delaying tactics, the new order did progress toward the end desired by the barbarians, and the stand-pat Chinese, little by little, had to resign themselves to it.

As the dust settled new problems were discerned for Court and Council to face. It became apparent that the barbarians should not be lumped together as one indistinguishable annoyance. There were barbarians and barbarians. Canton officials already knew this, of course, for they had dealt with Westerners before: the Governor of Kwangtung had pointed it out in 1841 when making his report on finances and explaining why they were at such a low ebb. It was not only that the warring British couldn't trade, he said. *All* barbarians were staying away from Canton, because of the British blockade at the mouth of the river: barbarian shipping had fallen off during the previous year by 80 per cent. The Council promptly issued an edict that other barbarians be encouraged to continue business as usual. "Kwangtung precedent allows the various barbarians to trade," it declared. "The respectful and obedient states naturally should trade as usual." It was hoped that if they were properly handled, that nation of barbarians known as America might be turned against Britain, and nip in to take away British leadership in trade while the others were busy fighting. Handling barbarians in this way, by pitting them against each other, was traditional in China and commended itself to the administration. The Council was now aware that America was a big country, and might prove quite useful as an ally against Britain. Unfortunately for the Chinese nothing came of this plan, the Western nations showing a vexatious tendency to stick together in their approach to China.

Now Ch'i-ying, brilliant man that he was, learned more details of the difference between various barbarian nations, and as he gathered the facts he sent the fruit of his learning to the Peking circle. He pointed out that they must distinguish between the rebellious British and the non-combatant Americans, French, Portuguese, and so on. It was a subject that needed considerable study. Only two years before, Peking had been lamentably ignorant about it, and the Councilors had read with slightly disdainful interest such primitive notes as these from Formosa:

"We find now that the eighteen white barbarians . . . are all red barbarians. Because their hair is slightly yellow, they are called red barbarians . . . they are all natives of the English mother country. . . . In addition, there are thirty black barbarians, all natives of Bombay. . . . These island barbarians from ancient times forward have known only love of gain and fundamentally are no different from dogs and sheep." [Swisher, p. 88.]

Ch'i-ying knew much more now. He had to. With his assistant barbarian-soothers he was in an unenviable position vis-à-vis Westerners that might be described as schizophrenic. On the one hand they were supposed to hold off barbarians, and had to keep assuring Peking that the creatures would get no closer than the outer fringe of the country at the five ports—if indeed they got that far. On the other hand was the pressing need to start again with the collection of revenue from those same unpleasant creatures, for when they failed to collect money, the haughtily withdrawn officials in Peking were very quick to rebuke them. It was necessary to exhibit to each other, and to Peking, proper sentiments of horror and revulsion whenever barbarians attempted to advance. It was, however, a distinct relief that barbarians did continue to make such attempts. In his heart, Ch'i-ying was pleased with the prompt action of the Americans who came crowding on British heels as soon as the Nanking Treaty was signed, asking that they too might use trading facilities at the treaty ports. How presumptuous, yet how reassuring! Of course the request could not be granted—at least, not immediately. . . . One individual American jammed up the works for a while and scared Ch'i-ying badly, by asking if he couldn't come to Peking and live there, working for the Imperial Court. Whoever he was—and barbarian records don't seem to have any trace of him—he claimed to be skilled in astronomy and mathematics: perhaps he was a Catholic who hoped to repeat history and emulate the scientifically minded Jesuits who had found favor in old Peking. He didn't get his permission, but the storm he raised with what was probably an innocent if naïve request was a long time dying. The Manchus reminded each other darkly of the barbarian ambassadors who had tried from time to time to get themselves installed as permanent residents in the Heavenly City. This sort of thing must never, never happen, they agreed. It was bad enough having barbarians at the treaty ports: His Majesty could not possibly consider anything closer to himself. The old regulations could not be added to or changed. "Let there be no compromising," the Imperial edict ended in warning.

Nevertheless, there was a good deal to be said—and Ch'i-ying said it—for permitting Americans and other barbarians to share amenities in the treaty ports with Britain. For one thing, how could Chinese customs officers be expected to tell barbarians apart? It could be done, no doubt, with practice, but to separate rightful traders from interlopers would make a good deal of extra work. Besides, in the one brief year since the Nanking Treaty had gone into effect, and before the newly opened ports could contribute much, customs revenue was showing a decided increase, and if treaty port facilities were extended to other barbarian traders, a further large increase could be expected. This was a powerful argument, and though the Council continued to save face for a bit by wavering, it was understood that they would consent, when all of a sudden the Imperial dovecote was again fluttered by impetuous American action. Ch'i-ying got news that another embassy was on the way, sent by the American President Tyler and headed by Caleb Cushing, and that Cushing's intention was to go to Peking for a personal interview with the Emperor, in emulation of the British Lord Macartney in the nineties. This was dreadful. Barbarians never seemed to learn that it was simply no use trying to do that sort of thing. The alarmed Ch'i-ying did not have to be told by the Council that it must on no account be allowed to happen, though they did tell him so in the firmest possible way. For thirteen months, from November 1843 to December 1844, Ch'i-ying was in constant communication in both directions, with the Grand Council and the Americans, on this point. Dealing with the Americans, he used all his tact, but however prettily he wrapped the message the meaning was always the same— No, no, no, Mr. Cushing was on no account to go to Peking. For the looks of the thing, the rejection was based on a point of protocol which, if it had failed to fill the bill, would have been replaced with any one of a dozen more. This point was that though American ships had been coming and trading in Canton for more than a hundred years, America herself had never paid tribute. How could she dare, therefore, set herself up to ask such a tremendous favor now? It could not be denied that the British had succeeded in getting an embassy past the barrier, but Macartney had been quite a different matter from Cushing. He had brought tribute from the English King. It would have been no use pointing out to the Manchus that this interpretation of Macartney's gifts had been repudiated, again and again, by the British. It suited the Manchus to say that tribute had been paid, and they had no intention of giving up their version of the facts.

Ch'i-ying explained, kindly and soothingly, that if the Americans wanted to ask the Emperor for anything they could always go through the usual channels, by way of an Imperial Commissioner; he would memorialize His Majesty. The system had always worked. There was no need to change it now. But however kind and soothing Ch'i-ying was, there remained the horrid possibility that the Americans weren't convinced. "Barbarians are by nature somewhat impatient," and Cushing, when he got to the East, might brush aside all objections, bypass the Commissioner, and sail straight to Tientsin. If this happened, the Council said, the Tientsin garrison must be alert, and not permit a single man ashore. Everyone was to be courteous and if the ship's captain wanted water or provisions he was to be supplied, but no one must get off. Fortunately Cushing paused at Macao, and Ch'i-ying hurried over to interview him there. (He felt that if the meeting took place in Canton, the other barbarians might think he was already showing favoritism. Ch'i-ying always tried to think of everything ahead of time, and ward off trouble that way.) The American was told that "his country's previous respect and obedience had long since come to the attention of His Imperial Majesty and would be sure to receive condescending consideration." But he must not go north, no indeed. It would be unkind to permit him to make such a journey. After having traveled an enormous distance across the sea, said Ch'i-ying, would it not be very troublesome to travel so much more, all the way to Peking *and back*, for nothing?

The barbarian ambassador was unreceptive: Ch'i-ying reported to Peking that he found Americans stubborn and hard to discourage. He had complaints to make, too, of the way the proposed new treaty Cushing presented to him was expressed in Chinese. The language was not clear; the phraseology was uncouth. The American barbarians' difficulty of understanding was much greater than that of the English barbarians, because the latter had Morrison and others, whereas the Americans had only Parker and Bridgman (missionaries who were serving the Embassy as Chinese secretaries) and these men didn't know many characters, and besides were versed only in the Cantonese dialect. Ch'i-ying said that the British interpreters, although artful and cunning, did know Chinese fairly well; one could discuss business with them. But Parker and Bridgman. . . . In any case the Commissioner was able at last to dissuade Cushing from his proposed journey, and induced him to hand over the ambassadorial credentials to himself.

With such a diplomatic triumph to his credit, it was easier to discourage the French when, in due course, they made a similar attempt to get somebody into Peking. Ch'i-ying was becoming quite an expert on barbarian affairs. In July 1844, he wrote:

"According to what Your slave has heard, the said country (France) and England are neighbors, only separated by a sea. The English barbarians were formerly under their control. Later when they became strong and large they rebelled and set up a state themselves. They were repeatedly at war. Although they ceased fighting and concluded peace, neither has accepted inferiority to the other. The United States was also a dependency of the English barbarians. Because they were oppressed by the English barbarians, one of their countrymen, Washington, led the people in a war of resistance. The French barbarians sent troops to help them, whereupon the English barbarians made peace and the American barbarians were enabled to set up a nation. Therefore the French barbarians have a grievance against the English barbarians but have greatly benefitted the American barbarians. Thus, last year the English barbarians' defiance of authority"—that is, the Opium War, actually over two years back, in August 1842—"had absolutely no connection with the French barbarians." [Swisher, p. 164.]

Obviously Ch'i-ying's source of information for this burst of knowledge was somebody on the French diplomatic staff. But he was capable of thinking things out for himself too, and a month later, in September, he reported one of his conclusions to Peking: "Your official finds that England, the United States, and France do not accept inferiority one to the other. They are constantly imitating each other in order to extol themselves. Thus as soon as the English barbarians had negotiated a treaty, the American barbarians sent Cushing here." And he was able to soothe the Grand Council a little later, when they examined Cushing's red-sealed credentials and shot off a sharp question to him:

"What is the purpose of the cake of vermilion contained in the bronze box in which the credentials were forwarded?"

"It is a wax model of the seal of his country's sovereign," replied Ch'i-ying, "attached to the letter in order to show sincerity and respect, and has no other use."

With an Imperial mandate forthcoming on these American affairs, the Commissioner requested that its style be kept simple and direct for the benefit of the representatives of the United States, as ordinary elegant court language would be beyond them. "Of all the countries, it is the most uncivilized and remote. . . . The different races of the world are all grateful for Imperial bounty. It is only that the said country is in an isolated place outside the pale, solitary and ignorant. Not only in the forms of edicts and laws are they entirely unversed, but if the meaning be rather deep they would probably not even be able to comprehend."

In spite of these alarms and difficulties, the Wang-hsia Treaty at last took form and was signed. Now all the Western barbarians would enjoy equal rights.

❖ ❖ ❖

The hesitations, setbacks, and advances that filled the months following the Opium War were of worldwide importance, but were at the diplomatic level, so that they had little perceptible effect on the ordinary working-class Chinese in the ports, and none whatever on the humble people who lived in the interior. These went about their affairs as they had done for centuries, without paying heed to barbarians at the seacoast, any more than they worried about the other barbarians north of the Great Wall. They tilled their fields, eating well in good times and starving in bad. Their clever sons racked their brains in preparation for those all-important examinations that might lead the way to security, even wealth, for the clan. The people tended their ancestral graves at the right season, brought up as many sons as they could but deprecated their daughters, settled their affairs before the New Year, and looked after their own. What had barbarians—red, black, or yellow—to do with these things?

These peasants did not realize, as the years passed, that barbarians sailing in and out of the river at Canton and trickling into four other cities, were making a dent on the surface of the life the Chinese knew. For one thing, silkworkers and tea growers were gradually becoming busier and more numerous than they had ever been before. For another, opium was seeping blackly through every corner of the country where in former generations it was unknown; still, it was now an old story, not directly attributable, in an unsophisticated peasant mind, to barbarians. The agent that altered the pattern most noticeably was Christianity. Even more promptly than the traders, missionaries of Christian creeds were hurrying to take advantage of the relaxation of laws—Roman Catholic and Protestant; German and English and American and Norwegian and French, each group with its particular interests and methods, its schools, hospitals, literature. Yet the greatest impact made on nineteenth-century China by Christianity had no direct connection with any of these.

The Taiping movement is comparable in a way to the Penitente offshoot of Catholicism in America's Southwest, in that none of the creeds would wish to claim what it became. The Catholic Church, rediscovering the Penitentes after having been cut off from them for many years, renounced them. The London Missionary Society wasn't called on, formally, to renounce the Taipings, but it certainly did not want to take them on, though in a strange way the Society started off that revolution, and started it, moreover, long before war opened the treaty ports to Western missionaries.

It will be remembered that Robert Morrison, that same Morrison whose proficiency in Chinese was praised by Ch'i-ying, had been sent out to Canton by the Society early in the century, and was instrumental, with William Milne, in setting up a printing press in Malacca. There were published Morrison's Chinese translation of the New Testament and other writings in Chinese that were used for the work of spreading the Gospel. Some of these tracts were contributed by a Chinese convert, a printer and assistant to the mission foreign staff whose name was Liang Fa, or, in the Cantonese style, A-fa. According to Professor Latourette, Liang was "apparently the first ordained Protestant evangelist" in those parts. He and the other Chinese Christians had a great advantage over Western missionaries because with very little trouble they could go into and out of China, making direct contact with prospective converts on the spot. Liang did this a good deal. Preaching was only one method of spreading the all-important message, and he didn't depend wholly on it. The printed word went farther and was likely to last longer, so Liang, accompanied by other Chinese converts, very bravely carried a lot of literature from the Malacca press, every time he went in, and distributed it wherever he felt it might do most good. He reasoned that his likeliest prospects would be among the educated, who by nature cared for religious disputation and would be able to read the tracts easily, so he tried to time his tours of indoctrination with the season of government examinations. During such a season in 1834, in August, he and an assistant were in Canton, preaching at great hazard to crowds in the streets, and handing out booklets they had brought along. The two men had taken up their position near the Examination Hall, deliberately choosing the hour when the candidates, released from their ordeal, were flooding into the street on their way to their lodgings, where they would wait anxiously for several days until the examination results were announced on the Hall notice board. That day Liang Fa and his assistant were able to get rid of five thousand booklets, and on the next day they distributed as many again. Among the thousands of men who received this unexpected gift was Hung Hsiu-ch'uan, a poor Hakka student from a village called Hua, in Kwangtung. Hung taught school to support himself, and was a candidate for the third degree. Like many others he had worked himself almost to death, hoping to climb the ladder of degrees and attain a better livelihood for his family. Preoccupied with the examination he had just written, fearful and hopeful in turn, he had no time to waste

on strange religious pamphlets, but he didn't throw away his handful of little books. Absently he put them in with his other belongings
when he got home. As things turned out, Hung had failed to pass.
He would have to wait another three years for his next chance. Disappointed, resentful, downcast, he went back to his village school.

What happened to him later has been a bone of contention among
many scholars ever since. Hung broke down. He fell into a strange
fever that lasted forty days, during which his parents thought him
dying. He was hardly ever aware of his surroundings, but lived in
another world, undergoing a series of experiences in dream or vision.
It seemed to him that he was carried to a heavenly sphere where
he had audience with an awesome, splendid figure with a golden
beard, who was seated on a throne. Hung understood that this was
the one true God, or Shang-ti, the Heavenly Ruler. Shang-ti called
Hung his son, and showed him the world far below them. He said
that Hung was to rule it. He gave Hung a sword and told him to
lead his country out of slavery by casting down the Manchus. Hung
Hsiu-ch'uan was to be Emperor in place of the Manchu usurper.
Many details in the dreams were recalled vividly by Hung after he
came to his senses. The general outline of his visionary adventures
was remarkably close to that of the Christian concept of God: at
least, a completely unsophisticated mind like Hung's might well see
a similarity. He had even noted another glowing figure with Shang-ti
who was spoken of by Shang-ti as his first son, though Hung gathered that all men on earth were sons of God: he was later to identify
this angelic creature as Jesus. The most remarkable fact about all
this was that Hung saw his visions before he learned anything at
all of Christianity. He had never so much as looked at the books
acquired from Liang Fa. Not until 1843, when a cousin happened
to pick them up and read them, did it occur to him to examine the
missionary's writings. The coincidences between these and his
dreams were many and striking. He was tremendously excited, as
was his cousin. Hung Hsiu-ch'uan really had been selected, then,
by a God already known to foreigners!

With a few friends and kinsmen he worked out various methods
of interpreting this God-worship. They baptized each other, according to the rules as he understood them from his books. Then, as a
first step to converting others, they banished or destroyed all the
graven images or pictures of gods they could lay their hands on.
Local officials naturally resisted the blasphemous iconoclasts, and

more than one of Hung's apostles lost his job; some went to prison. But, after a period of failure and misfortune, the band began making headway, and their success snowballed. Learning that there were wise men from barbarian countries who understood these mysteries, Hung at one time actually gathered the means to go to Canton and study Christianity with an American Baptist missionary, the Reverend Issachar J. Roberts. Roberts didn't pay much attention to this student, who was only one among many, and even for some reason postponed Hung's baptism when the Hakka asked to be accepted into the church. Hung was discouraged, and went back to his own country and his own interpretation of the Scriptures.

The two Kwang provinces, Kwangtung and Kwangsi, are remote in distance from Peking, and much of their area is cut off from the rest of the country by mountain ranges. Fugitives from the law and the Imperial troops often made for the Kwangs, where they could be sure of safety if not luxury. It was to this region that the last remnants of the Ming Dynasty had fled when the Manchus, in the seventeenth century, toppled their kinsman from the throne and attempted to kill off all the princes. The local people are traditionally rebellious and easily stirred up against far-off authorities. Hung's tribe, the Hakka, had a name for being especially intractable, but it would be fair to say that none of the Kwang people were easy to govern. They were tough and independent. Following the Opium War, times were hard for them and everyone was grumbling. The cash had been devalued, and a series of climatic disasters had added to the peasants' many trials. They were hungry and out of patience with the ruling classes, who were foreigners anyway—a mere two hundred years could not wipe out that fact in the Chinese mind—and they were ripe for change, even if it brought in a new religion. Smashing the old gods gave many of them a savage satisfaction. Then, too, Hung Hsiu-ch'uan was a stirring, convincing speaker, and he had other persuasive orators in his train. The band traveled widely, making converts everywhere. Then they found themselves fortified by a set of powerful, if incongruous, allies—the Triads.

The Triad, or Heaven and Earth, Society was one of the many secret organizations that have flourished in China as long as people can remember. They were probably the widest spread of all at that time, and had an influence that was tremendous among the submerged workers. Although most men joined them because it made a convenient cover for lawbreaking, protecting as it did all Triad members even though they were smugglers, thieves, and bandits, the Society declared itself centered around a noble-sounding cause, nothing less than the restoration to the Heavenly Throne of the Ming Dynasty. They claimed to have a genuine Ming prince waiting for the right moment. At that time, they declared, they would rise up in revolution and set things straight in Peking. Their stronghold was the city of Canton, but Hung's activities were not so far away that they did not hear of him, and the Ming prince was in that neighborhood as well. In due course, therefore, a large number of Triads fell in behind Hung's banner. He could not exactly keep them away from his God-worshipers, so he incorporated them: they would be useful fighters when the time came. The Triads produced their Ming prince, a weak, rather stupid man bearing the dynastic family name of Chu, called Celestial Virtue. Hung accepted Chu, at least for the moment: it was not difficult later on to supplant him in the minds and hearts of his followers.

Thus, hidden behind mountains, the God-worshipers increased in numbers, faith, and strength. Nobody outside the provinces paid attention to what was going on in the hills. Years passed. In February 1850, the Tao-kuang Emperor died, although in accordance with custom his death was not announced until 1851, and he was succeeded by the weakling Hsien-feng. An obscure cult far off in the Kwang provinces did not disturb the sleep of any official in Peking. Nor was there the slightest knowledge in the treaty ports, among the barbarian missionaries, that thousands of Chinese miles inland had found their own way to worship the Christian God, and were even then devoutly reciting the Ten Commandments.

Chapter Four

The development of Chinese-barbarian relations proceeded at an uneven pace. For Westerners it all depended on where they lived, or sought to live. Hong Kong, the domicile of the British Superintendent of Trade, John Francis Davis—who had succeeded Pottinger—offered fewest problems, for it was now a British colony. The settlement was practically a British creation in any case, no Chinese except a few fisherfolk having chosen to live there in the past. After the war it was Britain's stronghold, and also, though the British did not stress the fact, the center of the opium trade, as it had been before. The other islands occupied by the Westerners during the war, Chusan near Ningpo and Kulangsu near Amoy, were to be ceded to the Chinese in 1846, according to treaty. Though by that time the traders in Canton felt so aggrieved that they held Davis should not give up the islands, both of them were returned. Sir John, as he now was, was not spoiling for a fight.

In the other treaty ports, Ningpo, Foochow, Amoy, and Shanghai, the ordinary natives bore the invasion philosophically. They were not heirs to a tradition of independence and xenophobia, like the Cantonese, nor had they been indoctrinated through the years with contempt for barbarians. Their main complaint as time went on was that so many Cantonese came along with the foreigners: they didn't like their southern brothers. But the official class did resent the barbarians, and resisted the intrusion in every way. To begin with, there were tussles about accommodation for consuls. In the Chinese version of the treaty, rights of residence for the foreigners were ambiguously stated, as were the rights of entry into the towns. The foreigners, however, believed firmly that these rights had been granted to them. In most cases, firmness won the day, as it did for Rutherford Alcock, the British Consul at Foochow. Alcock found the local gentry, of whom a large proportion were Manchus, determined not to let him live where he wished, but he insisted on having his way, and he got it. He had to rise again to the occasion later, in what was called the Tsingpu affair; by insisting once more on getting his way, and beating down the officials, he became a hero to the disgruntled traders of Canton.

From the foreign point of view the best port to live in was probably Shanghai. There, Westerners had ample space, which they divided into districts that were to remain as they then were for a century to come—the French Concession and the International Settlement of British and Americans. It had been laid down in the treaties that barbarians could travel inland, but never beyond a point that could be reached in half a day's journey; this was later defined as thirty miles. Treaty or no treaty, only a reckless adventurer would have made such a journey very often from Canton, but the Chinese of Shanghai's province, Kiangsu, were more amenable. Many a barbarian went into the interior there, to shoot wildfowl or merely to look around or, perhaps, to convert the heathen. In the earliest days there was an occasional contretemps—on one occasion at least, a hapless Chinese bystander was peppered with shot intended for wild duck—but incidents like that, which would have led to murderous riots in Kwangtung, were managed at Shanghai without bloodshed. As the barbarians grew more confident, they broke the rules a bit and went a good deal deeper than thirty miles into the country, usually taking the precaution of wearing Chinese costume on these occasions. The authorities protested against such infringements, but with the passing of time their protests lost fire— everywhere, that is, but at Canton. Canton remained very difficult. Canton was the center of chronic controversy.

It was partly a question of habit. Like the Chinese, the Manchu lords of Peking were intensely conservative. Canton had always been the place set apart for segregating barbarians, snubbing barbarians, and holding off barbarians; therefore, that was where such duties must continue to be performed as long as China could get away with it. The old Emperor was the essence of conservatism, not that he had much genuine influence on his Grand Council during the postwar years before he died. He merely strengthened the tendency of the officials to hang back and remain in the past. They used every trick in the trade to drag their feet, as far as Canton was concerned. As we have seen, they also diverted all would-be foreign diplomats to that port where they could be the more conveniently dealt with.

As for trade in Canton, the angry barbarians complained that it wasn't going much better than it had done before the war, but in that they were not being quite truthful. Without the Cohong things did proceed more advantageously for the foreigners. Peking stood firm on the subject of opium and refused to legalize its sale, but the smuggling continued as before, technically outside the knowledge of the consuls. The traders' main grievance was that they were still confined to the old ghetto of factory buildings, which had been put up again since the holocaust of 1842, though the treaties stipulated (they claimed) that they should have free entry into the walled city. The gates remained closed to them, and what aggravated them most of all was that Sir John Davis seemed willing to let this infringement of their rights continue, by default. In vain did they urge him to take action. He did not catch their fire. He was soothed by Ch'i-ying, that master handler of barbarians: time after time he allowed the old Manchu to put him off. By implication; he asked, did it matter so much, after all? Why *should* Europeans be so keen to go into the city, anyway? They were perfectly well able to do their work without this privilege.

The Canton traders argued that this wasn't the point. It was their right to go into the city. They were being deprived of their right, and if they sat down under such injustice the Chinese would think them weak and contemptible, and would take further advantage. They must start as they meant to go on, with the upper hand.

Ch'i-ying had an answer to this. Ch'i-ying was always reasonable. He explained to Sir John that Canton city remained closed to foreigners because of The People. The People weren't yet in a favorable frame of mind for such a shock. One must take into account the Cantonese temperament; quick-tempered, xenophobic, more difficult altogether than the nature of the cultured Northerners. To prove his point, Ch'i-ying published in the city a proclamation about the barbarians, asking if they should or should not be allowed inside the walls; it was a test of public temper, he explained to Sir John, a sort of trial balloon. Nowadays we might call it a proto-Gallup poll. The reaction may or may not have been a genuine reply from The People; Sir John had no way of knowing, but it certainly vindicated Ch'i-ying if it was. Promptly, somebody hung up a placard in reply, declaring the British to be of "a dangerous deceitfulness of heart, untameable as the wild horse, and voracious as the vulture."

It ended with a threat to kill any Englishman who dared to show his nose inside the city.

"You see," said Ch'i-ying regretfully.

Soon afterwards a mob attacked the factories again, and Sir John dropped the subject. But the traders wouldn't leave him alone, and as time went on their gloomy prognostications were justified. Any barbarian who went outside the factory enclosure took a risk; it was worse than before the war. In 1847 two British sailors went into the city, in spite of the danger, and were set upon and nearly killed. There were other incidents as well, and Sir John determined at last to go into action. He was the readier for it because there had just been a change of government at home. The new Prime Minister was Lord Palmerston, who approved of a stiffer attitude in the East. Therefore Davis sent three gunboats full of soldiers up the river to Canton and past the city, where with the greatest of ease and no casualties the forts' defenses were destroyed and the Chinese guns spiked. It seemed as if this was all the situation had needed. Ch'i-ying immediately became conciliatory, and the firebrands among the foreigners congratulated each other. But once more the Manchu managed somehow to put Sir John off; he signed an agreement that the city would be opened, well and truly, in another two years' time—April 6, 1849. Presumably, two years would be enough to reconcile The People to the inevitable. However, by the time April in 1849 came around, Ch'i-ying had been replaced, and so had Sir John Davis.

Ch'i-ying's successor was both Viceroy and Imperial Commissioner in one. His name was Hsü Kuang-chin, and during his comparatively short term of office he proved to be a difficult man to handle, not only for the Western barbarians, though he disliked them intensely. He saw no reason to behave like Ch'i-ying and pretend to a fondness he did not feel, so there were no more soft words and placatory promises from that office. Sir John Davis was succeeded by Sir George Bonham, and he too was more abrupt and determined than the man he replaced. Nevertheless he didn't go at the city-wall problem bald-headed, as the traders wished him to. He believed that Ch'i-ying had told the truth about the Cantonese populace: he accepted the fact that they were refractory and independent, and it seemed to him that another forcing of the defenses might well do more harm than good to trading prospects, which after all he was there to further. He proposed alternative action. It was obvious long before

April 1849, that the Cantonese authorities had no intention of carrying out the agreement. Bonham suggested that when the time came and the Europeans were again refused entry, the British should send a mission to Peking. If, as was very likely, it should be turned back, they could blockade the Grand Canal, thus either putting a stop to all inland water traffic for the Chinese, or bringing matters to a showdown. He had in mind that in the past the mere threat of such a mission had always been enough to stir stubborn Chinese officials to action. But Palmerston didn't like the idea, because, as he said, such action might have the same adverse effect on future chances of trade as a forced entry into Canton. Nothing at all was done, therefore, by the British. On his side Hsü memorialized the Throne for instructions, and while he waited for a reply more mobs rioted in the city and made provocative proclamations, just to keep the barbarians reminded of how intractable the Cantonese still were.

A week before April 6, a reply came in the name of the Emperor: "Since the people of Kwangtung are now unanimous in their determination, and do not wish that foreigners should enter the city, how can, then, an Imperial order to that effect be stuck up everywhere, and forced proclamation be issued? The Central Empire cannot oppose the people in order to yield to men from a distance. Foreign nations ought also to examine into the feelings of the people, with a due regard for mercantile interests."

Thus April 6 came and went with no change in the status quo, and soon afterwards Hsü was honored by the Emperor. It was the most pointed way possible of administering a snub indirectly to the barbarians. Five years had now passed since the final signing of Opium War treaties. The sentiments of the factory foreigners can be imagined, but that is not necessary, since Rutherford Alcock, now posted to Shanghai, has put it all down on paper. He had never himself worked in the south, but he was a spokesman for the traders in that he agreed with them as to how Chinese should be handled. His own stern methods in the northern ports were successful, and he was much admired for this reason. In 1849 he published, anonymously, a series of letters that sum up the attitude of his school, especially its abiding faith in trade as a universal blessing. Among other things he said,

"The lesson of the past is very legibly written in the history of our relations—oppression in the Chinese, increased by submission in the English. Resistance of the latter followed by concession in the former may be read in every stage, and the influence of the late war, beyond the tangible effects embodied in the provisions of the treaties, has been limited very much to outward forms: there is reason to suspect that the policy of the Chinese has been masked, not changed. . . . They have no objection to the foreign trade as one of the elements of their own prosperity, though they much underrate its importance. . . . The practicability of maintaining our relations on their present unsatisfactory footing in the south must be very doubtful." [Alexander Michie, *The Englishman in China* (London, 1900), appendix.]

Alcock frankly expressed the feeling of the extremists that another war might soon be advisable unless the Europeans were willing to let the whole China trade come to a stop. The more the Chinese were appeased, the more difficult they were bound to become. "A rooted conviction in the minds of a whole population, derived from traditional knowledge of the humiliating and derogatory position voluntarily accepted by foreigners, cannot be effaced by a treaty, or even a short successful war which passed over the city that was the offending cause almost harmless (sic). . . . If it be the traditional policy of the Tartar dynasty to keep foreigners at the outer confines of the empire and in a degrading position, it may with better justice be the policy of Great Britain to obtain a direct action upon their centre, and freedom from idle and vexatious recourses." What followed makes strange reading today: "The right of a nation to interdict intercourse and commerce, and therefore to determine upon what conditions it shall exist, is but an imperfect right, and subject to such modifications as the rights of other nations to the use of innocent objects of utility dictate; and the refusal of a common right is an abuse of the sovereign power, and an injury to be resisted."

Of the opium trade he spoke casually and coolly: he lived in a totally different climate than ours. "They (the Chinese) believe to maintain this traffic we made war and dictated a humiliating peace, and that we are prepared to do so again, if they ventured on any interference. . . . These opinions may be false or true in their foundation, that is not the question, but, What is the influence they are calculated to exercise? Hostility and distrust can alone be traced to this source. . . . Accepted as *un fait accompli*, the best means of neutralizing and counteracting its bad effects are alone to be considered, since the enormous capital, large revenue, and inseparable connection of our legitimate trade with opium, as a means of laying down funds in China, involved in the traffic, precludes all idea of its cessation or removal. . . . As to any remedy to be applied to the evils of the opium trade, there seems to be none open to either Government but its legalisation, which would strip it of its contraband character, and remove from the emperor the open reproach to his authority, while it might be made to yield a large revenue to his treasury."

In spite of the fact that Alcock visualized a second war as a not undesirable possibility, he was not sure that the Superintendent should jump the gun by embarking upon a forcible entry into Canton. He weighed the arguments on both sides. "The entrance into the city is obviously a question of principle, not of any *direct* practical advantage in a *commercial* sense. The freedom from annoyance, and security to property, are more truly so, and of these two the latter, by far the most essential and important to our interests, seems only to require more storage room for goods, away from a dense Chinese suburb which renders insurance from risk of fire impossible . . ." especially, he might have added, considering the likelihood of fire in that particular part of China.

It would be wrong to say that the Consul was 100 per cent in favor of a war. He recognized a grave danger that would certainly accompany any victory Britain would win if she were to fight China again—the competition of other Western powers. In the light of later history his words make peculiarly interesting reading. "Russia, France, Spain, Portugal, Holland, and America, with their several jealousies and united rivalry with England, their missionary enterprises or commercial and political schemes clashing in their aim and development, are all capable of creating such turmoil, strife, and disturbance throughout the empire, if free access to the Court and the provinces were insisted upon by Great Britain, as could only end in the ejection of Europeans from China as formerly from Japan, or an intestine war in which European power would probably be involved on opposite sides, and to their mutual destruction as States with commercial interests in the country. These, again, might lead to attempts at territorial possession, suggested in the first instance, as in India, in self-defence, and afterwards continued from necessity. With Russia spreading her gigantic arms to the north and east, Great Britain on the south and west, Spain, Holland and Portugal with their colonies in the Chinese and Indian seas, a struggle for superiority on the soil of China for exclusive advantages of predominant influence might be centered in Peking and embroil the whole of Europe in hostile relations."

*   *   *

Whether they had meant it in just that way or not, the Imperial advisers had spoken no more than the truth when they described Canton's population as turbulent and unmanageable. They were soon to discover how accurate they had been, when a fair proportion of that population rose against them. In July 1850 the insurgent plotters of the Triad Society, who had long been waiting for their chance, felt that the moment had arrived because of the old Emperor's death. They spread the word, and a large number of conspirators made their way to a meeting place outside the city walls where it had been decided to start hostilities. They wasted no time in playing their trump card, the name of Celestial Virtue, Chu, the alleged scion of the Mings. Greatly daring, they affixed to a city gate their placard, announcing to anyone who could read that "His Sovereign Majesty" Celestial Virtue hereby called upon his people to join him in overthrowing the Viceroy, and offered a reward for the apprehension of Hsü. It had been many years since such an affront had faced any official of the Emperor: Hsü hardly knew how to contain his wrath. Furiously he collected crack troops and set out to catch and punish the malefactors. He did not know—not that it would have mattered, or held him back—that the so-called Ming prince was not really behind this manifestation, being at the time a long way off in the mountains with Hung Hsiu-ch'uan. In Hsü's estimation this would be merely a civil war, not unlike many others that had been fought in the past, and if he had been dealing merely with Triads he would have been right.

As it was, many of the Triad brothers even now were in ignorance of the God-worshipers with whom their leaders had made alliance. But they soon found out that the Ming pretender was taking refuge with a body of other rebels in a hide-out in the Kwangsi hills. When Kwangtung grew too hot to hold a Triad group, they naturally repaired to that hide-out and joined Hung's people. Now and then a Triad would allow himself to be baptized and become a God-worshiper, but conversion was not made a condition of his acceptance into the camp. By this time Hung's band had decided to call themselves the Heavenly Kingdom of Great Peace, T'ai-p'ing T'ien-kui, a name that was soon shortened in ordinary conversation to "the Taipings"—simply meaning Great Peace. Never was there a less apposite title, even in China where euphemism abounds. The Great Peace Rebellion was to devastate thousands of square miles of country and cause millions of deaths.

At first near Canton city, then deep into the countryside, the Imperial forces pursued their campaign furiously, showing no more mercy than Chinese troops ever did. They would torture their prisoners for information, then execute them in public, according to ancient custom, by decapitation or slicing. Red-haired barbarians who happened on occasion to witness such executions, usually performed in the mass, were appalled but not surprised: Chinese torture and public execution were notorious in the Western world and just what they would have expected of Viceroy Hsü's men. Hsü was under the impression for two months that he was waging war only against Triads, and for that time he was: Hung Hsiu-ch'uan was holding his hand and waiting. Not until the end of September did the Emperor's troops come up against any Taipings, when they had a horrid surprise; by chance, in pursuit of the enemy, they cornered Hung himself in a mountain cul-de-sac, whereupon Taipings fell upon them with fury, beating them off with many casualties, chasing them out of their headquarters in a nearby town, and occupying their barracks. The Great Rebellion was under way.

Like his Triad allies, Hung well knew that this couldn't have happened at a more advantageous time for his cause or a worse one for the Ch'ing Dynasty, since the old Emperor had just died and Hsien-feng was taking his place on the Dragon Throne. If the nineteen-year-old Emperor had been a stronger character . . . but he was not. Under the old Tao-kuang Emperor the Grand Council had taken firm control of affairs, and even in the palace the Emperor didn't rule; eunuchs were the real lords there. But things might have been different afterwards if the old man had chosen one of his elder sons, Prince Kung, to succeed him instead of the limp Hsien-feng; Kung was able and steady. Why the father chose Hsien-feng is explained in a story that may or may not be true, which is told in the fascinating, gossip-filled *Annals and Memoirs of the Court of Peking,* by Bland and Backhouse. China has always been a reservoir for particularly colorful anecdotes, and surely some of them, at least, must be true. As this one goes, the Emperor commanded all the princes to go out hunting one spring day in the Southern Park. Hsien-feng's tutor concocted a clever plan and coached his charge carefully. That day the young prince refrained from shooting or setting traps or doing anything at all to kill a beast or bird; he merely stood by and watched his brothers gaily bagging everything they came across. When at the end of the day they counted over their prizes, the youngest prince's bag was empty, and the old Emperor asked him why. The boy replied.

"It's wrong to take life at this season. Beasts and birds have their young to take care of. To kill them at such a time violates the harmony of Nature."

Such a Confucian attitude pleased the old father so much that he declared, "This is the conduct of a superior man," and named Hsien-feng as his heir.

Only nineteen when he acceded to the Throne, he was weak and easily led by the palace eunuchs. As far as the rebellion in the south was concerned he was a cipher. The Grand Council did the Emperor's thinking for him and made all decisions, merely asking for a Vermilion Pencil endorsement when this was necessary. But the situation changed somewhat when Hsien-feng's new concubine Yehonala made her appearance in the palace. Yehonala, a Manchu girl of good family like all the accepted concubines—most of these girls were well born; in any case the status of concubine was a perfectly respectable one in China—caught Hsien-feng's fancy from the beginning, and never looked back. She was to become Empress Dowager, the Tzu-hsi of the Boxer Rebellion, a redoubtable enemy of the West. She was unusually intelligent, but even her brains, in those early days of the Taiping Rebellion, didn't give her an understanding of its nature. The Rebellion was something unique in China's history. Time and again the country had seen invasion and civil war, but this was war of a novel sort, a great popular movement based on a religious idea that came from outside the Kingdom.

*   *   *

With the campaign well on its way, Hung put into practice many customs he had long been planning. Others he had already instituted, as for example his rule of celibacy for everyone except himself. A definite program for daily life was vital, since the Heavenly Kingdom was moving every day, and growing by thousands: discipline was everything, or nearly everything—a willingness of heart was also essential. According to his lights, Hung was strictly just. Whatever the Taipings owned in the way of food went into a common pool. Disbursement of silver was decided by the leaders for the good of all. Women and children were carefully guarded, sleeping in their own community center every night and marching under escort by day. This was done in order to avoid the mass rape that was one of the most fearsome things in Chinese warfare, in case the Imperialists should win any victory, and for his part Hung decreed that none of his followers were to rape anyone, or do violence to anybody but an Imperial soldier or a Manchu. Young Taiping girls did not have their feet bound—this was probably because Hung was a Hakka, and Hakka didn't go in for foot-binding. Taiping men, as soon as they joined the force, had to cut off their pigtails and let their shaven hair grow out. When it was grown they covered it with turbans: they were known as the Long-hairs for this reason.

The Taipings were feared of course, for they took towns and sacked them as they moved, but the populace soon learned that they were not to be feared as much as the Imperial troops, who wiped out every village they came upon, and after raping the women put the population to the sword, regardless of guilt or innocence. People would try to escape before the Imperialists arrived, and as there was nothing else for them to do they made their way to the nearest Taiping encampment and pledged their allegiance to Hung. Or if the Taipings got there first, before burning the houses they would warn the people to get out, ending up with a blanket invitation to join the procession. The dispossessed often discovered that existence was quite bearable under the Taiping flag. But the effect on the countryside was terrible—razed villages and forsaken farms marked the trail of the rebels everywhere.

As Emperor of the Heavenly Kingdom, Hung considered himself above the rule of celibacy. He maintained a chief wife, a girl he had married before the days of the Kingdom, and a number of concubines, but he had no eunuchs; there were no eunuchs anywhere among the Taipings. Women did the work in his palace, wherever he lived. Both he and the Ming pretender wore garments of the forbidden color, Imperial yellow. Hung dressed his children in yellow too, and saw to it that his soldiers used the color lavishly in their uniforms. On state occasions he wore a headdress copied from that of the Ming Emperors, a tall miterlike hat. One might have supposed that the presence of Celestial Virtue would be an embarrassment, or at least a confusion, considering how many members of the Triad Society had pledged their fealty to the Ming prince, but it does not seem to have troubled Hung. The two men had gone through the blood-brother ceremony, which made it all right as far as the Triads were concerned; Celestial Virtue himself said that he was a younger son of God, Hung's little brother.

Time after time, the Taipings defeated the Imperial troops, with the Triads fighting along with them in peculiar alliance. The combination worked. Though the Triads were ordinary insurgents, they reflected the fiery spirit of the Taipings who were battling for an ideal and believed fervently that their leader Hung Hsiu-ch'uan was the new Redeemer they had only lately learned about. It was not really necessary that all the Triads be converted, though many did make the change; they were, after all, fighting toward the same end, Peking. Hung had outlined his strategy. They were to move north, fighting as they went, along the West River as far as they could, then cross the watershed beyond Kweilin in Kwangsi. By this time they were thirty or forty thousand strong—the figures are impossible to pin down accurately—with only about one-third of them men of fighting age; the rest were women and children. It was an immense undertaking, but Hung was confident that Shang-ti would see them all the way; after Kweilin to the Yangtze and then east along the river to Nanking and the sea, with Peking the final object of the march. Their pattern of operation was always the same. They would move in on every town they came to, break the idols in the temples, sack the houses, make converts, and move on. Now and then they were overtaken by Imperialists. Then there would be a battle, which the Taipings nearly always won. Defeated and much reduced, the Imperial troops would fall back to recover, while their leaders wrote lying reports about another great victory over the rebels, which was sent back, ultimately, to Peking. Viceroy Hsü simply dared not tell the truth to the Grand Council, but there came a time when they found it out from other sources and he had to face the reckoning. He was removed from office—lucky to escape from execution, as he well knew—and replaced by Yeh Ming-ch'en, a man even crueler than Hsü, and more effective as a general. (He was also even less compromising toward the Western barbarians in Canton.) Yeh went at the rebel problem with fresh vigor. He took prisoner thousands of the enemy and no doubt some innocent parties as well, and excuted them all, or caused them to be executed. His name is still remembered for ferocity. Yet the rebels continued on their march. But Yeh's cohorts succeeded in holding them up for six months. It happened at Yungan, eighty miles south of Kweilin, in the last outpost of the outer mountain range. Yungan was the Taipings' first strongly walled city. They breached the defenses and occupied the palace, where they were able to make themselves comfortable in luxurious surroundings. To celebrate the victory Hung relaxed the rule of celibacy. A good time and plenty to eat were had by all, until the leader decided that they should go on their way, and then they found that the strong walls that had protected them were now a prison, for Yeh's men surrounded the town in great numbers. The Taipings were cooped up in Yungan for six months, until April 1852. Then they broke out, fought a sharp battle, and escaped with many losses. The Imperialists pounced on Celestial Virtue as he was making his escape under heavy guard, and sent their prize to Peking. There, the officials were jubilant. They had no thorough understanding of the Taiping movement, and thought that this Ming pretender must be the root of the trouble. Now they had him, and of course they killed him. But before he died, Chu wrote out for them a "confession," a long, puzzling story about the man Hung Hsiu-ch'uan. In executing the Ming pretender the Imperial party settled nothing for themselves. Rather, they were helping the self-styled Heavenly Emperor by removing his only rival, as from that time on Hung could claim the undivided loyalty of the Triad Society.

Again on their way, the rebels emerged from the mountains of Kwangsi into open country and arrived at Kweilin, a city set among sharp-pointed peaks sticking up individually from flat ground, as if Pluto had thrust up spears from the underworld. The Taipings tried to get into Kweilin as they had entered Yungan, but the stout walls resisted all their attacks, and the inhabitants held out against a month's siege. Finally Hung abandoned the attempt. His people continued through Hunan to the Yuen-ch'ang, a tributary of the Yangtze, where they managed to get together a great number of boats and carried on by water. Literally it was not all plain sailing, as they were ambushed from a bridge and the flotilla was burnt. The scattered Taipings recovered, however, and moved on to lay siege to Changsha. Like Kweilin, Changsha resisted, though this time the Taipings tried much longer to sit it out. At last, toward the end of November, Hung gave it up as a bad job. The Three Cities, Hanyang, Hankow, and Wuchang, clustered together at the confluences of the Han and Yangtze rivers, were an easier proposition: the Taipings took rich prizes there, burned Hankow, and were able once again to find boats for their journey toward the coast. Hung had led his people more than halfway to Nanking.

All through Hunan their only serious opposition had been organized by a man who was not, strictly speaking, a military person at all—Tseng Kuo-fan. Until a few months earlier, Tseng had been a high official at the Manchu court, nothing less than Vice-President of the Board of Rites. He was one of those Chinese who co-operated with the Manchus and accepted the Ch'ing Dynasty wholeheartedly. He was a native of Hunan, and happened to be on compassionate leave in 1852, for his mother had died and he obeyed Confucian doctrine, retiring from his post and going back to his native province for the proper twenty-seven months of mourning. There on his estate, Tseng saw at first hand what was going on, and realized better than his Peking colleagues how grave the situation was. He set straight to work rounding up the local peasants, most of whom he knew from childhood. He drilled them and trained them and welded them into a well-disciplined body which he called the Hunan Braves. To help him in this work he had a friend named Li Hung-chang from Anhui, the next-door province; Li had been dispossessed by the Taipings and chased off his property, so he had a vested interest in the project. The Hunan Braves gave a good accounting of themselves and managed more than once to come off better than the Taipings. This was all very well, but Tseng knew that he must get official sanction for what he was doing, and he wrote off, as soon as he could, to Peking requesting it. If they approved up there, he would be appointed commander in chief of his troops and everything would be regular.

The Grand Council was startled by the proposition, and afraid of it, for they were always afraid of anything new. Tseng had no right to develop these unsuspected talents for military matters—he was a civil servant. It could not be allowed, they told each other. Next thing you knew he might take it into his head to lead his private army against *them*. It was awkward when the Emperor's first reaction was not theirs, when he expressed enthusiasm and admiration for Tseng's feat, but the Councilors knew how to manage Hsien-feng, and with a few well-chosen words they reminded him of the hidden dangers they had already sensed. Promptly Hsien-feng agreed with them: this sort of thing would not do.

Tseng Kuo-fan might have been suppressed then and there if the Emperor's beloved Yehonala hadn't spoken up. Hers was the voice of common sense. Alone among the people at court, she considered the very real threat of the Taipings. As she said, anyone who could cope with them should be encouraged. For herself she thought Tseng Kuo-fan most enterprising and praiseworthy, a superior man indeed. Hsien-feng changed his mind again and agreed with his concubine. The Grand Council was defeated. Tseng Kuo-fan was told to take his new title and go ahead with the good work. High time too, he must have reflected, for the Taipings were nearly on Nanking's threshold, and now numbered eighty thousand.

*   *   *

Like the other Western barbarians at the coast, the missionaries of the treaty ports were by this time all too well aware of the strange uprising inland, and naturally they pricked up their ears when they heard that the Christian faith, or something very like it, had somehow got mixed up in the proceedings. Distressed reports trickled out of Hunan from crypto-Catholic Chinese there who had inherited their beliefs from converts of centuries earlier, and still continued unobtrusively worshiping the Christian God, aided by foreign priests who dared penetrate the country to look after their flock. Evidently their habits had not been kept quiet enough. Some of them were hounded out by Imperialist troops and accused of alliance with the Taipings, and persecuted accordingly. The Jesuits of Siccawei, Shanghai, received this news and spread it, and missionaries of other sects began to ask each other what it all meant. Soon afterwards they had their answer from Hong Kong. A kinsman of Hung's, taken prisoner early in the campaign, had managed to escape his captors but found himself on the wrong side of the lines. He made his way to Hong Kong and took refuge in a Swedish mission, where he told the Reverend Theodore Hamberg all about Hung Hsiu-ch'uan and his revelations. The mystery was solved.

At first it must have seemed to the foreign missionaries a miracle of the happiest sort that the beliefs they had imported should have taken root in so unlikely a manner, and flourished unknown to them. They were eager to get in touch with Hung Hsiu-ch'uan as soon as possible and help him to Christianize the whole nation. But second thought, and third, and fourth, soon intervened. That claim of Hung's to have gone bodily to Heaven and talked face to face with God: his declaration that he was God's son . . . Was not such stuff dangerous and blasphemous? The reverend gentlemen were shocked. Then too, to which church would Hung choose to belong— Baptist? Lutheran? Roman? A good deal would depend on that. Moreover, would a foreigner be able to handle a man like Hung, who from all accounts was a savage? He had a great number of concubines; he was evidently a pitiless murderer; there were un- savory stories of intrigue at his palace, and jealousy, and injustice. Finally, there was the political aspect of the matter. Missionaries were not supposed to be actively concerned with politics in China, but it goes without saying that they sank or swam with the other foreigners, and depended heavily on their diplomatic representa- tives. To join forces with rebels would be considered treasonable by the court at Peking. The Emperor if he retained enough power would certainly expel barbarians if they offended him; he would push them all out, taking away the footholds that had so recently and laboriously been gained. *If* he retained the power . . . What if he didn't? What if the rebels triumphed? Well, in that case there would still be time to claim special treatment, from one Christian to another.

While these problems were being pondered in the missions, the Taipings in March 1853 moved into Nanking, killing twenty thou- sand people in the process.

Chapter Five

In Nanking the crusaders found any number of idols to smash, and had a splendid time doing it. They began with the famous Porcelain Pagoda, which they destroyed completely, and in their zeal also came near to murdering more than a hundred genuine Christians—some Roman Catholics whose church seemed to these home-grown monotheists a hotbed of idolatry. Fortunately the mistake was discovered and explained away in time to save the Catholics. It would have made Hung feel very bad if he had been instrumental in wiping out the first Western God-worshipers it was his lot to encounter since the ill-fated experiment with Issachar Roberts. He still felt akin to all Christians, and hoped to be able, once he had pacified his country, to unite with them. As for the Nanking Catholics, they prudently decided to join the Taipings, after they saw what happened to some other people who resisted the invaders; there were horrible scenes of carnage, as there often are following Chinese battles. The quality of mercy was not one of the Christian virtues that Hung Hsiu-ch'uan adopted. No person recognized as a Manchu was spared—men, women and children of the hated race were beheaded or burned to death—and it is no wonder that all the others deemed it wiser to merge themselves with Hung's followers. Within a week the city was quiet.

It was then that Hung's initial, astonishing drive toward a goal seemed to flag. The day of the Taipings was not yet at its noon, but Hung determined to stay where he was, in Nanking. This city was after all the proper place, he decided, for his throne and his dynasty. Not for a moment was he relinquishing his intention to overthrow the Manchu usurpers in Peking. A few weeks after the occupation he sent an army north under one of his most trusted generals, Lin, to do that task for him. But in person he was to stay where he was for the rest of his life. He liked Nanking. In its own right it was ancient and redolent with tradition, having been in the past the capital of the Ming Dynasty. Besides, it was for his purposes better placed then Peking, for the Taipings now had a double task— to keep what they had already won in the southwest, as well as to conquer the north's fresh territory. Under Tseng Kuo-fan the Emperor's forces were trying to fill every vacuum left along the Yangtze by the departing Taipings, and whenever they could they retook towns evacuated by the rebels. From his new stronghold Hung sent troops back to reaffirm Taiping dominion. Already Tseng's men were in possession of Hankow. The rebels snatched it back, and this time when they went away they left a garrison to guard the fort. It was clear that vigilance would be necessary for a long time. So Hung stayed in Nanking and enjoyed his glory, the central figure of a fantastic and splendid court. Those of his troops who were not occupied in the rear, or on the way to Peking with Lin, filled in their time and kept fit by wandering about the neighborhood to conquer such towns as Chinkiang, and keep the countryside unhappily alert. Inside the walls the community lived according to Hung's peculiar rules, much like Spartans, with the women segregated and the men sternly denying themselves wine and tobacco. Opium smoking was punishable by death. Like squires with medieval knights the young boys waited on the warriors. Nobles dressed in bright silks, and Hung spent much of his time interpreting the Scriptures in immensely long poems.

Now that the famous rebels had drawn so near to the foreigners in their settlements outside the Chinese city of Shanghai, the Western barbarians determined to find out more about them. In April, a few weeks after the occupation of Nanking, the British Governor of Hong Kong, Sir George Bonham, went to Shanghai and from there set out in HMS *Hermes* up the Yangtze, to interview the mysterious Hung Hsiu-Ch'uan. By mistake—the Taiping guards thought the *Hermes* was an attacking Imperialist craft—a few shots were fired as they came close to the city walls, but explanations were soon made and the Taipings apologized and were very nice about it. Bonham's intentions were to make contact with Hung, to affirm Britain's neutrality in the civil war, and to make it clear that her nationals must be left unmolested no matter how that war went. Most especially he wanted to declare the terms of the Nanking Treaty, in case Hung should inherit the government. Unfortunately for these hopes, the Governor was not to see Hung in person; his intentions were frustrated by conditions not unfamiliar to the British, namely, that the self-styled Emperor of China expected this barbarian envoy to kowtow to him. It was Macartney's dilemma all over again, and Bonham was held by the same laws that had held the noble lord: he could no more have kowtowed to Hung than he could to the Ch'ing Emperor in Peking, without falsely implying that his country was tributary to China. All this had to be explained through Bonham's interpreter, Meadows, later to become British Consul General in Shanghai. No offense was taken but there was as a consequence no meeting, except on lower levels. While the *Hermes* remained at anchor a number of Taipings came aboard out of friendly curiosity, and Meadows was able to go ashore and call on several princes. He was fluent in Chinese and conversed a good deal with them, and was very favorably impressed with most of what he saw and heard. One of the nobles showed a lively grasp of politics, cautioning him and his nation against the Manchus, who would certainly, he said, try to use barbarians against the Taipings if they could. When the ship left, Hung sent Bonham a long communication in poetical form, setting forth his "message" and making various declarations which scandalized the Western missionaries when they saw them—of his being the son of God, and other claims of the same sort.

Unaware of the judgments being passed on him, Hung then wrote cordially to his old teacher, Issachar Roberts, suggesting that the American come to Nanking, there to live and teach and preach the right true religion. Roberts was somewhat alarmed. He couldn't remember anything about Hung Hsiu-ch'uan's early contact with himself. Considering the wild statements this man was making, the situation seemed so delicate to Roberts that before making up his mind he went to consult with the American Commissioner. The Commissioner thought he ought not to go, because if it became known that an American missionary had joined the rebels, Peking would suspect the whole American community of non-neutrality. Most foreign missionaries in China are not noticeably inclined to listen to the cautious voice of officialdom, but Roberts was an exception, and stayed where he was. The other missionaries of the treaty ports buzzed with speculation about the poem Bonham had brought back. Could they, or could they not, afford to make advances to this strange man Hung who claimed to be of their faith?

To allow him to slip through their fingers might be a tremendous waste, and unwise as well, for he might possibly succeed altogether in his revolution and replace the Ch'ing Dynasty in Peking. However, one could not overlook the shocking, impious claims he was making. He was blasphemous. On the whole, the missionaries decided they were better off if they left Hung alone. Like Issachar Roberts they could not be totally indifferent to the effect any advances to Hung might have on the Manchus, especially as just at that time the Manchus were trying to persuade the British to lend them some ships so that they might pursue their campaign against the Taipings. The British intended to refuse. It was no time to irritate the court even further.

The attempt to get aid from the barbarians was almost the only sign of agitation that Peking deigned to show. For the most part, Peking behaved as if the Taiping contingent under Lin's command, for example, was not at all on the way to the capital. The courtiers busied themselves with their customary peacetime preoccupations, and exhibited the usual determination to maintain their wall against the West. No threat from compatriots would alter their attitude toward the newly arrived American Commissioner, a man named Humphrey Marshall. Marshall went to present his credentials in the proper way to Viceroy Yeh Ming-ch'en at Canton, though it was not a propitious time to visit the southern city, as the Triads were surrounding it. But Yeh was unavailable; Marshall was told that he was occupied for an indefinite period, chasing rebels in the country. Marshall therefore sailed to Shanghai, in hopes of getting his credentials presented there through the Taotai, Wu Chien-chang, who was concurrently the Superintendent of Customs. Wu was a merchant from Canton, one of the men who had always dealt with barbarians and who was reasonably ready to help them when he could, and Marshall thought he might be willing to forward the papers to the Viceroy of Kiangsu. But Wu had not received instructions to do this and he was afraid even to see the American. Marshall, tired of being shunted back and forth, then fell back on the old threat of frustrated barbarians in China and said he would move on to Tientsin since he couldn't get action any nearer home. This of course sent all the officials scurrying around in agitation. Once more Marshall was directed to Canton, and this time he found Yeh willing to be cornered and to accept the credentials.

I-liang, Viceroy of Liang-chiang, the two Kiang provinces, and another old hand with barbarians, memorialized the Throne in explanation of Wu's behavior, with an interesting little comment on his opinion of Americans: "The United States usually is not much trouble nor is the said barbarian chief tyrannical or proud: fundamentally there was no objection to having a personal interview with him at Shanghai, but it was feared that as other countries would imitate and come one after the other to request the honor of an interview . . . and as it would be hard to avoid the development of further complications, it would be better to have the said barbarian come here for an interview and have it over with." This was written on July 20, when the Taiping army was well on its way to Tientsin. But in the Chinese official mind, any foreigner was more to be feared than a Chinese be he ever so rebellious. As late as September 1 an Imperial edict gave directions as to the American Commissioner's reception in Canton, for the Council darkly suspected that Marshall was going to try to get more rights of some sort out of Yeh.

"Let Yeh Ming ch'en immediately devise means of blocking and controlling him as circumstances allow. If there are further demands, hold rigidly to the treaty as before and stop his wanton demands." [Swisher, p. 194.] Considering what was about to happen to Shanghai on September 7, this edict has a weird charm.

Already, various unpleasantnesses had overtaken Shanghai. As the Taipings moved toward the coast the port was bound to feel the effects of the war, the more so because it had been so flourishing. Shanghai had become the leading export-import center of the five ports: Canton would not have been able to compete at all were it not that it was the only city where Europeans could communicate with the elusive Chinese of position. The reason for Shanghai's growth was geographical: the territory was easier of access than Canton's from both sides, since the river afforded ample berthing space, whereas most Chinese who grew silk or tea found it nearer as a market than the southern ports. Also, Shanghai was only thirteen miles from the sea as against some ninety miles in the case of Canton. The most important traders of all, the opium smugglers, considered Shanghai very good indeed. They maintained several hulks —permanent edifices made of old ships—near the river mouth. A small amount of decorum in this trade was still preserved in the old way, and the smuggling was not exactly thrust on official attention. Chinese customs officers were more than willing to be bribed in return for blindness, and since the foreigners had won the Opium War there were no more men of Commissioner Lin's zeal to prohibit the trade, so the opium sellers were even able to keep a warehouse on the mainland, downriver from Shanghai. But though opium was important it wasn't the whole story. Legitimate trade too swelled steadily; the Customs men were busy with ordinary imports and exports—until the Taipings came close. Then things changed. Then, because the rebels traveled by river, the water-borne traffic of central China slowed down, and after the Taipings occupied Nanking it was cut off altogether. Nothing came through to the coast. The only trade Shanghai saw was what remained of the stock already in town, which was exchanged for new imports that kept coming in until the warehouses overflowed. There sat Hung upriver like a cork in a bottle. Shanghai ran dry.

The Chinese merchants of the city took to hoarding such currency as they had, and would not buy the new stock. Foreign importers too ran short of money, but ships kept arriving because they had already set out from their Western ports before their owners heard the news of the Taiping victory, and the foreign importers had to pay duty on all goods coming in whether or not they wanted them. As pockets emptied the importers went to complain to their acknowledged leader, the British Consul Rutherford Alcock, who had made a name for his firm stand when defending British trade. The merchants asked if they need really go on paying duty on goods they couldn't sell in the country. They argued that the Chinese authorities, because they had allowed things to come to this distressing pass, should not expect to profit from the miserable situation. The Chinese had not done their job: they had not maintained order or kept trade possible, so why should they be paid anything? Alcock replied, as he had to do, that the terms of the treaty were clear and duty must be paid, but the traders continued to struggle. Could not some kind of credit scheme be worked out, so that they needn't hand over any cold cash until the currency shortage was relieved? They could sign bonds, and settle up later when the money flowed normally once more.

As always, Alcock saw the merchants' point of view and he wasn't averse to the suggestion. In any case there was nothing else to do —the Taotai's various stratagems weren't helping the situation, though he had set up a post in the interior which gave some access to the Chinese selling produce—so Alcock allowed a credit scheme to go into effect. The British Consulate was for that period virtually a bank, accepting bonds from foreign shipowners and permitting ships to come and go on his responsibility, while he promised the Customs to pay later. But Sir George Bonham didn't approve when he arrived on his fact-finding mission, and put a stop to the practice. He pointed out that it was improper for England to arrogate to herself the job of duty collecting on behalf of China. The Consulate must not serve as a deputy Custom House for Peking, and on leased Chinese territory at that. The bond system must cease forthwith.

Britain was the final authority in these matters and all the foreign traders accepted the dictum of Bonham, though they grumbled about it. But then there was a new development. In May 1853, a bare two months after the occupation of Nanking, Amoy was entered and occupied by a band of rebels who were not Taipings, but Triads. Each Taiping victory in the interior had been making conquests easier for these Triads, who were running a parallel rebellion of their own. Except for a few converts who had joined Hung back in Kwangsi, none of them accepted his religion and his disciplinary laws, so they were not a part of his forces, but they were by no means inimical to the God-worshipers; they found it very convenient to take advantage of the chaos Hung's troops brought into existence. The Triads were not visionaries like Hung, but fought for what they could get out of it, regularly moving in the margin of Taiping activity and creating a crucial problem in the treaty ports. The foreigners of the settlements had learned already to fear the Triads perhaps more than the Taipings. They were aware that there was a difference—not that the knowledge was much comfort when war was brought to their doorstep.

With the Triads in Amoy and taking over all government offices including the Custom House, the Shanghai traders watched with painful interest to see what might happen to their colleagues there. A few weeks brought the answer—nothing too bad. The rebels didn't seem to be particularly xenophobic; their hostility was concentrated on Chinese authority. As for trade, in a way things had never been so good for the foreigners, because nobody bothered to collect import duty nowadays. Ships came and went without paying for import or export. Unofficially Amoy had become a free port. There was never a great deal of business going on there, but for the first time, Shanghai traders envied the merchants of Amoy. Alcock, however, knew better, and so did the important traders. In the long run this wasn't good, and it set a dangerous precedent, for Peking would very quickly show her displeasure. Without customs revenue the Manchus would lose their last reason for tolerating the barbarians: however grudging that toleration was, it had to be cherished. When businessmen came clamoring to the Consulate, asking Alcock why they couldn't be as lucky as their Amoy opposite numbers, Alcock gave them Bonham's answer: that Amoy was different because there was now in that city no Imperial Customs whatever. Amoy shippers were forced to smuggle, whereas in Shanghai there was still a customs service; there was no solution for Shanghai traders. Besides, he said, Amoy was too small to create an incident, even in Peking where people were touchy, but a large part of the national revenue came from Shanghai collections and would be missed immediately.

On September 7 the inevitable happened and the Triads moved into Shanghai's walled city. Fortunately for the foreigners, they maintained their record of non-molestation of foreign devils. But inside the city they killed many Chinese, sacked the best houses, and either moved into or burned down the government buildings. Of these the Custom House, which was an old temple, stood on the Bund in the British settlement. In their eagerness to do a thorough job the rebels, augmented by mobsters from the city, came into the sacred area to loot the temple. Foreign anxiety during those early days was cruel. For the first time some of the settlers, new to China, heard shots and shrieks from the victims, and saw a mob at work—an unnerving sight, though the old-timers who had lived in Canton were able to shrug it off as an old story. However, even they were disturbed by the news that their best friend among the Chinese, Wu Chien-chang, had been taken prisoner on general principles, and thrown into prison. The foreigners could not take that lying down, and two of them, Americans, went to Wu's rescue and got him out, and found him refuge in the British settlement. Wu was as eager as any of the barbarians to pick up the pieces of the customs service and keep it going, since he was directly accountable to Peking, and there would come a day when the taxgatherers turned up demanding money. He tried quite valiantly to start things up again, but time after time he failed. As foreigners were under their own laws, not China's, the Consuls were by treaty responsible for all legal taxes to the Emperor of China.

Thus the question of collection of duties was once more posed to the British Consul, in default, and this time it was even more urgent. On the day the Triads destroyed the temple, for example, there were twenty-six ships waiting for clearance in the river—an average figure. The captains knew their duty to the owners. They clamored for permission to get on with the job; to load or unload, or both, and then to sail away after as quick a turnaround as possible. Alcock had no authority to hold such men. He could only reason with them and try to persuade them to do the honorable thing in paying their duty, but the honorable thing was hard to do without a Custom House, and the Consul's powers of persuasion didn't work. For some days Shanghai was a free-tariff enthusiast's dream, until Alcock and his American colleague Cunningham refused any longer to take the risk. Alcock knew he need not worry very much any more about Bonham, who was shortly going to retire to England. In the local English newspaper, the *North China Herald* of September 17, the two Consuls published declarations. A government "temporarily incapable of enforcing its rights," said Alcock, was not a government to cheat, and action would shortly be taken. After a day or two he announced that the British Consulate was once more in the banking and customs business, under what he called a provisional system. He stood ready to underwrite the duties of any shipper, as he had done before. This time, however, the third party of the big three refused to play the game: the French preferred to give up their status as honorable gentlemen and forget about duty. As soon as the other nationals saw French ships moving in and out freely, they started imitating this example. When even the Americans did it, Alcock had to admit defeat. He was beset from all sides. The Taotai, though figuratively dead, refused to lie down and kept trying to organize a system that would work, from a ship moored off the Bund. This complicated matters even more for Alcock, and did not help the customs revenues. The Consul therefore abandoned his provisional system once again, and it was open season for the import-export trade. For ten months no duty at all was collected in Shanghai.

It should have been, but probably was not, a comfort to the Shanghai barbarians and Chinese alike that their troubles were as nothing compared with those of Peking. In October the Taiping army sent out by Hung came steadily toward the capital until it reached Tientsin's outskirts, only a hundred miles away from the city of the Throne, where courtiers were paralyzed with terror, and every sort of confusion reigned in the streets. Fortunately for them, the rebels by that time were sorely in need of a rest. They were being closely followed by government troops trained by the Tseng method, who harried the enemy effectively even though they seldom went in for direct combat. The southerners also suffered grievously in an autumn chill they had never before known, and the staple food of the country—millet—was new to them and lay like so much poison in their unaccustomed stomachs. If the Taipings had been just a little more fit they could have taken Peking and found it an easy task, before the court got round to defending itself. Years of fancied inviolability had led the Manchu military men to neglect their defenses. Corruption had undermined the army, whose soldiers were underpaid and half-starved, and it was about to collapse. The courtiers were in as rotten a state as the army, and as the Taipings advanced they could think only of saving their belongings, which they packed up and carried off as they ran away. The wonder was that the Hsien-feng Emperor was not in the vanguard of the fugitives, since he was not—to put it mildly—the sturdiest character in China. Rumor said that he was all prepared to decamp, but his spirited concubine, Yehonala, may have persuaded him not to disgrace himself in this fashion. At any rate he stayed in Peking, putting his trust in a friend from Inner Mongolia, the Prince of Korchin, Seng-ko-lin-chin. Prince Seng didn't let the Emperor down. He brought in cavalrymen from his country. They were tough soldiers, each worth about ten of the Peking Bannermen, and they soon stiffened the city's defenses. Seng chased the Taipings well back from Tientsin. They were good, experienced fighters in their own sort of country, but they had never yet stood up to cavalry and it was too much for them. Dispersed by the Mongols, they faded into the countryside as guerrillas, and when in the early spring the Taiping General Lin died, their imminent threat disappeared forever. This debacle, however, did not affect Hung's strong position in Nanking.

In the meantime, the Triads in Shanghai had not been forgotten by Tseng Kuo-fan, and his Imperialist troops ultimately came trailing along in belated pursuit of them. The government soldiers came in ships which had been frugally hidden upstream all this while, as long as their leaders hoped that other craft might be borrowed from the barbarians. This fleet was brought as close as they could get it to the walled city, and an attack on the rebels began that continued for months, incidentally harassing various residents of the French Concession, a part of whose area was in the way. Occasionally a shot fell short among the alarmed French, usually from the gunboats, which swayed public sentiment strongly over to the Triads. In spite of this, the Frenchmen in charge of the concession decided that it would be more politic to side with authority. They were finished with neutrality; they must protect their nationals. Therefore, while the British and Americans were still cogitating over neutrality, the French offered their help to Peking to rid Shanghai of the insurgents. The help was speedily accepted, and the French congratulated themselves on having got in ahead of their fellow treaty members by making friends with the exclusive Manchus.

But they were not so simple in Peking: they understood. There the constant jockeying for position among the three treaty nations was always observed with bright-eyed interest, and if the Grand Council and the Emperor disliked the British most of all the barbarians, it was because they were strongest. It seemed natural to the officials to work away at undermining them by pitting the other barbarians against them. This was an ancient Chinese method long before Britain formulated her theory of the balance of power. The Governor of Kiangsu memorialized:

"The barbarians are arrogant and untractable and have long been so. Since the opening of the five ports to trade they have increasingly ignorantly vaunted themselves. The honest people of Canton became steadily increasingly resentful. . . . From their arrival at Shanghai, the popular temper has been mild, and the people have not been antagonistic. The said barbarians are greatly pleased at this situation, vastly different from Canton, and have constantly courted popular favor. Their purpose is particularly questionable. Wu Chien-chang is thoroughly conversant with barbarian psychology and understands them deeply. The American and barbarian chiefs have also repeatedly spoken of this. Wu Chien-chang has therefore secretly allied with the American and French barbarian chiefs in order to isolate the strength of the English barbarians." He went on—this was in April of 1854—to tell aggrievedly how the British had refused to allow government troops across to the north city wall through their settlement but did permit "recruited rebel groups" to go across that land, and also sold food to the rebels, and allowed munitions to get in to them. "The rebels regarded the barbarians as close allies; the barbarians regarded the rebels as profitable customers. The feeling of all English barbarians was merely fear that Shanghai's hostilities would stop. . . . Furthermore, there is a newspaper printed." He was referring to the *North China Herald.* "It makes the extreme statement that 'Chinese are hard to reason with and it is only by threatening them with force that we gain our ends.' As it is circulated among the various countries, the barbarian chiefs get ideas therefrom. Up to the present time its harm has been most extreme.

"It is noted that trade at Shanghai began with the English barbarians. In this trade the English barbarians are the greatest and the American barbarians are second to them. The French barbarians regard religion as most important and their interest is not in gain." [Swisher, p. 203.]

But any hopes Peking may have had, of dividing the British from the French in order to take advantage of each, were frustrated that year. The Crimean War had brought the two European nations together as allies, and though their representatives in Shanghai were doubtless not averse to a little sly undermining between merchants, a serious rupture of relations was out of the question.

In the import-export trade of Shanghai, everybody was smuggling —if smuggling is the proper word for the open business that was going on—and nobody had the whip hand: China was the only loser. Regardless of local rebellions, foreign trade must go on, and now the three main powers prepared for a new development respecting their treaties. The problem was a confused one, hinging on the fact that there were two of these treaties, the one signed first at Nanking in 1842 and the later one, between China and the two nations America and France, at Wang-hsia in 1844. In the Wang-hsia Treaty were two clauses that now affected the situation, according to the Westerners: one the most-favored-nation clause, and the other stating that a revision would be due in twelve years. The barbarians held that the first clause empowered the signers of the Nanking Treaty —i.e., the British—to take advantage of the second clause, to start revising in 1854 rather than 1856, because it was now twelve years from *their* date. It was certainly a questionable theory, but the traders determined to have a shot at it, and collected their forces in preparation for the tussle. Sir John Bowring replaced Bonham, who was retiring in any case, and the American Commissioner Marshall, who had hardly succeeded in presenting his credentials, now went home and gave way to Robert M. McLane. The Chinese observed these changes with perturbation, and noticed that the French, too, were shifting their officials. Indignantly they commented among themselves that these pushing, greedy people were ahead of things by two years. The revision clause was a nuisance in any case, and when the time did come, they said to themselves, must be resisted as stoutly as possible—Ch'i-ying was culpable: he shouldn't have permitted it to be slipped in. Certainly they would not so much as discuss it, they resolved, until 1856.

At the British Consulate in Shanghai, Rutherford Alcock welcomed the replacement of Bonham, because he had a new project about customs collection which he knew would never have met with the approval of the retiring Governor, but which might well gain Bowring's blessing. It was very much a departure from previous British policy, but the Consul had talked it over with McLane and the Taotai, and both of them thought it might suffice. Understandably, Wu was reluctant, but even he admitted that as a temporary expedient this idea, of an internationally managed customs service in Shanghai, was just about the only plan that would work, in the circumstances. Britain, France, and America, in conjunction with the Chinese, would set up a new Custom House, which, as the temple formerly used was still badly smashed up, would be in another building in the British settlement, at the edge of Soochow Creek. Many details had still to be discussed, but Bowring gave an assent to the preliminary plan, as did the American and French authorities. There remained the final word from the Chinese, for Taotai Wu was not empowered to make decisions of this magnitude, so McLane undertook to interview the Viceroy of Liang-chiang, I-liang. I-liang had been assistant to Ch'i-ying in the early Canton days, and was an experienced barbarian-tamer. He hardly hesitated at all over the international customs idea, which surprised McLane. But then, the readiness of Manchus and Chinese to permit foreigners to work for them was always taking the foreigners by surprise. By the end of June an agreement covering most of the important points had been drawn up and signed by all four powers, and a week later the three Western consuls announced that the Chinese Imperial Maritime Customs Service would be ready for work after July 12.

The new service was being inculcated, as the Taotai put it bluntly, because he hadn't been able to find an exclusively Chinese body of men which was sufficiently honest, watchful, and educated in foreign languages. (Again, Chinese readiness to face facts, shameful to foreign minds, surprised the Westerners.) The Taotai was to appoint at his discretion one or more foreigners "of undoubted probity" to act as Inspectors under his orders, and they were to have under their direction a staff of linguists and writers—Chinese and foreign—and a revenue cutter manned by foreigners. The consul of each of the three Western nations would select and nominate one Inspector of his own nationality. In disciplinary affairs a mixed court, of the Taotai and the consuls, was to try cases of alleged exaction, corruption, and so forth. This agreement gave a good deal of power to the consuls, and was later to be severely criticized by the Chinese on that account. Another facet of the agreement which was to give rise to trouble was the extraterritorial standing of the Western Inspectors, who were being paid by Chinese funds yet were not directly accountable to Chinese justice. A third complaint often made was that the foreigners were being paid on a far higher scale than the locals. But such as it was, the service was ready, and three foreign Inspectors were speedily selected. For the British there was Thomas Francis Wade from the consular office, who was destined to live in history as the man who romanized Chinese characters. The American nominee was Lewis Carr from the U.S. diplomatic service, and the French came up with a man with the un-Gallic name of Arthur Smith. None of these three men was to remain long in his new post, and each would have been surprised to know that the international customs was going to be anything more than a stopgap contrivance, destined to cease its activities at the end of the civil war. Yet the Customs Service was to play a great part in China's destiny, and would last a century. It would spread far beyond the limits visualized by Alcock. It would be the supervisor of China's transport. It would create a modern post office for the nation, and would educate thousands of young Chinese. The secret China of the nineteenth century would give way to a new nation, struggling toward democracy, in the twentieth. Much of the change came, in the beginning, from that little building at the corner of Nanking and Kiangsi roads in Shanghai.

＊   ＊   ＊

Before he joined in the new battle of diplomacy, the recently arrived French Minister, de Bourbolon, sailed in the French *Cassini* up the Yangtze just as Bonham had done, to take a look at Nanking and the rebel empire. The American, McLane, soon afterwards did the same thing, in the U.S. frigate *Susquehanna*. Both French and American envoys came to much the same conclusion as Bonham's

—Hung was a controversial figure, best left alone. They could not possibly do as the Taipings wished and join in the attempt to overthrow the Manchus, especially now, with the treaties (they hoped) coming up for revision. Not long after these visits, the barbarians even showed themselves ready to abandon their neutrality the other way around, and offered to help Peking against the Taipings. But Peking did not rush to accept the offer; Chinese distrust of the barbarians was deep. The Court still felt—however erroneously—that it could cope with its own people, whereas barbarians were different. Time and again the Imperial edicts contained such phrases as, "We must maintain extreme calm and cut off the gradual development of (the barbarians') covetousness," and one can hardly say that they were being overcautious, at that.

Nevertheless the three Western nations' representatives set to work on the tedious preliminaries of discussion. Endeavoring to get in touch with Manchu officials, they approached Taotai Wu. They were used to him and he was used to them, and he was foolish enough to try to help them a little, handing them on to the Viceroy of Kiangsu, Hsu Nai-chao. Hsu, too, did not choke them off immediately, but memorialized the Throne on their behalf. The Emperor was so irritated by this sign of what he considered weakness that Hsu and the Taotai were both immediately removed from their posts, and when McLane offered to go upriver to interview the Viceroy, an Imperial edict slapped down the suggestion. Let McLane go to Canton, said the edict. Rules were rules. When McLane retorted that it seemed oddly difficult, even when one did go to Canton, to find Yeh Ming-ch'en at home, the argument availed him nothing. Peking wanted to delay and discourage the barbarians, and arguments were no use.

Realizing this, Bowring and McLane in October did what so many of their predecessors had often threatened to do, and sailed straight to Tientsin to force the issue. Among the courtiers, when the alarming news arrived in Peking, there was great perturbation. Troops far up and down the coast were alerted. Before the affair was over Prince Seng-ko-lin-chin himself was called in, just in case. Alarm ebbed a little when it became obvious that the foreigners were not bringing with them a large army. Evidently they really did want to do just what they claimed—interview somebody with authority. But though they talked and talked with the underlings sent to meet them, and exerted great powers of persuasion, they were no match for their adversaries. These, their minds sharpened by fear of the Emperor and Grand Council at their backs, would not at first give an inch, but kept insisting that no interviews could take place at Tientsin. Still the barbarians persisted.

"Medhurst is the most crafty," the officials reported to the capital. They were speaking of the British Chinese Secretary, whose Chinese was very good. "Although they said they came to Tientsin for treaty revision and to present a bill of grievous wrongs, what goes on in their minds is inscrutable; there is no assurance that they are not hiding some evil plan and are intentionally picking a quarrel with us. Yesterday they wanted to come ashore for a walk, but Your slaves informed them that as the Tientsin volunteers were very numerous and the temper of the people violent, there might be some misfortune and then their friendly purpose would be lost. The said barbarians desisted." [Swisher, p. 242.]

Yet some of the more sophisticated officials realized that a blank refusal of all the foreigners' requests would only lead to disaster, and now and then a particularly brave spirit ventured to hint as much to his superiors. The newly appointed Governor of Kiangsu, Ch'i-erh-hang-a, was one of these. On his mind was the considerable sum of uncollected customs that the barbarians still owed the Treasury; they might well refuse to pay it, he said, if they weren't allowed even to make contact with the government. In a memorial he said, "If the country is short this amount, it will be a great inconvenience."

Communications by the dozen flowed between Peking and Tientsin while the barbarians waited. Officials at the frontier hopefully reported that it was getting awfully cold—the end of October was drawing near—and with luck, the barbarians wouldn't be able to endure conditions much longer. But after ten days' wait, those stubborn fellows sent an ultimatum, declaring that if no Imperial rescript was forthcoming within three days more they would return to Shanghai and *report to their superiors*. The implied threat stirred the court to a slight concession. Ch'ung-lun, a Manchu of some importance, was sent to Tientsin with the proper powers. It is true that he arrived at the last possible moment and purposely interviewed the foreigners, on November 3, in an open space in front of the Taku forts where the weather was especially bitter, but at least there he was, and they could put their message on record. What they had to say was no surprise to Ch'ung-lun or the Grand

Council. Between them the barbarians wanted much the same treaty revisions: permission for their ministers to reside at Peking; free access to important officials at all the treaty ports; abolition of *likin* stations; free travel permitted foreigners within the country; legalization of the opium trade and so forth. In their hearts the Westerners entertained small hope of getting any of this, but it had to be put down in black and white. In the middle of the meeting their colleague the French representative arrived—he had been held up by bad weather at sea—to add his voice, for what it was worth. As an indirect reply the Manchu spoke about the Shanghai back customs. He made no headway on that, and the others made no headway on the treaty. When the talking was all finished, the barbarians sailed away.

"Everything must be handled calmly," the Emperor summed up. "Do not entertain their requests. If you take special pains to control them rigidly and check them courteously, how far will these barbarians' cunning get them?"

Chapter Six

Up to autumn in 1856, life on the China coast moved in its uneasy way much as it had done for two years. Nobody was richly satisfied with the situation, but at least it was no worse. In spite of many quarrels between its officers and the traders, the new Customs System was working, and Shanghai especially turned over a lot of revenue from duty. In all the treaty ports save Canton the Christian missionaries taught and fought and infiltrated, now and then asking themselves uneasily if they shouldn't be doing more about Hung Hsiu-ch'uan. Peking remained haughtily secluded, and so did the Imperial High Commissioner Yeh Ming-ch'en in Canton. Yeh continued to supply an effective bottleneck whenever other Chinese officials' privacy seemed threatened by importunate barbarian diplomats; though the exasperated diplomats preferred to believe that this fat official was doing what he did out of personal, idiosyncratic xenophobia, there can be no doubt that Peking knew and approved of his actions. Proudly he had memorialized in September of 1855,

"First McLane came to Canton in the middle of the month; in the latter part, Bowring, with several warships, also came to Canton, and sent a man to give notice and to fix a date for an interview, insisting that it be in the *yamen* to accord with propriety. Your official answered that he was really so desirous of a meeting that, no matter what the place, he should consent, but as the *yamen* was inside the city it was virtually impossible to agree. They stayed in Canton some three weeks but never came back to repeat the request." [Swisher, p. 303.]

Always suspicious, Yeh thought the foreigners must be in league with the Taipings, but in this he was mistaken. It was however a natural error—Chinese officials were preoccupied with the Taiping problem, which often took their minds completely off the barbarians on the coast. Tseng Kuo-fan's campaign made headway along the western periphery of Hung's zone of influence, but within Nanking Hung seemed as solid as ever on his throne. True, the daily life he led in imperial state didn't move as smoothly, somehow, as it had done under the arduous conditions of the march. His princes had now too much time to intrigue, and they brought off successfully one very unpleasant plot, by which a loyal official was legally murdered. Yet the occupation of Nanking and the Taiping incursion generally seemed after a fashion to be settling down. China was adapting, as she always did. The rebellion was being digested. Trade between the interior and the coast was picking up; once more there was plenty of silk coming down to the ports for export. The ordinary Chinese were getting used to the Taipings and the foreigners were getting used to China, with all its irritations—most foreigners, that is, but there were exceptions. Here and there was a man obsessively looking for annoyance, a man longing for trouble, a man like H. S. Parkes, Her Majesty's Consul at Canton.

At twenty-nine, Harry Parkes was an example of the second generation of foreigners in China. There were other young people like himself—their families were a part of the Eastern scene, and they themselves had been born there, or had come out at an early age to join their parents. Such another one was the bright young man of the Customs Service, Horatio Nelson Lay, whose father first saw the Orient because he was agent for a mission society: H. N. Lay at the age of fourteen had left his English school and gone to China, there to study the language under Gützlaff. Parkes too came out at fourteen. He was Mrs. Gützlaff's cousin, and like Lay he studied Chinese with the opium-boat preacher. Such men were presumably better fitted to cope with the natives than their forebears had been, because of their proficiency in the language, but even so there was still a shortage of Chinese-speaking barbarians, and newcomers had to depend heavily on interpreters. Harry Parkes for this reason held his post and also held in his hands a good deal of power; too much, undoubtedly, for a man of choleric temper. But it must be admitted that his work in Canton was bound to elicit choler, and the affair of the *Arrow* was certainly a wonderful chance for him to blow off steam.

It all began with the fact that the British permitted Chinese shipowners, if they were resident in Hong Kong, to sail their craft under the British flag under certain rules. The *Arrow* was a lorcha—that is, a ship with European hull and Chinese rig—belonging to one of these Hong Kong Chinese, manned by a Chinese crew and captained by an Englishman. In the ordinary pursuance of trade she lay at anchor off a little island called Dutch Folly, near the factory quarter of Canton, on October 8. Her captain was aboard and the ensign was flying. Technically speaking, the ensign shouldn't have been, for the *Arrow's* registration had expired a few days before; as the craft had been at sea at the time, and as the authorities weren't inclined to fussiness on such points, the matter had been overlooked. Certainly the Chinese weren't aware of this circumstance until later, when they were very glad to find it out. That day, in spite of the Englishman on deck and all the rest of it, a party of Chinese officers suddenly boarded the *Arrow*, hauled down the colors, and carried off twelve of her crew. Their reason, as it was to be explained by Yeh, was that some of the men—two, to be exact —were recognized as pirates who were wanted by the law: evidently the others were just scooped up in the general excitement, but in the following dispute all this is not very clear. Parkes's indignation was high. According to treaty, since the *Arrow* was a British ship, no matter how many malefactors there might be in her crew they were to be protected until the British authorities could be told about it, when the latter were bound to take the proper course.

Parkes wrote to Commissioner Yeh demanding that all twelve men be returned forthwith, in as public a manner as that in which they had been snatched. After this restitution, he said, a proper investigation of the charges would be made. In a lengthy reply Yeh retorted that the lorcha wasn't an English ship: she had been built in China and she belonged to a Chinese. "It is useless therefore to enter into any discussion respecting her," he said. As for the men, though there were undoubtedly "several great offenders" among them, he was returning nine of them, retaining three for more strict examination. He did return them along with the letter, but not in the manner which the consul had demanded; besides, Parkes had demanded the whole dozen, and he angrily sent the insufficient nine straight back to the dispatcher.

In a day or two the affair had become the overpowering topic of Parkes's world. He wrote reports to Bowring in Hong Kong, and got replies; on the eleventh he himself went to the colony and had a talk with the Admiral, Sir Michael Seymour. Back in Canton he interviewed naval Commodore Elliot, who fully concurred in his view "that if any reparation be due for so gross an insult, it is only by active measures on our part that such reparation can be obtained." Again he wrote to Yeh, and Bowring backed him up with a letter of his own. The Commissioner must send an apology and an assurance that the British flag would thereafter be respected, and this must happen within forty-eight hours, or else. By this time the Englishmen had discovered the fact that the *Arrow's* registration was not in order, but they refused to be embarrassed by that. It was an affair between themselves and the lorcha's owner, they said; it had nothing to do with the fact that the *Arrow* was English and had been flying an English flag which the Chinese had forcibly and impertinently lowered. The correspondence between Yeh and the British became monotonously repetitive from then on, with Parkes repeating his allegations and demands, and Yeh replying just as he had done before. Yeh's only fresh contribution was a promise that from that day forward, Chinese officers must not "without reason" seize and take into custody anybody aboard a foreign lorcha. But as he added that foreigners, for their part, must no longer permit Chinese subjects to register craft under foreign flags, the general effect of the letter was hardly placatory.

The forty-eight hours' grace was more than over when Commodore Elliot, with the eager Parkes aboard his ship, set out with a small escort to collect a debt. It was their plan to capture an Imperial junk in full sight of the world, thus convincing the Chinese that crime does not pay. They did get a junk flying the Imperial flag, and took it back in triumph to Whampoa. Unfortunately it soon became clear that the vessel didn't belong to the government, but was privately owned, and they had to let it go. (Yeh rather rubbed this in.) On October 22, under threat of another ultimatum, the impenitent Commissioner wrote yet another repetitive letter, this time with a slight variation in his falsehoods: the *Arrow* at the time the Chinese boarded her, he declared, wasn't flying *any* flag *at all*. However, there was an accompaniment to this letter—not nine men this time, but ten.

Parkes sent them back. He repeated that he wanted all twelve of the original party, plus publicity, plus an apology. Before nightfall Yeh sent back all twelve, but still Parkes was not happy, for with them was "no officer of rank or letter of apology," he said com-

plainingly in his report to Bowring. Back they went, therefore, and
the war began in earnest. Sir Michael Seymour went into action.
With little trouble and no loss of life, the British took possession
of four forts, the Barrier Forts, below the city and followed up by
capturing two more: all of them were dismantled and their ammunition removed. Parkes then wrote again to Commissioner Yeh, but
the Chinese remained stubborn, and in a belated reply merely re-
capitulated the old arguments, threatening the wrath of the multitude—that notorious Cantonese multitude, reportedly so much
fiercer than any other Chinese mob—in case things should get any
worse.

Jubilant over the easy victory, Bowring in Hong Kong began
to wonder if the time might not be ripe to settle "*vexata quaestio*
of our entrance into the city." He added, "This would be a crowning
result to the successful operations of Her Majesty's naval forces;
and at such conference with the Imperial Commissioner many local
arrangements might be made." Obviously, Sir John even now had
no inkling of the nature of his opponent, or of the relations that
existed between the Imperial Commissioner and his masters in Peking. Yeh simply had no power to change the local arrangements.
All he could do was obstruct to the best of his ability; that was
what he was ordered to do. Yeh was an able man at obstructing:
the talent wasn't to prove particularly fortunate for him, but there
it was: a high official in old China didn't have an easy time of it.
In obeying Imperial commands he might well bring down disaster
on his Emperor as well as himself, but disobedience meant certain
disaster. There was no choice. Sir John Bowring, the fair-minded
Briton with his firm theories on free trade, could no more understand Yeh's predicament than he could appreciate the problems of
Neanderthal man. One might have expected better, however, from
the China-trained Harry Parkes.

The feeler was put out: Yeh would have none of the suggestion.
That permission-of-entry business, he said, had been shelved for
good in 1849, and he had no desire to discuss it. Such straightforward
lying fairly took away the breath of the British, but when they had
recovered themselves they went at the war with more verve than
ever. They shelled the Commissioner's house in Canton and forced
him to move out. They shelled the city walls and broke them down.
Triumphantly they walked into the forbidden city (which was a
disappointment, after all those years—a lot of mud houses, they

told each other scornfully), and entered the Commissioner's house, which had already been thoroughly looted; then they went back to their ships and continued shelling. Yeh from a new residence sent out notice to his people that he would pay thirty dollars for every English barbarian head brought to him. He also sent word to the French and American officials, calling them to witness how badly he was being treated by the English. Their expressions of sympathy were somewhat cool: if Chinese were to begin collecting barbarian heads, they implied, they couldn't be expected to approve. They also did not forget the most-favored-nation clause of the old treaty. If Britain managed to negotiate improvements, they would benefit. No, in the last analysis the French and Americans would stand by their colleague. Americans realized this obligation the more keenly when they took the Commissioner's advice and started evacuating their nationals from the factory district to Macao. By that time the Chinese had gone back into their forts, for the outnumbered British could not continue to occupy all the places they captured; over-excited, some Chinese blasted off at an American corvette on her way to assist in the evacuation. In retaliation the Americans naturally silenced the offending guns once more, but with that incident the affair seemed closed. Without further mishap, the French and Americans removed themselves from Canton. Parkes was disappointed by this American forbearance, and so was Bowring, but though they wanted help they paid no attention to an eager voice now sounding from Nanking. On October 30, Hung sent a long letter to Bowring. It was an interesting missive, describing the career of the Taiping movement and offering help to destroy "the Mandarin dogs of the Tartar Government." All he needed, he truthfully said, was the tools to do the job. "Grant us a loan of supplies, or lend us steamers, and give orders to your police to appropriate thirty or fifty of the junks lying in Hong Kong, for the use of our soldiers, and we will proceed straight up the river to Polo, and there land, and fighting on shore will utterly exterminate the vagabond (followers) of the Tartar Government," he promised. The British were not interested; they were not even sure if the letter was genuine, since pirates were in the habit of claiming to be Taipings. In any case they didn't want Hung for an ally, being convinced that he was a dangerous crackpot, and they would not permit any native armed junks in the river near Canton.

Parkes would not believe that Yeh told the truth when he spoke of the Cantonese people's unshakable opposition to allowing foreigners into the city. He determined to call the Commissioner's bluff, and held several meetings with leading citizens to find out from their own mouths how they felt about things. Here again he seems to have been strangely naive. The merchants and officials would naturally not speak up in the open way one would expect of British citizens. They hinted cautiously that Yeh was not their ideal representative, and made courteous protestations of their liking for foreigners: what else could Parkes have expected? when it came to the test, they backed down. On December 14, when the factory district was almost empty and only a score of British remained, Chinese set fire to the buildings. The fire had its own way for two days, and when it died down at last the whole neighborhood had been destroyed. Of the famous merchants' ghetto, the Chinese shops Hickey had visited, and the drinking dens of Hog Lane, only charred rubble remained.

Parkes's sanguine idea that Yeh was bound to compromise himself with Peking by persisting in his intransigent course was as wide of the mark as it could be. An Imperial edict of December 12 proves it. A rapid summary of the early events of the *Arrow* War as Yeh had reported them gives the picture that the Grand Council saw, a picture of British haughtiness, injustice, and impotence all at once. ". . . because our marine forces arrested the bandits . . . the English barbarian Harry Parkes seized the pretext to start a quarrel, boldly dared to enter the Canton River, and harrassed Lieh-te Fort. He also fired empty cannon shots at Ta-huang-chiao Fort, and from October 27–29 attacked the city wall, setting fires. . . . On the 29th, when he gathered together two or three hundred men and scaled the wall, Lieutenant Colonel Ling Fang and the gentry . . . met and hurled them to their death. On November 6, when the barbarians came out from the Thirteen Factories anchorage and pounced on Tung-ting Fort, our troops blew up a warship, killed their admiral Michael Seymour, and killed or wounded more than 400 barbarians and rebels." This statement was inaccurate, of course—for one thing, Sir Michael wasn't even wounded—but the Grand Council preferred to believe it, and also believed what followed in the report: that the city wall was now fortified, and twenty thousand Chinese soldiers and marines stood ready to scatter the foe. Moreover, they believed that even the Americans and French were turning against the British: "They are quite isolated," the edict said. "Yeh Ming-ch'en understands barbarian affairs thoroughly and can certainly find means to control them, so he is ordered to act as circumstances require."

The paper went on to discuss Bowring's demands for access to the city: "We regard all these as attempts to further their advantage. The barbarian mind is inscrutable. . . . As at present the interior is still disturbed, how can we have another disturbance on the coast? . . .

"As Yeh Ming-ch'en has long held office on the ocean frontier, we trust he will be able to manage satisfactorily and relieve somewhat our indignation and anxiety. If these chiefs, having been defeated repeatedly, acknowledge and regret their wrongs and come to beg an armistice, the said governor general can himself find means to handle them in order to end strife. If they are still tyrannical, there can be no compromise settlement to give rise to a train of demands." [Swisher, p. 326.]

Only one subdued comment cast a shade on the general tone of approval. A Peking official—Metropolitan Circuit Censor Han Ch'ing-yün—pointed out that Yeh could have avoided the whole thing at the beginning: ". . . the governor general merely sent soldiers on board a barbarian ship to seize bandits; as he failed to notify them, he gave the barbarians a pretext. If on the other hand he had ordered the coastal forces to defend the forts, he would not have been taken unawares." [Swisher, p. 328.]

* * *

By the beginning of 1857, the British Foreign Secretary, Lord Clarendon, had to face the likelihood of all-out war against China. The situation was strange: the *Arrow* incident had resulted in a "contained" war, with British forces completely engaged in naval action against a district of China—an important district—that was still being ignored diplomatically, from Peking. But then, Peking persistently ignored everything diplomatically, all the more easily as there was no method of communication. In the other Chinese treaty ports business continued as usual, but without Canton this state of affairs couldn't go on much longer. The obvious next step would seem to be the old, tried-and-true feint toward Tientsin and Peking direct, which would presumably shake some sort of action out of the Grand Council; it always did. But Sir John Bowring wrote

repeatedly that this was the wrong way to go about things. Canton
was the trouble spot, he said. Peking always referred annoying questions to Canton and there managed to obstruct all business; therefore the clever thing to do would be to wipe out Canton as a refuge,
once and for all. After the city had been captured and placed under
adequate control, he argued, there would be plenty of time to tackle
Peking. A start had been made, but with the slender resources they
had the British could do no more. They would need five thousand
men, said Bowring. He suggested that most of these troops could be
supplied from India.

Clarendon was not opposed to the idea of sending more troops,
especially since he had been giving much thought already to the
necessity of treaty revisions in Peking. In preparation for future
moves, therefore, he directed Bowring to sound out the Americans
and French as to their attitude if the British should determine to
subjugate Yeh and force the matter of treaty revision to a head.
The French were willing to go along: the Americans, though they
were clearly in favor of action, didn't quite commit themselves. All
three plenipotentiaries, however, signed an agreement to support
one another. For a while the outcome of Bowring's requests was
in doubt, for there was a good deal of criticism in Parliament of
what was going on in Hong Kong and Canton. However, a general
election in the early spring of 1857 silenced the opposition by returning Palmerston to office, and Clarendon was able to get on
with the plan. He named the Earl of Elgin and Kincardine Her
Majesty's Plenipotentiary with Full Powers. Under this splendid
title Elgin started out, accompanied by fifteen hundred men; he
was to get seven hundred and fifty more, plus some Indian troops,
from India, when he arrived in Hong Kong. His duties were roughed
out: from Hong Kong he would go to the mouth of the Peiho in an
attempt to communicate direct with Peking, and though it did not
seem likely that the Emperor would give way this time any more
than he had done in the past, plans were made for every eventuality.
Supposing Elgin were actually to get in touch, he was to ask for
war reparation, a proper execution of the treaty terms as they then
stood, and compensation for British losses incurred at Canton. Still
presuming that this business could be finished satisfactorily, Elgin
was then to make another attempt to get the right of diplomatic
representation in Peking, and when all these affairs had been settled
he was to arrange future ease of communications with high Chinese

officers, and better commercial facilities. But—failing all these pleasant eventualities, the plenipotentiary was to use coercive measures. Since it seemed very likely that he would fail in all the first-named respects, the future looked promising to Parkes and Bowring. At last they were going to get some, at least, of the support they wanted, though their dream of five thousand troops did not look as if it were going to come true.

Unfortunately for their hopes, just in time to spoil everything, the Indian Mutiny boiled up. Elgin was already on the way; he heard of it in Ceylon. The situation rapidly worsened, and even with the best will in the world for his mission, he had to divert most of his China-bound troops to Calcutta, where they were badly needed. For himself Elgin found that he had the summer on his hands. He could not go to the Peiho without an escort of certain strength, nor did he wish to make a solo trip of it, and neither the French nor the American representative was able to go with him at that season. He reasoned that his idle presence in Hong Kong would do more harm than good, and he was probably right: the Chinese were already gossiping happily that the barbarians had fallen out among themselves, and there was a rumor that Bowring and Parkes had been recalled in disgrace to London. Accordingly Elgin went to Calcutta and stayed there until autumn, when he returned to Chinese waters. He still encountered delays, as one is apt to do in the East, but by December several decisions had been taken, chief of which was that Canton was, after all, to come first.

In the meantime Russia had lined up with England and declared her support. Neither she nor America, however, wished to take part in active combat against the Chinese. Only the French were willing to go so far; unlike the other two nations, France had a genuine grievance in the fact that a French missionary, Father Chapdelaine, had been murdered in the interior but the authorities had always refused to do anything about it. Elgin and Baron Gros, early in December, sent an ultimatum to Yeh Ming-ch'en. His reply was the usual one—he hardly varied the formula—and on December 15 the barbarians moved in on the island opposite Canton, occupying Honan Point. Yeh still refused to make any concession, whereupon they assaulted the city. The combined allied forces fell short of five thousand and were heavily outnumbered by the Chinese, but there was little resistance: the fight was over by the end of the month, and British and French detachments entered Canton city.

A French captain captured the Governor, Po-kuei, on January fifth (all high Chinese officials having run for cover), and Yeh Ming-ch'en was nabbed on the same day by Commodore Elliot. He was put into preventive detention aboard a British ship that was anchored off Tiger Island; he must have been glad to go, for a man of his experience could have been under no illusions as to the outcome of any interview he might otherwise have had with his masters.

When all the early jubilation was over, the victors faced a problem. How could they administer a Chinese city as large as Canton? It was out of the question unless they called in the help of the locals. Po-kuei seemed very anxious to be helpful, so he was reinstated as Governor, but he was now answerable for all his acts to a commission of three foreigners: Parkes, another Englishman, and a French officer. A young Consular interpreter, Robert Hart, was named as secretary to this body. Canton was garrisoned by foreign troops, and later a police force of mixed nationality was organized. Martial law remained in force. Commissioner Yeh still languished in durance, and the barbarians were not happy about the situation. They felt that Tiger Island was too near Canton; his presence, wrote Elgin to Seymour, "tends to disquiet the public mind." It was decided to send him to Calcutta, and this was done. There Yeh spent the rest of his life, which was far longer than it would have been if he had remained in the hands of his compatriots after such a humiliating defeat. The Chinese records of Yeh's ups and downs in Peking favor during the time of the Canton war are eloquent, if indirect, testimony of how far removed was their mentality from anything the Western barbarians appreciated. The Court had not heard of Canton's fall on January 17, and an Imperial edict of that date declared,

"Although the said chiefs (i.e., the English and French plenipotentiaries) realized that their argument was faulty, they boldly made requests hoping for some gain. The said official (Yeh) refuted them reasonably and explained matters adroitly. His rhetoric was entirely appropriate. We trust that the said chiefs have no place left to stick their beaks." [Swisher, p. 346.]

Then came a memorial from Canton, bearing all the disastrous news. Yeh's subordinates instead of Yeh himself now spoke, and they placed his actions and judgment in an entirely different light. Po-kuei complained that Yeh never told him anything: for example, the barbarian chief Reed, the new American envoy, had been in communication with Yeh, shortly before the debacle, but "At the time the governor general did not notify me at all," said the governor. "Afterwards, when Your slave finally learned of this, he was greatly astonished. . . . Your slave has worked with the governor general for years and knows that he works cagily and secretly, and when he spoke this way must have things under control. Moreover he had received various provincial officials and said emphatically that he could guarantee that there would be no trouble. Consequently, everyone kept his mouth shut. Anyway, as no symptoms had developed, Your slave could not oppose him outright.

"Then unexpectedly, on December 16, ten ships of the various barbarians sailed up Canton River. The governor general sent orders that unless the barbarians made a move the soldiers and volunteers were not to pick a fight. There was a stalemate for several days, and then on the 24th the barbarians sent a communication to the five provincial officials, Tartar general, governor general, governor, and the two deputy lieutenant generals. Again the governor general consulted no one and it is not known how he replied. Then on the 27th the barbarians again communicated with the five officials, and still the governor general gave us no notice. Moreover, he sent orders to various gentry that they were not to go unauthorized on board the barbarian ships, and if they disobeyed they would be specially punished. Consequently these gentry, Wu Ch'eng-yüeh and others, just looked on.

"On the 28th cannons roared on all sides. The governor general finally mobilized the village trainbands, but they were not all assembled by the 29th when . . . Kuan-yin Shan inside the city and the forts both inside and outside the North Gate were occupied by the barbarians. Your Slaves then sent for Wu Ch'eng-yüeh, who along with various gentry, went to the barbarian ships to find out what they wanted. The barbarians' language was proudly contemptuous. . . .

"Suddenly, on January fifth, the barbarians burst into the *yamen* of Your slave Shuang-hai, seized the governor general and led him to a barbarian ship. Your slaves were grieved beyond measure. . . ." [Swisher, p. 346 f.]

To this disingenuous account, the Imperial reply was prompt. "If Yeh Ming-ch'en, as Imperial Commissioner in charge of barbarian affairs, could not accede to the unreasonable demands of the barbarians, he should have found means of bringing them around and, on the other hand, discussed suitable plans for their management with the Tartar General, governor, et al. . . . Patently obstinate, smug, perverse in administration and unworthy of the responsibility entrusted to him, Yeh Ming-ch'en is ordered immediately degraded."

Po-kuei was named as acting Viceroy for the time being—the title called "Governor General" in this version being translated, more properly, "Viceroy"—and the first punishment meted out to him was commuted to something milder. Another edict shows that the misunderstanding of alien natures was not all on one side:

"Yeh Ming-ch'en has managed miserably and cannot deny his guilt. But the barbarians have taken him to a barbarian ship with the idea of extortion and are sure to come out with rash demands. The Tartar General and acting governor general can tell them that Yeh Ming-ch'en has been degraded and is beneath consideration, so the barbarians will have no ground for extortion and realize that it is useless to hold him. . . . As these barbarians have no standing enmity toward Mu-k'o-te-na (the Tartar General) or Po-kuei and as Po-kuei is now acting governor general, he is ordered to explain plausibly and see if they have any feeling of remorse. If the barbarians withdraw from the city and ask to trade, the said Tartar General and acting governor general can act according to circumstances so as to show management. If the barbarians bring up indemnity for goods destroyed by fire, tell them that the Chinese forts and residences which they burned are very numerous and if we discuss indemnity, their account would not equal ours. Besides, it was the barbarians who started hostilities and all nations are free to decide who was right and who was wrong. . . ." [Swisher, p. 349.]

The loss of Canton was a severe shock to the Emperor and his Council. Most reverses seem to have come as a shock, always, to Peking. In their seclusion they cast about, seeking some way to minimize the calamity. By the first of February they had come up with one or two ideas that seemed to them constructive. Might not the Americans be swayed to take the side of the Chinese in this argument, if they were nicely treated, if they were given special favors? It was possible: their troops had not taken part in the hostilities, at least. No doubt that villain Yeh Ming-ch'en had mismanaged them, just as he had mismanaged everything else, but there was a chance that things might now be set right with them.

Cantonese officials were commanded to investigate this avenue. As for Canton, of course it must be taken back as soon as possible. The people of the countryside must be mobilized; ultimately they could get rid of the impertinent intruders. There couldn't be more than a few thousand foreigners left in the garrison, and the Chinese could easily muster far more than that. Orders were sent, commanding the officers to organize preparations for the great day of deliverance.

In the middle of all these disrupted plans, a new complication appeared. For a while the Court simply couldn't be bothered to consider it. There were pieces to pick up, a calamitous condition to be remedied; it was just like barbarian impertinence not to leave Peking alone at such a time. In sum, Lord Elgin had dared to write, addressing his letter direct to "The Senior Secretary of State at Pekin." It was dated February 11. The barbarian spoke at length, giving his side of the story of Canton and Yeh Ming-ch'en's behavior, but the nub of the letter came later, when he announced that he and Baron Gros, the plenipotentiary for France, would soon be proceeding to Shanghai, "where they will be prepared to enter into negotiations for the settlement of all differences existing between their respective Governments and that of China, with any Plenipotentiary duly accredited by the Emperor of China, who may present himself at that port before the end of the month of March." With a few general observations on the settlements he hoped it would be possible to make, Elgin ended on a politely worded ultimatum: if no suitable plenipotentiary should present himself before the end of March in Shanghai, Elgin would have recourse to whatever measures he might deem best. The calm assurance with which he wrote was doubtless fortified by the knowledge that his three fellow plenipotentiaries from the allied barbarian nations were by prearrangement sending similar letters, though the Russian and American versions carefully refrained from threats. By a clever maneuver, the old difficulty of getting these letters delivered more or less directly to the high level desired had been circumvented. H. N. Lay of the Customs Service was working for the Chinese—actually on their payroll—and was also fluent in the language: nobody in the Chinese world knew quite how to turn him away when he arrived on the doorstep of the Viceroy of Liang-Chiang, or the two Kiang provinces, in Soochow. This official forwarded them to the right address.

Reluctantly the government concentrated on the new problem

by telling the Canton officials to step up their warlike preparations. Nobody considered acceding to Elgin's demand for a plenipotentiary to meet him in Shanghai, and Elgin himself was not surprised by this silence, though he pretended to be. At the end of February he himself went to the treaty port, and there he found a sort of an answer, though he would not receive it as such. Not as person to person, but by message in a letter from the Viceroy of the two Kiangs and another official, the Senior Secretary replied as he had been directed to do, purely in order to procrastinate a little more. (The officials of the day clung blindly to the belief that barbarians ultimately grew tired and dropped their demands, if only one could put them off long enough.) The Secretary explained that he could not in propriety communicate at all with barbarians. He recommended that all four plenipotentiaries go to Canton as usual, there to treat with the Viceroy. But this time the barbarians were not pliable. Elgin sent the note straight back and reminded the Secretary that in accordance with a certain clause in the Treaty of Nanking, he himself must correspond directly with some officer equivalent to his own rank. He had now no choice, he said, but to carry on to the north, where he could find for himself officers of suitable importance. When he had sent off this warning he prepared for the journey. The other three plenipotentiaries, Count Poutiatine for Russia, Baron Gros for France, and William B. Reed for America, proposed to go with him, and once again the party borrowed H. N. Lay, to accompany them as interpreter. Elgin wrote to Sir Michael Seymour requesting as many gunboats as the Admiral could send; these small craft would be necessary for crossing the bar at the mouth of the Peiho. He did not wait for their arrival; the party set off on April 10, 1858.

Peking hummed distractedly. The government was muddled as to the proper course to pursue, and dithered between outright resistance in Canton with the help of mob action, or a little appeasement of the barbarians by making trade conditions easier. They were late in coming around to this idea, but it was a tried and true rule that barbarians cared only for trade, really, and Peking felt it would be a sound experiment. Tempt the intruders with trade and all should go well; the barbarian powers would surely call off their dogs. On the other hand, said some pessimists, barbarians were inscrutable, so it might be as well to strengthen their defenses at Tientsin, just in case the envoys didn't rise to the bait immediately and go south again. Word was sent to all coastal authorities along the way from Shanghai not to supply food to barbarian ships. Another thing the Chinese might do, they decided, was to go on working on a potential split between the warlike nations, France and England, and the more peaceable ones, Russia and America. Just in case the worst came to the worst and they had to negotiate, the Russians and Americans ought to be softened up in advance. So the Chinese talked and sent letters, and on April 14 the four barbarian envoys with their staffs and escort ships arrived in the Gulf of Pechili, anchoring five miles from the Taku forts at the mouth of the Peiho.

The Governor General of the two Kiangs, Ho Kuei-ch'ing, had been watching events with close attention. An intelligent man, he wrote a memorial that arrived in Peking on the fifteenth of April. [Swisher, p. 408.] In it he reported accurately as to the strength of the naval reinforcements that were on their way, and went on,

"Your officials humbly observe that the four chiefs who have come with joined masts to Shanghai have acted very obstreperously. The English barbarians actually returned Your officials' reply ordering them to go back to Canton and await a settlement, and went direct to the north. . . . Their attitude is indeed detestable. It is reported that the English barbarians have come after a decision was reached in their country; that the French barbarians are in their pay and will join them in making trouble; that the Americans and Russians are taking advantage of the strife to follow in their wake hoping for benefits gratis." Prejudice apart, this was really a very fair summary of the situation. He continued, ". . . On examining the (English) communication to Grand Secretary Yü-chang, there are no improper expressions, but they regard the fact that 'ministers have no intercourse with foreigners' as a slight to them and use this as an excuse for wanting to go to Tientsin. It is obvious that though these barbarians are mercenary they have an air of false pride and are afraid that others will belittle them. May we not beg Your Majesty, with Heavenly grace, to seize this wedge to formulate a plan and send an Imperial Commissioner to Tientsin to flatter them a little, discuss the general situation with them personally, and then send them back to Canton in order to avoid other complications?"

This perceptive official went further, and discussed Peking's plans to counterattack in the south: he didn't think much of them.

He pointed out that the interior was still in turmoil. "In the event of another coastal conflict, interior banditry and external grief will both be upon us and how will we handle them?" Turning to the barbarian question, he remarked that things had changed since early days when the Commissioners Lin and Hsü had held office and had really *controlled* the barbarians. The war had changed things, with the resulting opening of the treaty ports. "Now the barbarians have repudiated treaties, occupied our (provincial) capital city, abducted our high official, and every red-blooded man is gnashing his teeth in bitter anger, wanting to eat their flesh and use their hide for blankets." Yet—Ho was not so sure any more of the climate of temper in Canton. At the beginning of the occupation it would have been easy to call on popular fury and recover the city, but three months had gone by. The barbarians had strengthened the forts. Trade was going well, "so while public spirit is starved, public greed is gratified." One couldn't rely on the Cantonese, and to use other soldiers would be to draw them off the rebels. Thus the present policy for barbarian management, as Ho saw it, was self-evident: "Employ soft to manage hard; devise means to manage in accord with Imperial Edict; and not talk promiscuously about going to war." The barbarians' trip to Tientsin couldn't be prevented, but after all, barbarians had always kowtowed at the Emperor's gate and begged for mercy, so why shouldn't they do it again? "It is humbly requested," said the tactful governor general, "that Your Majesty's Heavenly Favor condescend . . . to appoint an Imperial Commissioner to meet them, flatter them a little so that they will have no quarrel to pick, settle general conditions by negotiation to get them to cease hostilities and restore the (provincial) capital, and then tell them to return to Canton and discuss treaty provisions separately, in order to relieve the immediate crisis." Later, when things had settled down, there would be plenty of opportunity for vengeance and Heavenly punishment. . . .

"This memorial is very lucid," was pensively written in the Emperor's vermilion pencil on this paper.

It was therefore not against a blank wall of negativism that the four barbarian envoys made their first attack by persuasion, from the new vantage point of the Gulf of Pechili. For ten days they waited, during which time a number of officials paid unofficial calls on Poutiatine and Reed, duly attempting to soften them up against the day when China might need friends in the negotiations. On

April 24 the barbarians sent word that they had arrived, and requested that a plenipotentiary of suitable rank and authority be sent
to treat with them—within six days, said Lord Elgin. Within the six
days they actually got a reply, this time; they were informed that
T'an T'ing-hsiang, the Governor General of Chihli, would wait on
them. The plenipotentiaries hesitated: did Viceroy T'an have the
full powers necessary—powers to match those of Ch'i-ying and
I-shan in the old days, when the Treaty of Nanking was hammered
out? When T'an replied, they considered that he was being evasive.
More action was indicated, and for himself Elgin would have em-
barked on the next phase immediately, pushing his way to Tientsin,
but that the additional fleet had not yet arrived. So he and Gros
waited, while a stream of visitors called on Poutiatine and Reed,
chief of whom was T'an himself. Over and over the governor general
discussed matters with the barbarians—tariffs, permits, treaties, and
the possibility that the two comparatively friendly nations might
act as peacemakers between the potential belligerents. In his reports
T'an's attitude varied according to the day's conversations. Sometimes he was hopeful, but more often than not he spoke despairingly
of the unreliability of barbarians—the perfidy of Poutiatine, the
weakness of the Americans, the general futility of treating with
them at all. As the day for the trip upriver approached, the Russian
count warned T'an that it would certainly happen—worse would
happen—if the foreign envoys didn't get permission to come outright to Peking. T'an hinted to his masters that it might be well
to give in. He ventured to remind them that it was constant official
refusal to communicate, in Canton, that had driven the barbarians
to their previous excesses. After all, had not Jesuit barbarians, in
the old days, lived quite peaceably in Peking? Now, all these barbarians asked was permission to visit the city now and then: the
Russian barbarian had even suggested that they could come by
land, thus avoiding coastal troubles: "it is not an impossible way
to mollify the barbarians," said the poor Viceroy.

He had got by with it: T'an did not. The Vermilion comment on
this memorial was long and angry. The Russians wanted the land
route so that they could spy, said the Emperor. As for the Jesuits
of the old days, they had been scholars, well controlled, but these
new foreigners "would come and go as they wish and their greed is
insatiable." When T'an said that if Peking was not voluntarily opened
the barbarians would surely force their way in, he was told that he

was getting hysterical. Perhaps he was. If so, he had reason. On May 24 the British and French were ready, and they moved in to the river. There was some resistance from the Taku forts, but a battle of less than an hour and a quarter silenced the fort guns, and the whole party then proceeded, without further incident, to the vicinity of Tientsin. There for a time they halted, but T'an knew they would not wait very long. The ensuing correspondence between the luckless Viceroy and his pig-headed superiors is enough to wring the heart with pity, especially as his post lasted only as long as he took to convince them of what he knew. When at last he had hammered his facts home, he was removed in disgrace. An old actor in the drama, who had long been retired, was now dusted off and sent back to duty.

"June 2, 1858. Edict (to the Grand Secretariat). Order the brevet rank of board vice-president conferred on Ch'i-ying, to take charge of barbarian affairs."

Chapter Seven

Ch'i-ying had been out of favor since the old Emperor's death. He had incurred the wrath of a number of officials by indiscreetly suggesting that they were redundant, whereupon they persuaded the new Emperor to denounce him and allege that he "oppressed the people to please foreigners," as well as exaggerating the threat of British strength. Since then the old Manchu had lived quietly. No doubt he was pleased at this chance to get back into the swim. He would never have been rash enough to point out, much less rub in, that he had been right after all about the British, but that fact hadn't escaped the observation of several nobles who now sponsored his appointment. Ch'i-ying went to join the other Commissioners in Tientsin, Kuei-liang and Hua-sha-na, who were not pleased that they should be subordinate to this newcomer. Kuei-liang, a Manchu, happened to be father-in-law to Prince Kung, a half-brother of the Emperor: he got on to Prince Kung, who promptly wrote a strong protest against the arrangement and sent it to the Emperor. Barbarians were naturally insatiable, he declared, and Ch'i-ying had never been firm enough with them: "in Ch'i-ying's previous handling of barbarian affairs, if he did not humble himself to give in to them, he mumbled what was taken for consent, feared barbarians like tigers and treated the people like grass, and brought about a great disaster with evil consequences to the present." The Prince went on sarcastically, as his rank permitted him, that if submission to the barbarians was the Emperor's wish the other two Commissioners could be as submissive as necessary, without Ch'i-ying's help. Whereas if that wasn't the aim of the exercise, Ch'i-ying of all people was not the man to be trusted to put up resistance.

This objection, even when bolstered by Kuei-liang's and Hua-sha-na's and other dissenting voices which spoke of Ch'i-ying's "conciliatory methods," did not change the minds of the Emperor and his Council. They felt that a bit of Ch'i-ying's specialty, conciliation and soothing, would not come amiss when the enemy was massing in strength at their very door. But they reckoned without full knowledge of the enemy's resources: the enemy had a secret weapon, which was to be wielded by—of all unexpected people— the British interpreters. The story of the part these interpreters played in the negotiations is unusual. In theory, such people are nothing but machines for translating, even though in practice they have been known to damp down insults, cover up gaffes, or even for one purpose or another suppress part of the truth. H. N. Lay and Thomas Francis Wade were something more in this affair than mere interpreters. From the beginning Elgin not only permitted but encouraged them to take active part in the conversations; indeed he usually left them to discuss affairs by themselves. He knew they were experienced in Chinese matters; presumably they understood the mentality of the Imperial Commissioners where he, a newcomer, did not. Lay's position was especially odd. He was in the Chinese Customs, which meant that he was a paid employee of the Chinese: just how much he was an employee is indicated by the story of how he joined the Service in 1855. At that time Wade had just completed the six months he had contracted for in the Customs, and felt that he'd had enough. He wanted to get back to his first job with the Consulate, where he would have more time for his beloved Sinological studies. According to the way things were done in those early days, Sir John Bowring took it for granted that he was to recommend Wade's successor as the English Inspector of Customs, and that his recommendation would be accepted without question. He was ready and waiting with two candidates; he favored a man named Gingell, Vice-Consul at Foochow. But H. N. Lay, acting Vice-Consul at Shanghai, keenly wanted the job and saw how to go about getting it. Unlike most young foreigners in his position he had many Chinese friends. He was aware that the Chinese resented the British way of pushing into the Customs men of their choice, without waiting to see what the Chinese might want. After all, as they told each other (and Lay), it was supposed to be a *Chinese* Customs. Lay therefore prevailed on influential Chinese friends to back him up in his application for the post. They did so, and though it was a struggle, they had their way and Lay got his appointment. Still, he was no turncoat, and at Tientsin he championed the British point of view. In fact, he behaved more harshly than the other British did toward the Emperor's representatives. They complained to no avail.

When Ch'i-ying arrived in Tientsin he sensed that all was not well: the British and French Ministers made no attempt to see him, and this was strange. Ch'i-ying got in touch with Count Poutiatine, and the Russian gave him a hint, telling him that if he was going aboard the British ship he must be on his guard. Ch'i-ying did not understand. The dramatic aftermath was reported to Peking by Kuei-liang with a mixture of shock and satisfaction.

"Later, at the American quarters," said Kuei-liang, "he was suddenly shown the seal copy of the treaties previously concluded (i.e., the Nanking treaties). Ch'i-ying was amazed and asked how they came by this document. He was told by the American chief that when the English barbarians captured Canton and Yeh Ming-ch'en was taken prisoner, they took China's 'Management of Barbarian Affairs Yellow Chest'; not only did it contain their American treaty, but also several years' accumulation of Edicts and memorials which were all taken by the English barbarians. . . . After Ch'i-ying returned to his official residence he became more nervous.

"Yesterday . . . the English barbarian, H. N. Lay, sent a threatening communication. Your slaves and Ch'i-ying met him together and just when we were arguing the treaty, the English barbarian Thomas Wade brought before us a document. It was Ch'i-ying's secret memorial on the state of barbarian management for that year. The language greatly disparaged barbarians. Besides there was the *Vermilion endorsement* of Emperor Hsüan-tsung (Tao-kuang).

"Your slaves were astonished beyond measure. For several days they have heard reports that the English barbarians, because they had previously been deceived by him, wanted to take revenge. His ill fate is unfathomable. . . ."

Such a disclosure would have rattled a man of any nationality, but it was more than embarrassing to these gentlemen; it was a calamity of the worst description. The Emperor had lost face, that was the worst, but they had all lost face, Ch'i-ying most of all. And this downfall had taken place before barbarians. Really there was no measure to the horror of it. Even beyond the shock—and life had to go on, one did one's duty—Ch'i-ying had become acutely unwanted at the conference. He had been there because they considered him *persona grata* with these dreadful people, and for no other reason, but he wasn't *persona grata* in the least, he was a laughingstock. The Commissioners knew they had to get him out of sight immediately. It was not necessary to say so in the memorial: they put it more delicately.

"As Your slaves think that Ch'i-ying's personal fate actually involves national prestige and if these barbarians are allowed to have their way with Ch'i-ying it will be a great impediment to peaceful settlement, . . ." it would be a good thing to recall the old man to Peking where he could "report on barbarian affairs personally." [Swisher, p. 489.] Nobody had illusions as to Ch'i-ying's future, for there was never much sentimental nonsense in Peking Ministries about standing up for one's own staff. Just as soon as the calamitous news hit the Council there was a rush to put on the record a spatter of accusations against the wretched old man, the most vociferous accusers being those who had recommended his appointment. Ch'i-ying himself did not run for cover. On the contrary, he went to Peking before there was time for the Imperial summons. Technically this was an offense punishable by death, as so many actions were in that perilous world. They told him he had deserted. They put him on trial for having hurried to Peking, as if his other crimes were afterthoughts, and a fortnight later, Ch'i-ying was condemned to death by strangulation. Then, to show mercy, the Emperor commuted the sentence to permission to commit suicide. Ch'i-ying died saving a shred of his honor, by strangling himself.

Did the British realize that they had signed the death warrant of an old Manchu who had been friends with them? Lay must have known. It is questionable whether the others did, but Lord Elgin had some inkling of the blow his mission had dealt, after it happened. On the date of the great exposure he wrote a few significant words to his wife:

"I have gone through a good deal since we parted. Certainly I have seen more to disgust me with my fellow-countrymen than I saw during the whole course of my previous life, since I have found them in the East among populations too timid to resist and too ignorant to complain. . . ."

The remaining Imperial Commissioners were free of Ch'i-ying, but they made no progress anyway. Daily they had exhortations from Peking to stand firm, but whatever they said, the barbarians stood firmer. Two clauses in the proposed treaty were so abhorrent to the Imperial mind that the poor Commissioners were in a tremble merely to think of them: the British barbarians said they must have a resident ambassador in Peking, and they also insisted on the right to go into the interior and trade. Since these were the very root of what the English had been pushing for, the Commissioners came up against a blank wall every time they tried to wash out the clauses. Finally Peking made a definite suggestion. The Commissioners should try the roundabout approach and appeal through the less aggressive members of the barbarian quartet, Count Poutiatine of Russia and William Reed of America. To a certain extent the Chinese were successful, in that these two ministers did intercede and talk to Elgin and Gros, transmitting the sad protests of Kuei-liang and Hua-sha-na on a personal ground—that if these two clauses went into the treaty, Kuei-liang and Hua-sha-na would assuredly lose their heads. It was an ingenious argument and it could have been true, though as a matter of fact it wasn't. Kuei-liang had already discussed the matter in several dispatches to his superiors, and had dared to warn them that they might have to give in, at least on the resident embassy.

"The English and French barbarians are always thinking of going into the city to live and, while they have not occupied the villages, they have forcibly taken over private residences and are constantly stirring up trouble, . . ." he said. "In the past they have been most irked by China's contempt and so want to acquire residence in the capital as a matter of prestige. If we could just send officials to look after them suitably they might repent out of gratitude and be able to resolve their former suspicions; even if they did not meet their obligations, their numbers would not be great and we could still manage them. But these barbarians have many cunning devices and whether or not they are harboring any subtle motives, Your slaves do not venture to claim firm control of them. From this dilemma we see no escape." [Swisher, Chapter 10.]

There seems no fear of beheading implicit in this document; in any case the emotional appeal did the Chinese no good, for Elgin was annoyed. He felt that his colleagues were letting him down, and to some extent he was correct: the fact was, the four Western ministers were not aiming for the same ends. France did little trade in China, so Baron Gros wasn't interested in the rights of free entry to the interior. Poutiatine and Reed could afford to be relaxed, as

they knew that whatever gains the other two men made they would
be in on, because of the most-favored-nation clause. Also, Russia had
her own designs on China and was not too keen on pushing a British
ambassador into Peking, whereas Reed, who hadn't yet seen most of
Ch'i-ying's papers and the Edicts that the British snaffled in Canton,
still lived in a fool's paradise, believing that America had a special,
secret hold on Chinese affections. [Stanley F. Wright, *Hart and the
Chinese Customs* (Belfast, 1950), p. 126.] Thus none of the others
were in as truculent a frame of mind as Lord Elgin's. Elgin himself,
for that matter, didn't really carry a chip on his shoulder. He was
no Harry Parkes. But he was wary, and like the other British in the
know, he still smarted from those discovered secret papers. As the
discussions started off he had written to his wife:

"I made up my mind, disgusting as the part is to me, to act the
rôle of the 'uncontrollably fierce barbarian,' as we are designated
in some of the confidential reports of the Chinese Government which
have come into our hands." [*Letters and Journals of James, Eighth
Earl of Elgin*, edited by Theodore Walrond, London, 1872.]

He had to use all the firmness he could muster during the last
phase of the talks. Poutiatine and Reed delivered the proxy plea.
"Well," wrote Elgin, "I sent Frederick [Bruce, his brother] to the
Imperial Commissioners, to tell them I was indignant beyond all
expression at their having attempted to communicate with me
through third parties; that I was ready to sign the Treaty as it
stood; but that, if they delayed or retracted, I should consider negotiations at an end, go to Pekin, and demand a great deal more,
etc. . . . Frederick executed this most difficult task admirably, and
at 6 P.M. [June 26th] I signed the Treaty of Tientsin. . . . Though
I have been forced to act most brutally, I am China's friend in all
this." [Elgin's *Journals*.]

Elgin's character should interest any student of British foreign
policy, for he was a typical privileged diplomat of that era, the sort
of man who maddened British colonials by dropping in on them
where they lived and worked and sweated, told them where they
were wrong, and went away again. He was an aristocrat and he
could afford to have ideals and principles, yet, sooner or later, he
delivered the goods. Full of misgivings, nagged now and again by a
wounded conscience, he nevertheless worked on the side of the
British. It was the great dilemma of his period.

The terms of the treaty he had signed were in the main as follows: There was the much-discussed permission for an ambassador to live in Peking (though already this clause was somewhat softened by the suggestion that the right of an occasional visit might be substituted). Protestants and Roman Catholics were to be protected by the Chinese from the Chinese. British subjects were entitled to travel to all parts of the interior, save to those places held by the Taipings. British ships could trade on the Yangtze River. Five more ports were to be opened to the barbarians. The tariff rates fixed in the Treaty of Nanking were to be revised so that all duty on goods might be paid at once, at five per cent of the value. The epithet "Barbarian" was no longer to be used as applied to British subjects in official documents. The Chinese agreed to pay indemnity for the war and other losses in Canton—such as the burning of the factories—amounting to four million taels, which corresponded to one million, three hundred thousand pounds sterling. Similar treaties were signed with the other three powers, though as we have seen certain clauses in the British treaty were not insisted upon in theirs. It should be noted that the clause entitling British subjects to travel inland everywhere save for Taiping-held localities automatically placed the British on the side of the Emperor as opposed to the rebels. It is an obvious point and a circumstance that could hardly have been avoided, but it was to become significant later on.

The formalities completed, the Imperial Commissioners suggested that all negotiations for a supplementary treaty in which the tariff questions should be settled ought to take place in Shanghai, where the Custom House was located and most trade was now done. They were in a great hurry to get the barbarians away from Tientsin, but Elgin saw in the proposal a gratifying zeal on their part to wind up matters, and he read in their pledge to follow close on the heels of the barbarian mission a good augury. The Emperor had by this time seen the treaty, and would hardly send his Commissioners to Shanghai if he didn't mean to abide by it, reasoned Lord Elgin, who had not yet learned that the world doesn't always play the game according to one's own set of rules. He was cheerful as he sailed back to Shanghai, though the news he got when he arrived rather dampened his spirits. There was more trouble in Canton: the "braves" were harassing the occupying forces. Elgin decided to insist to the Imperial Commissioners when they arrived that all this must stop: a word from the Emperor would surely be enough. It would also be wise, however, to make a show of force, and he arranged with Admiral Sir Michael Seymour that a large part of the British fleet should go to Canton as soon as was practicable. *The Times* had recently printed something unflattering about Yeh Ming-ch'en, now safely stowed away in Calcutta, and though Lord Elgin was ruffled afresh by events in Canton, in fairness he felt that the newspaper article had been unjust to this defeated enemy. The captain who took Yeh to India had reported favorably on his prisoner, saying that he was courteous, civil, and not at all troublesome. Elgin wrote,

"I suppose that there is no doubt of the fact that he executed a vast number of rebels, and I, certainly, who disapprove of all that sort of thing, am not going to defend that proceeding. But it is fair to say that rebels are parricides by Chinese law, and that, in so far as we can judge, nothing could have been more brutal or more objectless than this Chinese rebellion. They systematically murdered all—men, women, and children—of the dominant race, and their supporters, on whom they could lay their hands. Certain Americans and Europeans took them up first because they introduced a parody of some Christian doctrine into their manifestoes. But these gentlemen are now, I think, heartily ashamed of the sympathy which they gave them." [Elgin's *Journals.*]

For reasons not quite clear to Elgin, the Imperial Commissioners did not after all follow close on the barbarians' heels to Shanghai. In fact they were working away like beavers in Peking with the Emperor and his Councilors, trying to figure out holes through which they could wriggle away from that treaty, which had come as a terrible shock. All Lord Elgin knew, however, was that they were not now coming until the autumn, that it was extremely hot in Shanghai, and that he had another important mission which he might as well go about accomplishing in the interim—the drawing up of a treaty with Japan. He didn't know quite what to expect of Yedo, as Tokyo was then called, but the country had been entered after centuries of exclusiveness; opened by the Americans, who now had officials in residence; and Whitehall had been given to understand that the way lay open to the British as well. Elgin had a magnificent present for the "Tycoon," or Emperor; a steam yacht sent by Her Majesty the Queen. On the last day of July he sailed for Nagasaki, having appointed delegates for the supplementary treaty negotiations. One was his secretary Oliphant—though Oliphant went with him to Japan—and the other was Wade. He also insisted that Lay take part in the proceedings as usual, though once again the Customs Inspector's position was ambiguous.

Plotting in Peking, the Imperial officials worked out a scheme that seemed to them admirable. They called it the Secret Plan. The Commissioners were to go to Shanghai according to the standing arrangement, and plunge into discussions as though tariff revision was their only aim in life. At the same time they were to introduce behind stage a magnificent lure, so that the barbarians would willingly abrogate the most obnoxious clauses in the treaty—no less a bait than the offer of free trade at all the existing ports. If the barbarians need no longer pay any duty at all, would they not willingly forgo all the rest—ambassador in Peking, rights of inland trade, new open ports, no travel up the Yangtze? Of course they would, because as everybody knew they were dogs and sheep, avaricious and interested only in gain.

However, they seemed to be punctual-minded dogs and sheep, and those who were waiting in Shanghai now grew restless and troublesome, asking when the talks were going to begin. This was reported to Peking by that intelligent man Ho Kuei-ch'ing, Viceroy of the two Kiangs, who had advised against another Peking plan of stepped-up attacks in Canton when the envoys were enroute to Tientsin. Ho kept a clinical eye on barbarian temper in Shanghai, and noted that the American and French chiefs were getting restless, so he deputed Hsüeh Huan, who was officiating Superintendent of Customs, to keep them busy, taking up "miscellaneous minor items in the tariff schedule," as he said in a memorial, and discussing them one by one, as a means of keeping the barbarians under control. Still they were restless, until there came the inevitable moment when they threatened to break off negotiations and go back to Tientsin, or else go back whence they came, there to wait until the end of the year. No doubt Wade and Lay were the instigators of this intransigence, for they could guess the reason for the delay. They knew, backwards and forwards, the Chinese technique of polite stalling. Hsüeh Huan made "plausible explanations" and cleared up, item by item, the schedules to be discussed, while August wore on. Meanwhile Elgin arranged his treaty with Japan with magical smoothness and swiftness, and it is not wonderful that he should have fallen in love with that country, so different in every way from China. When it was time to go he jotted a sad little note:

"August 30th . . . We are again plunging into the China Sea, and quitting the only place which I have left with any feeling of regret since I reached this abominable East—abominable, not so much in itself, as because it is strewed all over with records of our violence and fraud, and disregard of truth." [Elgin's *Journals.*]

His arrival in Shanghai precipitated events. For one thing, the peace he had demanded for Canton had not been bestowed on it; the braves were still needling the occupation troops. Elgin made a scene about that, insisting that the official in charge, Huang, be recalled immediately. He was assured that all would be done. Then he had to crack the whip over the negotiators.

"After consulting with the American and French chiefs for three days," reported the observant Ho Kuei-ch'ing, "(he) wanted to weigh anchor and go home without saying why or without a word about when he would be back to negotiate. Hsüeh Huan realized that it was already autumn and the rivers would soon go down and we would not have to worry about their going to Tientsin, but that the most important principle in controlling barbarians is confidence." Moreover, the waters would rise again in the spring. . . . The talks had better commence, so let the Commissioners come. Peking took his advice and slipped the leash.

On the eve of the beginning of discussions, Ho wrote a long memorial, the result of deep thought, in which he indicated boldly that he was opposed to the Secret Plan: he was opposed to the slightest suggestion of free trade for China. He appreciated, far more than did his superiors in their Pekinese ivory tower, how necessary the customs revenue was to the nation. Border control too must not be sacrificed. "If we did not collect import and export duties, there would be no inspection. This would mean allowing the barbarians to take our native products and trade in the interior; turning over the economic lever of the empire to the barbarians while our people perish and our capital is depleted. It is Your official's stupid opinion that we must recover the economic lever, and tariffs cannot be lightly abolished."

It is interesting that Ho still reposed great confidence in Lay, whose apparent apostasy was regarded by his Chinese friends as a clever disguise of genuine sentiments of loyalty to China. No doubt, in Ho's view any Chinese statesman might have behaved in the same way.

"H. N. Lay is the most crafty of the barbarians," he now continued. [Swisher, p. 522.] "In the winter of 1855, the former governor, Ch'i-erh-hang-a, sent an offer to that chief to employ him as Shanghai Customs Commissioner with generous pay. The barbarian still feels grateful and looks out for smuggling for us, so in recent years barbarian customs have been three or four times as much as when the port was opened. The said barbarian was afraid of being disliked by various other barbarians, so he also accompanied them to Tientsin and made a great display of violence and ingratiated himself with the barbarian chief in order to show his public spirit. When he returned to Shanghai he was as compliant as ever in our employ. 'Who bells (the tiger) can remove the bell'; so we must continue to hold him responsible for all the barbarians."

The history of Chinese-Western relations is dotted with such individuals as Lay, who captured the confidence of the Chinese and kept it for reasons mysterious to most of their compatriots.

As a result of the Governor General's strong objections to the Secret Plan, which were backed up by the expert Hsüeh Huan, now released from his stalling duties, the Emperor and Council actually relinquished the idea, though they hated doing so. The only shred of it retained was their determination to keep Peking's gates closed against any barbarian minister, but even this resolve, during the early part of the negotiating, was kept under wraps. The Westerners were represented officially at the talks only by the British. The treaty the Americans had made at Tientsin hadn't mentioned the subject of tariff, and the French had made it clear that they were not particularly interested in any trade article but silk. However, it was still of course advisable that they should know what was going on, so each country appointed a delegate to consult offstage with the British during the talks. For America this delegate was Wells Williams, secretary of the American Legation, and France appointed her Consul in Shanghai, Edan.

As if there were no Secret Plan lurking in the background, no outraged Emperor fulminating to his ministers and his favorite wife in Peking, the discussions proceeded smoothly. Lay was the star at these meetings. He had at his fingertips all the Shanghai Customs figures for the past three years, and knew exactly what was needed for reference at every stage. The most important revision hammered out at these talks was that for a nearly allover tariff on a 5 per cent *ad valorem* basis, tea and silk only excepted. This was a most welcome simplification. Stanley Wright, historian of the Customs, calls the schedule finally drawn up "a reliable and comprehensive document." [P. 129.] Apart from the main tariff figure were other questions, all directly connected with the Customs: transit dues, tonnage dues, aids to navigation of a uniform Customs system to all ports, and—a most important and significant innovation—the legalization of the opium trade. Of course this had always been one of the most cherished aims of the British merchants, ever since William Hickey's day and before, but the matter had grown vastly more complicated through the years, though the various points of view had not altered. In Peking, some officials still deprecated the use of the drug, but by this time even such self-made hermits realized that the habit was too widespread to eliminate merely by passing laws of prohibition, and they were now in favor of recognizing it, in order to control trade and use. Besides, recognition and legalization of opium trading would mean that the commodity could be taxed direct from Peking. As things were, the trade was taxed unofficially, but the money went into the pockets of the local authorities, who naturally preferred to leave matters untouched. Twice as much opium was coming into China in 1858 as had been smuggled in at the time of the Treaty of Nanking. Reform would cut down provincial revenue, just when provincial chiefs needed all the money they could get to pursue the war against the rebels.

This was another point on which all the barbarians didn't see eye to eye. William Reed wanted opium prohibited outright. The treaty clause had never prevented American traders from dealing in opium with as much enthusiasm as their British colleagues. Reed, however, took the official U. S. attitude. In the end he submitted to the majority, writing to Elgin, ". . . my deliberate judgment was and is that the trade must go on as it is, with all its mischief and disgrace, unless Your Excellency will undertake to adjust and regulate it." His Excellency did so undertake and he succeeded, though as Wright somewhat defensively points out, Elgin never insisted on the legalization clause, and it was not extorted from the Chinese; in proof of this he quotes Lay as reporting,

"The preparation of the tariff devolved upon me, at the desire of the Chinese no less than that of Lord Elgin. . . . The Chinese Government admitted opium as a legal article of import, not under constraint, but of their own free will deliberately." [Wright, p. 133.]

If Lay too sounds defensive, this is hardly to be wondered at. The opium trade had long been under fire at home and abroad, from missionaries and liberals who felt guilty about the Opium War. Even now that the trade was to be legal, the door was not exactly flung wide open. Tax collectors and prohibitionists did agree on one point, that strict control was necessary. It was decided that opium could be sold by the importer only at its port of entry; only Chinese could then take it inland and distribute it. The ordinary transit dues regulations wouldn't be applicable to its transport either; such dues were left to the Chinese retailers to arrange—in other words the drug was not to be classed as an ordinary commodity. Yet, as Wright says, "The British had at last got their desire: for good or for ill the trade was now legalised." [P. 133.]

Finally the Imperial Commissioners came face to face with the burning question: how were they to soften that terrible clause about the resident British minister in Peking? How could they avoid this intrusion which seemed blasphemy to them, apart from being so very inconvenient? Bereft of their Secret Plan, they bore down heavily on a compromise proposal. They told Elgin that Peking wouldn't be a satisfactory center for an ambassador because it was not really a central, clearing-post sort of city. Contrary to what he seemed to believe, they said, there was no form of federal government in China. The provincial governors looked after most provincial affairs, and Peking officials looked after Peking affairs; it was as simple as that. Then there was the climate. Peking's climate was awful, they assured Lord Elgin—no Englishman could possibly live there the year round. Humbly they begged that the Queen of England might forgo her right to keep a permanent minister in Peking, and use her option instead, of sending somebody now and then to visit the place, transact necessary business, and go away again. So persuasive were they that Elgin's determination wavered. He didn't quite agree to the compromise, but he did consent to a delay while he wrote to England asking for further advice on the subject. It was his private opinion that the visiting-envoy idea might work out better for Britain in any case. Elgin was in a hurry to wind everything up, for he was determined to make a journey up the Yangtze. We learn from a Chinese memorial which is quoted below that his American and French colleagues had the same desire, but were dissuaded. Elgin couldn't be dissuaded. He thought the trip would be the "crowning act" of his mission, and would forestall some of the criticism he felt sure would be leveled at his treaty in England. He had already heard adverse comment on it from Hong Kong, and it rankled, though as a seasoned diplomat he should have been used to such pinpricks. Of the Yangtze he said,

"The Treaty only provides that it shall be open when the Rebels have left it. I daresay this will give rise to comments. If so, I shall have anticipated them, by going up the river myself. I shall take with me my own squadron (what I had in Japan). . . . We shall visit a region which had never been seen, except by a stray missionary. I shall lose by this move some three weeks, but I do not think they will be really lost, because it will give so very complete a demonstration of the acceptance of the Treaty by the Chinese authorities, that even Hong-kong will be silenced." [Elgin's *Journals*.]

Acceptance? At the same time Lord Elgin was cheerfully getting ready for the voyage and writing such words, Ho Kuei-ch'ing and the Imperial Commissioners toiled over a long memorial that they knew would send the Emperor into frenzies of indignation because they dared to so much as hint at acceptance. To soften the blow they started out with a bit of comment they thought would please him. William Reed had offered to co-operate with China, and had really seemed friendly.

"It is apparent," said the writers, "that the present temper of the barbarians is not that of Tientsin." It was no use: the Emperor endorsed this with the dubious note, "How can this kind of talk be believed? If it goes no further than urging us to use them and if we use barbarians to restrain barbarians, then it is possible." [Swisher, p. 539 ff.]

The paper reads almost like a dialogue, it is so interwritten in Vermilion characters; but the memorialists tried hard. "In the management of barbarian affairs at this time when a settlement has just been made, it is difficult to get one's hand in. For instance, the matter of residence at Peking was brought up repeatedly before they were willing to forego permanent residence. . . . If other clauses are reopened, under the circumstances they are certain to fail." Trying hard to show the Emperor a brighter side, they pointed to their triumphs of diplomacy: had they not talked the barbarians out of trading in salt? They had been very firm about salt, and it had taken ten days to wear down their antagonists, but in the end they had won. Also, due to their efforts no arms or ammunition were to be imported. And beans and bean cake were not to be carried out of Niu-chuang and Teng-chou in any but Chinese ships. Furthermore, barbarians wishing to travel and trade in the interior —except Peking, where they weren't allowed at all—would have to get passports from their consuls, and these passports would have to be examined and stamped by Chinese local officials wherever they went, a process which would eliminate promiscuous barbarian renegades. To cheer up the Emperor even more, they added, "Moreover those who travel are mostly missionaries." The Vermilion endorsement snubbed that: "At first they propagate gospel; later their motives become inscrutable." To the further memorial comment, "Originally they were not prohibited by law; now with passports we can examine them," the Emperor retorted, "Even if they are examined everywhere, how does that help the situation?"

The dialogue continues. The memorial: "Barbarians naturally are most resentful of annoyances and if these accumulate perhaps eventually they will be discouraged."

The Emperor: "To hope that they will discard their former attitude is really to talk in one's sleep."

But, said the memorial, stressing facts that His Majesty would never accept, there is simply nothing else to do. "Only when China's army is efficient, supplies adequate, artillery effective, and ships strong can we do as we please and repudiate anything. Speaking for the present, we can only eliminate the worst and call it a day."

But they *had* managed to stave off unwelcome barbarian would-be visitors up the Yangtze, they pointed out—all, that is, but the British. "Your officials negotiated with them personally, urging them this way and that, over and over again, and finally cut them off with forthright argument. The American and French barbarians, blankly dispirited, accepted our advice not to go up the Yangtze at once. But the English barbarians were stubbornly adamant. . . ."

A long final word by the Vermilion Pencil has a very angry tone. "On reading this memorial, We were involuntarily vexed. Even more exasperating, in your negotiations you not only have been unable to abrogate, but even beyond the original treaties have actually allowed the English barbarian steamers to go up the Yangtze. If they do not return, how will you manage?"

That worry at least could have been spared him, for Elgin had every intention of getting back for continued negotiations as soon as possible, and he had accepted the Chinese estimate of three weeks needed for the voyage like a true foreigner, unversed in Celestial vagaries as to numbers. The squadron left Shanghai on November eighth: it was not to get back until January 1, 1859, after frequent occasions when ships went aground, and one when the largest vessels couldn't clear the shallows at all. The Plenipotentiary started out in a mood of pleased excitement: "We are going into an unknown region, along a river which, beyond Nankin, has not been navigated by Europeans. We are to make our way through the lines of those strange beings the Chinese Rebels. We are to penetrate beyond them to cities, the magnitude and population of which fabulous stories are told; among people who have never seen Western men; who have probably heard the wildest reports of us. . . ."

Near Chinkiang, a town that had been taken and retaken by the combatants, he got his first sight of a typical civil-war battleground, and its desolation shocked him; he had an impression that the few people who had not gone away were glad to see the British and hoped for free trade and protection from the rebels. More likely, they hoped for peace from any quarter whatever and had only the vaguest idea of free trade, but Lord Elgin's mind was set in those grooves, and the happenings of the following day were hardly calculated to instill in him more charitable feelings toward the Taipings. The British were going past Nanking. Through outlying Taiping strongholds, Elgin had sent letters ahead informing the rebels that the British squadron was coming upriver past their forts, that they were neutral, and expected not to be molested. But some vessels from the Imperial navy, taking advantage of the squadron's presence, sailed up too in their wake, and came closer than the Taipings ever permitted. As soon as their presence was spotted from the forts, when the British were almost past, the Taiping batteries blazed away. Even after the British hoisted their flag of truce the shots continued, and the British fired back. Their casualties were one killed and two wounded: their anger was high.

"We have passed the town"; recorded Elgin, "but I quite agree with the naval authorities, that we cannot leave the matter as it now stands." Though we might raise our eyebrows, the reaction was natural; the British reasoned that if they didn't take prompt action their return journey in the future, downstream, would be even less comfortable. Some of the squadron went back to Nanking next day and reduced several of the Taiping forts, after which Elgin gave orders to resume the journey, "as I did not want to have to hand over the town to the Imperialists, who are hemming it round on every side. . . . A set of Imperialist junks set to work to fire at the town as we were leaving off, throwing their shot from a most wonderfully safe distance."

At this supremely inopportune moment, a letter was delivered from a Taiping official to Lord Elgin, begging him to join his British forces with theirs and annihilate the Imperialists. In reply Elgin pointed out warmly that he had just been attacked by the Taipings and had retaliated. Another communication arrived immediately, with strongly expressed apologies and explanations of the mistake. Nothing more was said at that time on the subject of an alliance. The British continued, when seeking their nightly anchorage, to stay nearby Imperialist shipping. When they came to Anking, rebels who had not heard of the Nanking incident again mistook the squadron for the Emperor's ships and fired on it. Once more the British "taught them a lesson." But Elgin's early excitement over these encounters was ebbing, since from his point of view it was all small stuff. Though he saw no civil-war fighting with his own eyes, according to reports it was very desultory on both sides. If nothing happened to change Chinese ways, he reflected, this war might well carry on for years to come. And the cities disappointed him, too, for they did not live up to reports of their enormous population, let alone their great splendor. Admittedly Ouchang (Wuchang) of the Three Cities was a fine place and must be as large as Canton. Kuei-liang had sent word ahead to these cities, and the Governor General was waiting to receive the party with a reception—the most sumptuous Elgin had yet seen in China, he said, though the formality of the proceedings was daunting. "It is rather hard to make conversation when one is seated at the top of a room surrounded by some hundred people, and when, moreover, one has nothing to say, and that nothing has to be said by an interpreter. However, the ceremony went off very well."

Hankow was the upper limit of navigable waters and it was time to turn back—past time, as a matter of fact, since it was now December 10. Lord Elgin looked forward to England; he did not think he need tarry long in Shanghai. As the ships approached Anking on Christmas Day, everyone held his breath. Would the rebels shoot at them again? The rebels didn't. On the contrary, Wade received more apologies and special assurances of safety. At Wuhu a strange gift was sent aboard from the rebels; "They have sent me a letter written on a roll of yellow silk, about three fathoms long," wrote Elgin. "It seems to be a sort of rhapsody, in verse, with a vast infusion of their extraordinary theology. It is now snowing heavily. . . ." In fact this

silk scroll was a fascinating specimen of Hung Hsiu-ch'uan's calligraphy in the type of poem he habitually wrote, an exposition of
his religious experiences as well as a recapitulation of the whole
story of Jesus according to the Taiping faith, ending with a warm
invitation to the British to join forces with the enlightened Taipings
and "extinguish the stinking reptiles" of Peking. There was a prose
postscript, inquiring in a typically allusive way if the Reverend
Issachar Roberts was by any chance on board. If so, said the letter,
he should come and talk to the community in Nanking. Roberts was
not on board; he was still at the coast where he need not be embarrassed by unorthodox Taiping Christianity. But another missionary
was there, a representative of the London Missionary Society who
had come along to investigate the general situation, and he went
with Wade, Lay, and Oliphant when these three paid a visit to the
city. (Elgin of course could not compromise Her Majesty's mission
by including himself in the party.) The four Englishmen were handsomely received by one of Hung's princes of high degree, and spent
a day unique in barbarian annals, though it is to be feared they
didn't appreciate it. Oliphant was patronizing and the missionary
was shocked by Taiping theology as the prince expounded it. As for
Elgin when he heard their reports, he dismissed the whole thing with
an indifference bordering on contempt. In at least one respect he
was mistaken:

"Whether the original Taiping chief, 'Hung-Seu-Cheun,' is still
alive or not, we have not been able to discover. Some say he remained shut up with about 300 wives. At any rate he is invisible."

Back at long last in Shanghai, he immediately sent off a dispatch
to London with a summary of the facts he knew financial circles
would want to have. He said shrewdly, "My impression is, that British manufacturers will have to exert themselves to the utmost if they
intend to supplant, to any considerable extent, in the native market, the fabrics produced in their (the Chinese) leisure hours, and
at intervals of rest from agricultural labour, by this industrious,
frugal, and sober population. It is a pleasing but pernicious fallacy
to imagine, that the influence of an intriguing mandarin is to be
presumed whenever a buyer shows a preference for native over foreign calico."

All seemed set fair for the future, but that dispatch was written
on January 5.

Chapter Eight

Elgin had no way of knowing that the continued unrest in Canton was instigated from Peking, but he could not help noticing that the Emperor's Grand Council didn't seem much troubled by the situation. They paid no attention to his demand that Huang, the Viceroy of the Kwangs, be removed from his post. It suited them that the disorders should go on. Any counterirritant should serve to keep the barbarians busy, and put off indefinitely the day when the supplementary trade treaty would be ready for signing. Even the delayed return of the British Plenipotentiary from his Yangtze journey, though it made the Emperor nervous—what was the fellow doing in there anyway all that time, if he wasn't chumming up with Hung Hsiu-ch'uan?—was welcome to the Imperial Commissioners because it gave them a genuine reason and excuse for postponement. But it was touchy work nevertheless for these men while they waited, for they had to juggle Western impatience against similar impatience in Peking, and soothe barbarian tempers about many things. First Canton, then the treaties; first the treaties, then Canton: and while everyone waited for Elgin to come back, the Emperor commanded Seng-ko-lin-chin, the Mongol prince who had beaten back the Taiping General Lin and scattered his forces, to repair and strengthen the fortifications at the mouth of the Peiho. Taku must not be taken so easily again.

The Imperial Commissioners had reason to think they were not doing too badly on their mission, during the long wait. Ever since the original treaties had been sent to the West for ratification, they noticed that the barbarians who waited with them for Elgin to return seemed placated, somehow; not so quick to lose their tempers. The Commissioners dared to grow hopeful. In a memorial dated January 9, 1859 [Swisher, p. 546], they developed a new idea for keeping barbarians out of the Imperial City when the time came to exchange the ratified treaties. It was a prospect that had been worrying the Emperor, they knew. It had grown out of that cursed treaty; a liberty barbarians should never have been permitted to contemplate. Could the foreign envoys not be persuaded to do their exchanging in Shanghai? That would spare the Emperor the pain of the first visit at least.

"None of the barbarians want to go to Kwangtung to negotiate. When the various matters have been settled and the ratifications exchanged, the Imperial Commissioners at Shanghai will again ask for an Edict of confirmation, so that the barbarians will understand that there is someone in sole charge of foreign affairs and not be constantly proposing to go north." The phrase "foreign affairs" was written in the new, foreign-approved style, which means "outside nations affairs," rather than the old way much disliked by Westerners, which means "barbarian affairs." It is interesting that the Chinese should thus show themselves as working around to the idea of a regular body of foreign experts; the change also indicates that they intended to live up to their lesser promises, whatever their intentions regarding the big ones. A few days later they were glad to hear unofficially from the British Consul that Her Majesty's Government had ratified the treaty, including the compromise that concerned the British ambassador's occasional visit to Peking instead of his residence there. This success inspired the Commissioners to make further efforts to soften, if they could not cancel outright, the other hateful treaty clauses. Elgin had returned; they reported: "His attitude was fairly compliant." They were now thinking hard of how to exclude foreign trade from inland waters. If nothing further could be done, at least the unwelcome travelers were going to be under control, because the system of passports and inspection they had evolved could be used as an effective deterrent against most would-be visitors. "The matter of residence at Peking has been eliminated already. As to occasional visits, Your officials ordered Judicial Commissioner Hsüeh Huan to reason repeatedly with H. N. Lay without success." [Swisher, p. 549.] They tried a bit of tactful threatening: "Your officials have also had their subordinates divulge to the barbarians the statement in the Edict previously received, that if the barbarians come to Tientsin again, they could not be treated as they were last year and that we should certainly open fire. They still said they were not afraid."

So far so good—with reservations. But every day the barbarians were growing more restive about the trouble in Canton, and the Imperial Commissioners were at a loss, as they couldn't elicit any response on this subject either from Canton officials or Peking. What were they to do? The Westerners continued to press for the removal of Viceroy Huang Tsung-han of the two Kwangs, and also had their knife into three minor officials in the south. They now declared they wouldn't negotiate with the Commissioners at all until these people were removed from office. The Commissioners felt that the barbarians, if they got much angrier, might take steps. "The barbarians' steamers, without regard for winds, swiftly sail the seas and almost always leave without notice. If in the end they do go to Kwangtung and start trouble again, the implications will not be slight."

This was one of the points on which Peking refused to be stampeded. Lord Elgin accordingly announced that he would do something about it in person, on his way home to England. He left Shanghai toward the end of January, and in Hong Kong he kept his word and superintended preparations for an expedition into the country near Canton city. He stayed in the colony long enough to hear a report on the proceedings, which were pronounced as satisfactory; they proved even more satisfactory when the news was brought to Hong Kong by Lay himself, on February 23, that Governor General Huang had at last been punished. It was true that he hadn't been deprived of his post as Governor General, but he no longer held the rank of Imperial Commissioner of Foreign Affairs. Elgin felt that England's honor had been satisfied with that. Moreover, the Canton braves had been quelled for a time. Elgin was all the more inclined to cheerfulness because his brother, the Honorable Frederick William Adolphus Bruce, had been appointed Minister to the Court of Peking, and would—presumably—soon pay his first visit to the Imperial City, according to the treaty. He would have to go in any case, to exchange ratifications.

"I am really and truly off on my way to England, though I can hardly believe that it is so," wrote Lord Elgin in his journal on March 3. "The last mail brought me not a word either from Frederick or about his plans; only what was very satisfactory, the approval of the Government of my arrangement respecting the residence of the British Minister in China."

The hopes of the Imperial Commissioners, as to doing the rest of the treaty business in Shanghai, were dashed. Inscrutably, the for-

eign Commissioners insisted that they must go to Peking for the exchange of ratified treaties—or that some other accredited official
must go—and then they all departed for their separate countries,
to report on what had been done. Informed of the barbarians' in-
scrutability, the Councilors made the best of a bad bargain and began dreaming up ways to render life in Peking as difficult as possible
for the intruders. There were all sorts of sumptuary laws. The envoys must bring no more than ten attendants apiece. They must not
bear arms. They would not be permitted to ride in sedan chairs
within the city walls, and as soon as the treaties had been exchanged
they must leave the place. Said an edict of March 29, "If you explain
clearly like this the barbarians must needs bow their heads and obey.
The three other matters can be elucidated when occasion affords
and if one can be eliminated, hereafter there will be one less hard-
ship to bear. If complete abrogation is not possible, restrictions must
be placed on the three clauses to keep the barbarians from making
endless demands." [Swisher, p. 555.]

In spite of Ho Kuei-ch'ing's daring bluntness throughout his correspondence about the commission and the treaties, he was in this
edict honored by being elevated in rank to the job that had just been
taken away from the Viceroy of the Kwangs—Imperial Commissioner of the Five Ports, which meant of Foreign Affairs. Automatically this placed him in a position of authority over the other
Commissioners. Another edict of the same day's date went out to
Prince Seng-ko-lin-chin, warning him to be on guard, as the returning Western envoys might bypass Shanghai and sail straight for
Tientsin. He must of course tell them to turn around and go to
Shanghai, but if they persisted in trying to enter the Peiho, or dared
to fire on the Taku forts, Seng-ko-lin-chin must hit back. The Mongol willingly made a note of this command: his forts were strong
now, and the river well defended by obstructions.

In the event, Bruce and his colleagues didn't bypass Shanghai,
but by the time they were on their way, Seng-ko-lin-chin had a new
plan. In April he memorialized the Court [Swisher, p. 559]: if the
barbarians still insisted on coming to Peking instead of exchanging
ratifications in Shanghai, they had better go around the mouth of
the Peiho and sail to Peitang, a small port farther up the coast. This
was to keep them from taking inland the great fleet that rumor said
they were bringing along. From Peitang they would be able to sail
upriver only sixty *li*, after which they would have to disembark and

go on by land to Peking, "or perhaps by land from Pei-t'ang to Tientsin and by boat to the vicinity of T'ung-chou." The Emperor approved of this latter route. It was about the only thing in the whole project that he did approve. In the weeks that elapsed between the Mongol's memorial and the actual arrival of the Western envoys, the Emperor and Council kept dithering about the coming ordeal, commanding the Commissioners, Kuei-liang and his assistants, to go on trying to modify the clauses, and to keep everything down in Shanghai. It was no use, said the Commissioners; the barbarians were as inscrutable as ever. Only John Ward, the American, was a peaceable, approachable man. They reported that he would even have been willing to exchange ratifications in Shanghai, if it hadn't been for the bad example of the other ministers. Naturally, when the French and English insisted upon going to Peking, he elected to do likewise. John E. Ward was a newcomer who had taken no part in the preliminary hostilities or any of the history of the treaties. His errand was purely and simply to make a formal exchange of documents.

In spite of all their flurry and tenacity, the Peking government kept in mind that things would probably work out for the worst: the envoys would come to the Imperial City. Between their orders to general and commissioner, therefore, they made arrangements to lodge the Westerners, and in characteristically fussy manner they changed these arrangements several times. Over and over they repeated the rules: no sedan chairs, no more than ten attendants, and so on. They seem to have slipped back into the mentality that governed barbarian affairs in the days before Canton was captured, when foreign envoys were sent from Shanghai to Canton to present their credentials, and meekly obeyed the Emperor's orders. It did not seriously occur to any of them that the foreign commissioners might not obey Seng-ko-lin-chin's orders, and go around Taku to the fort next door.

It happened on June 25, 1859. Rear Admiral Sir James Hope, Seymour's successor, was in command of the fleet. De Bourbolon represented the French, and Bruce of course the British. Ward came along with a couple of American ships. They all sailed to the familiar Peiho mouth, watched over by the Taku forts, and were surprised to find their way barred by large booms and miscellaneous junks and hulks. Hope asked the local officials to clear the way; in reply, they told him that there had been Imperial orders to the effect that he must take his party to Peitang, and that they must regretfully refuse to clear the river. Some of Hope's men got to work and moved some of the obstruction out of the road. Hope then sent an ultimatum to the guard and tried to force a passage with eleven gunboats. According to Chinese versions of the affair, one of these gunboats fired the first shot, at the forts. This may or may not be true; what is certain is that the gunboats were suddenly subjected to a volley that surprised their crews with its fury and vigor. A brisk exchange followed, by which the forts were badly damaged, but so was the squadron: three gunboats were lost outright, and others put out of action temporarily. Seng-ko-lin-chin's jubilant declaration that he had sunk all the squadron but one must be put down to pardonable exaggeration in the first flush of surprise and joy. Never mind: it was an extraordinary victory. The Westerners sent a detachment of men ashore to continue the battle on land, but the forts were still well enough manned to withhold their assault, and eighty-nine Allied troops were killed, with several hundred wounded. De Bourbolon and Bruce sailed back to Shanghai, leaving the rest of the fleet to follow when the pieces had been picked up. It was a great humiliation altogether for the Allies, and the celebrations that went on in Peking can be imagined.

The Court quickly calmed down, however, and settled on a follow-up strategy. It had always been their desire to bring about dissension between the Western nations, and now they saw their chance. The British wouldn't have the face to reassume negotiations, they reasoned, but the French might want to carry on with their own exchange, and since it was a British gunboat that had fired the first shot, the Manchus were willing to let bygones be bygones for the French and Americans. An offer therefore went out to these ministers repeating their former directions; they were to wait at Peitang—not Taku—for someone to come and fetch them and take them on to Tientsin, where again they must wait until Kuei-liang and his colleagues came to meet them. Ultimately they would accompany these gentlemen to Peking and continue with the treaty business, as planned. The sumptuary rules were repeated: no large retinue, no sedan chairs, and so on. The French did not accept this proposition, but the Americans, in the person of J. E. Ward, did. Poor Ward followed the dictates of common sense—after all, it wasn't his fight and he had his orders from Washington—but he was ill rewarded for his efforts. The courtesy of the first official communication did not endure. His two ships obediently sailed on to Peitang on June 29, and there he remained for a very long time while his hosts talked it over at leisure. The other Westerners were later to claim in all sincerity that the shabby treatment afforded Ward was deliberately insulting; that the Imperial party were feeling their oats, and humiliated the American in order to demonstrate to their people that they could kick barbarians around with impunity. It seems more likely, in view of some of the documents, that much of their behavior was due rather to ignorance and suspicion. Putting it without exaggeration, they weren't accustomed to entertaining Westerners, and they naturally suspected all people from Outside. Seng-ko-lin-chin warned the Council, while Ward cooled his heels in Peitang, "Just after the rupture we must be doubly cautious. If we once stoop down, the barbarians are sure to be arrogant again. We have finally come to the conclusion that in conciliation, the slower the better." [Swisher, p. 572.] Moreover, there were many small matters to arrange in advance: what to do with two prisoners the Chinese had, one Englishman and the other, as they erroneously thought, an American. He was Canadian actually, but the Allies wisely never told the Chinese that, as they rightly thought it would jeopardize his chances of being released. Within the palace opinions were by no means unanimous as to the wisdom of letting Ward in, even after he had been informed that he might come. There were protests and arguments and changes of mind. Ward was told he could have his interview on July 5, then it was put off to the eighth, and then it was put off again. He heard that the Russians were already in the city waiting to exchange their documents, but he was never allowed to communicate with them. It was July 20 before the American party—Ward, S. Wells Williams, and W. A. P. Martin —were permitted to set out for Peking, on a journey that took several days: It was August 9 before the Imperial edict was issued setting the actual day for the ceremony, and the sixteenth before the business was done. Even at that, they finally exchanged the documents in Peitang after all. All this time the Americans were practically imprisoned, in most uncomfortable conditions, and the minute the signatures were affixed they were hustled away and sent back to Shanghai. However, Ward had delivered a letter from President Buchanan to the Emperor—the first time an American President had written direct to this imposing personage and actually got it through—and when he left he took with him a reply from the same august being.

According to China's code, her Court had maintained its dignity, and they had reason to be proud. But as the noise of the firecrackers died away, sober thoughts of the future intruded. The Councilors had no illusions: the British would be back for revenge, and the French, who had spurned special favors, would no doubt be with them again. Seng-ko-lin-chin once more built up his defenses at Taku, and was commanded to fortify Peitang as well, though this order for some reason was never implemented. No one must relax: the enemy no doubt had spies everywhere. Even at the moment the Emperor made his plans, the Russian barbarian ships were in the vicinity, said his Councilors; they were hanging about, spying. Orders went to Ho Kuei-ch'ing to keep himself and the court informed as to barbarian actions, especially British actions. Ho replied with alacrity. The Shanghai barbarians seemed stirred up in the most mystifying manner over what had happened to Ward in the north. [Swisher, p. 628.] Medhurst, the English Consul, in an interview with the acting Customs Taotai Wu Hsü, had really gone off the handle about it, saying that Tientsin was a trap and that Ward had been treated in Peking like a captive chieftain; furthermore, that the barbarian merchants were furious and planned to go to Tientsin in the spring to get even. "As his speech was incoherent," said Ho, Wu Hsü and the others explained that his attitude was mistaken. They said that Ward had been treated with courtesy in Peking "and even received an autograph letter promulgated by His Imperial Majesty, a superlative favor." It is not hard to picture the furious indignation of the Westerners on two counts, in defense of Ward and yet in criticism of his having let down the side by going to Peking at all. It did not improve British and French temper that they now had to tread in the American's footsteps, diplomatically speaking, and trade on sufferance, claiming support from the most-favored-nation clause. Ward did his best for the common cause, and lost no time in demanding that two new ports, Ch'aochou and T'ainan, be opened in accordance with his ratified treaty. Though Peking as usual tried to back out of the agreement or at least put him off, claiming that they need not do this until the other treaties had been settled, Ho Kuei-ch'ing's counsels prevailed in the end and the ports were opened. The Imperial Commissioner's method of carrying his point is interesting: he made the port-opening appear like a concession on the Emperor's part, to soothe Ward's feelings for any slight he may have fancied he had received. The Chinese were genuinely puzzled by the American's bitterness over his Peking ordeal, as can be seen by a memorial from Ho, dated October 4, 1859:

"It is finally learned that when John Ward was in Peking, unaccustomed to the diet and accommodations and besides being in a solitary, isolated position, he was anxious to return south and therefore did not venture any demands. Actually he deeply regretted this failure to realize his heartfelt desires." Moreover, when he got back to Shanghai, Ho went on, the English and French made fun of him, saying that his treatment was no better than that of a messenger boy and that he was "utterly incompetent. . . . Thus they ridiculed him." [Swisher, p. 631.]

In those leisurely days, nobody saw anything strange in the state of affairs by which, in spite of the rancorous battle of Taku, in spite of the coming struggle that everyone knew was inevitable, the Allies and the Chinese tacitly appreciated the fact that trade need not —in fact, must not—be suspended. The Westerners wanted the money and the Chinese had to have both the profits and the resultant revenue. Though the trade clauses in the supplementary treaty were no more ratified for the British than the rest of the treaties, one of them now brought about an important development in the Customs Service. Hitherto Shanghai had been the center of Service activities to such an extent that the only foreign inspectors lived and worked at that port. Examination of imports and exports and collection of duties at other treaty ports were therefore less scrupulously done, since Chinese officials had not yet become thoroughly indoctrinated with the Western attitude, and this arrangement, though it suited venal officials, was unfair to such traders as had to take their goods through such ports. It was also of course disadvantageous to the national treasury. The new rules provided for expansion of the foreign inspectorate to all ports. But if the Chinese regretted this alteration, as some of them naturally must, they were appeased by another reform: no longer were foreign candidates for the jobs to be recommended, i.e., selected, by their own Consuls. Selection and appointment were to rest entirely with the Chinese Superintendent. In other words the Customs were now going to be truly Chinese in management. It will be remembered that H. N. Lay had already obtained his post through Chinese support, against the will of the

British official who had hitherto recommended all British inspectors, but he had had to intrigue and struggle to get it. That was all changed by the new rules. To organize the expansion and appointments, a high officer was to be appointed by Imperial Commissioner Ho Kuei-ch'ing, who was advised by his colleague Hsüeh Huan to name H. N. Lay, and accordingly did so. Lay thus became first Inspector General of Customs, a title inevitably shortened in everyday usage to "I.G."

These changes brought down on Bruce's head a good deal of criticism from English merchants who hated to see British control of the Customs relinquished. Tom Meadows had recently been made Consul for Shanghai, and he was most violent and outspoken in his objections. He said he found something repellent in Englishmen who were willing to give their first loyalty to a foreign institution, and though he named no names, he didn't have to. [Wright, p. 136.] Bruce ignored Meadows and similarly minded others, and gave Lay all help possible in his complicated task. Ward, who had only recently returned from Peking, was the cause of more complication when he spoke up for the non-British foreign nations and pointed out that the Service Inspectorate, though nominally international, had hitherto been a pretty exclusively Sino-British concern. He suggested that the number of nationals should be based on the proportion of trade each country pursued with China. It was a proposition that sounded all right but was impossible to put into practice: however, certain adjustments were made in the new set-up, and other Commissioners than British began to appear in the lists. Lay had other considerations to worry about which seemed to him more immediate, chiefly the question of Canton. This port, which had once been the only place in China through which goods could get through, was now the stepchild of trade. The opening of the other ports, especially Shanghai, had dealt a tremendous blow, and when the British stormed the forts in 1857, after the factories were burned down, what little regulated trade there was almost vanished. There had been sporadic attempts to revive it, but the activity of the Canton braves and Western countermeasures were not exactly encouraging. Customs posts had been set up at different places, but none of them worked very well, and Lay was not surprised, when he went to look the land over, to hear that Canton customs revenue had gone down 50 per cent in the past five years. A man of exceptional ability was needed to nurse the Service back to health, and

Lay found him in the person of Robert Hart, who had once served as interpreter to the Allied Commissioners at Canton and was now in the British Consular Service there. Lay's attention was drawn to him by a long memorandum Hart wrote at his request, summing up the local situation, and the I.G. promptly invited him to take on the job of Customs Commissioner for Canton. Hart successfully applied to Bruce for permission to resign his consular post, and moved into the new station as soon as he got it. Lay went back to Shanghai.

There he was a busy man. Apart from his customs work, he had fallen into his old role, since the debacle at Tientsin, of go-between for East and West. As he had long been very friendly with Ho Kuei-ch'ing and Hsüeh Huan, and as Ho especially was rapidly rising in his career, this was a valuable bridge for the West, and Lay seems to have made the most of his opportunities to patch up relations behind the scenes. The Chinese officials told him that the root of the trouble was nothing new; it was still, as it had always been, the clause about ambassadors having free entry to Peking and all the attendant complications feared by the Manchus. Even the compromise arrangement, they said, in its very anticipation was enough to send the Emperor and his advisers into fits of resistance reckless enough to result in such calamities as the closing of the Peiho at Taku. Ho and Hsüeh themselves, better informed on Western mentality than their masters, saw clearly that the retribution that was surely coming would be overpowering, even to Seng-ko-lin-chin, the hero of the hour. Though they kept attempting the impossible and entreated Lay to persuade Bruce that he should give in and call off his dogs, they were not really foolish enough to expect any success in this endeavor. They listened to Lay's explanation as to just why this one surrender, of the rights of free entry for envoys, could not be accepted by the barbarians. Lay told them that the Emperor's jealously guarded hermitage was bound to be harmful to His Majesty, even if he could preserve it, because as long as the Western nations had nobody in Peking to watch over their interests, the Peking officials would back down on the treaty promises, and every time this happened, the Westerners would make war and force the Chinese to set matters right. As for the compromise the Imperial Commissioners had insisted upon making, it had already turned out disastrously: the very first test had shown that. Look at the way Ward was treated when he went to the capital city as an accredited

envoy! He had been first ignored, then dealt with like a servant bearing tribute. (If Ho Kuei-ch'ing felt like taking exception to this
statement, he held his tongue. It seemed that East and West would
never look at these matters in the same light.) But Hart was to be
much appreciated by the Chinese because he never raised his voice
or used the hectoring tone of Lay, Gordon, and others. Lay asked if
the Emperor could really desire these seasonal battles. Wouldn't it
be a better solution to give in altogether and let foreign ministers
live in Peking permanently? There was no need for them to communicate with the Emperor direct: the Chinese should maintain a
special committee of experts on foreign affairs to deal with them.
Ho and Hsüeh thought this an excellent idea, and were later to persuade their government to set up the nucleus of a Ministry of Foreign Affairs, but all this was in the future. They knew as well as Lay
did that first there would have to be a settlement by fire.

                    *   *   *

It was not as if the Peking masters were languishing in a vacuum,
waiting for the crisis. They were much occupied with another matter, the threat of the Taipings, which had gone into an acute stage.
Urged on by dangerous successes on the part of the Imperial forces,
who were besieging Nanking, Hung permitted one of his trusted
princes to go on an audacious venture. Early in 1860 this general
led his troops out of Wuhu, upstream from Nanking, and drove in
a southwesterly direction as if he intended to occupy the port of
Hangchow and cut off the Imperialists at Nanking from a large,
vital length of the coast. The Imperialists fell for the feint; in quick
alarm they abandoned the siege and pursued the rebels. The Taipings now doubled back and caught them in the open, and trounced
them. They ran for Soochow to the north, but the Taipings followed
and whipped them again, afterwards moving into the famous old
canal city. Shanghai Westerners viewed all this with pardonable
alarm, for they were now completely surrounded by the rebels, and
Bruce made an important decision: if or when the time came he
would defend not only the foreign settlement but the Chinese walled
city as well against the Taipings. It was merely another feature of
the very complicated situation that he should thus align his country
with Peking against Peking's enemy, while at the same time he laid
plans to assault Peking. But British policy was now set, and Bruce
was not being inconsistent within these limits: the English foresaw

an aftermath of the assault with an Emperor grown friendly; a tamed Emperor. If Hung had already overwhelmed Peking it would have been different, but he hadn't.

＊ ＊ ＊

Thoughtful foreigners marveled at the Emperor's tenacity. According to repute he was a weak debauched creature who had lately suffered an illness variously described as paralytic and dropsical. Where, then, did he get the stubbornness and audacity that rang through the few edicts he presumably published that came to foreign eyes? They explained it away: no doubt the edicts were written for him by his advisers. In Peking, where people lived near the Imperial Palace, guesses were probably nearer the truth. There it was said that Yehonala, the I Concubine, wielded more influence than ever over her husband since she had borne him his first and only son in 1856. Long after, the widowed Yehonala told a high official that she learned a lot about foreign affairs during her husband's lifetime because he always let her classify his memorials. Possibly he went further than that and let her dictate some of his comments and edicts. She was a spirited, haughty woman with a patrician scorn for barbarians, and the gossips were doubtless right when they called her the power behind the flaccid figure of the Emperor. She was even believed responsible for Ch'i-ying's death, though it doesn't seem likely that he could have escaped the ill-wishing of a number of officials he had angered, with or without the I Concubine's enmity. Otherwise the story rings true. The unbending pride, pigheadedness, and irrationality of the Emperor's style are not out of character for Yehonala, nor is the ignorance that blinded other eyes as well as hers to the future. It was not ignorance all the way. One is bound to be impressed, as Lord Elgin was, by the shrewdness of some of the Emperor's vermilion-pencil comments. Back in China as ambassador extraordinary to demand an apology for the Taku hostilities, he wrote after the Allied victory in Peking, on November 10, 1860:

"The gossip is that the Emperor is occupying his time at Jehol by marrying a fourth wife (a rather expensive proceeding) and getting tipsy. I am afraid he is not much worth; although, if the papers in the vermilion pencil which we found in the Summer Palace, are his writing, he is not such a fool as people suppose."

＊ ＊ ＊

Slowly the matter progressed. Bruce sent an ultimatum to Peking in March. Elgin complained that everything was being slowed down by the vast scale of England's and France's preparations. The leaders were being given far more men than he thought they would need—twenty-five thousand—though he declared that the whole affair would be far quicker, neater, and cheaper with five thousand. His protests were ignored by the aroused government.

Sir James Hope had succeeded Seymour as admiral, and Sir Hope Grant was named as general over all the forces, some of whom came from India—the Sikh Irregulars, who with their splendid physiques and dark skins struck terror to peasant hearts even before the Allies left Hong Kong and Shanghai. There in the southern cities it was necessary to draft some thousands of coolies for transport. Elgin saw his brother Frederick Bruce for the first time since the Taku rebuff, but it was not a long visit: according to the rules Bruce had to stay in Shanghai until the troops made it to Peking. A vast array of ships, French and British, gathered at a rendezvous not far from the Peiho. On July 26 they sailed together to anchorages off Peitang, intending to land on the thirtieth and assault the forts there, which they fully expected to find bristling with defenders. To their surprise, the forts seemed totally deserted and the river was not blocked. In any case disembarkation was impossible on the soft ground under a heavy rainfall that held up all day, so they spent the night of the thirty-first aboard, and made their landing in unpleasant conditions enough the next morning—mud, heavy cloud, and stretches of shallow water—but there were no hostile manisfestations, and the shore was still deserted. On examination the forts were found to possess for armaments two wooden guns, nothing else: a score of peasants were camping under the roofs. Where was Seng-ko-lin-chin?

For weeks the Mongol prince had kept anxious watch on the sea, kept up to the mark if that were necessary by a constant flood of memorials and edicts from Peking. As soon as he realized what a great fleet was approaching, however, prudence intervened in his plans and he took away his troops from Taku and Peitang, determining on the spot to use harassing tactics instead of outright attack. According to one of the British staff officers, Robert Swinhoe, the English soldiers joked about the disappearing general and declared that he was in reality a runaway Irishman from the Royal Marines named Sam Collinson: you had only to look at his methods, they said, if you didn't believe it. According to Western ideas of valor,

Seng-ko-lin-chin's strategy was weird and wonderful, and so if they had known it were the ideas of his masters, who continued with their plots and plans of diplomacy up to the last minute. They invested great confidence in the hope of turning Ward against the Russian, Ignatieff, and vice versa: both these men had accompanied the fleet again, in their usual positions of observer. Another possibility dreamed up by the Councilors was to stir up trouble between the French and British, so that all the Allies might start fighting among themselves and forget about Peking. Such things *had* happened in Chinese annals: why should they not happen again? There were other plans too, which changed with every hour. The barbarians should be permitted to come into Peking, the barbarians must not be permitted to come into Peking; Ward should be asked to mediate, Ward must on no account be asked; negotiate, do not negotiate. . . . All this time the Allies were landing at Peitang. The "Tartars" did not remain completely invisible, for a reconnaissance party of French troops came upon a considerable force of them. Unfortunately, though the French numbered two thousand, they did not fight because they hadn't been specifically ordered to do so, and the Chinese got away, a circumstance that added to their self-confidence.

On August 4 the deep thinkers of Peking were forced to give up any hope of negotiation rather than war or capitulation; Ward told their representative flatly that there was no chance of it. It was discovered that they couldn't even communicate directly with Elgin or Gros, these gentlemen having borrowed a line from the Chinese book and refusing to talk at all until Bruce's ultimatum should be honored. The terms of this were two; an apology for the occurrences of 1859 and prompt payment of an indemnity. It was at this point that the Allies seem to have tried to introduce to their enemy the principle of the flag of truce, which, in spite of its use on Elgin's voyage up the Yangtze, clearly remained a mystery to them. Seng-ko-lin-chin wrote about white flags in a memorial dated August 8 [Swisher, p. 677]:

"Between 9 and 11 in the evening of the 4th . . . two barbarians on board the grounded steamer went ashore north of Pei-t'ang, each bearing a white flag, with the two characters 'Cease Fighting' written on them, as well as bolts of white cloth . . . they said they had no official papers, but that our cavalry was stationed too close and it was feared that they would damage the explosives on board and thus destroy harmonious feeling. If either party had occasion to send persons to communicate, they must carry white flags and must not be harmed. . . . The barbarians, having no answer, flung the bolts of white cloth on the ground, saying they would leave them for us to use in communication. Then they returned to the ship. . . . Your slaves all agreed that as the English barbarians sent white flags, although they could not be relied on, actually these barbarians were admitting defeat and so proposed to send a communication to these barbarians fixing a time for an interview." This attempt came to nothing, as the barbarians didn't seem to understand. The memorialist continued, "As these barbarians' trickery has a hundred manifestations, their two characters 'Cease Fighting' were almost certainly intended to dampen our martial ardor, catch us unprepared, and wait for a chance to cause trouble. So orders were immediately sent to cavalry and infantry regiments to intensify their guard and not allow the least carelessness. They respectfully copy the American barbarian communication, make a replica of the 'Cease Fighting' white flags and respectfully present both for Imperial inspection."

The inhabitants of Peitang must have been more eager than the troops for the campaign to get under way so that the soldiers would move out and leave them alone. The officers gave a few futile orders that looting must not take place, but looting did take place, though there was not much to pick up in the poor village. Only such houses as were occupied from the beginning by officers escaped the sack: according to Swinhoe the muddy little streets were full of smashed pottery, torn books, and ripped-up scrolls. At last, on the twelfth, the move began, though Lord Elgin remained aboard his ship for the time being. The armies' route took them past the back of the Taku forts, which they took without very much trouble: Elgin watched the battle from a nearby hilltop. It was over by noon on the twenty-second: three days later in the *Granada* he sailed up the Peiho to Tientsin and arrived on the twenty-sixth. There, on the second of September, his old friend Kuei-liang, Imperial Commissioner, and another official came to see him. As they assured him that they brought word of complete agreement with the terms of the ultimatum, Lord Elgin was pleased to grant them audience. When it came to the crucial point, however, they backed away from signing the declarations, or convention as Elgin referred to it, saying they would first have to send it to Peking for approval. This was the familiar old run-around, and Elgin would have none of it. He was not displeased in his heart, however, to be subjected to the delay, since it gave Sir Hope Grant the time he needed for bringing his forces up. Next time Kuei-liang asked for audience Elgin refused it, and the march was resumed. The army didn't make good time, but then he had expected that. On September 11 Elgin was encamped twenty miles past Tientsin when a pair of officials of really high degree came to talk to him: Prince Tsai of I, who was a cousin of the Emperor's, and a man introduced as President of the Board of War. Impressive though these titles were, Elgin refused to talk things over until he should have reached Tungchao, twelve miles from Peking. Later, however, the dignitaries wrote to him in so conciliatory a tone that he had second thoughts about his decision. Sir Hope was growing uneasy about supplies, and would have liked to take even more time on the road. Why not feel out chances for making an honorable peace then and there?

Accordingly Elgin sent a small party ahead, under the leadership of Sir Harry Parkes and Wade, to talk things over. They came back with good news: these high-placed Commissioners were already at Tungchao and had said they were waiting to sign the convention at last, for which errand they had full power, without needing further recourse to Peking. Arrangements were made for the signing: Elgin, Gros, and Sir Hope would move on with a picked escort to the meeting place, while the main army waited behind. To make everything ready, Parkes went back to Tungchao with a party composed of Elgin's private secretary Henry Brougham Loch, a correspondent of *The Times* named Bowlby, twenty-two members of the British army including nineteen Sikhs, and thirteen Frenchmen. September 17 was the date fixed for the meeting. On that day, Seng-ko-lin-chin's men attacked the main army, at the same time falling on the advance party under Parkes and carrying them as prisoners to Peking. The fact that the party was carrying a flag of truce has always been cited as a particularly devilish feature of the betrayal, but it is quite likely that the "Tartars" still didn't understand just what a flag of truce was.

The attack on the main Allied army came to nothing; the assailants were easily beaten off, but the question of the prisoners was grave. Shocked as he was, Elgin concluded that the betrayal had not been a coolly calculated affair. It was more likely, he thought, a last-minute inspiration of Seng-ko-lin-chin's, but whoever thought of it first, the immediate reaction in Peking was joyful. To think that they had bagged a couple of barbarian chiefs! The official even memorialized at great length, urging the Emperor to follow up the daring blow by pressing on to Taku and burning the barbarian boats, exterminating all that were left of their vile sort. Obviously an old-timer, he repeated a long-outdated theory: "Not only are rhubarb and tea vital for the lives of the barbarians but actually, if we did not trade with them, the commercial barbarians would defy the military barbarians completely, so in the end China would still have her profit from barbarian customs." [Swisher, p. 681.] Elgin and his Allies quickly sent word that if their people were not sent back within three days' time and the convention was not signed within that limit, they would assault Peking. He sent this message to Prince Kung, who was now evidently the man in charge: the Emperor, it seemed, was not well. He was staggered to get a cool reply that they could have their men back as soon as the Allied army and fleet had left the country. Remarkable, thought Lord Elgin, considering that after five engagements with the enemy he and his brothers-in-arms had lost twenty soldiers at most. Another ultimatum elicited a softer reply, but Prince Kung was still trying to drive his bargain, so the army moved forward.

In Peking there was pandemonium. In spite of Prince Kung's audacious words, noblemen had for days been fleeing from the city with their families and portable valuables. Now the Emperor too made his escape to Jehol, or rather, in the polite language of his circle, he went on an autumn tour of inspection. Up to the end, said the gossips, Yehonala begged him not to go, and twice she succeeded in postponing the shameful exodus, but panic overcame him at last, while the avengers were still some days' march off. Fortunately for His Majesty the enemy was very slow-moving. Elgin complained bitterly that their delays took the sting out of all his threats: when he said, for example, that they would be on the way by October 1, they lingered until the fifth.

Now that they were officially at war, the brutal code of international usage left the troops officially free to plunder as they liked. When Swinhoe reached the town of Chiang-chiahuan where the Russians had already encamped and the others proposed resting, he saw scarifying scenes. The Cantonese coolies had taught their companions that pawnshops in China make good pickings—pawnshops there are used as storehouses as well as lending establishments

—and everyone had gone straight to these, as well as sacking the ordinary shops, so that the streets were littered with old clothes which poor peasants had pawned, thrown away when the looters made for gold and jewels. Sikhs marched around, clowning in women's garments and strange headdress. Beautiful wooden carvings were ripped out of houses and destroyed for no reason whatever. Swinhoe and several sober companions went out on a tour of mercy to collect the women of the town so that they might be placed under protection in one house. They came upon a group of females of all ages, who had swallowed opium in an attempt to commit suicide and die with their virtue unscathed. The poor creatures would not believe in Swinhoe's good intentions, and put up a terrific battle before they could be loaded into a cart and carried to their refuge. On the way, one mother tried earnestly to strangle her small daughter. Army doctors saved all but one of the opium-swallowers. Later some coolies were apprehended raping another woman, and by order of the officer in charge the chief offender was put to death. All this distressed Swinhoe, but if he had known the customs of the country he would have been even more dismayed, since it is very likely that many of these women, and certainly the raped peasant girl, succeeded in killing themselves as soon as their deliverers were out of sight.

On October 3, Elgin was reassured at getting a letter signed by Parkes and Loch, who were together. It had been sent on by Prince Kung, and though it was obviously written under duress, it showed that they were alive. No mention was made of the other prisoners, however—an ominous omission. Again the armies lumbered on, making for the Emperor's Summer Palace outside the gates of Peking, which was known as Yuan Ming Yuan: it was from there that His Majesty had fled. They got there on October 7. Yuan Ming Yuan was the pride of the dynasty. In a city of lovely palaces it was considered the loveliest. It was built in the eighteenth century, during the reign of Ch'ien-lung, designed at his command by the Jesuits he patronized: white marble buildings of mixed Chinese-Rococo style, surrounded by fountains and gardens and French-style clipped trees like those of Versailles. [C. R. Boxer, "Jesuits at the Court of Peking," in *History Today*, September 1957.]

"I have just returned from the Summer Palace," wrote Elgin in the evening of that day. "It is really a fine thing, like an English park—numberless buildings with handsome rooms, and filled with Chinese *curios,* and handsome clocks, bronzes, &c. But, alas! such

a scene of desolation. The French General came up full of protestations. He had prevented *looting* in order that all the plunder might
be divided between the armies, &c. &c. There was not a room that
I saw in which half the things had not been taken away or broken
into pieces. . . . Plundering and devastating a place like this is
bad enough, but what is much worse is the waste and breakage.
. . . War is a hateful business." Yet it was Elgin who in the end
had the place burned to the ground.

Swinhoe too described the splendid gardens and rooms, and the
throne room where the floor was covered with treasures. General
Montauban, pointing to these, said to him—Swinhoe was being
shown around by a Palace eunuch who had been left behind—"See
here, I have had a few of the most brilliant things selected, to be
divided between the Queen of Great Britain and the Emperor of
the French."

As he strolled around the rooms observing these beautiful objects,
says Swinhoe, the French officers suddenly began grabbing whatever they liked. "Gold watches and small valuables were whipped
up by these gentlemen with amazing velocity, and as speedily disappeared into their capacious pockets. After allowing his people to
load themselves as fast as they could for about ten minutes, the
General insisted on them all following him out, and kept on repeating that looting was strictly prohibited, and he would not allow it,
although his officers were doing it without any reserve before his
own eyes. . . . The French camp was revelling in silks and bijou-
terie. . . . One French officer had a string of splendid pearls, each
pearl being of the size of a marble (this he afterwards foolishly
disposed of at Hong Kong for 3,000 l.); others had pencil-cases set
with diamonds; others watches and vases set with pearls." [Robert
Swinhoe, *Narrative of the North China Campaign of 1860* (London,
1861), p. 298.] Next day every vestige of control was swept away,
and when Swinhoe rode over to look at the palace again, "officers
and men, English and French" were rushing through the buildings
like furies, smashing, snatching, spoiling, and wasting everywhere.
Inevitably there were quarrels, and finally there was a great selling
bee of silks and furs and porcelain and silver and gold and paintings
and jewels of all sorts.

In the middle of the rush for loot, on October 8, Parkes and Loch
with six other prisoners were handed back. Parkes and Loch had
been very badly treated the first two days, after which their captors
became cautious and began conciliating them. For another forty-

eight hours after their return, the Allies waited anxiously for news of the others. On the twelfth nine more made their appearance: the rest, including Bowlby of *The Times*, were dead, and ultimately all bodies but one were found. The story told by the survivors was a grim one of torture and starvation: their hands had been tied behind their backs very tightly, and the bonds were then soaked so that they would draw even tighter. Elgin had liked Bowlby very much. The tales of the ex-prisoners and the sight of the victims' bodies sent emotional temperatures sky-high. What punishment could be inflicted upon the Chinese—or, rather, upon the Emperor who was responsible for the atrocities? Elgin pondered the matter deeply. More indemnity? There were two arguments against that: first, the economy of the country would be destroyed if any more money than the indemnities already demanded were taken out, and second, in the end it would be the wretched people who would have to pay, through taxes. The Emperor would hardly suffer at all. Execution of the officials who ordered the capture? That would be difficult, since there was no doubt the true culprits would blame some "miserable subordinate" and hand him over. If the Allied generals were to demand the person of Seng-ko-lin-chin, the Chinese would assuredly refuse to give him up, and Elgin frankly did not know what he would do then. Finally he decided to destroy Yuan Ming Yuan—burn the place and raze it to the ground.

"It was the Emperor's favourite residence, and its destruction could not fail to be a blow to his pride as well as to his feelings." [Elgin's *Journals*, p. 366.]

The French refused to agree to such an act of vandalism—Swinhoe was bitter about that, considering how eagerly they had looted the place—so the British alone set about the job. Apportioning the buildings to different companies, they methodically set fire to the interiors of the marble houses; the splendid throne rooms, the carved walls and delicately latticed windows that looked out over landscaped gardens and fountains, the staircases and graceful curved roofs with their jewel-colored tiles. There was much to do: merely setting the fires took two days. As smoke rolled in great columns to the sky, the avengers kept finding more and more ornamental groups of houses and temples to destroy. Until the end, looters were busy unearthing new treasure. In an outhouse they found the two carriages brought by Lord Macartney to the Ch'ien-lung Emperor in 1793, and they were as good as new; the Emperor had never used them.

Chapter Nine

The treaties were at last ratified. Before the ink was dry they had been carried out of Peking, at least the English ones, in the care of Loch, who had orders to take them back to London as fast as the ship would go. Loch was delighted: after his kidnaping, London was going to look very good to him. Lord Elgin too was delighted, for the packet carried proof that everything the Allies had demanded was ceded by Prince Kung. The smoke from the Summer Palace disappeared into the sky and the embers cooled, while Elgin made himself as comfortable as he could in a splendid house belonging to Prince I, but he didn't find his quarters cozy. Like many other foreigners he felt that Chinese houses, however lovely their gardens and grounds might be, were austere and unpleasantly open to the elements. The palace that had just been made over to him to use for the British Legation would have to be altered radically before his brother could move in with a suitable staff. A novelist who knows old China has given an accurate description of the sort of lodging Elgin had:

"You must not expect too much. . . . Chinese gentlemen live in what you would call great discomfort. . . . Wenkwang has no fire by day, except a charcoal brazier, but puts on furs and wadded clothing; he does not sleep on a comfortable bed, but on a quilt laid on a brick kang, which is heated in winter; his chairs are all rectilinear and rectangular; his table has no linen cloth; his floor is tiled and uncarpeted; his walls are undecorated except by scrolls; his windows are without glass, closed to sight by thin paper and against rain by wooden shutters—but then they all open to an inner courtyard, and are sheltered by a portico; his rooms extend to the roof tiles, except that some may have a paper ceiling." [H. B. Morse, *In the Days of the Taipings* (Salem, Massachusetts, 1927), p. 111.]

Waiting for Bruce gave Lord Elgin plenty of time for reflection. Between tours of Peking, when his eyes rested on the prospects of the Forbidden City and other hitherto mysterious purlieus, he came to the conclusion that though his mission was not quite complete even now—for the Emperor in Jehol cast a threatening shadow over all official interviews, yet refused to return—he had not done too badly. He was satisfied that the Emperor would not dare to revoke the treaties now. Prince Kung really did have full power to treat with the Allies, and that gentleman had learned a good deal about barbarians in the past few days: he would from that time on urge his colleagues to treat the visitors from Outside with common sense. Yes, Kung was all right, but there was no point in overdoing the cordial approach, which Elgin understood the French were. He disapproved of the news he had heard, that Baron Gros went to call on Prince Kung without waiting, as was proper, for the Manchu to make the first move.

"The Jesuits think they can curry favour with the Chinese by making him condescend," observed Elgin scornfully. [*Journals,* p. 369.]

The brotherhood of battle had evaporated. Now that the Allies need no longer stand together in the face of threat from Peking, they were scrambling apart, each for his own country, each trying to get ahead of the others. Elgin was sure that he at least knew how to behave with haughty Manchu officials, and he sat tight and waited. Sure enough, Prince Kung arrived promptly to pay his respects. It was one up to Elgin and a small slap in the face for Gros, but if the truth were known, the nation to come out ahead in the race was neither France nor Britain, but Russia. It must be admitted that the Bear had a good start: there had been Russians in Peking the whole time that other foreigners were being kept out, for more than a hundred years. The Manchus didn't consider them quite as foreign as the others, which of course they weren't. Now Ignatieff succeeded in a shrewd maneuver. He knew that Prince Kung, for all his smooth politeness, was hating every minute of the intercourse he was forced to maintain with the barbarians, and fearing the demands they might yet add to those to which he had submitted. Ignatieff told Kung that he would intervene with the British and French and persuade them to moderate these demands and remove their troops—in return for something he said he was sure the Manchus had no use for anyway; the rough, sparsely populated province of Primorsk, which held the port of Vladivostok. In ordinary times the Manchus would not have considered relinquishing any of their territory whether or not they used it, but these were not ordinary times, and Prince Kung was unaware, or did not believe, that the British and French were planning to withdraw their forces, and didn't need Ignatieff's urging to do it. He agreed to give up Primorsk to Russia.

By the time all these matters were settled it was late in the year. The Allies must hurry to get their men and equipment out of the cold north, if they didn't want to be closed in by ice, and they had no intention of setting up their legations then and there, because of all the alterations and appointments that would have to be made. Bruce arrived to take over, but it was a visit of only a few days. The real residence was to begin in the early spring of 1861, but as caretaker Elgin left a vice-consul, Adkins, to spend the winter in Peking. Elgin too had learned wisdom during his contacts with Chinese bureaucracy, and knew that all his arrangements, however enthusiastically his opposite numbers had agreed to them, might well be upset as soon as his back was turned, especially when the Emperor came back. Everybody expected excitement in that event. Ignatieff, preparing to report in person to the Czar that all his business was nicely settled, made a handsome offer to Adkins: "If you fear any trouble, go over to the Russian mission: they will take care of you." But the Emperor continued to linger in Jehol and preserve his untouchability, though he also continued to send regular messages to his Regent with advice as to how to confound and frustrate barbarians.

Altogether, Prince Kung was in an unenviable position. He was forced to put up with indignities that must have outraged him to the core. Elgin mentions lightheartedly of that famous first visit, "We ended by photographing the Prince, a proceeding which I do not think he much liked." The Prince managed to keep his temper through all this sort of thing, though it must have been a traumatic experience. He had also to bend himself to new, perplexing tasks. One of the first of these was to cope with the payment of the huge indemnity mentioned in the treaties and the convention. China owed twenty-four million pounds each to England and France, and the convention provided that this debt was to be worked off on the installment plan in quarterly payments out of the Customs revenue, one-fifth of the gross proceeds for the country, each quarter. Men were to be especially appointed to receive these moneys, and more men were to be appointed to check the amounts and make sure they were correct. All this work was to be done within Customs precincts, which, as Wright points out, made of the always versatile Customs Service a debt-collecting agency, on top of its other duties. The collection and banking of the indemnity funds were in most cases left to the Superintendent, or Taotai, of each port, but it was the Chinese themselves who insisted that the delicate work of assessing, checking receipts, and keeping records and registers had better be under the supervision of foreign Customs employees. When it came to naming the man who was to handle all this, Prince Kung and his associates inevitably asked for H. N. Lay. Until he himself broke the story off short, Lay's cordial relations with the Chinese ran in an unbroken line through the archives. It is strange to think that this man with his long record, the man on whom so much depended, was barely twenty-nine years old when the convention was signed. It did not matter to the Chinese: he was H. N. Lay, and that was enough.

Lay or no Lay, however, it was clear that these Manchu gentlemen not only did not mind but actually preferred that an Englishman should be in charge of monetary operations such as the indemnity collections. As time went on they proved such preference again and again, resisting all helpful suggestions that they put their own people into the higher posts. They wanted things to remain as they had been at the beginning. The Chinese were wistfully certain that only in such a way could they be sure of the figures. When customs duty collection was left to Chinese exclusively, as one of them naively explained, they often didn't get anything in Peking at all. It should be pointed out, however, that Chinese venality has never been the cut-and-dried villainy it seems to Western minds. Westerners naturally thought the Chinese hypocritical. They heard the Orientals uttering pious maxims and saw them constantly flouting such noble principles in everyday practice, and put the discrepancy down to sheer flagrant cynicism. Yet from their own point of view the Chinese were not being hypocrites, any more than a Westerner is hypocritical when he says politely to the person who has just scalded him with a hot cup of tea, "It doesn't matter in the least." There were many occasions in the life of a Chinese when it was actually incumbent on him, according to his rules of propriety, to take bribes in public office or otherwise commit dishonest acts. If he was doing it for his family's good, the harm he did the public was outweighed by the virtue of his motive. This does not square with our code, but it does with his. Thus the officials who dealt with Wade in setting up the new Customs Service were eager to keep on Lay, or if they could not have Lay, some other Westerner would do. Their experience with Westerners had taught them that the odd creatures were more to be trusted than not, and no official would deny that probity in other people, especially people collecting large sums of money for one's own government, is a good thing. The officials said all this, unblushingly. It was their candor as much as the truth of the statement about their own standards that shocked foreigners, but the Chinese are a practical people, whose reticences are to be found elsewhere.

The Regent and his advisers now found it useful to adopt Lay's suggestion of a few months earlier, of a special committee whose duty would be to treat with foreigners. The men who constituted the first Ministry of Foreign Affairs, which was called the Tsungli Yamen, were Prince Kung himself with Kuei-liang, who was now Secretary of State, and Wen-hsiang, Vice-President of the Board of Revenue. The President himself was up in Jehol with the Emperor, but Wen-hsiang was a useful man because of his knowledge of financial affairs—the very first duty of the Tsungli Yamen being ways and means to pay off the indemnity. These three, then, were the Chinese overlords of the centralized Customs administration, though they intended to work through Lay. The Yamen was not long to be made up of only three members. By the end of a year it had grown to six, and was to expand after that to ten or eleven, as its functions too expanded when more and more foreign affairs had to be handled.

Everything seemed to be going smoothly, if painfully, to the Chinese, when their paragon Lay upset the machinery by requesting sick leave before taking up his new duties. He wanted to go back to England on a long holiday. His reasons seem good enough. Lay had been stabbed in the stomach during a battle with the Taipings in Shanghai in 1859 when he was a member of the Volunteer Corps; as he told his children later, he had only just managed to get out of that fight holding his entrails in place. The wound had never healed properly, and in the intervening months his schedule, what with interpreting for visiting plenipotentiaries and traveling all over the place to organize Customs ports, not to mention the time he put in in Shanghai between trips, acting as peacemaker and explainer of

West to East and and vice versa, was enough to break down a healthier man. All this could not be denied, but the pressure on him to postpone his departure was great. Prince Kung was especially eager for him to set up the new Custom House at Tientsin before taking off. His British colleagues implored him to make the effort to visit Peking and be sworn in, and Bruce went so far as to threaten him with replacement if he persisted in refusing to do this. Bruce and the other British felt that the moment must be grasped while it was available, for they had in mind, always, the possibility of the Emperor's return to Peking and a consequent cancellation of much they had accomplished. In spite of all the argument, Lay went home to England. His reasons for taking such a rash step may not be fully evident even today, but a rumor that went the rounds at the time, that he had actually refused the appointment in the belief that the Empire's days were numbered, was probably as false as most other China coast rumors. Lay didn't think the Empire was all that tottery. He had faith in the *status quo*, and felt great enthusiasm for the Service he had done so much to create. Probably he simply did feel very ill indeed. He was to pay dearly for his lapse in strength: by the time he returned he was supplanted by Hart, the man whose career in the Customs he had done his utmost to further. It is only fair to add that Hart himself did his best to dissuade Lay from departure, and did not deliberately steal the post.

Before he left, his old friend Hsüeh Huan decided with him that Lay should select two men to act together in his place until his return, as Officiating Inspectors General. These were Robert Hart and the Commissioner of Customs at Shanghai, G. H. Fitzroy. Then Lay went, and in May 1861, Robert Hart went to Peking for the swearing-in. The rest cure Lay had hoped for in England didn't turn out quite like that, for he found Customs affairs waiting for him at the other end too. British merchants in China had been stirred up and alarmed by the reorganization of the Customs Service. In the old slipshod days they had often been able to take advantage of the fact that the inspectors were Chinese. A little bribery here and there saved much money in duty that wasn't paid. It would be different now, and the British merchants had a number of high-principled arguments against the new order, saying among other things that no true-blue Britisher ought to pledge his allegiance to a Chinese service, despite the clause in the Treaty of Nanking specifically permitting British subjects to serve as Chinese officials. Once more, though in very different circumstances, Lay found himself interpreting East to West.

While the British-French adventure in north China was still under way, the foreign civilians of Shanghai, left with fewer guards than usual, naturally felt stripped and defenseless. The Taipings had made Soochow their new center, and Soochow was much too near for comfort. Bruce came to the conclusion that sooner or later the rebels must understand their position and either stay at a certain distance from the city, or take their chances against action from the Westerners. According to the rules of international law the Allies were neutral in a civil war such as this, but Bruce held that neutrality need no longer be observed if his charges were actively threatened, and to overstep a certain boundary line, not yet decided in his mind, constituted such a threat. Like the other foreigners he should have liked to see the matter completely cleared up for the sake of trade as well as safety, and now that the Imperialists had knuckled down he was of course more than ever set against the rebels. He was thoroughly convinced that the Taipings were nothing but pests, and—since an Englishman in his position must have things on a moral basis—that the Chinese people would be far better off without them. To be sure, there were some Westerners, even Britons, who argued with him that the Taipings weren't as bad as all that, and pointed out that trade from towns held by the rebels was now as good as it had ever been. Bruce did not believe them. He disapproved of the missionaries who had begun to visit Soochow: he felt that it didn't look well, and very nearly forbade such travel on the part of his nationals, at least. Then there occurred a grave incident that went a long way toward proving him in the right: the Taipings attacked Shanghai.

It started in July, just at the time the Allied forces were on their way to Peitang, but the crisis didn't come for another month. The Taiping leaders sent a letter addressed to The Honorable Envoys in Shanghai, in which they made the perplexing statement that they were on their way to the city to draw up a treaty, as they had been invited to do so. Who had invited them? Bruce dismissed the claim contemptuously as a trick, but the Taipings in later discussions certainly seemed firmly convinced that such an invitation had been sent to them by the French. It may be that some French Jesuit had said something that was misconstrued. In any case the rest of the message was clear—the Taipings intended to attack the walled city of Shanghai as they had done before, pursuing their campaign against the Imperialists, and so that they might not injure any brother Christians or non-Chinese they warned the Europeans to mark their churches and other buildings with yellow flags. Bruce angrily sent back the letter unopened. He also sent a warning that the city of Shanghai—the walled city—would be defended by Westerners, but this warning went astray and the Taipings never got it. On August 18, with a rather small body, the Taipings made their first attack. They weren't expecting much resistance, and the hot fire of the British and French surprised them considerably. In the following days they made several more attempts on the walled city, but the guns of the Westerners easily kept them off, and they withdrew to Soochow with heavy casualties. Their leader, the Ch'en-huan, wrote an angry letter to Bruce. If that was the way the Westerners were going to behave, he said, they would find that trading on the river with Taiping cities would not be as easy and pleasant as it had been hitherto. Such a threat worried the merchants who had been doing well on the Yangtze, but all the other foreigners were relieved and thankful that the rebels had been driven away. They welcomed the activities of Ward's Ever Victorious Army.

Frederick Townsend Ward, the "filibuster" as he was called—the word meant "mercenary" in those days—was one of a number of foreigners who for some time had been infiltrating the proceedings in China. The white mercenaries of the East are interesting. There have always been buccaneer types who explored the world as long as there was something to explore, but the secondary adventurers, or filibusters, who followed them to China are a little different. These stayed in the country they had sought out and lived with the natives, and—usually more for gain than for principle—fought for them as well, and generally played an important if transient part in history. China in the nineteenth century, bereft of the barriers that had protected her in the past, was particularly attractive to such characters. Ward was an American, born in Salem. Quite unofficially he offered his military services to the Peking government, and they hired him on the spot, directing him to organize an army of foreigners and Chinese to fight the Taipings. Recent events had proved to them that Western methods of making war were superior to theirs, and they felt no chauvinistic reluctance about acquiring this technique the quickest and easiest way. Ward's band won a few triumphs over the Taipings in the Shanghai vicinity which delighted his Imperial employers: they gave his bobtail outfit the resounding title of Ever Victorious Army, and hoped for more and better things. The Westerners of Shanghai soon conquered their first distrust of a man willing to fight for the Emperor, because it was nice to feel that they were being protected, and within a year Ward's army won their downright approval.

In parallel fashion the Taipings were acquiring Western adherents of their own. The one we know most about was an Englishman named A. F. Lindley, though there were others. Lindley wrote and published his memoirs, probably for propaganda, just before the Taiping Rebellion came to an end, otherwise we should not have heard of him, since his side lost the war and official history has a way of forgetting the details of lost causes. In any case, the Taiping movement never had many articulate friends among English-speaking people. Yet the story is well worth preserving. Lindley, or as he signed the memoirs, Lin-le, had nothing but scorn for the British policy in China as represented by Bruce, which is to be expected, since he spent his time on the opposite side and saw things completely differently. Where Frederick Ward had walked into his occupation in deliberate, straightforward fashion, Lindley fell into his by chance, led to it in the most romantic possible way. He went out to Hong Kong in 1859 and there found a post as second officer in a merchant marine ship. One day a pretty young Macanese girl appealed to him for help, saying that her father was marrying her off against her will. The people of Macao are of mixed blood—Portuguese, Chinese, and sometimes a dash of Filipino—but their ways are those of Portugal, and Marie was no doubt carefully chaperoned. Nevertheless she managed to talk to the handsome young Englishman, who of course fell in love with her on the spot. He helped her to escape from Hong Kong to Shanghai, and then arranged his work so that he could be near her new residence, where she had found refuge with sympathetic relatives. When the girl's scorned suitor discovered her whereabouts and kidnaped her aboard a lorcha, upriver to Chinkiang, the distracted Lindley followed and snatched her once more from the villain. In so doing, however, he and a foreign friend committed violence: he and the other man, as well as Marie, were now fugitives from treaty-port justice. Lindley had learned to know and like some of the Taipings, for his ship had stopped at Nanking more than once and no doubt he had done them a few favors in the gunrunning line. He now took his young woman to Nanking and left her in the custody of the prince, the Ch'en-huan, where she was safe with a family. From then on he threw in his lot with the Taipings, campaigning with them, fighting Imperialists alongside them, but most of all traveling up and down the river for them, since as a foreigner he could go into Shanghai and bring back supplies. Naturally he became more and more pro-Taiping and anti-Imperialist, extending his resentment to the Westerners, including his compatriots, who felt the other way about things. He made many bitter comments on the subject of opium-running—the use of opium was against Taiping law—and those who lived by drug traffic: his enmity included much of foreign activity in China.

"At Chin-kiang is established a corps of the foreign mercenaries of the Imperialist maritime customs, an organization patronized by the British government as a means of securing the indemnity money guaranteed in payment of the British expenses for a war undertaken to avenge the capture of the opium-smuggler *Arrow*, and apparently to facilitate the opium trade in general," he said sourly. [*Ti-Ping Tien-Kwoh* (London, 1866), p. 109.]

Lindley's descriptions of battles are detailed and spirited, but he is frank as to what Chinese fighting was. "The ordinary phase of Chinese warfare—watching, flag-waving, and yelling at a safe distance." [P. 345.] The main idea seems to have been for the cavalry troops to sweep the flag at full gallop so that the point of its staff described a large figure eight. The sight of a line of flag-waving horsemen rushing straight at one was supposed to strike terror to the heart, and in fact seems to have done so. When the Imperialists invested Anking in 1861, Lindley was there. "The Manchoo warriors girded up their loins, that is to say, tucked up the bottoms of their petticoat inexpressibles, fiercely wound their tails around their cleanly shaven caputs,"—as a good Taiping Lindley scorned the pigtail in favor of the Taiping uncut locks, for which they were known as the Long-hairs; they were worn in a kind of bag-headdress—"made a terrible display of huge flags, roaring gongs, horridly painted bamboo shields, and a most extravagant waste of gunpowder, and moving forward with terrific cloud-rending yells, established themselves safely out of cannon-range of the walls, and proceeded to complete the investment of the doomed city by building themselves in with a formidable series of earth-works and stockades, from which they could neither climb out nor enemies climb in.

As a rule, the Chinese never fight unless they are obliged to. Not that they are so cowardly as some Europeans have mistakenly seemed to believe, but rather from those singularly refined traits of reasoning which, with these peculiar people, border closely on the absurd. . . . If a determined resistance is *certain,* those who should attack content themselves by safely fortifying themselves at a distance . . . but should the determination of the defensive party be doubtful, then an attack, with no little impetuosity and daring, will almost surely take place."

The idea naturally occurs to one that against such a foe it is not surprising if Ward's Ever Victorious Army, in the early days at least, should have found it necessary to maintain strict standards of discipline and valor. Its resounding title bore little if any resemblance to reality—a rough, tough gang of mercenaries who had no political convictions and were motivated purely and simply by the hope of loot. Their greed was sharpened by the fact that the Manchus seldom gave Ward any money for his soldiers, and what pay they got was largely filched on its way down to the lower ranks. The mercenaries would fight to capture a town, and after taking it they snatched whatever booty they could find, then abandoned the campaign altogether until they had squandered everything they made out of their prizes. Yet they did well enough for a time against the Taipings, since they had far better equipment than the primitive weapons wielded by most of the God-worshipers. Ward himself was of better caliber—a good fighter, with plenty of courage.

*   *   *

By the terms of the treaty, five new Chinese ports were to be opened to foreign trade, as well as two more on the island of Formosa. In North China the new ports were Tientsin, Newchwang, and Chefoo; further south the cities were Kiungchao and Swatow. As the ice melted in early 1861 the Allies felt eager to get started on their new schedule, not only at the ports but along the Yangtze, inland. The situation was of course complicated by the fact that the Taipings held many of the river cities, but the British felt that this could be managed. Before Lord Elgin left he had talked it over with the Admiral, Sir James Hope, and Hope agreed that he must make an exploratory voyage along the route Elgin himself had once traveled, upriver to the Three Cities, to investigate the temper of

the rebels. After all, those threats after the abortive attack on
Shanghai might mean that they would turn awkward. In February
Hope set out with a large party, which included Harry Parkes.
They did not really expect trouble, and they didn't get it—a missionary, Muirhead, even went overland and met them at Nanking, quite
safe and well. There the Admiral landed three of his party to go
into the city with Muirhead and talk things over, while he continued
up the river with the others. Everywhere it was the same, peaceful
and reasonable. The Taipings promised to permit foreign trade along
the river without opposition, but Hope wanted more than that, and
on his return journey to pick up the other members of the party from
Nanking, he got it. The Taiping princes heard his proposition, that
a line should be drawn thirty miles from Shanghai and Wusung all
the way around, beyond which no Taiping must stray toward the
city. This, too, they promised to accept, and for the moment the
Admiral was satisfied, though Bruce knew he would have a struggle
to satisfy the Manchu government: they didn't like the idea of the
Westerners making any pact at all with the rebels. Hope's job
was to clear the way for traders and he had done it as best he could,
but in his report on the trip, and in that of Parkes, a very gloomy
picture was drawn of the devastation wrought by the Taipings on
the countryside. They had happened to be at Wuchang just as news
came that the rebels had captured a town fifty miles off, and the
Englishmen said they were appalled by the reaction of the populace.
These unfortunate people fled the city in "junks and boats of every
description," as Parkes wrote, "bearing slowly away upstream the
bulk of the population of three cities, which a few days before we
had computed at 1,000,000 of souls."

It is perhaps natural, and then again perhaps not, that the Admiral
and Parkes should have placed the blame for this situation wholly
on the Taipings, without pausing to consider that the populace
would have fled just as swiftly from Imperialist attackers, if things
had been the other way round. They would have feared any army
whatever, including the Ever Victorious Army. Poor devils, they
had had plenty of experience of both sides, but Hope did not see
it that way. He was becoming more and more convinced that the
Taipings were the scourge of China. It was more convenient to
believe it, and Bruce was wholly of his mind. They knew by that
time that neutralism was on its way out.

※   ※   ※

It would be a mistake to assume that the Imperial court, though rusticating, was enjoying a peaceful holiday. There was never any peace among Manchu aristocrats. In Peking the palace had always seethed with intrigue, and in Jehol it continued to seethe. For all her advance in status, or perhaps because of it, Yehonala had powerful enemies among the nobles who accompanied the party, and the head of this faction was Su-shun, President of the Board of Revenue and a man to be feared. Another who did not like Yehonala was Prince I, that same one who had parleyed with Lord Elgin on the road to Peking, and caused the Parkes party to be taken prisoner. These men and others did their best to undermine Yehonala's influence with the Emperor. Her co-wife and senior, Hsiao-ch'en, didn't worry them; she was a good-natured nonentity, but Yehonala was clever and ambitious; besides, there were old enmities among the Manchu clans in which these foes were involved. The ailing Emperor was not difficult to work on. Palace scuttlebutt had it that they told him all sorts of unpleasant things about Yehonala, the most serious being that she was carrying on with a handsome young officer in the Guards. While they were about it they filled his ears with poison on the subject of Prince Kung as well, because Kung was one of Yehonala's faction. Yehonala had never been a fool, and she knew quite well what was going on. Secretly she prepared for a crisis, sending word to Prince Kung that he must send troops up to Jehol at the double—friendly troops of her own clan, for the Banner Corps already in Jehol were all on the side of Su-shun. She knew she must work fast. Already the Emperor had given signs that he was turning against her, and her little boy, the heir apparent, had been removed from her custody to be placed in the house of Prince I.

There is no telling what might have happened if the Emperor had lived a bit longer. Fortunately for Yehonala, he died on August 23, 1861, before the intriguers had managed to solidify their position to perfection. The day before his death he was able to follow dynastic tradition in formally naming by edict the son of Yehonala, Tsai-chun, as his successor. The child was not quite six, however, and a regency would be necessary. For this task the Emperor designated eight men to form a co-regency, under the title Imperial Assistance in National Affairs; among them were Su-shun and Prince I. The conspirators must have thought that all was well for them, until it transpired that Yehonala was not out of the picture after all, for the Emperor had left in the hands of his two chief wives, Hsiao-ch'en and Yehonala, his great seal, which empowered them to give the final word on any edict the co-Regents might issue. The women had a veto.

Though they were infuriated, the co-Regents of course kept up appearances. In one of their first edicts they conferred on both widows the honorific title of Dowager Empress, but this was not enough to satisfy Yehonala's friends in Peking. One of the censors memorialized the Council, demanding that the older Dowager Empress be made sole Regent, in place of the men appointed by the dying Emperor, and the co-Regents were disturbed by this: they countered quickly with an edict pointing out that women were ineligible to rule. The veto-holding Dowagers of course refused to approve this statement, but they were forced to do so in the end because the co-Regents promptly went on strike and did no business at all until they had their way. It was a most exasperating state of affairs for everyone involved. Then the struggle grew hotter. The older Empress's brother-in-law came to Jehol as a messenger for the pro-Empress party, and was not permitted to so much as see the widows. However, he stayed in Jehol and worked away, and at last, through the intervention of that time-honored palace power, the eunuch, he got in touch with the ladies. Quickly they laid their plans, which hinged on the arrangements that were being made to transport the Emperor's body to Peking for a state funeral. The entire court was also moving back. Certain rules of ceremony had to be observed in this process. The great coffin must be carried by hand, and scores of men came along for the purpose. Every fifteen miles a shelter was prepared, and the procession spent the night there, guarding the coffin: as the distance from Jehol to Peking was one hundred and fifty miles, the journey was bound to take ten days. Two factors worked in favor of the Empresses. For one thing, they were bound by etiquette to get to Peking well ahead of their husband's body, in order to prepare sacrifices and ceremonies to welcome it when it arrived. For the other, all the co-Regents must stay with the coffin, from beginning to end of the funeral trip. Once in Peking, the Empresses would have friends and troops to take care of their fortunes.

Su-shun and his party were not happy when they saw the Dowagers set out for Peking, knowing that they themselves must lag on the way. The ladies would be in the city within five days unless something could be done to stop them. Su-shun therefore made an extremely courteous gesture and sent his own bodyguard with the Empresses, with private instructions to assassinate them on the road. The young officer of the Guards who had been named as Yehonala's lover may or may not have been guilty of that crime: at any rate he now proved his loyalty to her by riding ahead of the funeral procession, where the co-Regents were all held like so many prisoners, and catching up with the women's party in order to warn them. In any other country Yehonala would probably have advertised the intrigue at the top of her voice, and executed the false captain of her accompanying guards, but this was China, where etiquette reigned supreme. Without showing any agitation, she sent some of the men back along the trail to inquire of the co-Regents if all was well and her husband's august coffin safe. Yes, was the reply—everything was all right. In reward for their efforts the messengers were given a thousand taels—over three hundred pounds— and this golden hint was sufficient: the Dowager Empresses arrived alive and well in Peking on October 31.

After that it was comparatively simple. The ladies issued an edict attacking the co-regency, which in customary fashion blamed the members for everything that had gone wrong in governmental affairs for the past several years. It was their fault, said the decree, that the foreign chiefs had fought their way to the city and humiliated the people, and it was their fault as well that the Emperor had died, because they had persuaded him to stay on and on in Jehol, which didn't suit him. They had sinned furthermore in issuing the edict that confuted the censor's nomination of the elder Dowager Empress as Regent.

The time was ripe. Supported by Prince Kung and plenty of clan troops, the Empresses arrested the co-Regents as they arrived, and a week later they had Su-shun beheaded; the other conspirators got off with lesser punishments. Immediately after this business was concluded, a new regency of the two Dowagers was set up, with Prince Kung as their chief adviser. To soften the fact that both Regents were female, their regency was called "Listening from behind Screens to Reports on Governmental Affairs." [Arthur W. Hummel, *Eminent Chinese of the Ch'ing Period*, p. 132.] It seems odd to think that at this time Yehonala was considered comparatively unimportant, being the junior of the two: she was included chiefly because she could read and write and the older Empress couldn't.

The confirmation of Prince Kung's importance was hailed by the foreign ambassadors as a good augury for Sino-Western relations. The Empresses were as yet an unknown quantity, but the ministers felt confident that they could depend on Kung. And now, with so much deadwood out of the way, everything pointed to the next step, a hard and fast settlement of the Taiping Rebellion.

Chapter Ten

For one reason and another the Reverend Issachar Roberts had for years put off what might be considered the duty of accepting Hung's invitation to come and preach the Word to the Taipings. In the autumn of 1860, however, when it became rather the fashion among foreign missionaries to go to Soochow, only half as far from Shanghai as Nanking, and take a close look at the creatures, Roberts decided at last to run the risk. He found the Ch'en-huan at Soochow and was very well treated by him; after a few days the prince took his guest to Nanking, and Roberts had an audience with the Emperor Hung himself. It was a privilege granted to few persons by that time, and Roberts had only one interview with his former pupil. He stayed on in Nanking for fifteen months. Though a foreign colleague would drop in from time to time and he was not cut off from the Western world, he was not quite easy in his mind. There was polygamy, there was an erratic system of baptism, and Roberts was pained to observe that the original rules of austerity that had governed the Taipings were now all but forgotten, perhaps because the Emperor remained so withdrawn. The soldiers behaved much like any other Chinese soldiers, squabbling over loot and women. "The eccentric but earnest Issachar J. Roberts," as Latourette calls him, must have broken under the strain: it is difficult to account otherwise for what happened at the end of his sojourn.

"In a paroxysm of rage, he fled from the city," says Lindley [*Ti-Ping Tien-Kwoh*, p. 567], and all but fell aboard a British gunboat that happened to be lying in the river outside the walls. Weeping hysterically, he told his story. The place he had been living in belonged to one of the Huans, or chiefs, and this Huan had quarreled with one of Roberts's servants, a boy of the age when most young Taiping males were supposed to be serving in the army. The quarrel was about this: the chief considered the boy a deserter, which he probably was. Roberts said that the chief did "with malice aforethought murder one of my servants with a large sword in his own hand, in my presence, without a moment's warning or any just cause," and afterwards jumped on the corpse's head. It was indeed a frightful tale, but in the disgusted words of the British Consul of Ningpo, Roberts's opinion was not worth much, for a few months later the boy who had precipitated the scene turned up in Shanghai alive and well. The Westerners who had been churned with pity and terror felt more confusion and embarrassment than relief at this reincarnation. The implication of the missionary's emotional involvement with his servant was better ignored, they thought. It was not the fault of the Taipings, but missionaries in general did not visit Soochow so often as they had before.

On the other hand, relations between the foreigners and Peking grew more and more cordial: the past generation of haughty Manchus would never have recognized their Imperial city. First the British, American, Russian, and French legations were staffed, then came other Western nations claiming their rights and setting up their embassies, until the sight of foreigners became a commonplace to Peking residents and shopkeepers, and the Tsungli Yamen actually opened a School of Languages. In the Imperial Palace, the Dowager Empresses and those of their households who shared Yehonala's violent prejudice against outer barbarians were gently but surely undergoing brainwashing by Prince Kung and his assistants. On both sides a good deal of mystery was dispelled. All this led to an inevitable conclusion. In 1862 when the Ch'en-huan's army again attacked Shanghai, the foreigners finally abandoned their nominal neutrality outright, and proposed helping the Imperialists to push the rebels out of the thirty-mile belt, once and for all. General Ward, who had been improving his army and pursuing his campaign without benefit of foreign approval, now won social recognition among the Shanghai Europeans, which mattered not a bit to him, and practical aid from the British and French, which meant a good deal. He had rid his army of the useless beachcombers who made up his first force, and now had a hard core of Filipinos, or as they were then called, Manila-men, officered by Americans for the most part. He had also recruited a number of Chinese and trained them to fight in the newfangled Western way, with less screaming and flag-waving, and more shooting and stabbing. It was turning into a good army. Ward had taken Chinese nationality so that the American Consul might not deport him, and had gone so far into his new role as to marry the daughter of a Chinese banker, called by the foreigners Taki, who acted as paymaster to his troops. This money was made up from donations by Shanghai Chinese merchants and officials, and was not always regularly obtained, but Ward managed after a fashion, and his soldiers, though they were badly and sporadically paid, did their fighting for the sake of the loot. For more than a year the headquarters of the Ever Victorious Army had been Sungkiang, southwest of Shanghai.

Now Admiral Sir James Hope, who had in the past opposed Ward and even held him prisoner aboard ship until the American escaped, joined his ex-captive with a mixed force of English and French sailors and marines. Between them the armies drove off Taiping attacks made by far greater bodies of men. Ward was already in touch with the redoubtable warrior Tseng Kuo-fan and his associate, Li Hung-chang: now that Yehonala's star was in the ascendant, these two men whom she had long favored were also on the way up, Tseng having been appointed Viceroy of the two Kiang provinces, and Li acting Governor of Kiangsu. Admiral Hope gave signal proof of the new order by running a dangerous errand for Tseng Kuo-fan: he sent British ships up the Yangtze past Nanking to Anking in Anwhei, where they loaded nine thousand Imperialist troops and brought them downstream to Shanghai. Neutrality could not have been more dead. Very soon the French formed a mixed army of their own, with French and Chinese soldiers.

The Chinese thought Ward must be immortal, though he was wounded often enough and bore many scars. He never carried a weapon, but led all attacks with a cane in his hand and pointed out to his men where he wanted them to fight. Fate overtook him at Ningpo, an important port on the south border of Hangchow Bay. For months the Taipings had held the walled city of Ningpo, but following their usual policy they had left the foreign settlement unmolested. The situation changed on May 6, 1862, when the "Imps," as the Imperialist troops were known to irreverent foreigners, attacked them. From within the walled city the Taipings for the first time in Ningpo attacked foreigners in reply, by firing on British and French warships anchored in the harbor. This was more than enough incitement for the foreigners. The ships fired back, and the attack was followed up by their sailors going ashore and wresting the walled city from the Taipings. Then Ningpo was handed over to the Imps, and Ward brought down some of his army to help them mop up the countryside. On September 21, when this mixed force was attacking a city ten miles from Ningpo, Ward was mortally wounded. His death was mourned by an imposing array of Chinese officials. Li Hung-chang memorialized the Throne about it, and in reply the small Emperor was reported to be "filled with admiration and grief," which is interesting if true. No doubt the Regents thoroughly realized that their cause had suffered a great loss, but the problem of picking out a successor to Ward was not the Regents', but that of Tseng and Li. Ward had two officers he had trusted more than the others: Burgevine and Forrester. Forrester was thought to have more character, but he had suffered a protracted spell of imprisonment with the Taipings, from whom he had been ransomed at considerable cost, and he declared frankly that he would rather not take on such a responsibility as Ward's place would entail. This left Burgevine, a French-born American, and for want of anyone else—though he seems to have borne a name for bad temper even then—Burgevine was appointed by Li Hung-chang to step into Ward's shoes.

It was an arrangement that didn't work out. For one thing he caused a great scandal by killing some of his Taiping prisoners in a peculiarly cruel manner, blowing them from the mouths of cannon. For another, he couldn't handle his men as Ward had. They grumbled and jostled for position, and made demands. For a while Burgevine kept them quiet with the improvements he made in the army quarters at Sungkiang; he also raised the rank of a number of officers, and enlarged the whole force. But all these changes cost money, and he couldn't get it—not even the bedrock amount he had to have—to pay his men. Taki the banker kept putting him off, though the pay fell badly into arrears. Li Hung-chang did not much care for Burgevine, and persuaded the British to provide him with a Captain of the Marines, a man named Holland, to act as Burgevine's military secretary. He did this without first consulting Burgevine, who took it ill. Added to all these troubles was the competition that raged under cover between his army and the Imperialist troops, led by a brother of Tseng Kuo-fan. It was this General Tseng, of course, who sent the dispatches to Peking, and General Tseng had a way of leaving Burgevine's name out of his

reports. The crisis came when, toward the end of the year, his employers directed him to take his army, which now numbered six
thousand, to meet Tseng Kuo-fan's troops at Nanking and help
them to invest the city. The Ever Victorious men refused to budge
from Sungkiang until they had been paid what was owing. Burgevine applied to Taki for money; Taki put him off by saying it
would be ready in January. On the appointed day Burgevine and
his bodyguard went again to Shanghai to see the banker. There is
some confusion as to just what happened. Burgevine said that
Taki tried to put him off again, though the money was in the office.
At any rate there was a violent quarrel. The American slapped the
Chinese across the face, directed his bodyguard to grab the money
that was there—some forty thousand taels—and marched out with
his spoils, which he took back to Sungkiang. He was arrested as soon
as Taki laid charges against him, but Li Hung-chang realized that
the prisoner could not be beheaded as he would have been if he
were Chinese: for one thing, fifty loyal officers threatened to resign
if any harm came to him. Burgevine was simply dismissed. A month
later he tried to get himself reinstated; it is rather surprising to
read that his request was backed by the British and American Ministers, but Li Hung-chang would not hear of it.

Burgevine then took some of his friends from the Army and with
them defected to the Taiping side. It should be explained that any
account of the Taiping Rebellion is bound to be confused by the
desertions and counterdesertions that constantly took place. It is
a pattern characteristic of Chinese military procedure, so it might
be said that to this extent at least, Burgevine had adapted himself
to the customs of the country. The renegades were disappointed
with their reception by the enemy; instead of being given high
posts in the Taiping army they were all but submerged, and regretted what they had done. A few months later Burgevine had to
surrender in battle to Gordon. Li Hung-chang would have had his
revenge then, but the foreign element still felt some compunction
about letting down one of theirs, and the American Consul saved
Burgevine by arresting him and deporting him to Japan. Burgevine promised to stay away from China, but he could not bring
himself to keep his word. In June 1864 he came back to Ningpo and
rejoined the Taipings. Once more he was captured, in '65; this time
the foreigners left him in Chinese custody on the understanding
that he was to be shipped up to Soochow, which by that time had

been regained by the Imperialists and their allies, but on the way he disappeared. When the American Consul demanded that he be produced the Chinese presented their regrets and said there had been an accident and Burgevine was drowned. To prove it, they turned his body over to the Consul. He had certainly been drowned, no doubt about that, but just how accidental the death had been will never be known.

*   *   *

Almost anyone might have foreseen that Burgevine would come to an unhappy end. What could not have been guessed by anybody in China, native or foreign, was how the whirligig of time was to bring round the strange fate of that darling of the Chinese bureaucracy, H. N. Lay. His career was to suffer an eclipse which was more sudden than that of Burgevine's, if not as violent. The two men had little in common otherwise, unless one counts their swift, hot tempers and the fact that both of them brought it on themselves—though one of Lay's descendants, naturally enough, claims that none of these bad things would have happened if the I.G. had only stayed in China that spring of '62, instead of going back to England. *"Les absents ont toujours tort!"* he says bitterly. [A. C. Hyde Lay, *Four Generations in China, Japan and Korea* (Edinburgh and London, 1952), p. 8.] But according to Wright, admittedly a cousin of the Hart family who has studied the affair from first to last, Lay's performance was really extraordinarily high-handed.

For some time there had been in the air the idea that China could well use some ships of her own instead of depending, as she did, on the fleets of foreigners. Whenever there was need of water transport, especially on the Yangtze, the Chinese chartered these foreign-owned ships: they had never fully developed the hopes of post-Opium War days and built similar craft for themselves. Though the pressing need in 1862 was for ships with which to pursue Taipings, for three years the Customs people had been thinking of acquiring revenue cutters of their own. It was obvious that Chinese ships might be used for both purposes, as well as for chasing the pirates that infected the coast. Naturally there were few if any trained seamen in the Chinese forces, but the success of the Ever Victorious Army and its French counterpart suggested that a similar arrangement on naval lines might be a very good thing; a sort of Ever Victorious Navy, headed and staffed in the beginning by foreigners, who could train Chinese as they went along. As officiating I.G., Robert Hart talked this over on many occasions with Prince Kung. The Tsungli Yamen grew keener and keener on the proposition. Hart pointed out that Lay was conveniently in England at the time, and was the logical agent to purchase such a fleet and see that it was adequately manned. The Yamen decided that this would be the way to go about it. Once again, therefore, the Service was to be used in an extra-customs capacity: Lay found himself functioning as a naval recruitment agency. Hart wrote to him in March '62, with definite directions: Lay was to purchase and equip a steam fleet, staff it, and get it out to China without delay. Letters came thick and fast after the first one, urging him on behalf of Prince Kung to waste no time. Among the commentators on the affair who defend or criticize Lay for what happened after that—and they are many, for it became a famous quarrel, though not between Lay and Hart themselves—H. B. Morse has made a statement with which one might reasonably differ. He says it should have been a simple task to supply the fleet, but Lay complicated it. With all due respect to a famous expert, the task really could not be described as simple. Lay had not only to find his commander in chief, work out the list of vessels needed, find them and outfit them: he had to clear it all with his Foreign Office, which naturally looked askance at British nationals who did naval or military service for foreign governments. The commandership was not a post that could be filled by some renegade willing to risk official displeasure: it was a dignified job. In the event, Lay had little or no trouble on that score, because he was in excellent standing with the Foreign Office and the other Ministries in London because of his record in China. During his stay at home he was even made a Companion of the Order of the Bath, an honor seldom given to one as absurdly young as Lay then was: people were later to claim it went to his head.

It was never explicitly stated that the project should be exclusively British in personnel. Lay seems to have made some effort at the beginning to bring in a few French officers, but this never came to anything: in the end, the personnel *was* all-British. For commander in chief he selected Captain Sherard Osborn, R.N., later Admiral. The two had met when Osborn captained Lord Elgin's ship, the *Furious*, in China and took the vessel up the Yangtze to

Hankow. The Foreign Secretary approved Osborn's taking the post
and granted the Queen's licence to the captain and Lay, to serve
the Emperor of China. He could hardly have hesitated, especially
as three of the fleet's gunboats were bought from the Royal Navy
and the other three built to order in British shipyards. A storeship
and a tender were obtained from private owners, and these completed the flotilla; eight ships in all. There were a few points the
Foreign Secretary, Lord John Russell, wished to be clear on: what
flag would the ships be flying? This was a question not to be answered offhand, for China had as yet no particular standard emblem.
Lay wrote to Peking for directions and in the meantime designed
a flag on his own. When he received word from Peking as to what
the Yamen wanted, he combined the two ideas in one pattern. This
flag survived the fleet and continues even today as the Customs
Service's special ensign. It is green with a diagonal orange cross and
with various differences for the Customs Marine Department, for
the I.G.'s personal flag, and so on. Another slight irregularity slowed
up proceedings for a bit. Lay had no definite authority for everything
he was doing—no cut-and-dried document signed by Prince Kung.
It wasn't the way of the Chinese Government to give such documents; they had always considered their word-of-mouth commands
to be sufficient. So they were, inside China, but the British Government wanted something in black and white, so Lay obtained a
document from the Prince that satisfied Russell, especially since
it was accompanied by a large remittance for the considerable expenses involved. Lay, however, overlooked the fact that the Chinese
in their communications never gave him the wide authority he took
for granted, to make such agreements as he did with Captain Sherard Osborn before the flotilla set out for China. It was these agreements that caused all the trouble that followed, and Lay must have
been obtuse indeed not to foresee the Chinese reaction. Osborn
cannot be blamed, since he didn't know the country as Lay did,
and was assured by his friend that it was all perfectly regular. Lay
himself was floating around in euphoria, giving interviews to the
press in London, ordering this and canceling that, and dealing in
dazzling sums of money.

The contract that was soon to alarm and offend the Chinese
provided that Osborn in his post was to be answerable only to
Lay, and that Lay in turn was to be sole intermediary between
the Emperor and Osborn. No mention was made of Tseng Kuo-

fan or Li Hung-chang, those two powerful men in whose hands lay all the management of the contra-Taiping hostilities. Osborn was to command the new navy for four years, stipulating that there should be no other European naval commander in chief, and was to have entire control over all vessels of European construction, as well as over native vessels manned with Europeans who were in the Emperor's employ. Lay would "procure from the Emperor" the necessary authority to cover Osborn's acts as commander in chief. Osborn undertook to act upon all orders of the Emperor *which might be conveyed direct to Lay,* and would not attend to *any orders conveyed through any other channel.* Worst of all, Lay engaged to refuse to be the medium of any orders of the reasonableness of which he was not satisfied.

What was most astonishing about this set of rules was that a man of Lay's experience should have thought he would get away with it. Not only was he flouting Tseng and Li; he was offending the entire Tsungli Yamen and the Imperial crowd—in fact, every man in China who had the education to understand what was going on. It was probably the other side of his nature, the bullying side that had so shocked the Chinese Commissioners and even Lord Elgin during the talks at Tientsin when Ch'i-ying was so confounded, that was now uppermost in the I.G. There is no trace in his behavior at this time of the patient, intelligent man who did so much to organize the customs, and gave his Chinese friends the germ of an idea that evolved into the Tsungli Yamen. It is the haughty, overbearing Lay who wrote in his retrospective account of the affair:

"My attitude toward the Chinese was this: if I help you to collect revenue, you must do whatever is right by foreign questions: if you do not I shall cease to help you. I used my influence to coerce them. . . . I pursued this course, not only because it was inherently a right one; but, to take lower ground, because I was convinced that if in my administration I was not true to certain principles, I could not hope for the success at which I aimed. I was ambitious of obtaining the position of middleman between China and foreign Powers, because I thought I saw a way of solving the problem of placing pacific relations with China upon a new footing. . . . The Chinese Government was too rotten a reed to lean upon, and the foundations of the structure I was endeavouring to build up had to be artificially created. My position was that of a foreigner engaged by the Chinese Government to perform certain work *for* them but not *under* them. I need scarcely observe in passing that the notion of a gentleman acting *under* an Asiatic barbarian is preposterous." Anything more preposterous than that final sentence could hardly be imagined, from a man who would never have had his first job in the Customs if it had not been for the Asiatic barbarians, as he now called them, who rallied to his cause.

Lay got to Peking in May 1863, well ahead of Osborn, who was sailing with the fleet to Shanghai. There he found that the Tsungli Yamen would not for a moment consider sponsoring Sherard Osborn in such circumstances, and he plunged into argument to save the situation, his strongest point being that Captain Osborn had no official sanction from Britain to serve under any less lofty personage than the Emperor himself. By the terms of the Queen's Licence, as Lay truthfully pointed out, the Captain couldn't possibly take commands from provincial officials. When he got nowhere with this, he turned to Bruce—the foreign envoys were involved in the struggle, all through—and cited Major Charles Gordon, who by this time was directing the Ever Victorious Army, as a case in point and a horrid example of what should not be going on. He declared that Gordon, who had received permission from the Foreign Office to act as general of the Army, was contravening British law in that he was subordinate to Tseng Kuo-fan and Li Hung-chang. Lay's reputation as an expert in such matters rather cowed Bruce, and he nearly did what the I.G. strongly urged—withdraw Gordon from action until that state of affairs should be rectified. Lay was confident that such a withdrawal would force the Chinese to give in to his own demands, since it would certainly hamstring the anti-Taiping campaign: the war was going too well for Peking to please Lay, for he saw that the Chinese were growing confident enough to defy him. However, Bruce wouldn't go the whole way with Lay. He realized that he couldn't apply such pressure without protest from the other envoys. Gordon's status, therefore, was not dragged into the quarrel.

The gods seemed determined to destroy Lay. Not content with one battle, he now attempted to take on another, and aimed to grab complete power in the Customs. He declared that all Customs revenue thenceforth should come direct to him. His should be the decision as to how it was expended. Until then he had been sharing responsibility with two Chinese who were powerful officials, but

their power didn't deter Lay from stating that they were superfluous
and must be removed from their posts, leaving him supreme. Worse,
when he was asked for an accounting of the money he had spent,
he retorted that he was busy and would make his financial report
in his own good time. As if this were not enough, he put the seal
on by demanding an Imperial palace for his residence in Peking.
Nobody but a member of the Imperial family had ever possessed
such a house. The Chinese in government were completely furious
with Lay, and bided their time.

When Sherard Osborn arrived in Shanghai with his eight ships
in September, he was shocked to hear that the terms of the agreement had been turned down. He was expected to serve merely as
Assistant Commander in Chief under Tseng Kuo-fan and Li Hung-
chang. Prodded by Lay, he struck an attitude immediately: this
would never, never do. To add to his displeasure, the agents of Li
Hung-chang lost no time in tempting his ratings to desert and come
over to the Governor's service: Li was shrewd enough to see that
the fleet would probably come to pieces, and he could always use
trained men. Some of them succumbed to the prospect of opportunities to loot freely before Osborn got his flotilla out of those dangerous
waters and sailed it up to Chefoo. There he left the ships and proceeded to Peking, where he joined Lay against the Tsungli Yamen.
For three weeks the arguments went on. Osborn stood by Lay in
every particular, declaring ringingly that he was either commander
in chief serving the Emperor through Lay, or nothing at all, in
which case he must disband his force and send all the men home.
The Tsungli Yamen chose the latter alternative, and that was that.
Captain Osborn was out. There remained the question of the ships.
Osborn appealed to the foreign envoys and said that it would be
disastrous to turn over such unmanned vessels to the Chinese, as in
all probability they would ultimately find their way into the posses-
sion of pirates and even Taipings. Of course they did belong to the
Emperor, but that didn't mean that money-hungry princes wouldn't
find ways of getting around that fact. The American Ambassador
Burlingame, as well as Bruce and the French envoy, agreed with
Osborn. The American War between the States was going on, and
Burlingame saw complications if some of the ships fell into Con-
federate hands and were used to harry American shipping from
New England around the Chinese coasts. All the foreign diplomatic
gentlemen thought that the fleet must be sent away from the East,

and so it was decided. The ships were sent to England and India; the men who hadn't deserted were repatriated. Egypt bought three of the vessels, the Indian Government took two, one was sold to defray running expenses, and two later found their way to Japan. Wright says that though much of what the Chinese had spent was lost in the process of resale, the difference was finally made good by the British [Wright, p. 250], but the Chinese have always claimed that they lost heavily.

If the outcome of all this gave Captain Osborn any cause to doubt his wisdom, he didn't show signs of misgivings, though he appealed to his fellow foreigners for reassurance, asking them if he had not done right. The chorus of affirmative answers must have made him feel like a hero. Everyone in the legations assured him that a true British gentleman could have done no other. Even the Chinese Government took no revenge on the gallant Captain, but gave him ten thousand taels over and above the salary he had coming to him. When at last he was gone, however, and the foreign flags had done waving, it was Lay's head that rolled. He was no longer to be connected in any capacity with the Customs: he was out. Even with him, however, the Tsungli Yamen behaved gently. When Lay was retired in November he received a golden handshake for his five months in Peking—£14,000.

The natural man to take Lay's place was Robert Hart. Already he was well acquainted with the duties of Inspector General—his colleague Fitzroy, who had nominally shared his task, didn't know Chinese and had long since slipped into second place. Hart was appointed, but the once-bitten Tsungli Yamen was shy about giving him as much rope as had hanged Lay, and its decision not to let him reside permanently in Peking was approved in general by the envoys. Nobody wanted another Englishman getting mixed up in political affairs that should not concern him; megalomania might strike again. It was decided that Hart should live in Shanghai and visit Peking when his duties demanded it. In practice, though, he was so tactful, so unlike the Lay of the recent past, that the Tsungli Yamen changed its mind, and in 1865, by official request, Hart moved to Peking as a permanent resident of the Imperial city, where he in fact resided until 1908, forty-three years in a house with a garden of princely proportions that far exceeded most legations and would have met with the entire approval of Lay.

*   *   *

Captain Charles George ("Chinese") Gordon, whose position vis-à-vis the Viceroys annoyed Lay so much, was an officer in the Royal Engineers who had already seen service in the Crimean War. In 1860, bored and restless in his job as Field Works instructor at Chatham, this man, destined to be so celebrated, heard of the Elgin expedition to north China and volunteered for duty with it. He arrived in time for the last stages, and was in on the sack and destruction of Yuan Ming Yuan. Gordon expressed all the proper sentiments of horror and regret over that affair, and also shared in the loot, later presenting his most splendid souvenir to his corps headquarters at Chatham—the Emperor's throne. As one of the men left to take care of the British troops he stayed in Tientsin for eighteen months, building barracks, until General Staveley drew him into the anti-Taiping campaign. By training and talent he was particularly fitted for reconnoitering and mapping the territory within the thirty-mile limits around Shanghai, which had been delineated by the foreigners as the area from which the rebels must be kept. He was so good at his work that Staveley mentioned him in dispatches: "Captain Gordon was of the greatest use to me. . . ." Gordon could invent ways to get the men across fortress moats and up city walls. The flat countryside was full of marshes, rivers, and canals, but with his scientific approach these barriers lost their effectiveness. He was also exceedingly courageous, and took great chances to gather information about the terrain. He became so well-known in service circles that when the Chinese government appealed to their new allies for somebody to lead the Ever Victorious Army, he was the natural choice. Since Burgevine had been removed, his successor, the Marine Captain Holland, first acting as secretary to Burgevine, had been unable to hold the unruly troops in order. The American officers professed to resent his British nationality, and in several engagements since his accession the Army had come out the worse for wear. Until the British produced Gordon it looked very much as if the Army would have to be disbanded altogether. Major Gordon, as he now ranked, assumed command at the end of March 1863. A devout, buttoned-up man, from the beginning he was convinced that God was on his side and that the Taipings were wholly responsible for the poverty and misery he saw around him in the countryside.

"Words could not depict the horrors these people suffer from the rebels, or describe the utter desert they have made of this rich province," he wrote in a letter. "It is all very well to talk of non-intervention, and I am not particularly sensitive, nor are our soldiers generally so, but certainly we are all impressed with the utter misery and wretchedness of these poor people." [French, *Gordon Pasha of the Sudan* (Glasgow, 1958), p. 46.]

In his first interview with Li Hung-chang he confidently declared —as indeed he had declared before his appointment—that the rebellion would be crushed within eighteen months. It was a reasonable assumption, given the probability that his Army would do its part, for Tseng Kuo-fan's troops on the other side of the Taiping-held district were closing in on Nanking. They had Anking in Anwhei. The Taipings were already surrounded. However, Gordon had to whip the Army into shape before getting to work.

"You never did see such a rabble as it was," he wrote, after he had achieved some success in this task. He was forced to tame the three thousand unruly men, but soon they were moving ahead against the enemy with such effect that Li Hung-chang was in raptures, and referred to Gordon as "a glorious fellow." In those early days Gordon was not troubled, as Ward and Burgevine had been, with shortage of funds. He raised the pay of the soldiers and made— and enforced, with the death penalty—a rule against looting. He put his troops into uniform, a refinement hitherto missing. He obtained more and better heavy artillery, and organized water transport. He was the new broom, the scientist who supplanted the swashbuckler, and the Taipings hadn't a chance against his superior technique. Methodically, at place after place, he cut them from the coast, and aimed for Soochow after that, when his attention was distracted by a distress call from some Imperialists who had been ambushed when entering Taitsang, a city about halfway to Soochow, to the north. They had lost fifteen hundred men, and report said that ten thousand Taipings were in control of Taitsang. Gordon led three thousand men on foot and sent artillery reinforcements by boat. At Taitsang he bombarded one point of the wall until it was breached, and attempted to force an entry. The attack was repelled, but during a second battle there Gordon moved on and began bombarding another place in the wall. The defenders were taken by surprise, and when they divided their strength they were overcome by Gordon's Army. This had suffered an unusually large loss, as they counted casualties—two hundred and fifty. The places were soon filled, however, by a process peculiar to the era: Taiping deserters hurried to volunteer. At first Gordon was surprised by the ease with which Chinese seemed to change their allegiance, but he soon came to accept it, especially when the ex-Taipings proved to be very good soldiers. A few weeks later he noticed that more than half his personal bodyguard consisted of these men.

Like Ward, Gordon never carried a weapon, but went into battle carrying a cane with which he directed operations. His successes continued. Most of the time his strategy, like that of the Taitsang battle, depended on surprise. The biggest town that lay in his way toward Soochow was Kunshan. Gordon sent the larger part of the Army to attack the walls in the usual straightforward manner, then when the defenders were fully occupied he traveled by water, in his launch the *Hyson,* through canals and creeks around to the back of the city. He had only forty men with him and some big guns. The force made as much noise as possible, and the Taipings inside were so astonished and frightened that a stampede resulted and Gordon took the town. After a run of such defeats, Taipings became superstitious about Gordon, and many a battle was half lost before it began.

All did not run smoothly in the Ever Victorious Army. General Tseng, who had watched Burgevine with such a jealous eye, was even more jealous of Gordon, and did his best to disparage his rival. Soon the honeymoon between Gordon and Li Hung-Chang came to an end, over the old trouble, a break in the money supply. Gordon protested: Li found him short-tempered and peremptory, altogether less glorious than he had seemed at the beginning. Gordon's opinion of Li suffered more than that. It came to the point where the Englishman resigned his command, and the nation was treated to an extraordinary spectacle; one small officer (Gordon was not a tall man) behaving like a prima donna while the dignified envoys of the world's great Western powers begged and implored him to relent. In the end Gordon had his way and got money for the men. Before this blow-up, however, he had another battle with those same followers. It is one of the famous anecdotes concerning "Chinese" Gordon. After Kunshan he decided to abandon the old headquarters at Sungkiang and move the whole army up to this new city. The decision didn't meet with the favor of the Army, who preferred to stay close to Shanghai and its fleshpots. The non-commissioned officers were especially vocal in protest; they incited the rest of the men to mutiny, and sent an anonymous letter to Gordon, impertinent in tone, declaring that they would not move. Gordon made the non-coms line up before him, and asked who had written the letter. There was no reply. Gordon declared that if he was not immediately informed, he would shoot every fifth man in the line-up. During the protests elicited by this threat he spotted the man who talked loudest, pulled him out of line as the guilty one, and had him shot then and there, in full view of his mates. He then told the shocked, silent assembly that if they didn't come to heel within the hour he would do just as he had threatened. They came to heel.

The road was now clear to Soochow, but Soochow was going to be a tough proposition. Preparing for a long siege in the old-fashioned Tseng Kuo-fan manner, Gordon disposed his forces around the walls and settled in, though he hastened the operation in his modern way by cutting off every source of supply that the stronghold had. The siege began in September, and by the end of October the chiefs within the walls were breaking down. Gordon had private talks with at least one of them, the Na-huan, who was willing to engineer a surrender, and the surrender seemed so much a foregone conclusion that Li Hung-chang himself came to Soochow and set up camp so as to be there when it happened. So did a great personage on the Taiping side, the Ch'en-huan. In the preceding autumn this stout general had been suddenly recalled by Hung; at a late date the Taiping Emperor had shaken off his hermit's habits and seen the menace that Tseng Kuo-fan was posing to his city. He commanded the Ch'en-huan to drive north with his army and threaten Peking, so that the Imperialists would follow him and leave Nanking alone, as they had done when the prince led them on a wild-goose chase toward Hangchow. The Ch'en-huan obeyed, but Tseng Kuo-fan was not to be tricked a second time, and like General Lin before him the Ch'en-huan found that North China in the winter was too much for his men: they froze and starved. Unlike General Lin, the Ch'en-huan actually defeated Seng-ko-lin-chin in battle, but that was a flash in the pan, and he was suddenly recalled in the spring to the defense of Nanking. Returning to his master was difficult and costly. The Imperialists were close around the walls, on land and afloat in boats they had borrowed from the British, and when the Ch'en-huan's army ran the gauntlet into the city, many lost their lives in the fierce firing that impeded them. The Ch'en-huan found his Emperor stubbornly melancholic. He would not admit that he, the chosen King on earth, could possibly be in danger, and he only grew angry when the Ch'en-huan tried to persuade him to break out of Nanking and make a run for it to the western hills. There was a quarrel between these two old friends, but it was made up, and the Ch'en-huan, with as many men as he could muster, went on to Soochow to relieve the garrison there. With him went Lindley, sworn to vengeance for his wife, who had been killed during the fighting that greeted the prince's return from the north.

Lindley's adventures after that had no effect on the war's outcome, but they were exciting. His aim was to procure a ship for the Taipings with which to oppose the now notorious *Hyson* used by Gordon. With another foreigner the Englishman made his way from Soochow to Shanghai on this quest. He couldn't buy a ship from anyone, for it was against the law to sell weapons or craft of any sort to the rebels, but he stole a steamer by audacious action, locking four foreigners he had found aboard it into the cabin and taking them the whole way back to Soochow. He got there too late for the city's sake, but he handed the ship over to the Ch'en-huan, after exacting a promise that the prisoners in the cabin would come to no harm. Promise or no promise, they were murdered—Lindley always swore afterwards that it couldn't have been the Ch'en-huan who thus broke faith—and he himself was doubly a wanted man, for he had committed piracy. He managed to get out of China without being arrested, and made for England, where he arrived safely.

The Ch'en-huan found the Taipings in Soochow very shaky, and no wonder. He wrote to Hung, shortly before the end: "From this beleaguered city I indite these lines. Our provisions are exhausted; in the camp, the cooking pots are empty. The stove is cold and there is no drug that can allay the pangs of hunger. Corpses are carved in pieces and mothers sell their sons for food. For many days past we have been shouting 'Dinner is ready' at meal times, so as to deceive the enemy concerning our lack of provisions. Our plight is grievous, resembling that of the turtle in the tureen; our danger is as that of the tiger at bay upon the mountain precipice. Your Majesty has founded a new Empire, but if its roots be shaken, the branches are agitated. Soochow is your Majesty's lower jaw; if the lips perish, the teeth must speedily decay. As soon as you have been able to force a way through the beleaguering armies which invest Nanking, it behoves you to despatch troops to our assistance. I send these few lines beseeching you to take care of your health. Interrupting the whetting of my spear, I write this message, earnestly praying for your welfare." [Bland and Backhouse, p. 424.]

The Ch'en-huan did not set up residence inside the walls of Soochow, but camped nearby in open country, carrying on discussions with the men inside every day. They dissembled to him and didn't admit that they were planning to surrender, but they all were in the plot save for one man, the Mo-huan, and him they planned to kill. The Mo-huan suspected them, but was powerless to save himself. One night at a banquet the others stabbed him in the back; when he heard the news the Ch'en-huan fled back to Nanking. Next morning the eight other chiefs, who had been solemnly promised by Gordon that their lives would be spared if they surrendered quietly, marched out of Soochow and gave themselves up. They had reckoned without Gordon's allies, the Imperialists. They walked straight into the custody of General Tseng, the brother of Tseng Kuo-fan, who turned around and handed them over to Li Hung-chang. Within a few minutes they were all beheaded.

For some hours Gordon was unaware of what was happening. He had been caught up in the hideous scenes of the sack of Soochow, which outdid in ferocity anything he had yet experienced. Because he had promised the Na-huan protection, he tried to find this prince's palace, and on his way he was captured by a group of vengeful Taipings who held him all night as hostage, they said, for their safety, surrounded by terrified, praying women. He got out at last, in the morning, and when he reached his camp he was greeted with the news of what had happened to the princes he had promised to spare. Gordon nearly went mad with rage, shock, and humiliation. His honor had been impugned. He had been especially emphatic to the Na-huan's young son about his father's safety, so he took this prince's severed head in order to give it honorable burial, a thing very important to the Chinese, and followed his men back to Kunshan. There he brooded bitterly. His friend Dr. Halliday Macartney was seriously alarmed about his mental state when he found Gordon one morning sitting on his bed, crying. At sight of the doctor, Gordon pulled a grisly object out from under the bed, saying:

"Do you see that? It is the head of the Na-huan foully murdered!"

He lost no time, of course, in resigning. He wrote violently to Li Hung-chang, demanding that he too resign, but this did not relieve his feelings sufficiently: he actually took troops and set out again on the road to Soochow with intent to attack the Imperialists. Common sense intervened, however, and he abandoned that idea. In an attempt to calm him down, Li Hung-chang wrote to Macartney:

"Tell Gordon that he is in no way, direct or indirect, responsible in this matter, and that, if he considers his honour involved, I will sign any proclamation he likes to draft, and publish it far and wide that he had no part in or knowledge of it. I accept myself the full and sole responsibility for what has been done. But also tell Gordon that this is China, not Europe. I wished to save the lives of the Wangs [Huans], and at first thought that I could do so, but they came with their heads unshaved, they used defiant language, and proposed a deviation from the convention, and I saw that it would not be safe to show mercy to these rebels. Therefore what was done was inevitable. But Gordon had no part in it, and whatever he demands to clear himself shall be done." [French, p. 70.]

The Emperor's representatives sent a number of gifts to Gordon, along with ten thousand taels, but he sent everything back, and wrote on the blank side of the Imperial edict his refusal and regrets. It was February in '64 before he could be persuaded once more to resume his generalship.

*   *   *

Nanking was in worse straits even than Soochow had been, when the Ch'en-huan got back. Everyone was starving, and no more ammunition was coming through the gates: the Imperialists had stopped up all holes. The high officials had enacted fierce laws to deal with would-be turncoats and spies, so that the lesson of Soochow might not be repeated, but Hung Hsiu-ch'uan would not face facts. When the Ch'en-huan entered the audience hall, Hung sat on his throne and talked in a strange way, saying that he was bound to be protected; "I have at my command an angelic host of a million strong: how then could a hundred thousand or so of these unholy Imperialists enter the city?" The Ch'en-huan burst into tears and left the hall. When it came to the question of food, the Heavenly King was even more of a problem, for he handed out to his followers balls of kneaded roots, leaves, and grass, saying that it was manna, that everyone in the palace had been living on it for days, and that the populace should follow their example. Outside, among the waiting Imperialists, there were no members of the Ever Victorious Army, for it had been decided by the Westerners that this final conquest belonged by rights to the Imperialists and nobody else. Gordon did pay a visit to inspect General Tseng's arrangements to mine the walls, but it was purely in an unofficial capacity.

The long weeks wore on. The Ch'en-huan, who had given up arguing with his demented sovereign, took matters in his own hands one day and opened the gates in order to let out four thousand women. Because the Imperialists were not in active combat they were not cruel; they treated the women reasonably well and put them into a stockade where they were protected.

About a month before the end, the Taiping Emperor reached a new conclusion. Something had gone wrong. He ordered brought to him a cup of wine poisoned with gold leaf. Before drinking it he said aloud, "It is not God the Father who has deceived me, but it is I who have disobeyed God the Father." Then he downed the draught and died. [Bland and Backhouse, *China Under the Empress Dowager* (London, 1910), p. 72.] Because he seldom showed himself, the household was able to conceal his death for another eighteen days.

In June the Imperialists began exploding their mines. The first few were not strong enough to break down Nanking's massive walls, but finally enough powder was expended to do the trick. The invaders did not know that Hung was dead and buried. In the hope of capturing him they made for the Imperial palace, furiously opposed by Taipings who fought as bravely as if they were not nearly starved; by the time the invaders reached the palace it was blazing, for the Ch'en-huan had set it on fire. All the Emperor's wives had hanged themselves, and Hung's eldest son was dead. The Ch'en-huan made his escape from the city with Hung's second son and a page. The young prince was torn from his protector in the crowd; later he was caught by the Imperialists and executed. The Ch'en-huan and his page took cover in the country, where they were found and recognized by a party of woodcutters. The story told by the Chinese is that though the Ch'en-huan was much loved by the people, one of the woodcutters was tempted to treachery because the prince had with him so much treasure. The woodcutter gave him away to the Imperialists who were searching for him, but was later killed by his irate companions.

In the excitement that followed the capture of Nanking, it took some time to discover the buried body of Hung, but it was at last exhumed and his head cut off and sent to Peking, as were those of his brothers. General Tseng was told to send the Ch'en-huan alive to the capital, but he did not dare keep his illustrious prisoner too long, so deep was the veneration of all the other Taipings and even those who were not Taipings. He had the prince beheaded.

Though Gordon's exploits were not mentioned in the Imperial edict that was issued to tell the public all about the great triumph over the Taipings, the Chinese officials knew how much they owed him. They bestowed on him the Order of the Yellow Jacket, which had never before been given to a foreigner, and gave him splendid mandarin robes, and struck a gold medal in his honor. They also tried again to give him a large sum of money, but this he refused as he had done before. The British were less hysterically appreciative of his work—their hysteria came later, when Gordon was besieged and fell at Khartoum—but at least he was promoted to brevet rank of major-general.

Hung Hsiu-ch'uan's head, with that of the Ch'en-huan, hung over a Peking gateway until it rotted, and so ended the lesson.

Chapter Eleven

China's new frontier was in Peking. Here East met West every day, and put up such resistance, diplomatically speaking, as was possible. There were distractions of a more familiar nature, domestic problems which did not concern the Westerners: some of these, though threatening, were familiar to the government, and others were far away enough not to worry even the Chinese. One remote trouble was that of Cambodia; in 1863 France had set up a protectorate there, without important repercussions. Closer to home, and therefore more worrying, were the Nien-fei rebels. For a time they had combined with the Taipings, and after the latter were crushed the Nien-fei still troubled a large area, in Anwhei, Honan, Hupei, even Chihli and Shantung. They were fierce fighters, for the most part cavalry, and the Imperialists found them hard to grapple with. Even the favored Li Hung-chang and his colleague, Tso Tsung-t'ang, a very able general who had played a large part in suppressing the Taipings, were unable for a time to cope with the Nien-fei, and were temporarily reduced in rank, this being a commonplace punishment for high officials when things went wrong. Tso at last subjugated the Nien-fei, after which he went straight back into battle against the Mohammedans of the Northwest. They were a chronic threat. Early in the century, at the borders of Chinese Turkestan, a scion of the chieftain family of Hodjas, named Jehangir, had led an uprising against Peking which spread quickly through the Mohammedan communities of China. After a hard fight it was put down, and Jehangir was executed in Peking in 1828, from which date there were only two minor rebellions among the Mohammedans until the time of the Taipings. Then, with the Peking government concentrating all its energy against Hung's followers, the Mohammedans saw their chance and rose again. They wrought havoc in Shensi and

Kansu. With Taipings and Nien-fei out of the way, Tso Tsung-t'ang
was able to march against them, in a campaign which was to prove
long and arduous, though successful in the end.

All this, however dangerous at times, was an old story to the Chinese Government, whereas the diplomatic game was new. The
Tsungli Yamen's leading spirits, Prince Kung and Wen-hsiang,
coped very well considering how strange and trying their work must
have been. They had a lot to put up with: foreigners' scoldings,
foreigners' unmannerly insistence and shocking bluntness, foreigners' babble of progress—in short, foreigners. It must have been a
great relief after a day's talk to get home and feel oneself cut off for
a time from the intruders. Even so, on the surface relations were
cordial, and there was more social communication between East
and West than there was ever to be later until the 1911 revolution.
The young consular assistant Adkins, when he was left behind by
Lord Elgin to spend the winter of 1860–61 alone in Peking, was
often entertained by Heng-chi of the Tsungli Yamen in the Chinese
Minister's own house, doubtless because Heng-chi, who had been
Hoppo, or Customs head, in Canton, did not find Englishmen as
strange and terrifying as his Manchu colleagues did. Even the Manchus, however—Prince Kung and Wen-hsiang—behaved very nicely
to the first English ladies who came out to live in the British envoy's
residence, sending them plants and sweets from time to time. In
1866 the Yamen decided to make a friendly gesture on the occasion
of Hart's going home on leave, and selected a secretary of the Yamen
office, a Manchu named Pin Chun, to accompany him, not as an
accredited official but merely as a sort of observer of the foreign
scene. Pin seems to have been a heavy liability. "Though not an
envoy," said Morse [*The International Relations of the Chinese
Empire* (London, 1918), Vol. II, p. 187], "he was well received
in official circles in London and, the lead once given, he was equally
well received in the other capitals of northern Europe which he
visited in turn. . . . It was planned that the mission should also go
to Washington, but this was abandoned. In fact the delegate was
disgusted with the discomforts of travel in countries whose customs
he abhorred with all the dislike of a fossil and a Manchu. . . . His
tour was cut short, and he was allowed to sail from Marseilles on
August 19th. . . ." Europe does not seem to have cared much for
him, either. In a letter from his home in Ireland to London, Robert
Hart advised E. C. Bowra, a future Chinese I.G., who was with the

party and keeping an eye on their troublesome charge during Hart's absence, "Should the Prince (i.e., the later Edward VII) wish Pin to attend a levee, let him go, accompanied by yourself of course: *but don't let him take his flute!*"

To the foreign diplomats, their interviews with the Yamen and the busy back and forth of Robert Hart and his senior Commissioners constituted the center of Chinese existence. To millions of Chinese, however, all this held little if any significance. The peasants remained more interested in the weather than in international questions, and stepped-up missionary activity was soon to have bad reactions as well as good. Even in Peking, the legations did not make much impression on the people. The diplomatic corps numbered only sixty in all, and the residencies, though scattered, were all situated some distance from the city. This was by deliberate choice of the envoys, because the city streets were so dirty and smelly. The biographer of Britain's second resident envoy expressed the feeling of the foreigners:

"Life would be intolerable to Western folks if it were not removed from the sights, noises, and odours of the streets; and fortunately the ruling local principle of spaciousness lends itself to the solution without running counter to any native practice or prejudice. The Legations, the customs, and the missionaries are in their various degrees established in 'compounds' large enough to accommodate the members of their staffs in separate buildings with ample elbowroom, as in an Indian cantonment, interspaced with trees and sometimes gardens, the whole surrounded by a high wall and capable of defence. These seductive cases in a wilderness of garbage, in a city of great distances, naturally conduce to stay-at-home habits and to segregation. . . ." [Michie, Vol. II, p. 142.] Mr. Michie also complained that Peking was one of the most inaccessible capitals in the world: "The great tourist-stream passed it by," he said.

The legation crowd was exclusive, but there was another group more exclusive still, whose gaieties far outdid the foreigners' poor pastimes of racing, shooting, and duty dinner parties. This was the honeycomb of houses and cliques called the Imperial Palace, where the two Dowagers as regents presumably watched over the infant Emperor, T'ung-chih, and grieved for their dead husband. Decorous Chinese pretended that the conventions were being observed, and the Senior Dowager did live quietly, but with Yehonala it was different. She loved life, even the circumscribed existence that was all she knew. She loved plays and splendid spectacles and fun. Inside the palace walls she turned, as her husband and many Imperial ancestors had done before her, to the eunuchs for amusement. There had always been eunuchs to guard the Imperial seraglio and serve in secondary capacities that would in other circumstances have been represented by unmaimed men—always, that is, within the memory of the Chinese Empire. Courtiers feared these officials. Sometimes they grew too big for their boots, living as they did near the source of power, and various laws had been framed to keep them cut down to size. No eunuch could rise to higher rank than the Fourth Button. No eunuch in the Imperial household was permitted to leave Peking's city limits. Everything the lawmakers could think of was done to ensure that eunuchs should not capture power in the palace as had happened before, but it was a difficult situation, for ordinary men couldn't live close to the young heirs and rulers, whereas eunuchs could. Eunuchs could and did pander to Imperial fancies of all sorts. When a monarch was weak to begin with, and wanted too much of anything that was more weakening, there was always a corps of eunuchs ready to supply it. Yehonala's husband had been corrupted by eunuchs, at least that was what people said, and the world was suspicious of what might be going on now, in regard to her son. Rumor gave it ample cause to worry. Only two years after Yehonala was widowed, she was criticized in the only possible way, by the only class of person who dared to do such a thing—a censor, memorializing the Court. An Imperial edict replied:

"The Censor Chia To memorialises, saying that it has come to his knowledge that certain of the eunuchs who perform theatricals in the Imperial Household, have had their costumes made of tribute silks and satins taken from the Imperial storehouses. He asserts that they perform daily before the Throne and regularly receive largesse to the amount of thousands of taels. He asks that these practices be forbidden and discontinued forthwith, in order that all tendency towards vicious courses be checked.

"With reference to this Memorial, it should be stated that last year, although the twenty-seven months of Imperial mourning for the late monarch were drawing to their close, we issued a Decree forbidding all festivities, for the reason that His late Majesty's remains had not yet been removed to their final place of sepulture; at the same time we gave orders that the seasonal tribute in kind, and provincial offerings, should be forwarded, as usual, in order to provide eventually for the costuming of the Palace theatricals. . . . We seized the opportunity, in this same Edict, to abolish once and for all the custom of bringing actors to the Palace to be made eunuchs, holding it to be wise, while His Majesty is still a minor, that everything that might tend in any way to lead him into paths of extravagance and dissipation should be firmly nipped in the bud. The Censor's present Memorial has therefore filled us with real amazement. At a time like this, when rebellions are still raging, and our people are in sore distress, when our treasuries are empty and our revenue insufficient for the needs of Government, our hearts are heavy with sorrowful thoughts, and must be so, especially as long as His late Majesty's remains have not yet been borne to their final resting place. How then could we possibly permit such a state of things as the Censor describes? . . . It is imperatively necessary that the Emperor, in the intervals of his studies, should have about his person only honest and steady retainers, with whom he may converse on the arts and practice of government. If his attendants are evil men and make it their business to flatter his ears and divert his eyes with luxurious and effeminate pastimes, the result might well be to produce in His Majesty most undesirable tendencies. . . ." [Bland and Backhouse, *China* . . . , p. 86.]

Surely nothing could be more proper than these sentiments, but young T'ung-chih's upbringing was exactly what the edict said it must never, never be. He was flattered, his eyes were diverted, and he grew up—if that is the right phrase—with very undesirable tendencies. Yehonala's enemies always claimed that she did it on purpose. They credited her with superhuman talents for evil, and later declared that she never meant her son to amount to anything and planned from the first to maneuver for his early death. It is at least equally probable that she had no particular plan in his upbringing: a mother in her position didn't actually have much say in the matter. If she had ever had much maternal instinct, her experience in Jehol may well have killed it, when the silver cord was so rudely cut. In any case T'ung-chih grew up as his father had done, and in the meantime his mother amused herself with parties and theatrical displays, and played at politics in much the same spirit. She soon found a companion exactly to her liking, the eunuch An Te-hai; Little An, as he was called by the nickname-loving Chinese. Little An's rise angered a great number of people. It wasn't always sheer public-spirited indignation, for the men who were in a position to know the most about these matters were the same who had to pay court favorites heavily and secretly when they wanted special privileges, or even common justice. They hated and feared Little An, and Little An grew rich. After a while it was whispered that he wasn't really a eunuch, and that Yehonala had borne him a son; it must be admitted, however, that gossip in China, though splendidly uninhibited, is far more entertaining than dependable. What was indisputably true and no gossip was very nearly as shocking, the fact that An used sometimes to get dressed up in the taboo robes of the Emperor, just for fun; at other times Yehonala and he would put on fancy dress and go boating on the Palace lake. Once at an entertainment she even bestowed on him the royal jade scepter. It was all very sad. In 1866 two censors tried again to correct these frivolous habits, by memorializing:

"More care should be shown in the selection of the Emperor's body-servants. All the disasters that have overtaken previous Dynasties have been directly due to the machinations and evil influences of eunuchs. These creatures worm their way into the confidence and even into the affection of the Throne by their protestations of loyalty and faithful service; they are past-masters in every art of adroit flattery. Having once secured the Imperial favour and protection, they proceed to attach to themselves troops of followers, and gradually make for themselves a place of power that in time becomes unassailable. We, your Memorialists, therefore beg that this danger be now averted by the selection of well-bred and trustworthy attendants to wait upon His Majesty. There should not be about the Throne any young eunuchs of attractive appearance, creatures who make it their aim to establish influence over the Emperor and who would certainly turn it to their own ends so soon as he assumes the control of affairs." [Bland and Backhouse, *China* . . . , p. 88.]

The reply to this warning was prompt and approving. The memorialists couldn't be more right, it said, as to what had happened in the past, and the point was well taken. Because of this very history, eunuchs were absolutely forbidden to meddle in affairs of state. For two hundred years these "fawning sycophants" had not had a chance to practice their evil arts of intrigue, and certainly hadn't now, since the Empresses had assumed the regency. The document ended on a particularly high note, directing that if any of these "noisome flatterers" were trying to pervert the Throne's intelligence, the Empresses must be informed at once. Rash as the censors may have been, they were not rash enough to cite chapter and verse, or mention An Te-hai by name, and for the moment he went on his triumphant way unopposed. Three years later, however, he went too far, and even Yehonala couldn't save him. In a way it was her fault. In 1869, ignoring the hard and fast rule that eunuchs must never leave Peking, she sent him on a confidential errand into Shantung, to collect money. (She was extravagant and often short of funds.) According to the scandalized Governor of the province, "a eunuch named An and his followers passed through that place (Techow) by way of the Imperial Canal, in two dragon barges, with much display of pomp and pageantry. He announced that he had come on an Imperial mission to procure Dragon robes. His barges flew a black banner, bearing in its centre the triple Imperial emblems of the Sun, and there were also Dragon and Phoenix flags flying on both sides of his vessels. A goodly company of both sexes were in attendance on this person; there were female musicians, skilled in the use of string and wind instruments. The banks of the Canal were lined with crowds of spectators, who witnessed with amazement and admiration his progress. The 21st day of last month happened to be this eunuch's birthday, so he arrayed himself in Dragon robes, and stood on the foredeck of his barge, to receive the homage of his suite."

It sounds very pretty, but it was also blasphemous, and as soon as this report reached the eyes of Prince Kung he knew that his chance had come. Like most of the princes he hated An Te-hai, for whom Yehonala had been known to keep him waiting for audience. Unknown to Yehonala, he hurried to tell the Senior Dowager about it, and prevailed on her to sign a decree then and there to behead the eunuch. The Dowager was unhappy about it, knowing the strength of Yehonala's temper, but she couldn't hold out against Prince Kung; she only said as she signed, "The Western Empress will assuredly kill me for this."

The edict arrived in Shantung in time for the Governor to apprehend An and have his head cut off before Yehonala knew anything about the original complaint. At the same time eight or nine other eunuchs in the party were put to death, but one escaped and managed to get back to the palace, after which the secret was out and Yehonala heard what had happened. Her rage was terrible. She confronted her co-Regent, who quailed before her and said it was all Prince Kung's fault. Yehonala summoned him and made many threats, but by that time the first heat of anger had passed, and she probably realized that he was too important to be cast aside. Thereafter, however, she remained his enemy, and as for her co-Regent, from that time on Yehonala pushed her aside at every opportunity. The dead An Te-hai was soon replaced in her confidence and affections by another eunuch named Li Lien-ying, who became even more influential than his predecessor.

All this medieval, or at least Restoration, blood and thunder proceeded on a quite separate plane from that of the foreigners in Peking. While eunuchs dressed in silk and satin and postured on the palace stage, Robert Hart pondered the less colorful question of tonnage dues. For years Western merchants had been complaining that the high toll of tonnage dues collected far exceeded what was spent on the aids to navigation for which purpose they were levied. The Chinese hadn't provided many navigational aids, though the Treaty of Tientsin had mentioned lighthouses, buoys, and lightships to be supplied by arrangement between the Consuls at each port and the Customs Superintendents. In the Rules of Trade which supplemented the treaty the matter was spoken of more specifically, one clause stating that the maintenance of lights, buoys, and beacons were to be provided for out of tonnage dues. What with the events of 1860 and then the anti-Taiping campaign, however, little had been done to carry out these provisions, and now the traders were pressing for action. Save for lights on the Yangtze near Shanghai, which were maintained by the local Chinese authorities, the coast remained without aids, and it was a tricky coast too: navigation had been difficult enough with only five treaty ports: now that more and more cities were being opened, the necessity was urgent. That catch-all the Customs Service was clearly the organization for the job, so Hart was hard at work. For a beginning, he proposed to the Chinese that one tenth of the revenue obtained from the tonnage dues be set aside for improvements in navigational aid. This was agreed, and the money immediately went to defray the costs of several lightships and buoys. Later, in '68, Hart obtained permission to take far more of a bite from the same source, seven-tenths, and from then on he was able to start installing a well-thought-out system of lights, buoys, and warnings in many danger spots. The other three-tenths went to support the "foreign colleges" which had been inaugurated by the government, especially the Tung Wen Kuang, the language school mentioned before in connection with the Tsungli Yamen, which was fast developing into the most important of them all, becoming eventually the Peking University. During Hart's leave in '66 he went to a good deal of trouble to collect a staff for the Tung Wen Kuang, and found five foreign professors for the purpose. Thereafter the school seemed to sag for a while, probably because it was not being properly run, but after the professor of Political Economy and International Law, Dr. W. A. P. Martin, was made president in 1869 things went better. Martin was an American of long experience in China, who knew the language well and had assisted in translating many textbooks. Scholarly attainments are of great importance to the Chinese, and they respected Martin.

The navigational-aid improvements Hart first introduced were only a drop in the bucket. He foresaw that with the forthcoming entry of foreign craft into China's interior waterways—a future confidently expected by the foreign traders but secretly feared and opposed by the Chinese—the task of supplying and maintaining these refinements would grow tremendously. Even along the seacoast, increased shipping would call for more signals and lights. In the rivers, maintenance men would have to remove wrecks, conserve channels, dredge shallows, and, above all, issue correct charts. Someone would have to control berthing arrangements. The project would need more harbor masters, more trained men altogether. As Hart spoke of his plans to meet these needs a flood of protests came from the traders who kept up a constant battle against the Customs Service. They said it was no part of the Service's duty to take care of the tonnage dues: they said there should be a new, all-foreign office called, as in England, Trinity House, to handle the fund. The merchants pelted the British Minister, Sir Rutherford Alcock who had replaced Bruce, and the American envoy Burlingame with objections. But Hart outtalked them, arguing that the proposed Trinity House would cost so much what with overheads and salaries for more officials and the like that tonnage dues would have to be doubled to meet the costs, leaving no money over for Peking's foreign colleges. Moreover, its work would be taken out of Chinese hands, and in Hart's estimation that was worst of all, for he was always thinking of the day when foreigners could bow out of the Customs, leaving a trained, honest set of Chinese officials to run their own Service, a vision in which the Western traders didn't share. Hart convinced Burlingame and Alcock that he was right, and then went ahead with his plans, which entailed considerable expansion and resulted in the creation of the Marine Department of the Imperial Maritime Customs Service "in connection with, and in certain respects formed from, the Customs Service." [Wright, p. 297.]

Alcock, after six years in Japan, had returned in 1865 to take up his new post in Peking, and the outstanding problem on his mind was revision of the Tientsin Treaty. According to one of its clauses, this treaty was to be revised every ten years on demand of either of its signers. The British thought a revision advisable after the first decade, which would be in 1868. "To that important juncture all eyes looked forward," says Michie. [Vol. II, p. 180.] "The foreigners hoped for freer intercourse; the Chinese wished to restrict what already existed." The foreigners wanted China's waterways opened to steam navigation; they wanted the right of their traders to reside in the interior wherever they wished; they strongly desired the vexed question of "likin" and other internal and interprovincial taxes to be cleared up by abolition. They wanted to get rid of the coast trade duty of 2½ per cent *ad valorem* levied on all goods going from one Chinese port to another within the country. They wished to see the end of China's salt monopoly, "The Gabelle." They would have liked the right to own and work Chinese coal and iron mines, and to build railways and telegraph lines. Of course, the Chinese did not want to give in on any of these demands, not only because of their innate conservatism but because in the case of some of the claims, especially those concerning inland taxes, it was beyond the power of Peking to enforce decisions on the provinces. One of the excuses they had made before signing the Tientsin Treaty, that it was no use for the foreign nations to keep envoys in Peking since Peking didn't directly control the provinces anyway, was unfortunately true.

On both sides as the date approached, leaders canvassed for opinions. Alcock circularized all British Consuls in the ports, asking for suggestions, and a similar circular was sent around to the leading Boards of Trade in Britain. He was nearly swamped by the replies, many of which contained demands astonishing in their ambition. The Hong Kong merchants were especially belligerent. The Tsungli Yamen sent its own circular to all Viceroys and other high officials in the provinces, stating the terms of what they knew would be the new demands and asking the recipient's opinion as to how China could safely avoid making these concessions. Most of the replies, as one would expect, strongly opposed the idea of any concessions at all. Tseng Kuo-fan ventured to remind the Tsungli Yamen that no matter what was decided, it rested with the provinces to carry out those decisions just as they thought best—not that the Yamen needed such a reminder, but the foreigners did, and Tseng's word was doubtless passed along to its proper recipients. It remained for Li Hung-chang to give everybody a surprise. His memorial showed amazing balance and vision.

"It is often said that foreigners are crafty and malign and full of unexpected ruses," was one of his statements, "but is it not the fact that Chinese are the same; or rather that the outrageous craft and malignity of the Chinese exceeds even that of foreigners? The truth is, that at present foreigners are powerful and the Chinese feeble." He went on to ask why this should be, and concluded that the strength of the foreigners depended on their technical knowledge. Therefore, the sooner China obtained such knowledge, the sooner she would grow strong again. They could learn all about telegraphs, railways, locomotives, and steamships if they had them at home, and it was not true, as so many people alleged, that these inventions were harmful, since in foreign countries everybody had them. The terms of the proposed concessions did not scandalize Li Hung-chang. He said that audience with the Emperor, which the foreigners were expected to demand, had already been stipulated in the treaty and it would be "next to impossible" to withdraw it, but the envoys could be put off until His Majesty had attained his majority, after which he could receive them all at once in a side hall, as his father had received Japanese and Russian envoys in the past. It should be made quite plain that these audiences could take place once, or at most twice, a year. As for the suggestion that Chinese go abroad as ambassadors, which was another proposal that agitated most of the Viceroys, Li wasn't opposed to it, as long as embassies didn't cost too much. He was not at all in favor of another demand, however, that missionaries be permitted more latitude. He seemed to think they were all agitators in disguise. "At the present moment innumerable churches are being erected in every province, district and department for the explanation of their canon and the preaching of their faith; and the common people are one-half of them deceived, and the other half led to join them for evil purposes." No missionary could be allowed to make forcible conversions. "At the approaching revision of the treaty all possible arguments must be used with regard to this point, and on no account must any further clause be added." The other points, regarding salt and coal and inland steam navigation and so forth, Li said, were comparatively trivial. If such concessions weren't harmful the Chinese might as well give in. If they were bad, the Chinese must go on arguing. "The fact is, that the prosperity of foreign countries is inseparably connected with the welfare of the Chinese people; and instead of draining that people to the last drop, would they not rather prefer to use, without exhausting—to take, and still leave a residue?"

Here one might almost think that the Viceroy was being over-optimistic, if he did not then hint that if the foreigners tried coercion, the Chinese would have to fight back. On the whole, however, it would be better if they didn't have to; they weren't strong enough at the moment. Better to wait until "with large armies and abundant supplies, with no rebel or Mohammedan outbreaks in the provinces, and no difficulties in the capital—we can cope with them without hesitation." He reminded his readers that he had had several years' experience of the foreigners and knew their character: he had found that they acted honorably, without deceit or falsehood. Of course one never really knew about foreigners: still, there was Gordon. [Michie, Vol. II, p. 185.]

Perhaps Li's mild attitude toward the idea of Chinese embassies influenced the Tsungli Yamen; perhaps they needed no influencing, and were already in favor of it. Certainly they thought it over. Dr. Martin of the Tung Wen Kuang was asked for his advice, and he told them a good deal about ambassadorial duties and procedure. Toward the end of 1867 they took action of an unexpected kind. It was the end of Anson Burlingame's tour of duty and he intended to retire. During the round of his courtesy farewell calls, he visited the Tsungli Yamen. As one does, he asked if he could do anything for China when he got home, and one of the Ministers smilingly said,

"Yes, you might act as our Ambassador."

Everybody laughed pleasantly and the visit ended, but the Yamen remembered the conversation, and as things turned out, Burlingame *did* become China's Ambassador. They invested him with the Red Button of the First Civil Rank, as Minister Extraordinary and Plenipotentiary. In '68, with a party of undeniably international character—one Englishman, one Frenchman, one Manchu, one Chinese of high rank, and thirty Chinese small fry—the old man set out for a round trip of the Western powers, to represent Peking. It goes without saying that the Customs Service supplied the money.

Hart had great hopes of the mission, but a large number of other foreigners in China felt it to be merely another procrastination device of the Tsungli Yamen's, to put off the treaty revision. Feeling mounted: the traders wanted to force immediate action, embassy or no embassy, but Hart opposed them. He wrote to Clarendon, "China has, to my mind, entered upon a career of improvement, and will, step by step, develop resources, create industries, and achieve progress materially, intellectually, morally. I therefore am daily more inclined to believe that the true policy is to 'leave her alone'—not that I am satisfied with the rate at which she progresses, but that I think, given the conditions which do exist and cannot be ignored, China is most likely to come to good in the end with benefit to herself and harm to none, if allowed to go along at her own rate, than if dealt with after a fashion of which the chief characteristics would be constantly recurring acts of violence, and that foreign dictation which breeds revolt, and checks healthy growth and natural action." [Wright, p. 370.]

Hart was to suffer the occupational troubles of all middle-of-the-road advocates, not only because he annoyed both extremes but because he had also to cope with overenthusiastic allies. Though he approved of what Burlingame had set out to do, the American went too far. Once arrived in America, he was carried away by his own eloquence and described a China that didn't exist; a China completely transformed by Western influence, panting for progress. Certainly everyone was very glad to hear about it. With Seward in Washington, Burlingame signed eight additional articles to the American Tientsin Treaty, pledging to respect Chinese sovereignty. They also grappled with the vexed, chronic problem of Chinese contract labor and emigration. On China's behalf Burlingame promised to prohibit the usual indentured type of emigration, but permitted free immigration to the Pacific Coast of the United States, where coolies were much in demand for work on the new Union Pacific line. In return America pledged that she would not exert pressure on China to adopt innovations the Chinese did not want, and would use her influence with the other powers to persuade them to take a like attitude.

Glowing with triumph, Burlingame took his party on to London, and had an audience with the Queen. Clarendon was better informed than his opposite number in Washington, but he too assured the Ambassador that Great Britain had no desire nor intention to apply unfriendly pressure on China. He added a hint, however, that Great Britain preferred to deal with the central government rather than provincial authorities, since it was with the central government that the treaties had been made, and he went on to say that he was sure all the other Western powers would take the same attitude. It was to the Chinese Government's own advantage, he pointed out, to assume authority over the provinces, and to be prepared to exercise it when appealed to for the redress of local wrongs.

America and Britain supplied the mission's chief triumphs. They moved on, but after that the journey was more in the nature of an excursion than a political venture. They had a very good time in Paris but collected no promises from the French Emperor. They went to Stockholm, Copenhagen, and Berlin, but in St. Petersburg, in February of 1870, just two years after setting out from Peking, Anson Burlingame caught pneumonia and died. The Manchu official assumed Burlingame's position and led the mission to Brussels and Rome before they went back to China, where they arrived in October. From Peking's point of view it had been a success, but Alcock and Hart had no cause to be happy. All their discussions about treaty revision seemed to have been rendered useless. Alcock wrote glumly to an official in Shanghai that there was no evidence in Peking of that desire for progress which the mission in Europe had assured everybody was so ardent with China's rulers. "If any hopes are built upon its existence, therefore," he said, "I fear there is nothing but disappointment in store for those who indulge in them. Projectors of telegraphic lines, railroads, and other plans for the sudden development of the resources of this country are but losing their time, while the Government here shows no disposition to entertain their projects." [Wright, p. 372.] Hart felt as if he had asked for an inch and been given an ell he didn't want. He feared the reaction of China's enthusiastic new admirers once they learned the other side from the merchants, and he was right to fear it.

In a heavy atmosphere of the disapproval of their compatriots, Hart and Alcock finally produced the result of their revision parleys, the Alcock Convention, which was signed by the proper Chinese authorities in October 1869. The traders were as disappointed and angry as they had intended to be all along with what they considered the officials' waste of time and the footling advantages resulting from it. The other envoys, too, were less than enthusiastic. In vain did Alcock explain why he had not taken the highhanded approach the traders had wanted from him: "We are no longer dictating conditions of peace, but negotiating for reciprocal advantages upon an equal footing," he declared. At home, the champions of the merchants made strong representations to the Boards of Trade, and what they said made all the more impact because of reports arriving at the same time of much anti-missionary activity in the Chinese provinces. Public opinion swung sharply away from the image presented to the British by Burlingame. The finishing touch was a horrible affair at Tientsin in '70, where a mob, stirred up by rumors of atrocities committed in the French mission hospital there, attacked the mission and burned down all its buildings, as well as the French consulate. They murdered and mutilated the Consul and his assistant, ten nuns, two priests, four other French citizens, three Russians, and thirty Chinese converts. A conversation about this affair between Yehonala and Tseng Kuo-fan has been recorded (Tseng was at the time Viceroy of Chihli, of which Tientsin was the capital):

"*Tzü Hsi (Yehonala)*. When did you leave Tientsin?
Tseng. On the 23rd.
Tzü Hsi. Have the ringleaders in the massacre of foreigners been executed yet?
Tseng. Not yet. The Consul told me that the Russian Minister was coming to Tientsin and that the French Minister was sending a deputy to witness the executions, so that the decapitations could not be summarily carried out.
Tzü Hsi. What date has Li Hung-chang fixed for the executions?
Tseng. On the day of my departure, he sent me word that he expected to dispose of them yesterday.
Tzü Hsi. Have the Tientsin populace calmed down?
Tseng. Yes, things are now quite settled and orderly.
Tzü Hsi. What made the Prefect and Magistrate run away to Shûn-Te after the massacre?
Tseng. When first removed from their posts, they knew not what sentence would be decreed against them, so they boldly and shamelessly ran away from the city. . . .
Tzü Hsi. It would be a fine thing if we could secure ourselves properly against invasion. These missionary complications are perpetually creating trouble for us.
Tseng. That is true. Of late the missionaries have created trouble every-

where. The native converts are given to oppressing those who will not embrace Christianity (literally *eat the religion*) and the missionaries always screen the converts, while the Consuls protect the missionaries. Next year, when the time comes for revising the French Treaty, we must take particular pains to reconsider carefully the whole question of religious propaganda."

[Bland and Backhouse, China . . . , p. 77.]

The massacre had a tremendous effect on France, and its repercussions were not much milder in the other European countries and America. As for the Alcock Convention, which was to lead the way for all the other treaty revisions, it was killed. In July, a month after the Tientsin affair, Whitehall announced that the Queen would not ratify it.

Chapter Twelve

Though the Tientsin massacre was dramatic, it could not fairly be described as a sudden, astonishing explosion, for it signified a state of mind that had long existed in China. It might have happened elsewhere, in any one of a dozen places. If this hostility seems to have been aimed more at Catholics than any other section of the Christian church with missions in the country, that is simply because Catholic missionaries had been longer in China than the others, had made more progress, and were perhaps more enterprising than their colleagues. Catholics were zealous, and as France was the special guardian of most of the Catholic missions, and had declared this policy when she joined Great Britain against the Chinese in order to teach them a lesson in regard to Father Chapdelaine, the determined foes of Christianity naturally singled out the French for attack. Additionally inflammatory was the background of the ill-fated French mission at Tientsin. The property had been taken over by the French after their landing with the British in 1860, while the soldiers' depredations were fresh in the minds of the citizens. As if this were not bad enough, the authorities had also pre-empted for their use an Imperial palace, setting up in its grounds the French consulate, the mission buildings, and most particularly—to make assurance of offense doubly sure—the cathedral, which was built on the foundations of the palace temple. Already resentful, the populace was eager to believe the worst of the intruders. Catholic missionaries made a practice of baptizing moribund children, and during epidemics they did their best to induce people to bring in dying infants before it was too late. Prejudiced observers read the most sinister meaning into the sight of children being carried in to the hospital who never came out again, for the little bodies were buried afterwards in the mission's consecrated ground. Atrocity stories were whipped up about the French community, but they were not the only missionaries who were given such attention. In Hunan, in 1869, a placard was published which carried ten charges: it declared that Christians did not honor their ancestors or "the spiritual powers," and that missionaries required their converts to destroy their ancestral tablets. (The trouble with this sort of thing was that so much truth was woven into the nonsense that it was impossible to refute it cleanly and simply.) The placard also asserted that for baptism missionaries used an unguent made from the corpses of priests and administered a stupefying drug, chanting the while a magic charm that would keep the convert faithful forever to their erroneous beliefs. Furthermore, when a Christian convert lay dying, the missionaries would get his relatives out of the room and then, even before he died, they took out his eyes and his heart, which they used for making counterfeit money. Converts were taken away and sold to foreigners, and sometimes their bodies were used as bait in the fisheries of the Southern Seas. Missionaries served as spies for the trading bandits. [Morse, *International Relations* . . . , Vol. II, p. 235.]

After the massacre, the French made furious demands for justice from the Tsungli Yamen. They wanted to see that responsible officials were properly executed, whether they had offended by active malice or merely by neglect. Negotiations degenerated into a squabble as to who these officials were, a sort of haggle over heads. Anxious to make amends in the good old way, the Tsungli Yamen commanded quite a few beheadings, then paused hopefully to see if it was enough; it never was. Moreover, the French wanted the Chinese to pay an indemnity, and this they did without demur. Later, however, the bishop of the diocese, on being presented with that portion of the money his officials thought the mission should have, refused the greater part of it, retaining only enough to reconstruct his cathedral. One of the officials whose head the French wanted was a man named Chunghow, a Manchu who really seems to have been innocent of any part in the outrage. The Yamen refused to sacrifice Chunghow. Instead, they made him the messenger who was to carry the official Chinese apology to Paris. The terrors of such a trip into the unknown were alleviated for him by the presence of two French officials from the Customs Service who went along. They started out in October 1870.

This was the unpropitious moment the Tsungli Yamen chose for an attempt to set up a form of control over Western missions in China. They circularized all the legations, suggesting that missionary activities be defined and limited. One sees their point, but it was a tactless act at that particular time, and the foreigners refused to consider such a thing. As a result, anti-missionary incidents continued to blow up here and there, though they did not attain the scope and horror of the Tientsin massacre. Outrages against missionaries became a standard story in the Western press, and remained a part of the China scene up to the middle of the present century.

Arrived in France, Chunghow found that the excitable foreigners were now completely indifferent to him, to his apology, to China altogether; they were embroiled in the Franco-Prussian War and he couldn't even find an official who would accept his document. He had a few distressful weeks wandering through the provinces in search of an attentive ear, but it was no use, and he finally started for home with his apology undelivered. He went via America. He was in New York when a French Minister in Paris belatedly realized what he was after and called him back. Poor Chunghow obeyed, and in Paris was kicked around some more and ignored again, probably not out of planned malice so much as simple distraction on the part of the French. At last he got an interview with the President, who had just succeeded Napoleon III, and was able to present his document and listen meekly while M. Thiers scolded him. Actually, because of the war, he and China got off very lightly. Absent-mindedly, M. Thiers told him that France wasn't out for more beheadings: what she really wanted was a good, honest China that would live up to its treaty obligations. The President suggested that a permanent Chinese Legation in Paris would be a good thing, and then released Chunghow. [Morse, *International Relations* . . . , Vol. II, p. 258.] This tame conclusion to so much blood and thunder disappointed foreigners in China, for they had hoped for sharp retributive measures that would protect their own nationals in days to come. Hart commented in a letter,

". . . (China) does not deserve equal consideration till she gives equal facilities; that is my creed. At the same time she deserves— so does the devil—fair treatment at all times. The religious question ought either to be eliminated or Christian states go the whole hog, and protect converts against their pagan government. It is a serious question this: from a worldly point of view, I am of the former opinion, but, as a Christian, my sympathies go in the latter direction." [Morse, *International Relations* . . . , Vol. II, p. 261.]

*　　*　　*

In its reference to the selling of Christian converts and the use of their bodies as bait in fisheries, the anti-missionary placard in Hunan shows a lively appreciation of the evils of forced emigration. This scandal was growing with great rapidity. For centuries Chinese subjects had been forbidden by law to leave their country, but like so many laws this one was ignored widely, especially in those territories far away from the center of control. Near Peking, would-be emigrants obediently applied for permits when they wished to get out, not that many people did, but in the south scores of adventurous Chinese moved out quite as they wished, as they had always done, roaming to Formosa, the Philippines, the Malay Peninsula, and the Archipelago. Some went back and forth, but more stayed where they got to and settled there, founding large communities: some of their descendants, the "overseas Chinese," can trace their ancestry in their adopted countries as much as five hundred years. Whatever Peking may have thought, this form of emigration was a harmless seepage on the whole. The other sort of emigration, which grew with the growth of foreign shipping along the China coast, could not be called harmless at all. Many foreign countries needed cheap labor for large projects. Slavery from Africa had been stamped out, and Chinese so-called contract labor became its substitute. Inland were purveyors, or crimps, who collected people at so much a head and delivered them to the ships that were to carry them off. Some contract labor consisted of emigrants to the United States and Australia who went of their own volition, tempted by the comparatively high wages they would earn in these countries, but this could not be said of the hapless coolies sent off to Peru, the West Indies, and other areas of the Western Hemisphere. Some were frightened into submission, some bullied by debts, some shanghaied in reverse. They were crowded into barracoons to await loading, and when they were aboard and on the way, the conditions were hellish. Many of these unwilling passengers found their own way out of the agony. In 1856 the master of a Cuba-bound British ship, who had loaded his living cargo in Hong Kong, recorded, "The first day I had the first suicide, and on an average I had three suicides daily between Honging and until I passed the Straits of Sunda." Out of his 332 emigrants he lost 128, from disease and suicide. Still, it paid. He collected $70 passage money for each man he set out with, and when he arrived he probably sold the coolies at auction for an average of $400 apiece.

For a long time before the end, enlightened public opinion was opposed to the trade: when it was disclosed that in some ships as many as 40 per cent of the men died enroute to the West Indies, the British Government did something about it. Already a gesture had been made in 1852, when the British introduced strict regulations as to the conditions in which coolies might be shipped out to British colonies, but the contractors evaded this by moving their activities to non-treaty ports on the mainland and to Macao. Peking was not indifferent to the problem, but it was the same old story—it had little influence in the southern provinces. In 1860, a special agreement was signed by Prince Kung, Alcock, and the French chargé d'affaires that provided for a certain amount of protection for the coolies, but this convention had no effect on Macao, and there the trade continued to flourish. It was not always the ship's captain who won out. At times the emigrants rose in revolt, killing the captain and running his ship ashore: such mutineers occasionally escaped and scattered to their homes, though others were caught and punished. Then, in 1872, the *Maria Luz* took refuge in Yokohama Harbor from a storm. She was a Peruvian ship, homeward bound with a full cargo of more than three hundred coolies. One of these men escaped and sought sanctuary aboard the British flagship, where he described the dreadful conditions in which he and his companions were living. The British chargé d'affaires handed him over, as he was bound to do, to the Japanese, but at the same time he requested that they take suitable action. Their hands were free; no treaty existed between Japan and Peru. The Japanese held a trial, declared the case in favor of the coolies, and sent them all back to China. Again public conscience was stirred, and people talked indignantly of Cuba, where it was well known that life on the sugar plantations was hard for indentured laborers. The Tsungli Yamen appointed an official to visit Cuba and make an investigation in company with two foreign Customs Commissioners. Spain and Peru especially had an active interest in the results of this inquiry, since both nations had for some time been desiring treaties with China. After seeing the report the Tsungli Yamen refused to consider such treaties until the coolie traffic should be stopped; truly it gave an appalling picture. Eight-tenths of one group interviewed said they had been kidnaped or decoyed: mortality during the voyage had exceeded 10 per cent: the coolies were sold into slavery on arrival: they were treated with extreme cruelty by their masters. On the plantations, food was insufficient, the coolies had to work very long hours, and were often punished by rods, whips, chains, and stocks.

"During the past years a large number have been killed by blows, have died from the effects of wounds, and have hanged themselves, cut their throats, poisoned themselves with opium, and thrown themselves into wells and sugar cauldrons. It was also possible to verify, by personal inspection, wounds inflicted on others, the fractured and maimed limbs, blindness, the heads full of sores, the teeth struck out, the ears mutilated, and the skin and flesh lacerated, proofs of cruelty patent to the eyes of all. On the termination of the contracts, the employers, in most cases, insist on a renewal of engagements, which may extend to even more than ten years, and during which the same system of cruelty is adhered to." In the face of the evidence Peru gave up importing coolie labor and got her convention in 1874. Spain took longer to satisfy the Tsungli Yamen. Finally a stop was put to emigration from Macao, the last port, and Cuba was accordingly cleaned up: Spain was admitted to the diplomatic club of Peking in 1877. [Wright, Notes, p. 431.]

* * *

According to the way Westerners count birthdays, in 1872 the young Emperor was sixteen and still a boy. According to the Chinese system he was seventeen, for Chinese count a child one year old at birth, and everyone goes up one year more on New Year's day. The Emperor, therefore, was a man; he had attained his majority. In preparation for his enthronement the two co-Regents proposed to find him a wife. This was Peking, and no sentiment was involved. Each lady, the Eastern Empress, Tzu-an, and the Western Empress, Tzu-hsi or Yehonala, had a candidate selected from the list of eligible maidens, and each selection had much to do with the ladies' personal friendships and family connections. Tzu-an favored a girl whose clan name was Aluteh, a niece of that Chunghow who had just delivered the Tsungli Yamen's apology to the President of

France. Tzu-hsi wanted her son to marry one Lady Feng, whose father was a close friend of Tzu-hsi's champion, Jung-lu. Tzu-hsi had every reason to suppose that the Emperor would obey her, because like a good Chinese son he always did: this time, however, for some reason he proved balky and would not make up his mind straightaway. Therefore, according to the story [Bland and Backhouse, *Annals* . . . , p. 421], the two Empresses did a most unusual thing and let him look at both girls so that he could decide between them. As is well known, the custom was that no man should see his bride until after the wedding, but Manchus gave their women more freedom than most Chinese did, and T'ung-chih had his private view. Much to Tzu-hsi's discomfiture he chose Aluteh, and held firm against all argument. Naturally he married Lady Feng as well— he could hardly have refused, after compromising her as he had done—but Aluteh was ranked as Senior Consort and Lady Feng came second. Accustomed as they were to their own Western ways, the envoys expected that they would be invited to a grand ceremonial wedding with everybody standing or sitting in his allotted space. They were unpleasantly surprised when in February 1872, two gentlemen from the Tsungli Yamen called on them each in turn to announce that the wedding was to take place next day, and to request the foreigners, ever so politely, to stay indoors in their own houses while it occurred. The foreign diplomats were furious. It was an insult to their respective monarchs or presidents. Sir Thomas Wade, who was now British Minister, scolded the Yamen messengers in fluent Chinese: the Russian, General Vlangaly, gave them a lecture on manners: F. F. Low, the American, was sulky, and the representative of Spain went right off the handle. Fortunately for their feelings, and no doubt for the messengers as well, the German and Italian envoys were out of town. There must have been deep amusement that day at the Tsungli Yamen.

T'ung-chih liked his Senior Consort. He spent a good deal of time with her, though Tzu-hsi persistently tried to keep him away from her apartments and continually thrust the second wife, now called "The Discerning Concubine," on his notice. "She would . . . frequently instruct the eunuch Li Lien-ying to convey the 'Discerning Concubine' at night to the monarch's bedchamber, in the hope that she might present him with an heir to the Throne, and thus secure for herself (Tzu-hsi) a long and undisputed tenure of the Regency. As etiquette prescribes, Li would carry the Discerning Concubine

on his back, with only a cloak thrown over her person, and leave
her at the lower end of the Dragon couch, from which position it
was her duty to raise herself gradually till she reached the level of
the Imperial pillow." [Bland and Backhouse, *Annals* . . . , p. 421.]

It was no use, and Li Lien-ying made many a journey with his
living burden in vain. The horse, led to water, refused to drink, and
often avoided the drinking trough altogether by staying out all night
either in the stews of the city or at his senior wife's palace.

These domestic rivalries had to give way to the preparations for
T'ung-chih's enthronement on February 23, 1873. As soon as it was
over the foreign envoys pounced, requesting in one letter signed by
all of them the long-awaited audience which had been promised in
the treaties. Signators were the Russian, German, American, English, French, Dutch, and Japanese envoys. One excuse and another
kept the court from having to fulfill the onerous task until June, and
then at last it took place, with every detail cunningly arranged by
the Chinese to avoid awkwardness. The audience was held in the
Pavilion of Violet Light—a clever choice, for the Pavilion was outside the city walls and there was no squabble, therefore, as to
whether the envoys should or should not have permission to approach by sedan chair. It didn't matter how they got there, since it
wasn't a palace in the Forbidden City. The actual audience was
simple and short. First the Japanese Ambassador had his own audience, because he was the only diplomat with truly ambassadorial
rank. The others all filed in in a body. Vlangaly, as doyen of the
corps, made the speech of congratulation, and then the envoys
walked up one by one and deposited their letters of credence on a
table in front of the silent young Emperor. It was not part of T'ung-
chih's duty to address such *hoi-polloi* in his own voice: Prince Kung
made a speech for him in reply to Vlangaly's. Then the French
Minister had a private audience in order to make a formal reply to
the letter Chunghow had brought to Paris, and that was all. A simple affair, but when one considers what had gone on all the years
before, and how it happened to come about at all, it was an intensely
interesting moment, being the first audience ever granted by a Chinese Emperor at which the kowtow was omitted. A good deal of effort and history went into making that change. Commenting on it,
the *North China Herald* pointed out that the conventional reception of the Japanese Ambassador signified "an abandonment of arrogant claims of supremacy, and an evidence that China is con-

scious that a new era has dawned on this part of the world." [July 19, 1873.]

What the *Herald* did not mention about that bit of the ceremony was that the Japanese diplomat had come to his post on a special errand, the settlement of the Ryukyu sailors' affair. Both China and Japan had long claimed suzerainty over the Ryukyus, and both countries collected tribute from them. In 1871, sailors from these islands were shipwrecked on the wild east coast of Formosa, which island China claimed as her own, and were there killed and eaten by the Formosan aborigines who lived in the mountains: like their relatives of Borneo and the Philippines, they were cannibals. On the assumption that the Ryukyus were a Japanese affair, Tokyo wanted assurances from China that she would receive satisfaction for the loss of the sailors. Li Hung-chang had already agreed to this, and promised that the Chinese would subdue the cannibals of Formosa; moreover, he made no awkward counterclaims to the Ryukyus. But Li's colleagues refused to back him up in his promise to take care of Formosa. Sending out such a punitive expedition would be expensive, they argued, and they needed every penny, what with the wedding and enthronement and audience, and that everlasting campaign against the Mohammedans over in the northwest. Who cared about a wild, useless island like Formosa? Contradicting Li Hung-chang, the Ministers told the Japanese that they weren't interested in the eastern region of Formosa, had no control over it, and didn't claim any. The Japanese took this in good faith as an invitation to go ahead on their own. They organized and sent out an elaborate expedition which was accompanied by several American officers. Arrived, they quickly built houses and roads and settled in for a campaign of pacification. The Chinese were startled and then alarmed: why had they given Formosa away? They must take it back. They quickly informed the Japanese that they did, after all, claim Formosa, even the eastern portion: they would take care of the cannibals themselves. To prove it they immediately rounded up and sent off to the island about ten thousand men. In an access of caution all the stronger for being belated, Prince Kung added, so that there might be no more mistakes, that China claimed suzerainty over Macao and Korea, as well as Formosa.

This was a blow to Japan. Her feet were already set on the path of expansion and she had invested a good deal of wealth and effort in the Formosa venture. In the ensuing arguments during the latter part of 1874 the two countries came very near to war. Our old friend Sir Harry Parkes, now envoy in Tokyo, did what he could to keep the peace, as did Wade and the French Minister de Geofroy in Peking. One side effect of the scare pleased Robert Hart very much. He wrote to a friend, in July,

"The Japs are on Formosa; the Yamen disavows connection with the expeditions: the Japs do not know whether to push on or go back; the Chinese do not know whether (they) will have to fight the Japs or get them out in another way: that's the situation, and the result so far is that the Viceroy at Foochow has—authorized a land line of telegraph from Sharp Peak to Foochow! I ought to add that foreign ministers in Japan are against the expedition, arguing that it will do no good to Japan; while here the foreign ministers are all for the expedition, arguing that it will do good to China. So far the expedition is a fact, and so far it is rousing China from its long slumber." [Morse, *International Relations* . . . , Vol. II, p. 274.]

In the end there was no war. Japan claimed a huge indemnity of three million dollars, which China refused to pay. Japan presented China with an ultimatum: pay up by October or else. . . . China again did one of her rightabout turns and agreed to pay something, though not all—half a million taels. Japan accepted it. (As always, this personification of some geographical division's government is misleading. Of course what is really meant is that a group of Ministers in Peking, arguing among themselves, each obsessed with his own reasons for advising some particular course—farsighted or myopic, public spirited or grasping—several times decided on a policy, found it disastrous, and quickly switched to another. In Japan another group of Ministers with better-disciplined egos chose one direction and stuck to it. Unfortunately this is a clumsy way to sum it up: one takes the short cut.) The indemnity payment finished the quarrel, at least temporarily. Whatever else the muddle had done, it affirmed Japan's claim to the Ryukyus, and no doubt her Ministers saw the advantage of this in the long run, and took comfort.

This was the beginning of a long, bad time for China, when the outside world seemed in a conspiracy to snip off as much of her territory as possible. The French, for example, had always declared that their only interest in China was to spread the true religion, but their actions in the southern regions continued to belie their words. Already they had declared a protectorate over Cambodia. Not long afterwards they annexed that province of Annam known as Cochin China, and then they went further: in 1874, with Peking otherwise occupied over Formosa and palace intrigues, France insisted on opening up the whole country of Annam as the Allies had opened China, with rights of trade for foreigners in the ports, and foreign shipping in the waterways. As Annam was one of China's tributaries the new threat disturbed Peking, but the Tsungli Yamen could do nothing. Then there was the old trouble of the Mohammedan revolts, still unquelled, though General Tso Tsung-t'ang was containing it. He had dug in for a long campaign in the wild wastes of Sinkiang near the Russian border. The Russians too were inimical to the Mohammedans, and the warriors of Turkestan fought on two fronts; in 1871, in fact, Russian troops stepped over the border and occupied the Chinese territory of Ili, though Russia assured Tso that when the crisis was over the troops would be withdrawn. As things turned out, they never were.

To add to this list of complications there was Korea. Korea was an unlucky country, lying as it did in a position vulnerable to three neighbors. She had been invaded many times by Chinese and Japanese, but ever since the seventeenth century she had been a vassal of the Manchu Emperors, and sent a token tribute to Peking every four years. Like the Chinese, the Koreans were putting up considerable resistance to Western missionaries, most of whom in that country were French Catholics. In 1866, after a particularly bloody manifestation of Korean anti-Christian sentiment, a French naval expedition set out to teach the Koreans a lesson. Landing at the port of Kanghwa, the troops found no opposition, but neither could they find any Koreans with whom to discuss matters. They waited for days, but nobody appeared, and at the end of some weeks the French retired to China, having proved nothing at all. In the same year an American schooner was wrecked on the Korean coast, and the crew was treated well by the local officials, possibly because they hadn't arrived on a hostile errand. Another American schooner's crew had a different experience. Ashore in a Korean port city they acted roughly, and the local inhabitants not only attacked them, but carried the battle out to the ship itself. All communication between the *General Sherman*, which was the schooner's name, and the outside world ceased abruptly. For nearly two years nothing more was heard from it. At last in 1868 a group of foreigners, an

international selection headed by an American, sailed from China
to Korea ostensibly to solve the mystery of the *General Sherman:*
their true aim, however, was to make their fortunes, for they believed Korea to be full of rich temples and tombs which they intended to rob. They found no fortune and no trace of the lost
schooner. Three years later the Americans of Peking decided to do
something to follow up the adventurers' visit, which to their mind
constituted an introduction of sorts: an inquiry about the *Sherman*
might lead to a treaty, they told each other hopefully. Low, the
envoy, was the moving spirit of the project. He refused to listen to
a mild warning from Washington to the effect that Korea was a
tributary of China's, for when he turned to the Tsungli Yamen to
find out how matters stood, they gave the same sort of reply they
had given Japan when that country asked about eastern Formosa.
Low eagerly took this for a green light, though the Manchus gently
refused his request that they lend him, to serve as interpreter on
their mission, an American, Drew, who was one of the Commissioners of Customs. No doubt the Ministers thought this was really a
bit too much. The question was still in abeyance, however, when
Hart wryly wrote to Drew, who was a good friend of his,

"I hope you won't get shot, or otherwise mauled—but I am very
much of the opinion that the Koreans will fight: if they do fight the
United States will have the honour and glory of asserting Republican
principles, and of opening the last sublunary lock *vi et armis.*"
[Morse, *International Relations* . . . , Vol. III, p. 6.]

The Koreans did fight. The minute they sighted the American
fleet from their forts at Kanghwa, they opened fire. At the same
time they sent an appeal to Peking to come and help, but before
the Tsungli Yamen had to cope with this embarrassing situation the
Americans decided to imitate the British action at Taku—the successful one, of course. Their gunboats easily reduced the forts and
silenced the guns, and in the process many Koreans were killed.
So far, everything had gone just as it had at Taku the first time, but
after that something went wrong, somehow, with the program, and
Low found himself up against the same blank wall that had faced
the French admiral, for the Koreans simply withdrew into their
shell. All responsible officials stayed at a distance, in Seoul, and
would make no response whatever to his demands for negotiations.
He found it impossible to get letters to the city. He hadn't enough
men to make up an invading party, and he could not even send an

armed escort for messengers to Seoul. It was no good, and the fleet had to withdraw. Hart had not been called on to take sides in the affair and indeed could not, in his position vis-à-vis the Tsungli Yamen, but privately he wrote to Drew,

"If America goes no further in the matter, Korea will ripen like a pear, and then drop into the jaws of Russia." [Morse, *International Relations* . . . , Vol. III, p. 9.]

His powers of prophecy failed on that point, as it happened, for it was not only Russia's jaws that gaped hungrily at Korea; Japan swallowed her. As if that enterprising nation had been given a new idea by the Americans, in 1876 she sent a large naval force to Korean coast waters and proposed a treaty. Better prepared than the Americans, the Japanese managed to convince their taciturn neighbors that negotiations were in order, and the result was a treaty in which Korea was represented as an independent state, with no tributary connections with China. Such a proud status was not really to Korean taste, and after the treaty was signed her rulers again applied to Peking for protection and advice. As a result of a quiet word or two from the Tsungli Yamen, a few years later Korea consented to make treaties with some of the Western governments, in which documents Chinese suzerainty was taken as fact. Many Koreans resented the entrance of Western diplomats in their affairs, far more than they had minded about the Japanese. They didn't really want anybody interfering with their country, but if it had to be someone, Japan was a devil they knew.

*   *   *

The Western nations had imperceptibly formed a ring, a cartel, to manage China: they surrounded her like a bevy of Nannies. Ostensibly they were taking good care of the child, but nevertheless they watched it with anxious jealousy, each of the other, as if one or another, as soon as she had a chance, might snatch it away from the rest. Instead of committing outright kidnaping, therefore, they indulged in petty pilferings. At a tactful distance they also observed the latest developments at the Imperial Palace; here was one side of Chinese life in which they could claim no part; on such occasions they behaved like permissive Nannies who deliberately ignore nursery tantrums and quarrels.

T'ung-chih, the Emperor, though never what the insurance companies would call a good risk, had at least managed to get his be-loved Senior Consort with child, while the Discerning Concubine remained barren. This fact was of great import for Tzu-hsi, and became even more pressing when in December of 1874 her son picked up smallpox, probably in the slummy brothels he frequented. At best it is a lingering disease, but T'ung-chih sank rapidly. He turned over his powers once again to Tzu-an and Tzu-hsi for the duration of his illness, but Tzu-hsi realized that she would not enjoy these familiar perquisites beyond his death unless she did something quickly, since her hold depended on her status as the Emperor's mother. Supposing Aluteh should bear a son, Tzu-hsi could hardly push herself into a regency again, for Aluteh's clan was inimical to the Yehonala family, and it was Tzu-an who had backed the girl: Tzu-hsi had always openly opposed her. The question of T'ung-chih's successor, therefore, summed up Tzu-hsi's entire difficulty, and she did some hard thinking and clever plotting even before her son died. There were always wheels within wheels. Apart from the un-born son—if it proved to be a son—the most likely choice of an heir, according to the accepted rules, was the son of T'ung-chih's eldest paternal uncle, a baby named P'u-lun. However, Tzu-hsi saw no future for herself in P'u-lun as Emperor, and she reminded herself that she had a chance to object to the choice on a technical point: his father had not been truly born into the family, but was adopted. Adoption had always been accepted by Chinese custom, but Tzu-hsi felt that she could argue on this basis if she held firmly to the line that things are different with Emperors. The next strongest claim was that of Prince Kung's son. In her mind she counted him out immediately, for obvious reasons: she and Prince Kung were bitter enemies, and the boy, moreover, was nearly seventeen: he would mount the throne immediately if he were selected—no regency would be necessary.

T'ung-chih died on January 13, 1875. Wasting no time on ma-ternal lamentations, the Western Empress moved immediately, be-fore the factions opposed to her could get together. She called a meeting of the clansmen and high officials, declaring that a new ruler must be selected on the spot, and brushed aside the suggestion of Prince Kung that they wait until Aluteh's child was born, mean-while keeping secret the news of the Emperor's death (something that was easily done in those days of Imperial seclusion). Tzu-hsi could talk faster than Prince Kung; somehow what he said got lost in the excitement. When the baby P'u-lun's name was brought forward she played her trump card and spoke of the father's having been adopted. Tzu-an next proposed the son of Prince Kung, and Tzu-hsi ignored her speech too, as she had overridden Prince Kung's, and hastily went on to make her own suggestion—another small boy who was son of Prince Kung's next younger brother, Prince Ch'un, who had married Tzu-hsi's sister of the Yehonala clan. Now at last Prince Kung managed to make himself heard, and angrily demanded if the rules of primogeniture were to be completely ignored. But Tzu-hsi rushed ahead and put the matter to a vote. The other two candidates had a few supporters, but most of the officials were either hypnotized by the dynamic personality of the Western Empress or they were afraid of her, and her nominee was elected. There was no real justice in it, but Tzu-hsi swung it, and the little boy who was thenceforth known as Kuang-hsü was immediately summoned to come and take his place in the Palace. At the same time, Tzu-hsi canceled any trouble that might be brewing by commanding Prince Kung to go and sit with the dead Emperor's coffin, while faithful Jung-lu rallied round with his troops and surrounded the Palace. Once again the two Dowager Empresses—dowager this time once removed—were named as co-Regents. The forgotten widow Aluteh languished for two months and then swallowed opium and died, along with the child she still carried in her body.

Clever as Tzu-hsi had been, there was no possibility of fooling the public completely. They had already begun to mutter and ask questions about the strange choice of the new Emperor, and when Aluteh died so dramatically most people were deeply shocked. Inevitably, they whispered to each other that the redoubtable Western Empress had herself poisoned the young woman, or had at least forced Aluteh's father to poison her. Of course it is not impossible, but sudden deaths in China often did give rise to similar suspicions, and Tzu-hsi in the course of her long life collected a list of allegations that makes the stories against Lucrezia Borgia fade into nothing. Any direct action by Tzu-hsi need not have been necessary. As anyone can see, by indirect methods she had already given Aluteh plenty of incentive for suicide. For all Tzu-hsi's hardihood, however, even she was not quite indifferent to the beliefs of her era: she had a strong tendency to superstition, and knew she had outraged tradition by breaking the dynastic laws of succession. It did something to allay her guilty fears, perhaps, when she and Tzu-an pledged themselves to provide a direct heir for T'ung-chih as soon as Kuang-hsü should have a son. This boy would be posthumously adopted by T'ung-chih and would then be the next Emperor after Kuang-hsü. Apparently nobody dared to mention P'u-lun's name at this juncture, nor to point out that the accession of Kuang-hsü had contravened another law that Tzu-hsi had preferred to forget, which stated that each successor must be a member of the next generation below the last Emperor's. Kuang-hsü was a first cousin, not a nephew, of T'ung-chih. Nobody dared . . . save for one man, Wu K'o-tu, and he had not the means. Only censors could memorialize the Throne direct. In earlier days Wu K'o-tu had been a censor; he had written an interesting memorial when the Court agitated itself over the young Emperor's—T'ung-chih's—approaching audience with the foreign envoys. What bothered them was that old bugbear, the fact that the envoys would not kowtow. Wu took a comfortingly lofty line:

"As Mencius remarks, 'Why should the Superior Man engage in altercation with birds and beasts?' I have heard, and believe, that the rulers of foreign nations are deposed by their subjects for all the world like pawns on a chessboard. I have seen with my own eyes the foreigners who live in Peking walking abroad, preceded by the females of their household either on foot or in sedan chairs; the men folk following meekly in their rear, like servants—all unashamed. They have made some score of treaties with China, containing at least ten thousand written characters. Is there a word in any one of them concerning reverence for parents, or the cultivation of virtue and respect for the nine canons of rightful conduct? No! Is there one word in any one of them as to the observance of ceremony, as to duty, integrity and a proper sense of shame, the four cardinal principles of our nation? Again, no! All that they speak of is material profit. 'Such and such a clause implies benefits or profits for China.' They think only of profit, and with the meretricious hope of profit they beguile the Chinese people. These men know not even the meaning of duty and ceremony, wisdom and good faith, yet we profess, forsooth, to expect them to act as if they were endowed with the five cardinal virtues! . . . If we insist upon their reverently kneeling, in what manner will it increase the lustre of the Throne's prestige? If we excuse them from kneeling, how can this possibly affect the Sovereign's majesty?"

This memorial had its effect in smoothing over the inevitable, and Censor Wu K'o-tu was commended for it. Later, however, his outspokenness irritated T'ung-chih to such an extent that he was reduced three stages in rank, was no longer a censor, and thus could not write a memorial and send it straight to the Regents. He knew that what he had to say would never be forwarded by any high official entrusted with it, for the great Personages had so hedged themselves about that they cannily punished intermediaries as well as original offenders in these matters. The way Wu K'o-tu got around the difficulty at last was effective but drastic. He committed suicide. First, however, he so arranged matters that his memorial was bound to catch the public eye. He did it all in this manner: In accordance with sacred custom the late Emperor's remains were to be buried four years after his death, in the Eastern Mausoleum. During the interim, Wu K'o-tu waited for any further sign of the Regents' good faith in bequeathing on the late T'ung-chih an heir, who could worship at his ancestors' tablet and sweep the ancestral grave in the proper manner. No further pledge appeared, and Wu considered the first hasty promise insufficient. Therefore he carried out his plan. He volunteered to be one of the coffin's escort to the Mausoleum, and when in April 1879, the ceremony was over, he did not leave the vicinity, but moved into a small Taoist monastery nearby. For a week the old man—he was seventy years old—wrote busily, and at the end of that time he took poison and hanged himself. He left behind him a letter to his son, another abusive one to the abbot— he didn't like the abbot—commanding him to turn over the enclosed memorial to the local magistrate, and, finally, the famous memorial itself.

"You will find forty-five taels in my box, of which you may keep the balance after paying for my coffin and burial expenses," he said to the abbot in his letter. "As to my watch, and the other articles on my person, it is known at my home exactly what I brought here with me. . . . If you should dare to meddle with my private affairs, as you have been trying to do these past few days, it will only lead to your being mixed up in the case, which might bring you to grief. All I ask of you is that you notify the Magistrate at once, and that you do not allow women and children to come in and gaze upon my remains. There is nothing strange or abnormal here; death has become an unavoidable duty."

Certainly the memorial was plain-speaking and would have got Wu K'o-tu into severe trouble if he had stayed to receive his punishment. The Empresses, he said, had twice erred, and the present

Emperor had not received his great inheritance as he should have, from the hands of T'ung-chih himself, "but by mandate of the Empresses." He was heir to Hsien-feng, not T'ung-chih. Wu continued, "I therefore beg that the Empresses may be pleased to issue a second Decree explicitly stating that the great inheritance shall hereafter revert to the adopted son of His late Majesty T'ung-chih, and that no Minister shall be allowed to upset this Decree, even though the new Emperor be blessed with a hundred sons. If, in this way, the succession be rectified and the situation defined, so that further confusion be hereafter impossible, the House-law of the present Dynasty will be observed, which requires that the Throne be handed down from father to son." [Bland and Backhouse, *China* . . . , p. 132 *et passim.*]

Wu had outwitted Tzu-hsi. Remote beyond her power, he was triumphant. All she could do was point out that he had made a futile gesture: had she not already decreed exactly what his memorial was demanding? However, she was willing to say it again, and she did. She also gave posthumous honors to the dead hero. If the Chinese are right and ghosts care about such things, the honors must have pleased Wu K'o-tu, but what would undoubtedly please him more was the knowledge that Tzu-hsi was never to forget her promise to him. However adamant her soul, the old man had made his mark on it.

Chapter Thirteen

It sounded like the subject of a boy's book, like so many British international projects. This was on the order of Stanley's exploits in Africa, or could have been if it hadn't gone wrong. The British in India had recently subdued and annexed Burma. Their possessions thus brought them up to the southwestern borders of China. Inevitably their trade-hungry strategists thought of entering China there and setting up commercial relations, like those of the maritime border over on the east. Once already a British expedition under an officer named Sladen had attempted to follow an ancient trade route with this end in view, moving from India up the Irrawaddy to Bhamo and then overland into Yunnan. Sladen had been stopped, but the British were now, in 1874, ready to try again with an expedition under their Colonel Browne.

Browne and his advisers expected no trouble in Burma, but the Chinese border had a bad reputation. It swarmed with tribes who admitted no allegiance to either one country or the other. Outsiders, however, considered them the responsibility of Peking. Browne's people would need passports to cross the border, and the authorities in India sent word to Sir Thomas Wade requesting him to get the necessary documents. Instead of sending them around by sea, which had heretofore been the way the British in Indian-zone possessions and in China dispatched mail to each other, a new method was decided on: the passports would go by hand in the care of Augustus Raymond Margary, a young man from the Peking Consular office. Margary would travel across China and meet the expedition in Burma. A fluent speaker of Chinese, he could then return in his tracks as their guide and interpreter. With an escort of six Chinese Margary set off with the passports. They went by way of the Yangtze and Tungting Lake to Kweichow, Kweiyang, Kunming (then known as Yunnanfu) and Talifu, on to Tengyüeh, and then Manyün at the Burma border, and in spite of the gloomy warnings given them before they set out, had a remarkably easy time of it, meeting with no obstruction from anybody. The only dangers they encountered were natural hazards: broken terrain, tough mountain ranges, rivers without bridges, and a good chance of getting malaria, especially in the Salween Valley, called by the Chinese the Valley of Death. At Manyün Margary approached the official in charge with some natural trepidation, for this was Colonel Li Chen-kuo, known to Peking foreigners as a sort of liaison man between China and Burma —his mother had been Burmese—as well as leader of the gang that had attacked Sladen's expedition and kept it from getting in. Unexpectedly, Colonel Li was charming to Margary, and insisted that the Englishman be his guest as long as he stayed in Manyün. Margary reported to Wade that he was "an exceedingly courteous, intelligent and straightforward man," and that he had done everything he could to help the expedition. [Morse, *International Relations* . . . , Vol. II, p. 267.] Undoubtedly he had his orders from high levels in Peking. The little party had to wait some time at Manyün for a guard of Burmese soldiers who had been sent by Browne to take them on the rest of the way to Burma, through the dangerous bandit country. Finally the Burmese got there, and Margary set out afresh.

It may have been on this leg of the journey that his fate was decided. According to local stories told to the Commissioner of Customs, Mr. Rolla Rouse, stationed in 1934 in Tengyüeh, not only Colonel Li but all the officials along the route had been notified of Margary's imminent journey and were told to be as polite to him as they possibly could. One magistrate not far from Manyün, obeying the Imperial commands, hurried out when he heard the little procession approaching and stood by the roadside bowing deeply to the Englishman's sedan chair as it passed. Unfortunately for his good intentions Margary wasn't in the chair at all. He had got out and was walking in the rear with the soldiers, as he often did when he felt cramped. The chair was not empty, however; Margary had left his little dog in it. The magistrate had bowed to a dog! He felt humiliated to a degree almost impossible for a Westerner to comprehend. To us it would have seemed merely a good joke: to him it was a tremendous loss of face, and he blamed the Englishman for it. Who but an Englishman would have done such an extraordinary thing in the first place? . . . getting out of his honorable chair, and putting a dog into it? The magistrate suspected that the whole thing was a calculated insult. Of course he didn't show his feelings, but perhaps he planned revenge.

Margary with his Chinese and Burmese escort arrived in Bhamo and met Browne in January of 1875. Three weeks later the combined parties began the trek back along the same way the young man had come. They crossed the border without incident, but just afterwards a Burmese slipped a secret warning to Browne that the expedition was going to be ambushed. Taking counsel, the two leaders decided that Margary ought to go ahead with his Chinese and investigate the rumor. After all, he had already become friendly with Colonel Li, and he knew the language and the country. Browne waited where he was, and soon got word from Margary that the latter was with Colonel Li and that everything was safe and quiet. This was the last message ever received from him: Margary and all the Chinese but one, soon after that, were ambushed and murdered. In spite of investigations, nobody has ever been able to declare categorically who killed him, or why. It could have been the outraged magistrate. Mr. Rouse's informant was a Customs officer serving under him who was the magistrate's great-grandson, and who stated that the magistrate had received a grant of land from the Chinese Government as a reward.

At the time Browne didn't realize what had happened, and set off again toward Manyün: before they got there his party was surrounded and attacked, and had a hard fight to get out of it and return to Bhamo.

When Wade heard of the tragedy he was violently angry, which was to be expected. What is more surprising is that he should quickly have attempted to turn it to political advantage. Eight days after getting the news he presented to the Tsungli Yamen a list of demands only three of which had any bearing on the Margary case, though admittedly these were much to the point: a commission of investigation at the border, which should include British officers to act as observers: passports for a second expedition from India, and an indemnity of one hundred and fifty thousand taels. The other demands were far-flung, a grab bag of grievances that had long been waiting for an airing. Wade probably thought that the Tsungli Yamen, because they felt guilty, could be stampeded, so he demanded a more satisfactory form of audience with the Emperor, rearrangement of inland imposts, and various other concessions. The Yamen was not stampeded, and the long wrangle that followed featured a familiar name—Li Hung-chang, who was now Grand Secretary, firmly and purposefully appropriating more and more power. Li held, with his colleagues, that inland taxation had no connection, however remote, with the murder of an Englishman on the Burma border, nor could he perceive a relationship between the murder and the protocol of Imperial audiences. Yunnan was an inland district, he pointed out, so that none of the Maritime Customs rules applied to any hypothetical trade there.

Negotiations went on and on: the inquiry didn't commence at Yunnanfu until May 1876, though it was one point on which the two nations were most nearly agreed. Wade continued to behave like an angry man. He pounded desks, insisted, and used a loud voice, for he had decided that this was the only method by which one could make progress with the Chinese. More than once he threatened that if he and Great Britain didn't get their way they would withdraw from China altogether. It was a prospect that his hosts would have viewed with equanimity if they had not realized that Britain, retired from China, would most certainly return immediately as an invading force. Still the Chinese didn't give way until Wade actually flounced out of Peking and went as far as Shanghai. The Yamen then took alarm and asked him to come back for more talks. He did: again they dug in their heels and again he stormed out. "The petulant and peripatetic plenipotentiary," as Wright calls him [P. 408] covered quite a lot of ground during those months. When the inquiry at the border was concluded, Wade took umbrage because the acting Viceroy of Yunnan, Tsen Yu-ying, had been exonerated of any part in the incident. He demanded that Tsen be put on trial anyway, but the Yamen would not consider it.

All this desk-thumping made a bad impression not only on the Yamen, but on the rest of the diplomatic body. Until then the foreigners had worked together, carefully maintaining a surface appearance of unanimity. This time Wade didn't even go through the motions of inviting his colleagues to talk matters over. His frequent ultimata were unilateral, and the other envoys resented it, and shook their heads, and complained among themselves. Still, Wade finally got results that they had to approve, when the Chinese consented to a new meeting in order to discuss that long-postponed treaty revision. In August 1876, Li Hung-chang came to Chefoo to meet

Sir Thomas and talk it over. Chefoo with its lovely beaches had been adopted by the treaty-port foreigners as a summer resort, and practically everybody in the diplomatic service was there, unofficially, comfortably able to watch what went on. Wade opened the talks with a repetition of his demand for a trial of Viceroy Tsen and other officials. Li Hung-chang refused, as he had steadily done from the beginning. The point was abandoned—Wade no doubt thought the softening-up process had gone on long enough—and they got down to cases on the treaty. First the Yunnan affair was settled. The Chinese agreed that a code of regulations must be drawn up for Burma-Yunnan trade, and that a second expedition could come in as Browne's had tried to do. British officers could be stationed for five years somewhere in the border territory, perhaps Tali. China would pay an indemnity for the assassinations —by this time she was finding the murder of foreigners unrelentingly expensive—and an Imperial letter of regret would be sent to London. The next section dealt with official intercourse and protocol. Li agreed that Chinese ministers and foreign envoys must work out a hard and fast code of etiquette for the reception of foreign diplomats in Chinese cities, and ditto for Chinese diplomats abroad. There was also to be some rearrangement of treaty-port justice administration which would define extraterritoriality more satisfactorily. The third section dealt with trade. Some control was promised over the collection of *likin*. The inland cities of Ichang and Wuhu, and the coast ports of Wenchow and Pakhoi were to be opened as treaty ports: Chungking would get similar treatment as soon as foreign steamers managed to reach the upriver city, through rapids and gorges. Six other towns along the Yangtze, though not declared open for trade, could be used as ports of call. A commission was to examine the question of Hong Kong, which colony had long been a center of trouble. Its government was of course British and not subject in any way to Peking. With impunity, therefore, Hong Kong merchants had steadily refused to permit the installation of a Maritime Customs post anywhere on colony territory, and smuggling was rampant and completely open. Hong Kong's geographical position made her a great trial to the whole Customs system, and Hart had long found himself split between duty to his employers and necessarily cordial relations with the British governor. The Chinese tried to get around the difficulty by setting up a naval patrol around Hong Kong, upon which the in-

dignant Hong Kong merchants declared that they were being blockaded. The patrol was not withdrawn, but it didn't really work
very well. It was high time Hong Kong should be settled.

When the Chefoo Convention was finally hammered out, the other
foreign envoys didn't applaud the result. Critical though they had
been of Wade's highhanded methods, they complained that the final
terms were too easy on the Chinese. Wade's own countrymen in
China said the same thing. But even in criticism the different
diplomats did not present a united front; each had some special
objection apart from that of the others, and as much of the text
couldn't be ratified without common assent, the formal ratification
was delayed for years. However, many of the concessions went into
effect immediately, and the foreigners, in spite of all complaints,
were not above taking advantage of them. The Imperial letter of
apology was carried to London in January '77; after delivering it
the dignitary entrusted with the mission remained in the West to
serve as envoy for the Court in both London and Paris. This was
the first permanent Chinese Legation to be established in Europe,
but others were set up soon afterwards. Hitherto, and often later,
diplomatic work in London was done through Hart and his Commissioner of Customs in the city, J. D. Campbell, the Non-Resident
Secretary.

*   *   *

Peking seemed to her foreign residents a theater for international
drama, but most of the Chinese officials were far more interested
in their domestic affairs and problems than in the West. Until the
war in their northwest entered its post-hostility stages they considered it one of these domestic affairs, and pursued it accordingly,
after their own fashion. Tso Tsung-t'ang, surely one of the most able
generals the nation ever produced, carried on in the traditional
style, with no fuss or hurry, but he introduced one new feature.
Until his day, Chinese soldiers had lived on the land they fought
in, taking food where they found it in the villages, until the wretched
peasants lost all feelings of identity with their own armies and simply
hated armed men of any nation or creed. Even apart from this
bad effect the system was not good, for a commander could never
be sure his men would get enough to feed themselves, no matter
how ruthless their methods of robbery. Tso Tsung-t'ang thought

of a way around the problem. Wherever his army camped for a sufficient length of time—and Chinese wars could be static for months on end, consisting as they did of one siege after another—he made the men plant crops for themselves. They became self-supporting, and could carry on indefinitely without impoverishing the country-side to an extent where they would have to move out. No one in China had ever seen anything like it. By the middle of 1878 Tso was able to send to Peking the proud report that the war was over, the Northwest pacified, and the insurgent Mohammedans either whipped into submission or gone into lands beyond the border. All of Turkestan had been recovered, Kashgaria was quiet, and the revolt was finished, but one of the war's side effects, the Russian occupation of Ili, remained.

The Russians had promised that their occupation was not to be permanent; that they would get out as soon as the war was over. In all likelihood they had not expected the time would ever come when they would be called on to keep the pledge: they had underesti-mated the genius of Tso Tsung-t'ang. Now they showed no signs of withdrawing. The Chinese Government waited a decent length of time, but at the end of the year they sent an ambassador extraordi-nary to St. Petersburg, to arrange matters. They were now com-pletely broken in to the idea of international diplomacy, but there was still a dearth of trained men for such tasks, and the Yamen chose to send Chunghow, that same Manchu who was involved in the after-math of the Tientsin massacre. No doubt they thought he would be good at the new task, because he had already been to Europe and could rate as an expert in foreign affairs. Poor Chunghow was not at all equal to the job. The Russians outtalked and outguessed him, and after nine months in St. Petersburg he had made no head-way whatever. He must have been dizzy, for he signed—in a Black Sea resort called Livadia—a treaty that was disastrous; news of its terms startled all the West, let alone rendering Peking aghast. In it Russia got everything she could possibly want. The northern, richest part of Ili was ceded to her, as were the mountain passes commanding all the region. Russians were to have free access to western China and could trade as and where they liked. Because they argued that they had done China valuable service during the campaign by policing the district for Peking, and asked to be paid, Chunghow promised them five million rubles for that.

Naturally when the poor fellow returned to Peking he was rushed

into prison on the spot. For official reason the government gave
the same one they had used to explain the imprisonment of Ch'i-ying
in the old days: they said that Chunghow had returned from St.
Petersburg without waiting for the Imperial mandate to give up
his post. But since Ch'i-ying's day times had changed, and the diplomatic corps, with their odd Western notions of justice, set up a
howl of protest, saying that it was shameful to punish a man for
failure if he had done nothing wrong. The Russian chargé, who
rightly felt that it was more his affair than anybody else's, led a
protest movement. In his footsteps all the envoys expressed shocked
surprise at what was happening to Chunghow. For a while it looked
as if they were doing the poor Manchu no favor, as if the government didn't care a bit what foreigners might think and furthermore
didn't have time to reply to sentimental protests, for the Grand
Council was overwhelmed with memorials of quite another nature
that poured in from indignant Chinese officials. An influential censor
named Chang Chih-tung wrote at length, demanding that Chunghow be decapitated, since—as Chang said—this was the only convincing manner by which China could demonstrate how firmly she
repudiated the Treaty of Livadia. Chunghow *was* tried and condemned to death by decapitation, but luckily for him, before the
sentence could be carried out a good many incidents intervened.
Punishment of Chunghow was not the only preoccupation of the
Chinese: many of them were so stirred up that they were keen to
declare war on Russia. For once it might have been a feasible idea.
Tso Tsung-t'ang's seasoned troops were still there in the Northwest,
ready to go. The Manchus, however, were chronically averse to
making war, since if things went against their army they might
well be unseated.

While Peking seethed and Chunghow waited fearfully in his
cell, a little comedy played itself out. Fifteen years after his triumph
against the Taipings, in the spring of 1880, Charles George
"Chinese" Gordon was in India serving as private secretary to the
Viceroy, Lord Ripon. Time had not modified his eccentricity. He
did not at all like being Ripon's secretary, and as June rolled around
he handed in his resignation from the post. Unlike many of Gordon's
resignations, this was a conventional one, an act he was privileged
to commit without at the same time giving up his army commission.
He was still in India waiting for further orders from the War Office

when he got a telegram from Peking, from his old friend Robert Hart:

"I am directed to invite you to China. Please come and see for yourself; this opportunity for doing really useful work on a large scale ought not to be lost. Work, position, conditions can all be arranged with yourself here to your satisfaction. Do take six weeks leave and come." [Wright, p. 484.]

The cable was the fruit of many worried talks between Wade and Hart, who had become alarmed by the threat of Russian trade in China; such trade had always been led, though not monopolized, by the British, and even Hart with his adopted allegiance could hardly be pleased by the new developments. The two men would not have minded if things came to a pitch where the bellicose Chinese had their way and declared war on Russia, but if that moment arrived they wanted a few British officers ready to help, just as foreigners had done against the Taipings. Getting ready, Sir Thomas warned the Admiralty and War Office in London that they might possibly be called on to give leave—quietly—to some of their men, and Hart at the same time sent that cable to Gordon. Gordon, who couldn't possibly have known the facts behind it, leaped to the conclusion that Hart had been told by Li Hung-chang to send it. Gordon had long since forgiven the Grand Secretary for his part in that affair of the Soochow Huans. He was delighted with the offer. Without going through the formality of asking the War Office to grant him leave, he sent word informing them that he was on his way to China, a typically highhanded act that much annoyed his superior officers. As time went on their annoyance mounted, for Gordon all the way along the line gave interviews to reporters announcing what he intended to do when he got to China. He said he would do his utmost to dissuade the Chinese from war with Russia. This might well have infuriated the Chinese themselves, since such statements could have bolstered the Russians and made them balkier than ever. Fortunately all the reporters, typically skeptical, wrote in their dispatches that Gordon was no doubt merely covering up his real intentions, and was on his way to lead a new Ever Victorious Army. The War Office sent cables telling Gordon that he couldn't *have* leave. Gordon, who by this time had covered more than half the journey, promptly tendered his resignation from the army. The War Office refused to accept it. It was much like the good old days, and no doubt Gordon thoroughly enjoyed himself. Next, the War Office climbed down and asked Gordon for his assurance that he would at least not take military service in China, since such action, especially after all the publicity, would gravely embarrass Britain. Gordon gave his promise, and everybody calmed down for a while.

The trouble with all this was that Li Hung-chang had not been the instigator of the invitation to Gordon, and didn't know anything about it until the Englishman arrived in Shanghai. When Gordon discovered his mistake he was angry. Through the years he had grown more and more short-tempered, if that were possible. He didn't like much what he found in Shanghai, and was disappointed in his old Chinese comrades in arms when he met them and found them disinclined, at their advanced ages, to go adventuring once again. He blamed Hart for his embarrassment, and blew up in rage when he got a letter from Hart in Peking telling him to come straight up to the capital, bypassing Tientsin and Li Hung-chang. Hart's reason for this was that Li had been becoming more and more obstructive of Customs activity, resenting the Service's power, but Gordon took the directive as a personal affront, not to mention a challenge. He went straight to Tientsin to call on Li. A conversation with the Viceroy so impressed his weathercock mind that he telegraphed the British War Office once again and said that he was withdrawing his promise: he *would* take military service in China if necessary: he would stand by Li Hung-chang to the bitter end. How Li felt about all this is impossible to guess, but he may have found Gordon's emotional partisanship rather overpowering, even if gratifying. The Englishman proceeded to give him a long lecture that embodied quantities of peremptory advice, then went off abruptly to Peking to arrange matters there. In Peking, coldly ignoring Hart, he gave much more advice to the Tsungli Yamen. The gentlemen did not care for the substance of his counsel, and it could hardly be expected that they would. Gordon said they should avoid war with Russia at all costs, even if it meant paying an indemnity, but if war could not be staved off, they must move the Emperor and all the government to central China, and then conduct guerrilla activities, since they wouldn't have a chance otherwise. It was a statement that made even the Manchus raise their eyebrows. Gordon continued: China's forts and ships were no good at all. It would take the Russians two months at the outside to get to Peking. To go to war would be idiocy.

"Idiocy" was a strong word, too strong to be used to the Yamen's proud ministers, and the interpreter refused to translate it into Chinese. Gordon grabbed a dictionary that lay on the table, found the word for himself, and pointed out the Chinese translation to the ministers, so that there might be no mistake. Then he marched out of the meeting and Peking, going back to Tientsin and Li Hung-chang.

Hart wrote once a fortnight on all matters to J. D. Campbell in London, and of Gordon he reported: "Gordon is still at Tientsin. Very eccentric. Spending hours in prayer, and then acting on inspiration . . . has thrown up his commission—and will probably have a row, and throw up Li in a few days."

He was absolutely right. A few days later he wrote in another letter, "Gordon, poor fellow, after throwing up his commission to throw in his lot with Li, has now said good-bye to Li, and is on his way home again, and after writing to denounce me at the Legations and refusing to come near me in Peking, has now written to withdraw his letters, as he found he was mistaken. Much as I like and respect him, I must say he is 'not all there.' Whether it is religion or vanity, or softening of the brain—I don't know, but he seems to be alternately arrogant and slavish, vain and humble, in his senses and out of them. It's a great pity." [Wright, p. 486.]

Whatever ailed Gordon—and there are various theories as to that—the War Office at least still wanted him, and once more refused his resignation. He never went back to China. Five years later he came to his end in a very different sort of country, heroic and peculiar as ever.

To nobody's surprise Peking renounced the Treaty of Livadia, and Russia had to agree to reopen negotiations. The atmosphere of Peking grew calmer, a welcome change for Chunghow. Queen Victoria had sent a message to Tzu-hsi about him, and Wade added his assurance that the British would take the Manchu's execution very ill. Other foreign voices chimed in, fortified by the advice of one of China's own diplomats, the Marquis Tseng, a son of Tseng Kuo-fan and envoy to London and Paris. The Marquis too thought Chunghow should be spared, and at last the authorities commuted the unlucky minister's sentence to imprisonment, saving face by announcing that their decision had been reached because they wanted to show that China had no wish to hurt Russia's dignity. Later Chunghow bought his way out of prison, and in 1884 was restored, more or less, to Imperial favor. Wisely, from that time on he stayed out of public life.

For the new negotiations Peking named the Marquis Tseng, who was obviously not so guileless as his predecessor. They took no chances this time, however, and sent two foreigners with him as watchdogs, one of them a Commissioner of the Customs. Tseng set out for St. Petersburg in July 1880. Fortunately for China, Gordon had been far too gloomy in his summing up of the situation as far as Russia was concerned: the Russians did not share his contempt for China's military potential. Tso's troop movements worried them because they knew they couldn't guard the long Manchurian border adequately, and they had no illusions about their ability to march to Peking in two months' time. Altogether Tseng should have had an easy time working out a treaty satisfactory to his superiors, if it hadn't been for the vacillations of those superiors in Peking, who kept sending contradictory directions. Even so, he managed fairly well. His other adviser, Halliday Macartney, wrote to J. D. Campbell in London:

"They give us back the Tekkes valley and all the passes between Ili and Kashgaria ceded to them by Chunghow; still we shall not, as I fondly hoped we would, get back the whole territory of Ili. A part of that ceded to the Russians . . . will also be restored to us. . . . In the free-trade area which Chunghow opened to Russian commerce, Russian markets are only to enjoy this immunity until the cities shall have so far recovered from the effects of the rebellion as to be able to bear the imposition of a duty. The Russian caravans coming from Eastern Turkestan to be stopped, whereas Chunghow had given them permission to continue their march through the country to Hankow." [Morse, *International Relations* . . . , Vol. II, p. 338.] It was true that the indemnity had been increased from five to nine million rubles, but on the whole the treaty was a good one, and represented the first diplomatic triumph ever won by China. Not bad, thought the foreigners, for people who until a few years before had thought of intercourse with the outside world only in terms of war or tribute collection.

* * *

The year 1881 was marked by a milestone for the strong-minded Western Empress. For some time her co-Regent Tzu-an had been ailing: in March she suddenly died, and the inevitable rumor quickly started up in the city that she had been poisoned by Tzu-hsi. It was an accusation not wholly unreasonable. The dead woman had been only forty-five. Palace attendants, who always claimed to know everything that went on inside the walls, had overheard the two Empresses having one of their frequent violent quarrels not long before the death. The subject of their quarrel this time was one that often caused trouble in the palace; Tzu-hsi's favorite, the chief eunuch Li Lien-ying. The Eastern Empress had resented his arrogant manners, and taunted her co-Regent with the fact that his nickname among the populace was "Lord of Nine Thousand Years," a clever play on the Emperor's familiar title "Lord of Ten Thousand Years." Had the quarrel been enough of an irritation to Tzu-hsi to cause her to commit murder? It has never been proved, but the death of the Eastern Empress removed from Tzu-hsi's path one of the two people she considered her greatest enemies. The other one, Prince Kung, was still there, but the Empress knew how to wait for a good opening. Three years later she saw her chance and seized it, during the war with France.

Two of China's struggles with the outside world coincided at this time. To avoid confusion it is better to take them up separately, though developments on each front sometimes dovetailed with those on the other.

The Browne expedition to Yunnan, ill-starred though it was, sharpened France's ambitions in the East. She too wished to trade in Yunnan, and had for a long time made advances to this end in her steady encroachments south of the border in Annam, China's tributary. The French had gained a protectorate over Cambodia, which was the southernmost section of Annam, and had also taken possession of Saigon and three provinces in Cochin China, north of Cambodia. The last section separating them from China was that which lay between the border and Cochin China—Tongking. If only they could get a foothold in Tongking, they reasoned, their traders would be able to move in and out easily by means of the Red River, which ran from Hanoi straight into Yunnan. In 1874 French troops captured Hanoi. The King of Annam, who still considered himself a tributary monarch, appealed to Peking for help and got it in the shape of a band of soldiers known as the Black Flags. (Manchu-governed soldiers, it will be remembered, were called Bannermen.) The Black Flags shoved the invaders out of Hanoi and cleared them off the Red River: France was still recovering from the Franco-Prussian War and couldn't yet bring much weight to bear on them. A little later, however, the King signed the Treaty of 1874 with the French and the Westerners got back much of the advantage they had briefly lost: France "recognized the independence" of Annam and promised to protect the King from (other) foreign aggression and internal disorder, in return for which Hanoi and some river ports were opened to French trade all along the Red River, from the sea as far as Hokow in Yunnan.

This represented a transfer of allegiance from China's ancient suzerainty, and she protested. The King of Annam was an unwilling party to the new, forced friendship, and he persisted in sending the usual tribute to Peking at the proper times, in 1876 and 1880, during which occasions the Annamese envoys ignored the French legation and appealed to their old overlord for protection. After the 1880 visit the Marquis Tseng, as envoy in Paris, also protested, but he could get no satisfaction and French pressure went on building up in Annam.

Perhaps the gloomy prophecies made by some of the foreign envoys, that China's success in the Northwest would go to her head, were justified. In any case the Yamen didn't take the French actions lying down. In 1881 French traders on the way from Hanoi to Yunnan were attacked by Black Flag soldiers, and the French commanded the King of Annam to expel the "mercenaries" from his territory. He did not expel them—it is doubtful if he could have done so even if he had wished to—and the French again occupied Hanoi with a small force. After that the Chinese and French reverted to negotiation for a year, but in 1883 the French adopted a more belligerent approach and sent a strong expedition to Tongking. They easily subdued the Annamese forces and established themselves in several places close to China's boundaries and far too close for comfort to Canton.

Great Britain and America did not care for this development, though naturally they were not as alarmed as the Chinese themselves. The American envoy eagerly offered his services as mediator, but France did not in the least wish to negotiate. Hostilities continued in seesaw fashion, a number of minor engagements marked sometimes by a Black Flag victory, sometimes by a French. One of these latter gave Tzu-hsi the chance she was waiting for, when in the early spring of 1884 some junks on the Min River in the vicinity of Foochow were destroyed by French troops. As soon as the news reached Peking the Empress dismissed Prince Kung, with all his associates on the Grand Council, from their offices; the Imperial decree announcing this action referred to the Prince's attitude of "self-confident and callous contentment with the sweets of office." [Bland and Backhouse, *China* . . . , p. 155.] The men appointed in their places were not given the power their predecessors had held. Tzu-hsi brought in a change that the Court considered very dangerous, by declaring that from that time on the Grand Council, before bringing anything of an urgent character to the attention of the Throne, should confer with Prince Ch'un, father of the Emperor and also of course her own brother-in-law. The usual swarm of protests from the memorialists buzzed about the Empress, but she brushed them off. There was now no co-Regent or Prince Kung to oppose her.

She was supported by the fact that it appeared the French trouble might soon be settled. A young Chinese Customs officer, a German named Gustav Detring, who had served as Commissioner in Tientsin and grown very friendly with Li Hung-chang, was transferred to Canton where he got acquainted with some French officers. Detring had a taste and a flair for political intrigue, qualities which made Sir Robert Hart rather wary of him; in fact, Hart had deliberately moved him from Tientsin for this very reason. But Detring continued to pull strings, and in the south he so wangled matters that a document called the Li-Fournier Convention, after Li Hung-chang and one of Detring's French acquaintances, was signed in May '84, and seemed likely to end the threat of all-out war between the two nations. Fighting continued, however, for another year before a truce was called. During all that time France maintained the fiction that she was not at war, though at the end of August Peking declared that the situation could not be described in any other manner. In Foochow, says Morse [*International Relations* . . . , Vol. II, p. 359], French and Chinese fleets "lay facing each other for five weeks watching each other and showing their teeth; but it is characteristic of the situation that, on August 16th, all, including the French, dressed ship in celebration of the birthday of the emperor of China." Before the end of the affair the French blockaded Formosa and the British announced that they, too, considered a state of war to be existing. It was more like a slow-motion minuet than a war, but battles did take place; some lives were being lost; Hart for one was gravely worried about his whole Service. The French said they would intercept all rice-carrying vessels sailing from ports north of

Canton, and as most of these ships were British or American, the merchants protested and so did their governments. Long before the fighting ceased everyone was tired, but neither France nor China would give in until in January 1885, Hart got permission to act as mediator through Campbell in London. In April the combatants signed a protocol ratifying the Li-Fournier Convention terms, by which France's suzerainty over Annam was admitted and the French could trade in Yunnan, but for the Chinese side the Black Flags were not forced to retire inland, and the indemnity which France had claimed and for which she had fought for the past year would not be paid. The French were glad to ratify and be done with it, but the Chinese, especially some fire-eaters far away in Peking, were not so happy, and gave in only after further delay.

The document was signed in Paris by the French President for France and Campbell on behalf of China. Both the French and Chinese governments were delighted with Hart's success, and the President of France made him a Grand Officer of the Legion of Honor. But the Customs Service did not come out of the affair quite unscathed. Li Hung-chang was offended because he hadn't been called in for the final negotiations. Throughout the year's discussions Sir Robert had dealt direct with the Yamen, and Li did not like being bypassed, and held it against Hart. Then too, Detring and his friend Fournier were jealous of Hart's triumph, which was natural—it was their convention in the first place—but was not conducive to harmony in the Service. Hart had stolen Detring's thunder, the younger man felt.

We must now go back a few years to consider the Korean affair. Advised by China as her suzerain to open her doors to the West, Korea signed treaties with Japan and the five Western nations of America, Great Britain, Germany, Italy, and Russia. There was a good deal of anti-foreign sentiment in Korean hearts, especially that of the King's father, the Regent, and it broke out in July 1882. A mob set on the Japanese Legation and killed some of its inmates, then marched on the palace with intent to murder the Queen, who was the most unpopular member of the royal family. They failed to get hold of her. By that time both China and Japan had sent in forces to impose order. Both countries got something out of it: Japan an indemnity, and China possession of the King's father, whom they carried off and imprisoned in Paotingfu, where he was brainwashed, or, as they called the process in those days, re-educated. The Tsungli Yamen was determined to bolster China's suzerainty in Korea. They told Sir Robert Hart to set up a Maritime Customs Service there, which though separate and distinct from the Chinese Service should be kept under his general management. Hart did so, but when it came to selecting the local head of the Service the choice was taken out of his hands; Li Hung-chang appointed his own candidate, von Möllendorf, a German already on the staff in China. Like Detring, von Möllendorf liked to pull political strings, and Hart disapproved of him for the same reason he distrusted Detring, but the Service was now so big that Hart could no longer manage everything just as he would have liked, and von Möllendorf took up the new appointment in Seoul. The post was much to his liking, for he was expected to serve not only as I.G. in Korea, but as foreign adviser to the King as well. Surveying the situation, he decided that Russian influence was what the country needed. Secretly he entered into an understanding with the Russians, promising to use his influence on their behalf.

The Japanese had an excellent intelligence service and must have heard about von Möllendorf's promises as soon as they were made. Already they had reached the same conclusion as Hart about the danger of Korea's falling into the grip of the Bear. The Japanese were possibly—probably—at the back of a new mob action that flared up in Seoul the night of December 4, 1884, at the inauguration banquet of the Postal Service set up by von Möllendorf. A rabble broke into the banqueting hall and murdered the postmaster general, an important Korean: other officials rushed to the palace to save the King, and took him for safekeeping to the Japanese Legation. Ready on the mark, the Japanese envoy called out his guard. Very soon afterwards the Chinese envoy, Yuan Shih-k'ai, called out *his* guard too, but by the time they got into action Japanese soldiers had occupied the palace and other important points. The two forces met and clashed, and the Chinese drove the Japanese soldiers out of Seoul all the way to the port, Chemulpo, and aboard one of their steamers, while in Seoul the townspeople fell on every Japanese they could find. Several were killed. Later both China and Japan sent warships to Korea, but the Annam affair was still keeping the Tsungli Yamen busy, and as Tokyo well knew, they didn't have the means to back up their gesture. In the end Korea made an apology to Japan, and though justice did not warrant it, on the advice of Sir Harry Parkes, who had just been moved from

Tokyo to serve in Peking as envoy, she also agreed to pay an indemnity. Parkes could judge both sides and knew what might happen if Peking took too provocative and defiant a line with Tokyo.

Even so, the Japanese were determined to push the matter as far as they could. In the early spring of 1885 the Japanese Premier himself, Count Ito, descended on China to talk over the Korean problem. He declared that he made the trip because China's representative in Seoul was not important enough for such weighty considerations, and when he arrived in Tientsin he infuriated Li Hung-chang by saying that he wasn't sure if even the Viceroy would do. No, said Count Ito, he must proceed to Peking and talk to Tzuhsi herself. The impact of such an outrage had hardly made itself felt when Li and the Japanese noble learned that France and China had signed the protocol and made peace. Immediately Count Ito's attitude changed, losing its belligerence, and he came to an agreement with Li: both countries would withdraw their forces from Korea on the understanding that either could bring them back if necessary, after giving due warning to the other nation. (Diplomats still professed in those days to follow such rules of sportsmanship.) The two men agreed that a Korean army must be created: such an army must be organized and trained during the next four months. Of course four months would not really be enough, but those were the terms mentioned.

In March that same year, 1885, Sir Harry Parkes suddenly died. At his funeral Sir Robert Hart received a telegram offering him the vacant post of British Minister at Peking, and his reactions were sadly mixed. He was flattered, dismayed, tempted, and hesitant all at once. For twenty-four years the Customs had been his life and to a great extent his personal creation. Did he want to abandon it? On the other hand, he was fifty years old, which at that time seemed a considerably advanced age for a foreigner in China, and he had often suffered painfully from periods of hopelessness, especially during the Annam crisis when it had seemed for a while as if the whole Service would be destroyed. The post offered to him was better than that which Parkes had held: Hart would be plenipotentiary extraordinary. It was flattering. It was a great honor. . . . Hart cabled to his wife asking her advice. He warned her that if he accepted the offer he would get less pay and probably no pension, and it might also mean that his retirement would be postponed. Nevertheless it would be a splendid way to finish off a career. . . . "Why not try it?" he wrote musingly to Campbell. Lady Hart thought he should, and he made up his mind to do so.

There remained, however, the question of who would take over as I.G. Sir Robert's brother James had worked with him for years and knew his methods. With James in his place, Hart was sure the Service would be safe. Like so many men in those privileged days, Sir Robert would not have suspected himself for a minute of nepotism: it was not that James was his brother, he would have said, but that James was the right man for the job. His friends in the Yamen declared themselves agreeable to the suggestion. Certainly in their philosophy any accusation of nepotism was no argument against the appointment of James: it was just what they would have done themselves. It all seemed settled. In London Sir Robert's credentials as Minister were drawn up and signed and practically on their way, when he heard something that gravely disturbed him, that it was by no means certain, after all, that James Hart could step into his shoes. Li Hung-chang seemed to be engineering things so that the post would go instead to the Viceroy's favorite, Detring. Detring, a German! Sir Robert couldn't have that. Detring would be the worst possible I.G.: Detring lived in Li Hung-chang's pocket. Sir Robert turned down the offer and stayed where he was.

*　　*　　*

The next Korean crisis was brought on by Britain. She became involved in a serious dispute with Russia concerning the border of Afghanistan. Li Hung-chang's differences of opinion with Sir Robert Hart were not on a national basis; he favored Great Britain when it came to taking sides with Western powers, and at this time he was eager, even overeager, to signify that China wanted to back Britain against Russia. He pressed for a formal Anglo-Chinese alliance, but the British were in a hurry and felt they could not wait until such an alliance could be formally concluded: they wanted a naval base somewhere near Vladivostok, and they took one. In May 1885, British naval forces occupied Port Hamilton, a roadway among a group of little islands off the southern point of Korea, without so much as a by-your-leave to Korea or China. The Chinese were as surprised as the Russians by such arbitrary action, and they were not pleased, but matters had reached the stage where they could no longer put up a bold front. Instead, swallowing their chagrin, they suggested that the *fait accompli* be marked by official permission from Peking for a temporary occupation of Port Hamilton. It would save face for them and also emphasize their suzerainty over Korea. Immediately, however, Russia and Japan protested. Russia announced that if the British remained in Port Hamilton she would occupy some other place nearby, probably Port Lazareff. The argument had been going on briskly for several days before a small, forgotten voice was heard—Korea's. A Korean deputation including von Möllendorf came from Seoul to Port Hamilton to make a formal protest to the British Admiral Dowell. Von Möllendorf was eager to force a showdown; it was a good chance to get the upper hand for Russia. Already he had told his Russian friends that he would soon be able to arrange that the new Korean army be trained by Russian officers. The Korean Government learned of this promise just after the mission went to Port Hamilton, and did not like it. Koreans have always been notably stubborn and independent, a trait no doubt due in part to their unfortunate geographical position. Few nations have been so much fought over and traversed by other people: the Koreans have small reason to love anybody except themselves, and they were enraged when they found their foreign adviser preparing to sell them out to Russia. They threw out von Möllendorf. It was typical of the oddly unrancorous spirit of Hart and his Chinese Customs Service generally that von Möllendorf managed later to get himself reinstated there.

The Tsungli Yamen continued its attempts to bargain with Britain over Port Hamilton, and tried to make the British promise protection for Korea in case of a Russian attack. They got nowhere. British ships remained in Port Hamilton until the Russians had given a pledge not to occupy Korean territory, even if the coast became clear. Not until 1887 were the British satisfied, and then their ships sailed away. This was a cavalier way to treat China, but such an attitude was becoming the general rule among Western nations rather than the exception. Almost without realizing it themselves, the foreigners had fallen into a habit of treating the Empire with amiable contempt.

Chapter Fourteen

China has given no offence—has done no wrong—does not wish to fight, and is willing to make sacrifices: She is a big 'sick man,' convalescing very slowly from the sickening effects of peaceful centuries, and is being jumped on when down by this agile, healthy, well-armed Jap—will no one pull him off?"

This passage was in a letter from Sir Robert Hart to Campbell, written at the crucial moment, in 1894, when the Japanese had at last succeeded in precipitating a showdown battle with China over Korea. Japan was well prepared for it, having planned the war for years past. The Chinese were not. The fact was, Korea had progressed too fast to suit Tokyo. The Maritime Customs Service that Hart set up was well managed, and provided a steady source of income for the government. Korea had even paid off a small debt she owed to Japan, a payment that did not gratify the recipient. The Japanese had hoped to possess Korea through default and weakness. Russia shared Japan's fears of a strong Korea, but it was Japan that finally took action.

When von Möllendorf's plans for getting Russians to train the new Korean army fell through, the vacuum was filled in the obvious way by the Chinese. Li Hung-chang appointed Yuan Shih-k'ai, a promising young general, to oversee the task. Consequently the troops were shaped according to Chinese fashion, and, as the King was already pro-Peking, Korea became more and more Sinicized. This tendency was disapproved of by the Japanese, but they bided their time and waited for the right moment to strike. It seemed to arrive in April of 1894, when the pro-Japanese Korean, Kim Ok Kiun, who had plotted to bring about the *coup* of '84, was lured out of Tokyo where he had found refuge, and persuaded to go to Shanghai. There he was assassinated by the son of the postmaster general of

Seoul who lost his own life as a result of the abortive attempt. At the same time a similar plot against another pro-Japanese Korean who lived in Japan was nearly successful. The near-victim escaped, but two such outbreaks spelled far more than coincidence to Japan's secret service, and nobody was surprised when those officials declared they had traced the origin of both actions to the King of Korea. The impatience of Tokyo's militarist party could not be brooked much longer; they were delighted when the Tong Hak Society of Korea gave them their chance.

Originally the Tong Haks had been something of a metaphysical society dedicated to the promulgation of Eastern religions, but it had long since changed into a rebellious group that demanded reform of many kinds, including the expulsion of all foreigners from the country. Agitators who had their own causes to promote were glad to use the Tong Haks, but nothing important came of them until 1893, a bad year, when famine led to widespread distress and unrest. The Tong Haks were able to enlist large numbers of new members, and even more people joined them the following year when a number of new taxes were levied on the populace. Then the starving people, mainly those of the south, in the name of the Tong Hak Society rose up in rebellion. They made rapid headway against the ordinary militia. In May, a month after the assassination of Kim Ok Kiun, the situation was so alarming that the King sent to Peking, asking for help against the "bandits," a euphemism for insurgents that was to be used more than once again in this part of the world before long.

It was exactly the development the Japanese had been waiting for. In the treaty agreement of '85, China and Japan had pledged to each other that if one nation found it necessary to send armed men into Korea it would immediately inform the other. But China took her time about this matter of the King of Korea, and the Japanese tried to hurry things up. A man from the Japanese Legation called on Yuan Shih-k'ai, asking why Peking had not yet dispatched troops and urging the general to press the matter with Li Hung-chang. Yuan agreed with him and did so. Li then sent off 1500 men, on the same day duly informing Tokyo of his action. Almost immediately after that Yuan heard the disturbing news that Japanese troops, too, were on the way, on the point of landing at Inchon, though Tokyo had said nothing of this to Peking. Yuan, alarmed, asked the Japanese diplomatic body what it all signified, but the officials assured him that their forces were coming only to defend Japanese nationals in Korea from possible danger. Later they admitted that the soldiers might also, just possibly, help the King against the bandits, but they repeated that Japan had no other intentions in Korea: as soon as the rebellion was quashed, the men would go. Li Hung-chang was not a fool: he believed none of the assurances. He knew that Chinese and Japanese troops together in Korea spelled trouble, and he tried to undo the action already taken by commanding his army to halt where it was, in the south. Indeed, if there had been time he would have called his men back to China, for he knew how badly prepared they were. But Japan acted too swiftly for this: her troops kept pouring in. By June twenty-first fifteen thousand Japanese in uniform were stationed at Inchon, Pusan, and Seoul. Chinese armed troops in Korea numbered only half as many. The rebellion that had brought on the situation was now forgotten in Peking; the Chinese would have been grateful of any way to pull out. Then the Japanese put their cards on the table, ignoring the various requests they kept getting from the Western nations to agree to a mutual withdrawal of troops. They would not move, they announced, until Korea declared herself independent and the King reformed his government in the way they thought it should be done. Helpless, the King had no recourse, and the Koreans set to work on the reformation. Naturally, however, it dragged, and the Japanese hardly pretended to wait. A month later, July 22, they marched into Seoul, kidnaped the royal family and imprisoned them in the Japanese Legation, and put the King's father, Tai Won Kun, back on the throne to act as Regent.

Through all of this the Chinese troops were paralyzed, without orders to act. Li Hung-chang was under bitter attack at home because of what had happened. At last he was forced to apply strong measures, though he knew well that it would be hopeless. He sent more troops, but it was so much waste. At the end of the month the Japanese Emperor declared war on China, and the dreary game continued. The struggle was pitifully one-sided. Wherever the Japanese chose to go they went, meeting little or no resistance from the Chinese troops, who were old-fashioned in training and weapons. Li's men were chased out of Korea: the Japanese followed them into Shantung and Manchuria, then captured and occupied Weihaiwei and Port Arthur. By March 1895, it was all over and the Chinese had to sue for peace—the most humiliating defeat any of them could remember.

Worse followed. In the Treaty of Shimonoseki China recognized Korea's "independence" and relinquished all claims to suzerainty. She ceded to Japan Formosa and the Pescadores, as well as a piece of Manchurian territory called the Liaotung Peninsula, but this latter cession, on the peremptory demand of Russia, was canceled shortly afterward. China promised to pay an indemnity of 200,000,000 taels—a sum that was increased when the Liaotung Peninsula bargain fell through—and opened four more ports, including Chungking, to trade. At the same time she agreed to draw up a treaty of commerce with Japan; until then, Japan had not been included in the most-favored-nation group. Now Japanese could trade wherever they wished. Before, they hadn't been permitted to travel in the interior: now they could reside in China, set up industries, and manufacture articles for sale on Chinese soil. On the face of it the Treaty of Shimonoseki would not alter the position of other foreigners in China, but actually it was of extreme importance to the Western merchants. From now on machinery could be brought in and factories built. Japan would be able to manufacture piece goods of silk and cotton in China's vast hinterland, underselling British products. British plaints were drowned, however, in the rejoicing that was heard from the other foreigners, since because of the most-favored-nation clause they too were now made free of the country. Everyone talked about concessions and leases for this and that. Everyone snatched.

Years of isolation had done the unfortunate China an ill service. The mystery enhanced what foreigners thought of as her potential value: Westerners were convinced that behind the curtain must lie vast fortunes. The French immediately organized an exploration mission for Yunnan, Szechuan, Hunan, and Kweichow, to search for treasure—gold, copper, tin, rubies, and sapphires: gums, varnishes, ivory, musk, and flax: horses that in French imagination outdid the prides of Araby. Jernigan, the American Consul at Shanghai, complained sorrowfully that his nation alone was backward in taking advantage of the treasure hunt.

"The establishment of a bank in China or Japan by American capitalists would, at least, give the color of permanency to American enterprise in China. China, being a country incomparable in resources, and acknowledged to be the wealthiest in the world, the question may well be asked, why should not American capitalists recognize a primary principle in the extension of the trade relations of their country?" [U.S. Circulars, Foreign Markets, 1895.]

Peking soon discovered that her defeat by Japan was even more tragic than had been supposed, and nothing like so simple. The gates were thrown open to plunderers from everywhere. It is true that Jernigan, at least, didn't get his way regarding the bank. The United States Government was not interested in the hurly-burly of grabs which the other Western nations had joined, but that one omission made small difference to unhappy China. European nations were much on the spot, each clamoring for the privilege of lending the money Peking must have, with which to pay Japan. With their shares the Western countries rapidly expanded their privileges. Like a pack of wolves they slashed at China, each attempting to tear off the biggest piece. It looked for a while as if their victim would be openly partitioned between them, but the problem was too complicated: nobody wanted to go to war, especially as the Westerners found themselves able to do well by peaceful means. Therefore, France edged in closer from Indo-China and got the concession for a new railway in the southwest.

Britain moved in similar fashion along the border from British-controlled Burma. Russia proceeded to switch the Trans-Siberian railway from the north and run its lines straight across Manchuria. She had every intention of increasing her strength in that province and leasing Kiaochow Bay, but in '97 the Germans outwitted her by taking advantage of a massacre of German missionaries: they moved into Tsingtao on the bay and forced Peking to let them have concessions in Shantung, where the massacre had occurred. To counter their influence the Russians occupied Port Arthur and Talienwan in the long-disputed Liaotung Peninsula, and in 1898 Peking granted them a 25-year lease on the territory containing the two ports. France promptly grabbed a much longer lease—99 years—on Kwangchowwan in Kwangtung. Not to be outdone, Britain took a lease of similar length on the New Territories across the water from Hong Kong, and also moved into Weihaiwei on the understanding that they would stay there as long as Russia had Port Arthur.

Competitive as the Western nations were, they were allied against their prey. Once the broad outlines of their gains were described, they came to an amicable arrangement of the so-called "spheres of interest." Russia's accepted sphere was Manchuria and other northern areas, France had Hainan and the provinces north of Tonkin, Japan kept her hand on Fukien. Indeed, Japan didn't profit from her winning of the Korean war as much as the other nations: she was still too small and weak to defend herself against the West. Germany had Shantung, and Great Britain the Yangtze provinces. Each nation promised not to trespass on the sphere of another. Each nation held that it was entitled to develop—economically at least—the territory of its own sphere. At first glance the absence from this line-up of America seems remarkable: for a while there was a bit of American money in the railway concession from Hankow to Canton, but the businessmen involved allowed themselves to be bought out. However, it was not because of ethics that the United States refrained from joining the pack. She simply didn't have much investment capital seeking a home, because there was still plenty of American territory awaiting development.

America's disinterested position in the Far East lent authority to the "open door" policy set forth by Secretary of State John Hay. Late in 1899 Hay sent a note to the Europeans and Japanese who were engaged in tearing up China, in which he asked them all to pledge their word not to upset the balance in that country by interfering with treaty ports or giving preference in customs matters to their own nationals. The Chinese Maritime Customs should be left in charge of collections, said Hay, and the tariff rate fixed at the discretion of the Customs authorities. The nations involved agreed to these proposals. Doing as well as they were, they could afford to be reasonable. Britain especially could afford it, as she had already exacted from Peking a promise that as long as her trade in China exceeded that of any other nation, the Inspector General of Customs would be of British nationality. At any rate, for the time being customs revenue was an almost academic matter to Peking, since the huge indemnity owed to Japan swallowed it as fast as it came in.

*   *   *

The bitterness of paying this indemnity and the humiliation of being virtually dismembered as a country preyed on the minds of the Chinese. To be beaten by Japan, of all nations, was worst of all, for in Chinese eyes Japan had always seemed merely an impertinent little outgrowth of their own culture. There are at least two popular Chinese versions of how Japan came to be populated. According to one, a Chinese ship that had been chartered for a children's excursion, loaded with infantile passengers, accidentally slipped its moorings, and drifted across to the Japanese islands. There the children went ashore and founded the Japanese race, whose members retained their small proportions. The other tale is something similar but not quite so polite—the ship that landed on Japan was loaded with monkeys.

Myths apart, Japanese culture does derive mainly from China. The kimono, Japan's traditional dress, is that of the Ming Dynasty, a period in history when Chinese people lived much as conservative Japanese do today, sitting on the floor instead of using chairs. The Chinese had preserved toward Japan the arrogance they could no longer maintain in their dealings with Westerners, and now they asked themselves how such a state of affairs could have come about, with China forced to give way to these inferior Asians. Many a man pondered the question and came to the conclusion that it was the fault of the Manchu Dynasty. On the whole, however, even the malcontents didn't visualize outright revolution. They wanted reform in the government, with less corruption, more efficiency, and, most of all, a diminution of Tzu-hsi's power. In their minds she symbolized all that was wrong with the court—self-indulgence, extravagance, and neglect of the country's welfare. No doubt much of this resentment came from exaggerated stories of her behavior, for Chinese are a gossipy people and such tales have a way of growing more lurid as they are retold. It was being said that the Empress had killed her sister Regent because Tzu-an discovered that Tzu-hsi had given birth to a child by an obscure lover. There were people who could cite chapter and verse to give body to the story. Other rumors credited the Empress with the temperament of a Messalina. One fact that was more than a rumor—that she loved theatricals—was the foundation for whispers that she knew many popular actors far too well. Before Tzu-hsi defied custom, actors had not been frequenters of the palace, for they had the lowest possible status in society. The Empress didn't care about their social status: she loved the theater, and that was that. Of course people talked when she invited actors to give performances for the Court's private delectation. They were bound to, and since China was China, it was equally inevitable that they said worse things about Tzu-hsi—the most insulting thing possible: that she amorously pursued the low creatures, and frightened them so much that whenever they realized she had an eye on them, they ran away. A famous bit of scandal concerned an actor known as "Puffed Hair Chao." Chao was particularly good for his female impersonations: until well on in the twentieth century the stage in China, like that of Elizabethan England, required men to play women's roles. It may seem strange that a female impersonator should have a large following of female fans, but so it was. A contemporary journalist wrote of him,

"The reason Puffed Hair Chao is so passionately sought after by young women of the wealthy and good families is that besides being handsome he is extremely expressive in acting the parts of lewd women craving love and is able to depict to perfection the tantalizing walk of mischievous young maidens. His eyes are filled with such devilish seductiveness that even the most demure and self-respecting young woman develops a desire for sexual excitement." [Harry Hussey, *Venerable Ancestor* (New York, 1949), p. 292.] According to the gossip of the time, one of the Imperial princes caught his revered sister-in-law in a compromising position with this exotically alluring creature. It was very likely not a true story, but it was popular in the market place, and had its effect on the public mind. Besides, it was no mere rumor that Tzu-hsi was wildly extravagant and always needed money, though she was adept at thinking up new ways to get it.

What could not be alleged against her in truth was that she neglected the little Emperor Kuang-hsü. She didn't. She was determined not to make the mistakes she had committed with her own son. She made a point of keeping him close by, and when he was small she even took him into her own room to sleep when thunderstorms frightened him in the night. She was meticulously careful in selecting his tutors and companions.

At first the boy gave signs of repaying this maternal devotion—something Tzu-hsi must have found much against her nature to give—by developing unusually well. He learned quickly and took with eagerness to a heavy schedule of education. By the time he reached his majority he was a cultivated young man with a taste for independent thinking, a quality which, however admirable, was ultimately to cause his downfall. Yet in spite of all this care and the Empress's attempts to be friendly, Kuang-hsü was afraid of her. He had been four years old when she snatched him from his mother and had him crowned at midnight in the palace, old enough for the memory of the alarming experience to stay with him. As he grew up, the Empress's dominating manners continued to frighten him, and so did the lowering atmosphere of the palace, where eunuchs seemed to reign supreme. He must have heard there many stories about the power of Li Lien-ying. On one occasion in the coronation year, his own father, accompanied by the eunuch, inspected the new navy. Li Lien-ying behaved in a haughty manner which offended a censor, who wrote a memorial taking the eunuch to task for insolence. This was not only his privilege but his duty, but Li was enraged, and so in due course was his Imperial mistress; as a result, the censor was degraded. Kuang-hsü was a young man of principles and this incident must have shocked him. The navy itself was a sore point: Tzu-hsi had taken the money earmarked for the purpose of bringing it up to date, and spent it instead on a new Summer Palace, built on the ruins of a garden that was destroyed by the British and French during the war of 1860.

Of all the grievances the young Emperor had against his "Imperial Father," as etiquette forced him to refer to the Empress on state occasions, the most important was the affair of his bride. In the story there are reminiscent overtones. In spite of her intelligence, Tzu-hsi seemed to find it impossible to learn from experience. Her disastrous meddling with T'ung-chih and the Fragrant Concubine had left her determined as ever to handle Kuang-hsü's love life as she wished it to be managed. The time for his accession, unwelcome though it was to Tzu-hsi, was drawing inexorably near, and he must be married first. According to custom the court issued a decree which was in effect an invitation to tenders, saying that suitable maidens might now register their names as candidates for the post of Empress. One would be chosen, and it was understood that two of the aspirants who had failed to make the highest grade would be named Imperial concubines. That was the way it was always done. Disconcertingly, however, this time nobody registered at all save for two young sisters who were nieces to Tzu-hsi. Considering what had happened to the late Emperor's wife Aluteh, this should not have surprised the court, but Tzu-hsi was furious. Promptly she changed her approach to the problem and on her own picked out a number of eligible girls, commanding them to gather for the preliminary examination. They had to obey, and from the bevy she chose eight she considered most suitable. In fact she had already made up her mind that Kuang-hsü should marry her elder niece, a very plain girl, but appearances must be observed.

The ceremony sounds astonishingly like an Atlantic City boardwalk beauty contest. Each maiden, carrying a little sign giving her name and pedigree, had to walk up and down past an elite group of judges: Tzu-hsi, Kuang-hsü, and a number of Court ladies. When they had all done this, there was polite jockeying between the Empress and Emperor:

"You choose her," "No, no, Imperial Father, you must choose her," —until Kuang-hsü was prevailed on to make the decision. At such moments the Emperor always pointed the royal scepter at the girl of his choice. Kuang-hsü innocently pointed at the prettiest maiden, but hardly was the gesture completed when Tzu-hsi called out angrily and interrupted him by gesturing very definitely toward her ill-favored niece. The poor boy faltered and submitted, as he always did when Tzu-hsi bullied him; he pointed at the niece. When the awkward moment was over the Empress carefully avoided naming the girl of his first choice to either of the lesser posts. Instead she chose two sisters who were to be known as the Pearl Concubine and the Lustrous Concubine: the Pearl was destined to cause Tzu-hsi a lot of trouble, but nobody could have foreseen that. As for the poor pretty girl who was passed over, she considered herself disgraced, and went home and committed suicide. [Hussey.]

Married and of age, the Emperor was to ascend the throne. The ascension was two years late. His father, completely subservient to Tzu-hsi, had done his utmost (at her request) to put off the moment, rallying friendly courtiers to petition her to remain in charge, and Tzu-hsi had gladly consented, and retained her power that much longer. But now it was 1886, and unless the court wished to give the impression that the Emperor of China was too feeble-minded to reign, the moment had to come. Tzu-hsi realized it, but she did not retire completely even then. She called a meeting of the princes and officials and in the presence of the Emperor made a strong speech, reminding him of all he owed to her. She urged him to promise that she should remain in a position of "tutelage" to him, and that he wouldn't made important decisions without her help. Most especially he should not make official appointments or discharge officials: that should be her task. It was not love of power that made Tzu-hsi demand this right so much as sheer practicality.

Always in need of money, she had learned a good way to satisfy her needs: high officials would pay heavily to get an interview with her, and less important men willingly handed over large sums in exchange for official appointments. Though he realized this, the Emperor wouldn't have been able to resist such a powerful appeal to filial piety even if he had not been chronically terrified of Tzu-hsi. On his knees he made the required promises.

After the war with Japan and its distressing aftereffects, Kuang-hsü was plagued with the dichotomy that was affecting thoughtful men all over the country. He deeply resented the Western nations but at the same time knew far more about them than his father had done, and knowledge often breeds a sort of sympathy. As a boy he had made special efforts to learn English—an ambition none of his ancestors would have comprehended—and after learning it he read a number of books on Western subjects. Inevitably he became acquainted with ideas that conflicted sharply with the Chinese concept of his own divine rights. Even Tzu-hsi proved herself receptive, to a certain degree, of Western influence; long ago her trusted adviser Tseng Kuo-fan had been partly responsible for this when he brought her to the point of consenting to a course of study abroad for some of her bright young men. With her approval, or at least non-interference, for more than two decades the Tsungli Yamen had been sending youths to America, many of whom became outstanding statesmen in their generation. The Western-style college that had started under the auspices of the Yamen was now a flourishing institution, and had inspired the growth in China of a number of similar establishments. Nowadays, the world of the foreigners was considered neither mysterious nor beneath contempt, but after the disasters of 1895 it posed more of a threat than ever. China knew the West better but liked it less. Still, Kuang-hsü's outlook was bound to be influenced by his studies, whether he knew it or not, and he in turn influenced the mentality of the Pearl Concubine, his favorite. He talked to her of his dawning ideas about reform, and she listened and encouraged, and tried to diminish the Empress's hold on him.

At this time, T'an Ssu-t'ung, a native of Hunan, was busy with plans that filled the old-style Manchus with alarm. T'an was a scholar and the son of a scholar: his father held important posts, among them the governorship of Hupei. As T'an traveled and worked, he observed the state of local administration all over the country. He was thirty years old at the end of the Sino-Japanese

War, and like other patriots was filled with sorrow and shame by the outcome. It was clear to him that China would never be strong again until she purged herself of corruption and brought in measures of reform in the government. Already he had founded a society "for the promotion of Western learning" in Hunan. At the end of the war it developed into a club with political connotations, dedicated to reform. T'an's ideas spread quickly, and clubs of the same sort sprang up in other Hunanese districts.

At the same time an older man named K'ang Yu-wei was working along similar lines. K'ang had a number of original ideas, one of which was that Confucius had been misrepresented, and was in fact a political reformer. K'ang also preached the desirability of a world community. He had an alert mind, though his later history indicates that he was capricious. At that period he was in the vanguard of the courageous souls who demanded government reform. He wrote a paper that was famous as the Ten Thousand Word Memorial, protesting against the terms of the Treaty of Shimonoseki, and persuaded twelve thousand officials in eighteen provinces to sign it. Like T'an he organized a club: his was called the Society for the Study of National Rejuvenation, which had centers both in Shanghai and Peking. As K'ang made more and more of a name for himself, T'an went to Peking expressly to meet him, and also became friendly with K'ang's follower, Liang Ch'i-ch'ao, who lectured at one of the subsidiary clubs in Changsha. These three men played important parts in the short-lived period of reform that was to follow.

Their movement gained ground. One friend and adviser was an English missionary, Reverend Timothy Richard, who helped plan the strategy of the reformists: the campaign had an efficiency that earlier movements lacked. Moreover, its leaders had a friend at court, in the literal sense; Weng T'ung-ho, who had been the Emperor's tutor and now held the very important post of Grand Secretary. Weng was a most unusual court official. His sympathies were with the reformists, and it was through his intervention that K'ang's memorials for several years were brought to Kuang-hsü's attention. Later K'ang sent the Emperor foreign books dealing with reforms in Russia and Japan, and the Emperor read them. They had an effect: Kuang-hsü came to identify himself with the reformists. It goes without saying that Tzu-hsi was opposed to the whole concept, but the Emperor was grown up now, and with the loyal Pearl Concubine at his elbow he dared to defy his Imperial Father. The Court split in two, with the Northern or Old Mother's party standing out against the Southern, or Young Emperor's. Kuang-hsü had Weng on his side and various other men who seemed by contrast with the old guard to be freethinkers. Tzu-hsi was lined up with the Manchus of high standing who had everything to lose if change were countenanced.

The climax was hastened when Weng T'ung-ho introduced K'ang Yu-wei personally to the Emperor. Kuang-hsü got on well with K'ang, and Weng arranged matters so that his protégé got the post of Assistant Grand Secretary at the Tsungli Yamen. Thus it happened that the extraordinary period known as the Hundred Days Reform came about.

It started on June 11, 1898, with a proclamation by the Emperor that he was going to bring in some changes. He gave no actual details of his intentions with the first notice, but K'ang Yu-wei was named head of something described by Kuang-hsü as the new Office of Constitution—a sinister hint to the old guard that the Emperor was contemplating giving a constitution to the nation. Of course the Old Mother's party took alarm. They moved quickly: four days later Weng T'ung-ho was removed from his post and sent to the country, out of touch. In a further effort to batten down the hatches, Tzu-hsi called her faithful henchman Jung-lu to an audience and named him Viceroy of Chihli as well as Commissioner for North China. She also put him on the Grand Council.

It seems strange that the Emperor and K'ang should have been surprised by the removal of Weng T'ung-ho. They were dismayed, but not discouraged. Far from it: their reform program had only begun. The day after Weng disappeared from court, Kuang-hsü and his new secretary had an immensely long private audience that lasted nine hours. Shortly thereafter appeared the first of the reform decrees, an alteration of the time-honored examination system; a declaration that European studies must be added to the itinerary of scholarship subjects. On the heels of this startling announcement came another, still more shocking to conservatives: the Emperor wished his kinsmen the princes to go abroad, see the world, and acquire a foreign education. While the palaces of Peking buzzed with outraged comment there appeared another decree and yet another, more and more. Some were radical, others not so bad, but in sum they were warranted to send the old aristocracy into fits of apoplexy. The Emperor suggested that his male subjects cut off their queues. He appointed a number of new officials, and abolished a few ancient sinecures. He told the Manchus, many of whom had lived for generations on government subsidies, to get to work. He said that China ought to have more newspapers, and that the press should be free. He tried to build up the navy. He planned a system of good new roads.

All in all, it was an amazing performance. China was undergoing a revolution sponsored by the hereditary head of the state.

*   *   *

Tzu-hsi of course was not idle: busily she made plans to cope with the errant Emperor. Jung-lu moved his troops until he had a concentration of picked men in Tientsin, and another army was placed close to Peking. Early in the game, before Kuang-hsü got the bit in his teeth, an announcement was made that she and the Emperor were scheduled to inspect the army at Tientsin in a few months' time. This was not a routine exercise, but part of the Old Mother's careful preparation against the crisis. The Emperor and his advisers were not guileless: they knew something was afoot, probably in Tientsin, and they were determined to get in first. Unhappily for their cause the man they decided to trust was Yuan Shih-k'ai, now commander of the Newly Created Army in Shantung.

Yuan had suffered some of the obloquy attached to his master Li Hung-chang after the Korean debacle. In his new post he was probably too ambitious, and determined to suffer no more. The reason Kuang-hsü was inclined to trust him was that Weng T'ung-ho had always entertained a high opinion of him, and no doubt T'an Ssu-t'ung and K'ang Yu-wei recalled this fact. Yuan had also been heard to say that he favored the reformists' cause. To the reformists these reasons must have added up to a satisfactory total; and on this supposition a fatal mistake was made. In September, three months after the first decree, the Emperor summoned Yuan to Peking and appointed him Vice-President of the Board of War. During the audience, Kuang-hsü told the general that he was determined to press on with his program of reform.

Yuan kept a journal that survives, in which he noted his version of what followed. His name has been handed down in Chinese history as a prime example of perfidy and heartless ambition, so it is no wonder that his account does not agree in all particulars with that of the reformists whose goose he cooked. According to the journal, he had just returned from the Imperial audience when T'an Ssu-t'ung surprised him by making an appearance at his temporary Peking lodgings. Yuan says he hardly knew T'an, and was at a loss to account for this visit, but he was aware that T'an was "a trusted adviser to His Majesty," so he consented to a private interview. [Jerome Ch'en, *Yuan Shih-k'ai* (Stanford, 1961), p. 56 *et passim*.] After a little preliminary courtesy, T'an came swiftly to business. Was Yuan aware that the Emperor was in grave danger? that Jung-lu was plotting to dethrone and murder him? He hurried on: Jung-lu was no true friend to Yuan: on the contrary he had stood in the way, time after time, of Yuan's advancement. He was jealous. . . . After this startling announcement, T'an produced a document, a secret order that he said came from the Emperor, which directed Yuan to arrest and execute Jung-lu in Tientsin, take over his posts, stop the railway and telegraph services, and bring his troops to Peking, where he was to guard the Forbidden City (with the Emperor in it) and besiege the Summer Palace, the Empress's stronghold.

Admittedly, this was enough to scare any military man. In implied excuse for what he did later, Yuan in his journal declared that he never believed that these orders really came from the Emperor, for they were not written in the Vermilion Pencil, but in ordinary black ink. T'an Ssu-t'ung, however, told Liang Ch'i-ch'ao about it afterwards and declared that it *was* the Vermilion Pencil mandate he showed to Yuan Shih-k'ai. It is likely that Yuan was lying. In any case, by his own admission he now proceeded to deceive T'an. He tried to play for time, saying that there was no hurry about the affair, but T'an insisted on a flat reply then and there. Yuan pretended to capitulate. "If His Majesty cares to give us even only a scrap of paper, who dares to disobey and what cannot be accomplished?"

T'an said, "If you decide against it, please go to the Summer Palace to report to Her Majesty. You will get wealth and power there."

Yuan said, "What kind of man do you think I am? We both serve our Sovereign and receive his favour. The duty of protecting him is not yours alone. Tell me what to do."

The plot as T'an now outlined it was to turn the tables on Jung-lu at the trooping ceremony in Tientsin. Yuan replied that if His Majesty should ride into his quarters and order him to execute "the villains," he would kill Jung-lu as if slaughtering a dog. T'an was satisfied and went away. As soon as he had gone, Yuan Shih-k'ai went to Tientsin and told Jung-lu all about it, and Jung-lu went to Peking and told the Empress.

Two days later Tzu-hsi came in from the Summer Palace to the Forbidden City, called a meeting, and announced her second regency. Kuang-hsü was imprisoned in one of the lake palaces, the Ocean Terrace, and separated forever from his Pearl Concubine.

"The country is now passing through a serious crisis beyond my poor ability to cope with," went the edict signed by his name. "So, fearing for the future of our country, and realizing my duty to our ancestors, I have besought Her Majesty to condescend once more—" and so on.

K'ang Yu-wei and Liang Ch'i-ch'ao escaped, but six other reformists were captured and executed. T'an Ssu-t'ung was one of them: he could have got away but chose to go to his death. K'ang lived abroad, in Europe and America, for sixteen years and became —of all things—an ardent monarchist. He returned to China after the Revolution of 1911 and was soon involved in an attempt to restore the monarchy, but though it failed he was not punished: he was a famous scholar and nobody really worried about him any more, now that he was so old. He lived his last years peacefully in Shanghai, collecting antique porcelain.

As for Yuan Shih-k'ai, T'an had been quite right. He got wealth and power from Her Majesty for his services.

Chapter Fifteen

Kuang-hsü, tamed and secure in the Ocean Palace, was carefully watched by the servants of his Imperial Father, and the conservative Manchus thought they had put away their troubles with him. But the adventure of the Hundred Days was not a detached incident: it was only one symptom of a deep-rooted problem that could not be settled so easily as the Emperor had been. There were other symptoms. Though Kuang-hsü's friends and allies had been chased out or killed, the root of the matter remained and spread underground throughout the country. Reform had been lopped off, but the Boxer Movement, like the surviving branch of a tree, grew stronger as soon as its rival was removed.

The Boxers were a secret society that inherited its title from an ancient religious brotherhood. The name is not so much a translation as a foreigners' nickname suggested by the Chinese original, "Society of Righteously Harmonious Fists." Jung-lu, who did not care for the Boxers, had other theories as to their background and said their first name was "Plum Blossom Fists," and that the founder claimed to be a Manchu prince. It is not important. What matters is the strong influence Boxerism had on its members. Anyone who knows the Chinatowns of the Western world can testify to the hold these secret societies maintain over the men who join them, and the climate of China in the 1890s contributed much to the peculiar fervor of the Boxers for their faith. '88 and '89 were both famine years. China was full of discontent arising from the Sino-Japanese debacle and its attendant growth of Western power and interference. The resentment felt by the late lamented Reform party had been shared by the Boxers, but there were important differences between the groups. The Reformers had been educated, scholarly men. The Boxers, at least those of the society's early stages, were simple peasants. K'ang Yu-wei had placed his faith in appeals to reason: he had certainly been prepared to gain his ends by force if need be, but only as a last resort. With their limited philosophy the Boxers could imagine only one way of attaining their goal, freedom from foreigners—bloodshed—and they expressed this ambition with a double slogan: "Pao Ch'ing Mien Yang": "Strengthen the Ch'ing Dynasty and drive out the foreigners." It was nearly what the Reformers had been after, of course, but in these words it was not nearly as likely to offend the Empress and the other Manchus.

The movement was born in Shantung. Shantung people are stiff-necked, and their anger had long been boiling against the Germans who occupied important cities and claimed most of the province as their zone of influence; they had got a foothold when Shantung men murdered two German missionaries. Boxers hated missionaries more than any other kind of foreigner. Indeed, most peasants probably thought all foreigners *were* missionaries, for these were the only barbarians they ever encountered, since merchants and diplomats seldom traveled in the countryside. For this reason the engineers from abroad who were beginning to come into the country to build the new railways were victimized for many grievances in which they had no hand. "Drive out the foreigners! Kill the Christians!" shouted the Boxers as they wandered through the province recruiting members. Hatred of the teacher meant hatred of the taught. The Boxers included in their black list all Chinese converts to Christianity, and their grudge was not based wholly on ideological grounds. During the "battle of the concessions" and the fervent land-grabbing that had gone on since 1895, many missionaries had begun to arrogate to themselves the power held by their governments in China, and thanks to the peculiar mentality of Chinese provincial officials they got away with a good deal of bullying. The Chinese officials, always sensitive to what went on in higher circles, were well aware of the increased pressure being exerted by the West on their superiors, and they reacted according to tradition: when the big man feared the foreigner the little one feared him even more, and extended his respect to the most insignificant representatives of the master races. What made it worse was that many missionaries in China were persons of narrow vision. They never questioned that their viewpoint on right and wrong was the correct one, and that any Chinese thought, if it swerved from their line, must be mistaken. They would believe the word of a convert far more readily than that of his next door neighbor who had not been saved, and in village disputes involving such converts the Western missionary often stepped forward and championed the cause of his sheep. Such meddling wrought havoc in the community. It is no wonder that to the harassed countryfolk missionaries seemed like so many extra tyrants suddenly imposed on them. For the "rice Christians" who permitted themselves to be converted merely for material gain and then strutted about, aping their foreign teachers, no words could be harsh enough.

The Boxer movement soon spread to other provinces. Probably its strongest appeal lay in its supposed key to magic arts and invulnerability, through incantation and spells. "The Boxers . . . possess a secret Talisman," wrote a contemporary, "consisting of a small piece of yellow paper, which they carry on their persons when going into battle. On it is drawn, in vermilion paint, a figure which is neither that of man nor devil, demon nor saint. It has a head, but no feet; its face is sharp-pointed, with eyes and eyebrows, and four halos. From the monster's heart to its lower extremities runs a mystic inscription, which reads: 'I am Buddha of the cold cloud; before me lies the black deity of fire; behind is Laotzu himself.' On the creature's body are also borne the characters for Buddha, Tiger, and Dragon. On the top left-hand corner are the words 'invoke first the Guardian of Heaven,' and on the right-hand corner, 'invoke next the black gods of pestilence.'" [Bland and Backhouse, *China* . . . , p. 279.] Boxers identified themselves by special touches in their costume: red sashes, red ribbons on arms and legs, and red headkerchiefs. Their banners, too, were red, red being the lucky color in China. They held elaborate ceremonies in their temples, where by ritual they swore loyalty to their precepts and each other. Sometimes, as if possessed, they went into fits. The incantations they chanted, they claimed, bestowed upon them invulnerability to any enemy's weapons. Those who had faith in them were by no means all of the poorer classes. Even Tzu-hsi began to listen to the stories, and some of her close friends arranged that she should see a demonstration of Boxer resistance to harm. She may have been present at a trial made during the Dragon Festival at the end of May 1900, at a great Boxer camp in Chochou, when ". . . duly authorized officers of the Crown have seen recruits, who have performed all the dread rites, and are initiated, stand fearlessly in front of a full-fledged Boxer; have seen that Boxer load up his blunderbuss with powder, ramming down a wad on top; have witnessed a handful of iron buckshot added, but with no wad to hold the charge in place; have noticed that the master Boxer gesticulated with his lethal weapon the better to impress his audience before he fired, but have not noticed that the iron buckshot tripped merrily out of the rusty weapon since no wad held it in place; and finally, when the fire-piece belched forth flames and ear-breaking noise at a distance of a man's body from the recruit's person, they have seen, and with them thousands of others, that no harm came." [Putnam Weale, *Indiscreet Letters from Peking* (London, 1906), p. 9.]

The Boxers began putting their precepts into practice. At first in little villages, then in bigger towns, they attacked mission settlements, burning churches and killing the "secondary Christians," or converts, as well. Though many Manchus approved of these activities and began to talk jubilantly of how the movement would be the salvation of their clans, one of their number, Jung-lu, watched developments with a worried eye. He saw through Boxer pretensions. Writing to the Viceroy of Fukien residing in Foochow, an intimate friend of his, in 1900, the Commander of Forces said, "At the end of the 9th Moon of last year there were Boxers openly displaying huge banners in Chihli, on which was written, 'The Gods assist us to destroy all foreigners; we invite you to join the patriotic Militia.' At one place a Buddhist abbot was the head of the Society and he led on the mob, burning the Christian chapel there. Subsequently, while they were burning converts' houses . . . the magistrate came out and attacked them with his troops. The soldiers opened fire and the Boxers retreated, but their priest leaders were captured, and some thirty or forty were shot dead. This ought to have demonstrated to the people at large how nonsensical were the stories about the invulnerability of these mountebanks: our soldiers dealt with them as easily as if they had been trussing chickens!" [Bland and Backhouse, *China . . .* , p. 247.]

So active were the Boxers in Shantung that the Germans sent in troops to protect their missionaries as early as 1899. Tzu-hsi had not yet committed herself to the Boxer side, and the dispatch of foreign troops worried the court. It was decided that Shantung had better be governed by a stronger man than the one then in office, so they sent a Manchu named Yu-hsien to replace him. Instead of putting the Boxers down, Yu-hsien fell in love with their cause and became their devoted adherent. His example was soon followed by certain of the princes, especially Tuan. Tzu-hsi too was strongly attracted, but at first she dared not show it: the bitter fact was that the foreigners held the whip hand over China, and a show of pro-Boxer sentiment on her part would have been tantamount to a declaration of war on them. She waited. In any case the early days of 1900 were taken up by a more pressing problem. She wished to depose Kuang-hsü altogether and place the child of Prince Tuan on the throne as the new Emperor, so that she might rule once more as regent for a minor. Many of the ministers approved of the plan—Prince Tuan naturally headed the group—but there were protests too. The Grand Secretary ventured to prophesy that most of the viceroys and governors would not care for the idea, and to the Empress's vexation time proved him right. Tzu-hsi had to drop the project, and turned her attention once more to the Boxers.

Jung-lu was not the only official who was not of her mind on the subject. Yuan Shih-k'ai's was another dissident voice. For some time he had viewed with alarm the rapidly mounting disorders in Shantung. When in July 1899, he suggested strengthening a police force in that province he had deliberately laid down so many rules in his prospectus that the Court was forced to put him personally in charge of operations. As soon as he got to Shantung he made his own test of the famous Boxer invulnerability, placing some of them against the wall and directing his men to shoot. This time all the Boxers fell dead, but if Yuan hoped the exhibition would shake public faith in their creed, he was disappointed. People do not willingly give up their belief in the supernatural. Moreover, in spite of his efficient methods of suppression, the Boxers held out against him for a long time; by the end of 1899 they had killed so many people and looted so much property that Peking owed an immense indemnity to Germany, and the Tsungli Yamen felt compelled to change governors once again. Yu-hsien was sent to govern Shansi and Yuan Shih-k'ai took over his post in Shantung, becoming in reality what he had been in effect for many months. And he still had no use for the Boxers: in a memorial he put forth his reasons bluntly. They were not good fighters, he said: nearly five hundred of them, to his certain knowledge, had attacked a church and failed to take it. They were bandits who lived on their loot—inefficient bandits, at that. "How can they wipe out foreigners?" demanded Yuan in the memorial. "Even if they could recruit millions of people into their ranks, roaming about everywhere like spreading bush fires, what would happen to our country?" [Ch'en, p. 66.]

As Governor, however, he was more successful than he had been as a mere general, and soon he drove the pests out of his province. To be sure, they merely moved into Chihli, nearer to Peking where their sympathizers were thick on the ground, but Yuan's first duty was to Shantung. Now there were Yuan and Jung-lu in agreement, opposed to any idea of taking the Boxers seriously as allies in the Chinese struggle for survival. Both were trusted servants of the Empress Dowager, and as if two voices were not enough, a third official joined them in their opinion; no less a person than Li Hung-chang, now Viceroy in Canton. And none of them, in the end, was able to make Tzu-hsi listen to reason. There were others in the south and the east of like mind, those Viceroys who were reluctant to send soldiers to help the Empress in her mad venture. Throughout the siege the South was to behave as if no declaration of war had ever been made. Business went on as usual; though Sir Robert Hart was trapped in Peking the Customs posts everywhere continued to function.

* * *

Mrs. Sarah Pike Conger, wife of the American Minister, was a sincere Christian Scientist who believed that perfect love would conquer any danger; not that she saw reason to think overmuch of danger in the first two years of her husband's residence. She wrote many letters to friends and relatives, which were preserved and later published, and in one of her pre-Boxer communications there is a detailed description of a meeting with the Empress in December 1899. As Tzu-hsi had never seen a foreign lady and no foreign lady had ever seen Tzu-hsi, the ladies of the diplomatic corps, thinking it might be a good thing to correct this state of mutual ignorance, conveyed to the Tsungli Yamen their desire to pay Her Majesty their compliments on her sixty-fourth birthday. "After much delay and manoeuvring," wrote Mrs. Conger, "the audience was granted." On December 13 twelve foreign women, including the wife of the Japanese Minister, rode in sedan chairs to the Winter Palace. Each chair had five bearers and two "mafoos," or grooms; the Empress had sent a mounted escort as well, and after the Spanish Minister, as doyen of the corps, had joined the party with his four interpreters, eighteen more mafoos and sixty additional mounted escorts, the procession became almost overwhelmingly impressive. The ladies were magnificently entertained. At the outer door of the palace, eunuchs took over and carried them in court chairs; at the next gate they found a genuine railroad coach waiting, a present from France which was kept there in the grounds as a sort of toy. By eunuch power the ladies rode in this coach to another building where they had tea, and they were then received by the Empress Dowager and the Emperor in the throne room. Tzu-hsi presented each lady with a golden ring set with a large pearl, but this was not all. The party lunched with princesses galore, and had another audience with the Empress. "She was bright and happy and her face glowed with good will. There was no trace of cruelty to be seen. In simple expressions she welcomed us, and her actions were full of freedom and warmth. . . . She extended both hands toward each lady, then, touching herself, said with much enthusiastic earnestness, 'One family; all one family.' . . . Only think! China, after centuries and centuries of locked doors, has now set them ajar." [Conger, *Letters from China* (London, 1909), p. 69.]

Two weeks later came the news that an English missionary had been killed by the Boxers.

❋   ❋   ❋

The last normal reaction shown by the Tsungli Yamen in their dealings with the diplomatic body occurred when they made their apologies for this affair, promptly caught the murderers, tried them, and executed them. Soon afterwards there appeared an edict that gave everyone, Yamen and foreign diplomats together, something to think hard about, for it contained an ominous statement: there was a difference, it said, between seditious societies of lawless bandits and groups of law-abiding people who had merely come together to protect their communities. All over the Legation Quarter foreigners were asking each other just what this meant, but nobody except missionaries worried too much. Certainly the diplomats did not. It had been a long time since the Chinese had offered a genuine threat to the peace, and missionaries were always squawking. Still, more as a matter of form than anything else, the five chief Ministers protested to the Yamen.

Tzu-hsi waited quietly while Boxer activities stepped up. Thousands were coming forward to join the movement, and so much burning and murder went on that the diplomatic voices began to sharpen at last with alarm. It was against the Empress's nature and training to be too forthright, and after some weeks she obligingly issued another decree which denounced the Boxers by name. This reassured the diplomats somewhat, but not for long. Slowly they came round to the decision that they ought to demonstrate the strength of their respective nations, and despite the jealousy and suspicion that divided their ranks it was agreed that a show of naval force in March might be a good thing. However, such matters move slowly and the formal demonstration never took place. Instead, a few warships—American, Italian, British, and German—were sent to the China coast with orders to stand by, the first three nations being represented off the Taku bar and the Germans at Kiaochow. The main thing, the ministers agreed, was to avoid any appearance of panic. It was not until May 20 that they discussed the advisability of sending to Tientsin for marine guards to reinforce the men they already had, and the majority vote was against it, only the French and Russians being in favor.

On the twenty-eighth, however, the others accepted their way of thinking: even the imperturbable British had taken alarm. Boxers seemed to be swarming all over the countryside. Bertram Lennox Simpson, an English assistant in the Maritime Customs Service and private secretary to Sir Robert Hart, who wrote under the nom de plume of "B. L. Putnam Weale," reported, "The Peking-Paotingfu railway is being rapidly destroyed; Fengtai station, but six miles from Peking . . . has gone up in flames; a great steel bridge has succumbed to the destroying energy of dynamite. All the European engineers have fled into Peking; and, worst of all, the Boxer banners have been unfurled. . . . Of course Peking is safe, that goes without saying, but merely because there are foolish women and children, some nondescripts, and a good many missionaries, we will order a few guards." [Indiscreet . . . , p. 9.] As Putnam Weale actually wrote his book after the event, much of his heavy sarcasm is due to hindsight. The guards arrived a day or so later, and passed without incident into the Legation Quarter, upon which the same old Manchu who wrote about the yellow Talisman observed, "The people muttered curses, . . . but no one molested them. What does it matter? None of them will ever leave the city." The foreigners welcomed their protectors gladly, and were more than ever pleased with their company on the third of June when more disturbing stories made the rounds. A large party of European railway workers, on the way to Tientsin from Paotingfu, had been attacked and lost seven of their number. Also, two British missionaries who lived forty miles from Peking were murdered. Then on the fourth, the railway line to Tientsin was cut. Two days later a new Imperial edict was promulgated which contradicted the last, coming out decisively in favor of the Boxers and accusing the Christians of making trouble. Clearly, the Empress had the bit between her teeth. As a grand climax the foreigners' grandstand at the racecourse, three miles from Peking, was burned down. The significance of this gesture could not be ignored. Thoroughly frightened at last, all the foreign diplomats sent off to their respective governments, urgently demanding help.

The residents of Peking included a number, gifted at writing, who left vivid accounts of their experiences that rather overshadow the corresponding reports from Tientsin. Thus the reader is apt to sum up the Boxer Rising in terms of the siege of Peking, forgetting other aspects of it. Yet the affair was three-pronged. There is the well-known story of Peking itself, but also the tale of Tientsin and that of the peregrinations of rescuers between the cities. These last had a most unpleasant time. It was June 10 when two thousand troops representing eight nations—Britain, Germany, Russia, France, America, Japan, Italy, and Austria—started out from Tientsin by rail to cover the ninety miles to Peking and relieve their threatened compatriots. Admiral Seymour of the British Navy was in command. They were held up by disruptions of the line: four days later, still only halfway to their destination, they suffered their first attack by Boxers. More battles followed, until Seymour resolved to abandon the trains, turn back part of the way, and take his men up the Peiho by boat. But as the troops began doubling in their tracks, hampered by heavy supplies and many wounded, they were set upon by Chinese regulars, the Kansu followers of an ex-bandit general named Tung Fu-hsiang. Seymour now realized that the Manchu government had joined forces with the Boxers. The situation was so grave that he determined to go straight back to Tientsin, but this course was no more feasible than his earlier one. As the troops made their slow way along they were constantly harried, and there was ominous thundering ahead: Tientsin too was having her troubles. The night of the twenty-first, still on the road and lost in darkness, the tired men all but stumbled on a great fort, the Hsiku Arsenal ten miles from Tientsin. The Chinese manning it challenged the foreign troops and fired on them; then, to Seymour's surprise, his desperate forces routed the guard and took possession of the building. There they rested for a day or so before they could get in touch with their friend in Tientsin's foreign quarter. Fortunately for these besieged people, the garrison had been strengthened at the last minute by fresh Russian troops, but on the fifteenth Boxers had attacked the settlement and burned down a part of it.

The men aboard the ships anchored at Taku, thirty-five miles downstream and twelve miles offshore, had soon realized what was going on. They could see Chinese busily at work on the forts. Some of these were setting mines, and the foreign officers determined to act before more preparations could be made. They were faced by the same problem that defeated their predecessors in 1859—the bar, which must be crossed by small gunboats. Moreover, the forts were in far better state now and were guarded by four new destroyers which the Germans had built for China. However, the foreign naval forces were well supplied too, and had eight vessels—British, German, French, and Japanese—suitable for their purposes. The officers sent an ultimatum to the forts' defenders which was to expire at 2:00 A.M. on the seventeenth, and duly lined up in position to wait. An hour ahead of time the forts opened fire. Six of the ships returned the compliment while the other two, both of them British, crossed the bar unperceived in the dark and approached, unseen, close to the Chinese destroyers, casting off boats full of men as they went. British sailors leaped aboard the destroyers' decks while at the same time the rowboat crews made a surprise attack. Soon the Europeans were in command of all four craft, an extraordinarily valuable haul. Furthermore, within two hours attacking forces had landed, and dawn saw complete victory for the foreigners, who now held the Taku forts.

The Viceroy in Tientsin knew that this item of news would not please the Empress, so he simply failed to include it in a memorial he sent her later that day. Instead he gave the impression that the foreigners of Tientsin were doomed, and that everything was going splendidly for the Chinese. In a way he was justified. His forces were pouring shot and shell into the settlement: no one could have believed that its inhabitants would hold out much longer. Nevertheless one of the young men from the British community slipped through the lines on horseback and carried the word to Taku, where reinforcements had just arrived from Hong Kong and Port Arthur, and on June 23 a relief force moved upriver, into the settlement. On the twenty-sixth Admiral Seymour and his men abandoned the Hsiku Arsenal and joined them, and there everyone remained, still besieged, still fighting, until near the middle of July. It was then decided that they would never have peace or anything approximating it until the Chinese city, old walled Tientsin, was cleared of its twenty thousand enemy troops. Russians, British, Japanese, and Americans joined in the operation, and on July 14 succeeded in taking the city. Now, back to Peking, both in space and time.

What happened in Tientsin was no secret to the outside world, for Taku was a gateway through which news passed more or less regularly. Peking's foreign community was in a different position: no news went out and nothing came in. Having asked for help and heard that Seymour was starting with his relief expedition on June 10, they waited expectantly for the army to arrive that same evening. At about the time the trains should have got there some young Englishmen of Peking rode to the railway station just outside the Chinese city to meet them. As we know, there were no trains to be seen. Instead the riders perceived, and did not like, "thickly-clustering tents of Kansu soldiery" [Putnam Weale] in the open spaces outside the city walls. On their way back through the Chinese city after dark, the riders were stoned by those same soldiers off duty. Next day everyone was sure that Seymour would arrive, but the Englishmen were not eager to repeat their experience near the station. Sugiyama, the Japanese Chancellor, volunteered to meet the trains instead, and set out on his errand in a Peking cart, a hooded, two-wheeled vehicle of a sort much used in the capital city. He was not seen again. At dusk his carter returned, disheveled and spattered with blood, to tell his story: Kansu soldiers had lain in wait for the cart, had pounced on the Chancellor, and killed him brutally, afterwards mutilating the corpse. Two days elapsed after this murder, during which the foreign community did nothing in particular but wait with increasing anxiety for Seymour. The Court published a decree declaring that Sugiyama had been killed by bandits.

On June 13 the German Minister, Baron von Ketteler, went out walking in Legation Street and saw a Peking cart pass by, drawn by a trotting mule. Seated on "the customary place of the off-shaft," the Baron spotted a man whose appearance electrified him, as well it might—he was "nothing less than a full-fledged Boxer with his hair tied up in a red cloth, red ribbons round his wrists and ankles, and a flaming red girdle tightening his loose white tunic; and, to cap all, the man was audaciously and calmly sharpening a big carver knife on his boots! It was sublime insolence, riding down Legation Street like this in the full glare of day . . . and, withal, was a very ugly sign." [Putnam Weale, p. 31.] Von Ketteler dashed forward, dragged the man off the cart, and beat him with a walking stick until the fellow escaped up an alley and into the grounds of the Manchu Prince Su's palace. Then the Baron discovered another Boxer under the cart cover, and handed him over to the German Legation guards. The first man was not found, though he had certainly entered Prince Su's palace, and that was thoroughly searched. The feelings of the diplomats, especially those with dependent women and children in Peking, can be imagined at this point, and one forgets to be impatient with them for their earlier complacency. By this time the Legation Quarter had become the main refuge of Peking's foreigners, and missionaries from outside the city were flooding in as well. There was one other gathering place for Christians: the Catholic North Cathedral, or Peitang, diagonally opposite the Quarter on the other side of the Imperial City: the Cathedral was later to be besieged just as the Legation Quarter was. The Chinese domestics of the foreigners began to take leave of their masters on one pretext or another, but their places were more than filled by frightened native Christians who threw themselves on the mercy of the foreigners, and could not in decency be sent away.

On the afternoon of the day von Ketteler beat the man in the cart, a great mob of Boxers entered Peking through the Hatamen—the Hata Gate—not far from the Legation Quarter, driving terrified Chinese ahead of them in a stampede. The legation guards were alert, and kept up a steady hail of bullets which had a discouraging effect on the intruders and held them off from the Quarter. Nevertheless the Boxers managed to fire the nearby buildings that had recently been deserted by the refugees—houses of university professors, mission property, the Customs compound, and the East Cathedral. An attempt to rush the Legation Quarter in the dark was averted once again by machine-gun fire. In the morning, Putnam Weale says, Sir Robert Hart was still standing at his post, "looking terribly old and hardly less distressed than the wretched fugitives pouring in. His old offices and residences, where forty years before he had painfully begun a life-long work, were all stamped out of existence, and the iron had entered his soul." [P. 41.] Putnam Weale did not have a high opinion of Hart: Hart was generally unpopular at this time. His compatriots felt that a man with his great reputation as go-between and one who understood the natives should have warned the powers before the foreigners were brought to such a pass.

Weirdly, through all the hubbub messengers from the Tsungli Yamen continued to bring words of encouragement and cheer, assuring the Ministers that order would soon be restored and even asking advice on how this might best be done. The Yamen was not being as hypocritical as the foreigners bitterly thought: Court officials were not as one on the subject of what to do about the Legation Quarter. This was clear at a meeting of the Imperial Council held on the sixteenth, when several Ministers, though the sentiments of the Empress were well known to them and she was present, declared that the Boxers should be driven from the city. However, they were in the minority. Prince Tuan, the most rabid pro-Boxer of all the Manchus, backed up the Empress, and she would not permit the Boxers to be touched. (It was about this time that Tuan replaced Prince Ch'ing as President of the Council. Ch'ing did not care for the Boxers.) Tzu-hsi's determination was strengthened the next day, when a forged document was produced and shown to her, and she accepted it as genuine. It purported to be from the foreign Ministers and to be signed by the French envoy: it demanded her abdication and the replacement on the throne of Kuang-hsü, and also declared that the collection of the country's revenue as well as the disposal of Chinese troops should thereafter be handled by the foreigners. No doubt agents of Prince Tuan had fabricated the paper. It is strange that the Empress should have fallen for it, but she did: probably she wanted to. It gave her that much more of an excuse for siding with the Boxers, and soon she was to need an excuse, for they began to outrun themselves.

In the home-hewn philosophy of the rioters, next in line to the foreigners for vengeance were the "secondary Christians" or "second-grade barbarians"—the converts. Horrible scenes of murder were being enacted among these wretched people, all through the city and especially near the Legation Quarter. "Word came to us suddenly," wrote Putnam Weale, "that the Boxers had caught a lot of native Christians, and had taken them to a temple where they were engaged in torturing them with a refinement of cruelty. One of our leaders collected a few marines and some volunteers, marched out

and surrounded the temple and captured everybody red-handed.
. . . Christians and Boxers were all of them gory with blood which
had flown (sic) from the torturing and brutalities that had been
going on; so the Christians were told to line up against the wall of
the temple to facilitate the summary execution in progress. Then a
big fellow rushed out of a corner, yelling, 'I have received the faith.'
Our leader looked at the man with a critical eye, and then said to
him in his quietest tones, 'Stand up against the wall.' The Boxer
stood up and a revolver blew the top of his head off. With that
quickness of the eye for which he is distinguished, our leader had
seen a few red threads hanging below the fellow's tunic. The man,
as he fell with a cry, disclosed his sash underneath. He was a Boxer
chief." [P. 44.]

The Boxers now added another item to their black list: the "third-
class barbarians," or those who pandered to foreign needs by selling
things. On the seventeenth of June the gangsters set fire to the district of foreign-style shops that had grown up near the legations.
So far so good, but the flames quickly spread beyond control and
destroyed the whole commercial quarter, most of which was Manchu property. It also burned the Ch'ien Men, one of Peking's most
imposing gates, which led from the Imperial Palace to the Chinese
city. The Empress had to move from one house to another. It must
have been at this moment that she dallied with second thoughts
about the Boxers, but she had gone too far to turn back. Then on
June 19 she was reassured. The memorial from the Viceroy of Chihli
arrived from Tientsin, with all its glowing detail of victory here and
victory there, and the added, if unfinished, bit of news that the
impertinent foreigners had demanded surrender of the Taku forts.
This was something not to be borne, said Tzu-hsi. It was a hostile
act. China *must* rid herself of the foreign Ministers. Jung-lu kept
arguing, in his tiresome way, that she could not harm the envoys
because it was never done according to the international code, but
what did the Empress of China care for barbarian codes? One could
at least send the Ministers out of Peking, and let fate overtake them
on the way to Tientsin.

That afternoon Yamen couriers delivered to Hart and the eleven
foreign Ministers one ultimatum apiece, all in pretty red envelopes
and all alike. Because the foreign powers had demanded possession
of the Taku forts, said the letters, it was obvious that they desired
to commit an act of hostility, and the time had come to part. Within

twenty-four hours, namely by 4 P.M. next day, the diplomats and their guards, "who must be kept under proper control," and presumably, all other foreigners, must leave Peking for Tientsin.

The communications came as a terrible shock. For nine days the foreigners had been in ignorance of all events outside their own experience, and had lived in hopes of Admiral Seymour's arrival with his relief force. What did all this mean about the Taku forts? Why were the Tientsin foreigners endangering the lives of the Peking community? Indignation gave way to fear when the British Minister, Claude MacDonald, said roundly that the Chinese clearly meant to kill them all, and that this was merely their roundabout, Asiatic way of announcing it—in which, of course, Sir Claude was entirely correct. The Ministers gathered in the Spanish Legation to discuss the next move, while others hung about the legation gates, waiting for some decision. Von Ketteler wanted the eleven envoys to go in a body straight to the Tsungli Yamen and demand an armistice, but the other Ministers were against it. At seven that evening, having weighed their duty to stay against the lives of the women and children—though there was no guarantee that these would be saved, even if they accepted the ultimatum—the Ministers sent a meek note to the Yamen, in which the signators agreed to go, but pointed out that the time allowed them for preparation was wildly inadequate. They also requested a meeting with two of the Yamen princes at nine o'clock next morning.

When the note had gone, second thoughts overwhelmed the Ministers, especially when the other foreigners heard about it and reacted furiously. What! Desert the Chinese converts whose lives were dependent on them?—and, what was even less conceivable, lay themselves open to massacre on the open road? There were a thousand foreigners in the Legation Quarter; their caravan would stretch out for at least two miles and could be cut up by the Boxers in a few minutes. All night the argument raged, and by morning the Ministers, tortured with uncertainty, did nothing about preparing to go, but sat and waited for the Yamen's reply to their request for an interview. Surely some word would come before nine o'clock! But no message arrived: evidently the Yamen had spoken once and for all. Again someone suggested that the whole corps visit the Tsungli Yamen: again the idea was rejected. Finally Baron von Ketteler announced that he, at least, was going to the Yamen, because he had a long-standing engagement there for eleven, and he intended to keep it just as if there had been no intervening ultimatum. He would, if the gentlemen wished, make representations on their behalf once his special business was finished. The gentlemen accepted the offer. Then, scorning to take any extra guards and accompanied only by the usual two outriders and Cordes, his interpreter, the Baron started out in his official sedan chair, calmly smoking a cigar. Like Sugiyama he did not return. Within fifteen minutes the outriders came galloping back in terror. They panted that the Baron had been shot dead and that Cordes, badly wounded, had run away. German guards hurried to the spot where the assassination had taken place, but could find nobody, and nothing but bloodstained dust: the chair had been taken away and the bearers had vanished. Cordes turned up later, in the company of some American missionaries from outside Peking, who met him while they were making for the safety of the Legation Quarter.

The foreigners took this murder much harder than they had Sugiyama's, no doubt feeling that the Japanese were Asiatics like the Chinese, and used to that sort of thing. At least the question of departure had been settled. People who would kill a Minister even before the ultimatum expired could not be trusted: their safe-conduct was not worth a brass cash. The diplomats would stay where they were. As a matter of historic interest the big attack *did* begin early, at 3:49. All evening there was firing back and forth, and the night was full of noise. On the morning of the next day, June 21, the Empress Dowager issued an edict declaring war on the world and appealing to all her provinces for reinforcements. She added that China must mobilize the "patriots," meaning of course the Boxers.

It was so mad that there is something splendid about it. Every Manchu heart leaped with joy and pride, even Jung-lu's: he confessed it in a letter. "I lay awake all the next night thinking over this matter. Unable to sleep, more than once I sprang from my bed restless and excited with mixed feelings of joy and fear." To get back at the foreigners! To get rid of them, and own one's own country again! Then sober common sense took over, as it had a way of doing with Jung-lu, and his old misgivings on the subject of Boxerism returned. With discipline and firm leadership the rabble might turn out to be useful, but he wasn't hopeful. ". . . at the beginning of the movement, these Boxers were afraid to come together in large numbers lest the Imperial troops should attack and destroy them; from this alone we may reasonably infer that they are not devoid of the common instinct of fear. By themselves they cannot be fully trusted. . . . As a fighting force they are absolutely useless, but their claims to supernatural arts and magic might possibly be valuable for the purpose of disheartening the enemy. But it would be quite wrong, not to say fatal, for us to attach any real beliefs to their ridiculous claims." [Bland and Backhouse, *China* . . . , p. 248.]

The reports received by Tzu-hsi for several days after the edict were encouraging. The murder of von Ketteler had been praiseworthy, and now another foreigner was dead, a poor crazy professor named Huberty James, who had simply walked across no man's land into the arms of his captors. He was decapitated and his head hung up to encourage the others. From Tientsin came word that the foreigners there were practically wiped out; hundreds had been lost, said the Viceroy, while attacking the Taku forts. The Empress was in no mood to listen to Jung-lu's warnings, but an unpleasant incident strengthened her new distrust of the Boxers. Prince Tuan and several of his cronies, who may have been drinking all night, walked into the Imperial precincts early one morning at the head of sixty common ordinary Boxers. There in the courtyard outside the residence of the Imperial family they set up a great shout, demanding that Kuang-hsü come outside and be killed, and leave the throne free. If Tuan thought that such rough-and-ready methods would meet with Tzu-hsi's approval, he was badly mistaken. True, she had indicated her desire to depose Kuang-hsü and install Tuan's son, but Kuang-hsü was an Emperor, after all: one did not permit the mob to dispose of Emperors. Furious that the prince had dared to take such liberties, she stepped out of doors alone to face her would-be champions, and scolded the leaders until they were glad to slink away. For a while at least she had had far too much of the Boxers.

The besieged foreigners spent the days strengthening their defenses wherever this was possible, and quarreling a good deal. It was a long ordeal. For nine weeks until August 14, although there was a fortnight's respite after the fourteenth of July, they all—three thousand souls in the British Legation, all the other Legations having been destroyed, of whom two thousand were native Christians, and nearly three thousand mewed up outside the Legation Quarter in the North Cathedral—lived with the idea that each day might be their last. Though the Cathedral was a fortress in itself, it was poorly stocked with food and ammunition. The Legation Quarter was short on walls, but the besieged built barricades of whatever they could; Peking carts on their sides, filled with earth, and sandbags. As if in compensation they were fairly well off for food, with a good lot of rice and a number of horses; and there were several wells of sweet water within the compounds. They also started out with a fair supply of guns and ammunition. Nevertheless the odds were against them, and it is not denigrating their courage and endurance to say that they could never have survived if there had not been a hidden agency on the Chinese side helping them. Several times everything seemed finished, and then a lull would overtake the attackers. The final blow never fell. For this they were almost certainly indebted to Jung-lu, who dragged his feet, withheld arms from the Chinese, and never pressed the point home.

By July 13, however, the situation was at its worst. Chinese mines had been placed under legation houses and exploded. The area defended by the Japanese, though they were the best fighters of the lot, was shrinking dangerously as the besiegers pushed in. The ancient siege tactics of building battlements by night and edging in on the victim were proving distressingly effective. Then on the fourteenth something extraordinary occurred. Ever since the beginning, the diplomats had attempted to send messages out to Tientsin, giving them to converts who were willing to try to get through. They had never heard, of course, if any of these tries were successful. Now one of the converts, an old man, reappeared as if from the dead, bringing a letter for MacDonald and a story of his adventures. He had never got very far from the quarter, having been captured almost immediately. Of course his captors had beaten him, but afterwards they took him to Jung-lu, who asked him questions. Later someone gave him this letter, and here he was.

The letter was signed by "Prince Ch'ing and Colleagues," which was odd, since Prince Ch'ing, having offended the Empress because he was not pro-Boxer, had been replaced as President of the Tsungli Yamen by Prince Tuan. Nevertheless it sounded authoritative. It was quite cordial in tone, and written in the courteous pretence that all the fighting was being done against the Court's wishes. The writers said regretfully that it was no longer possible to carry out the original plan by which the Ministers were to go to Tientsin, since the Boxers would certainly prevent such traveling: therefore they proposed that their Excellencies should move to the Tsungli Yamen instead, in small parties and without bringing along any guards. The missive ended with a strong hint: if no reply was forthcoming by noon next day, the undersigned could not be responsible for the consequences.

That same day the walled city of Tientsin had been stormed and taken by foreigners, but MacDonald and his colleagues didn't know it, and were at a loss to understand the new move. Nevertheless, though bewildered, they were not struck senseless, and had no intention of walking into the spider's parlor. They replied tartly, by letter which the old man carried back, pointing out that there are rules of international procedure that govern the actions of diplomatic personnel, and added that they could see no merit in the idea of moving to the Tsungli Yamen from where they were. Next morning the firing was especially hot and heavy, and the British chief of staff was killed. Another young Briton had lost his life the day before, and that evening there was a double funeral, the ceremony proceeding under whistling bullets. In the middle of all this the old man of the Yamen letter appeared again, carrying two more messages. One was addressed to Mr. Conger, and was, astonishingly, a genuine telegram from Washington asking for news. The other was again from Prince Ch'ing and his friends, addressed to Sir Claude and carrying friendly assurances of continued "protection." What *did* it all mean? Nobody could make it out, but at the same time, slowly and irregularly, enemy firing seemed to abate, and by next morning there could be no doubt about it: the Chinese had suspended hostilities.

In his *Siege at Peking* [(London, 1959), p. 168], Peter Fleming points out that the Court and even the fire-eating Empress had plenty of cause on that day to pause for reflection. It had become evident that the Boxers were not as useful as they had hoped. Instead of working a miracle and ridding the nation of the foreign pests, they had merely embroiled the Imperial troops and then left them to do the effective work. As one censor pointed out, "When the Boxers first came, they claimed that they had supernatural powers, that they were invulnerable to guns and swords, and that they were capable of burning the foreign houses and exterminating the foreigners as easily as turning over a hand. Now they are different: first they evade by artifice, then they retreat and make no advance. Only the army of Tung Fu-hsiang has attacked with all effort day and night."

The complaint was incontrovertible and was only one of many.

Moreover, by this time protests from the Western world were piling up and in their very number could not be ignored. London, Paris, Berlin, St. Petersburg had all been heard from, and ships of these nations were steaming, full speed, toward Taku. The Russians had gladly taken the opportunity to move their ever-ready troops into Manchuria. The provincial Viceroys, save for "the foul Yü Hsien, who in the inaccessible province of Shansi continued to murder every missionary he could lay hands on" [Fleming, p. 166], were less than ever pleased with the way things were going: a strongly worded memorial arrived from thirteen of these officials in the south on that same unlucky July 14, advocating a complete reversal of Peking policy: protection of foreigners, suppression of Boxers, and an apology from China to Germany for the murder of Baron von Ketteler. The Manchus needed a respite so that they might think over the situation, hence the truce.

Contemporary descriptions of the next thirteen days describe conditions something like those of the even shorter unofficial armistice of 1918 in Europe. Chinese soldiers applied at the Legation gates for medical aid, and were given it. The combatants swapped or sold food between front lines. Jung-lu learned that the Legation Quarter, though not actually short of plain food, was missing fresh fruit in the hot weather: he promptly sent them peaches, and the Empress had several loads of fruit, ice, and flour delivered to the foreigners. All this time Sir Claude MacDonald was corresponding busily with the chatty if changeable Prince Ch'ing. There was a personal interview between the diplomats and a member of the Yamen who came to the British Legation for the purpose. Now that a few barriers were let down, the foreigners learned some encouraging facts about what was going on in Tientsin, so that when Prince Ch'ing again broached the subject of their going away, they dared to dally. They haggled over ways and means, and played for time. Finally Chinese patience was exhausted and the firing began again, but these fresh hostilities did not sever communications between the diplomats and the Yamen. Between bullets, polite letters passed to and fro, and foreign Ministers were allowed to write messages—in code, at that—for their governments, which were courteously forwarded by the Chinese. Life was still dangerous, and now the community was running short of food and ammunition, but a definite thaw had set in. In the perverse way that fate works, it was at this time, the end of July, that an alarming rumor swept over Europe and America to the effect that all foreigners in Peking had been wiped out. The people at home were gripped with violent emotions; grief and a longing for vengeance. When the news was at last contradicted, preparations were set in train in Tientsin for a relief march on the capital.

The besieged people in Peking would have been divided between fury and despair if they had known how long the arrangements for their relief were in the making. The powers had begun to play international chess with the situation, and like most chess players they needed time to think over their moves. For excuse they said that this time everything must be properly ready before the troops set out; nobody wanted more Seymour disasters. Moreover, the failure to save "Chinese" Gordon at Khartoum was all too vividly remembered. Each nation tried to contribute the lion's share to the relief forces, and this was not due to a pure desire to help. Squabbles and reassessments were the order of many days, but at last on August 4 the International Relief Force, or at least an advance army of 20,000 men, started out, planning to wait at Yangtsun thirty miles on for the rest to catch up. They traveled along the Peiho, as Seymour had intended to do when his trains failed him; they used junk and sampan, mules and horses. Leading the procession were the Japanese, and at the first battle, which took place at the Hsiku Arsenal early on the fifth, it was the Japanese, with their usual courage and toughness, who drove off the assailants. Next day as the force approached Yangtsun there was another encounter with the Chinese, and the foreigners gained victory so easily that they decided not to wait for reinforcements after all. The French Annamites suffered, and nobody was happy in the glaring summer heat of North China, but those who did not drop out—and they were the majority—plodded on in the wake of the Japanese, who met the most formidable opposition, the walled city of Tungchow, with their customary aplomb and on the twelfth blew up the city's south gate. China's troops were fleeing in disorder. Nevertheless, in Peking as the Relief Force drew near, the besiegers increased their fire, probably in a crazy hope of wiping out the evidence at the last minute, but on the night of the thirteenth there was a noticeable diminution of noise as the Chinese threw down their weapons and ran. Between two and three in the morning of the fourteenth the first rescuers arrived in the Legation Quarter; they were Sikhs and Rajputs who found their way in through the Water Gate. They were given a wildly joyous welcome, though they were so thirsty they could not for a while appreciate it.

Little by little throughout the day the rest of the Force trickled in, hot and exhausted. While they rested and the relieved people celebrated, outside the barricades the last stubborn Chinese soldier quietly evaporated. Manchus had been fleeing in all directions for several days, but the Empress, with Kuang-hsü and the palace household in her care, put off their departure until very late, no doubt clinging until the end to the hope of some miracle. But at last, early in the morning on the fifteenth, Tzu-hsi gave the order to move on. "Whoever thought it would come to this?" she remarked as she changed her clothes, putting on the dress of a Chinese peasant woman and adopting a suitable hair arrangement. Giving hasty directions as she superintended the packing—take this, leave that, bury the treasure deep in that courtyard—she found herself annoyingly impeded, wherever she turned, by the tiresome Pearl Concubine, who insisted on dropping to her knees and weeping at the Empress, no matter how often she was told to get out of the way. The Pearl Concubine's pleas concerned Kuang-hsü, at that moment waiting in his apartments to be told which of his household he might take along. The Pearl had an extraordinary idea that he should be left behind in Peking with her to look after him: this was so ridiculous that Tzu-hsi could hardly be expected to waste any more time arguing, and at last her patience snapped. Like the Duke in Browning's poem, she gave commands . . . and her eunuchs promptly dragged the Pearl Concubine out of the royal chamber and threw her down a well. Soon afterwards the Imperial procession started on the long road which was to take them to Sian by a roundabout route through Kalgan in the northwest, in order to confound any possible pursuers.

They had got away just in time to avoid the entry of the Relief Force into the Imperial City. Thick walls had to be blasted before these men could get in, and some token resistance was put up by a few Chinese guards who had remained on duty, but the troops made it and were just about to enter the Forbidden City by the same means when their officers told them to desist. It was the Russian commander in chief's idea that the rape of this holy of holies would sow seeds of resentment and trouble for years to come. At first the men were angry in their disappointment, but they forgot it in the rapture of sacking the rest of Peking. Soon they were out of hand. The looting, raping, and sheer bestiality of the following weeks far outdid the scenes of the Yuan Ming Yuan's destruction forty years earlier, nor did the Forbidden City remain inviolate very much longer. Many of the tales of looting are so much like those pertaining to the destruction of the Yuan Ming Yuan that they sound like sheer repetition: the French with their greed, the sightseers who calmly pocketed any *bibelot* that took their fancy in the Imperial bedroom, and so on.

Chinese administration was of course at a standstill, but the various commanders in chief arranged to divide the city into zones of responsibility, much as all China had been split, and within these limits the different nationals took necessary steps to ensure hygiene. The streets were cleared of rotting human and animal corpses. The wretched civilians came out of whatever holes they had bolted to, slavishly protesting that they had always loved foreigners, all the time. Hardly had the noise of shots ceased to reverberate when representatives of the various powers got to work trying to steal marches on each other. It was generally admitted that Russia had come off best by occupying Manchuria. On August 18 they held a victory march through the city which, since nine-tenths of the residents were absent, could hardly be called a successful demonstration; still, it was the thing to do, and it was done. Then the question arose as to negotiations. Who was left on the Chinese side to take part in them? The Court had run away. Nevertheless an answer finally came; the Empress had a tidy mind and a sense of duty, and she had given thought to this quandary. Prince Ch'ing had started out with her on her "tour of inspection" as a part of the Imperial retinue. She sent him back to Peking with certain instructions: he was to persuade Li Hung-chang to leave Canton and come to the capital city, there to represent the throne, deal with the foreigners, and play the old game, if he could, of stirring them up against each other—dividing and ruling. In theory this was an excellent idea: Li was well known to the foreigners and had a name for his technique in managing them. Unfortunately it was not the first time he had been summoned since the beginning of the Boxer Rising. Again and again Tzu-hsi had told him to come, but he always got out of it: he didn't approve of the affair and wanted no part of it. Now that it was all over he was in no hurry to pick up the pieces. He did bestir himself at last, and left Canton, but he was a month on the way to Tientsin.

✽   ✽   ✽

That morning of the fifteenth of August the Empress's party traveled in Peking carts to the Summer Palace, where they were joined by Ch'ing and other princes and officials, and two thousand troops. The procession almost immediately resumed its journey northwest. Peking carts are neither swift nor comfortable and progress was necessarily slow: nervously the outriders kept looking out for pursuers who never materialized. For several days the Empress retained her peasant disguise, and had to subsist on the humble food of poverty-stricken, war-starved villages: indeed, that is how the memory of her flight is kept green in North China even today, by a certain sort of bread served in Peking restaurants. It is a corn-meal muffin with a pocket of minced meat at one end; Chinese will tell you that when Tzu-hsi was once given corn-meal bread to eat on the road, her host was overcome with shame at having to serve such rough fare to his Empress, and slipped bits of meat into it to take off the curse. There were other hardships. The first night out the lady slept on a brick k'ang, or ovenbed; k'angs are warm enough, but very hard. At another village when there was no bed at all, in spite of having just murdered Kuang-hsü's favorite concubine, she shared a bench with him on which they sat back to back all night, dozing as best they could. Yet for the most part the indomitable woman was surprisingly cheerful, assuring the other refugees that all would be well. Only once, if Wu Yung, magistrate of the village of Huailai, is to be believed, did she lose control of herself. Soaked with rain, chilled to the bone, hungry and thirsty, the Empress was weeping when the party arrived at the local inn.

Things got better as they left behind them the war-scarred country around Peking. After Kalgan the caravan turned southwest toward Sian, but made a long break in the journey at Taiyuan, the capital of Shansi, where the passionately pro-Boxer Yu-hsien was Governor. His meeting with Tzu-hsi was fraught with interest. These two people had backed the wrong horse together, but any camaraderie on such grounds was out of the question. Yu-hsien could not possibly tell his Empress that she had made a mistake. Instead he blamed himself for everything and apologized with all his heart for the Empress's errors of judgment. He said that the trouble was that the Boxers had lost faith, and the virtue had thus gone out of them. Still, he said, he had not been idle: he had done to death every Christian in Shansi province, native or foreign. Tzu-hsi smiled on him. Properly dressed again, ensconced in state in the Governor's own *yamen*, she presided at a great banquet; then the talk turned once more to Yu-hsien's massacres. They visited the main courtyard of the *yamen* where the governor had brought death to forty-five foreigners—men, women, and children—and a number of native converts. The Empress was fascinated by Yu-hsien's account of the long day, and asked many questions: proudly he told her all about it— the tidy decapitations at the beginning, his impatience with the slow rate at which everything went, his decision to turn his soldiers loose on the Christians all at one time—and Tzu-hsi listened raptly throughout. He had done splendidly, she assured him at the end of the tale, but—here she spoke with a touch of warning gravity— the foreigners would doubtless make trouble about the affair in due course, and it might be less embarrassing for the Throne if Yu-hsien were to resign his governorship. Of course he did resign then and there, but he could have been under no illusions: he knew this would not be the end of it. A few days later, "Coffins are getting cheaper," said the Empress to the doomed man.

For some days she stayed on in Taiyuanfu, appreciating the flesh-pots and daily expecting to hear that her host had committed suicide, which would have been the honorable way out. But Yu-hsien disappointed his Empress and waited to be apprehended. In due course he was, according to the terms of the treaty, and in the list of Boxers to be executed his name led all the rest. However, this was in the future. In the meantime Tzu-hsi welcomed Jung-lu with real pleasure when he caught up with her party. She might have prolonged her visit if a false rumor of foreign troops on the trail had not alarmed her. At the end of September the court, well-fed now and luxuriously appointed, moved on to its destination, Sian, seven hundred miles from Peking. There the Empress settled down and stayed, in splendid exile, for a year. She thoroughly enjoyed life in Sian: it made a change.

Chapter Sixteen

As the dust settled there were a few Chinese and Manchu officials who found themselves unexpectedly popular, considering that the colleagues who had shared their anti-Boxer views were long since dead. The tables were turned now and pro-Boxers were losing their heads at such a rate that it seemed as if there would not be enough officials to do the work, but Tzu-hsi knew she could depend, even at long distance, on at least three men: Yuan Shih-k'ai, Jung-lu, and Li Hung-chang. Yuan, supple as ever, had managed to sidestep the issue, and though he never approved of the siege or the murders he avoided saying so. Jung-lu had spoken his mind, but he had a favored position and there was never a chance that he would put himself in danger. The surprising one was old Li Hung-chang, who did not scruple to scold the Empress quite rudely before she was forced to run for her life. She had just appointed him Viceroy of Chihli, the same post he had held with honor and success for years, until the Korea affair brought him down in disgrace. This appointment, made in haste because Tzu-hsi needed him once more, was accompanied by one of her peremptory commands to come to Peking forthwith. Li had gone as far as Shanghai before sending a blunt message which read in part,

"I am sincerely grateful for Your Majesty's gratifying confidence in me, but cannot help recalling to mind the folly which has now suddenly destroyed that structure of reformed administration which, during my twenty years' term of office as Viceroy of Chihli, I was able to build up not unsuccessfully. I fear it will not be possible for me to resume the duties of this difficult post at a time of crisis like the present. . . ."

Again Tzu-hsi commanded him to come to Peking. Li would not. He gave an interview to the London *Times* correspondent in Shanghai, declaring that he wouldn't go north until the Empress saw the error of her ways and made it up with the foreigners. Then he sent a memorial which Tzu-hsi received just before the Court ran away. History teaches, said Li, that before going to war it is better to make sure you are stronger than your enemy. In 1860 Hsien-feng had been driven from Peking by foreigners, and it was natural that Her Majesty's subjects should join her in the wish to avenge her husband. But since that time France had snatched Annam, Japan had pushed the Chinese out of Korea, and the three nations, Germany, Russia, and England, had grabbed much Chinese territory. China simply wasn't able to resist any of this, and recent battles had amply proved it. Only two or three thousand foreign soldiers had defended Tientsin against tens of thousands of Boxers and Imperial troops who attacked the foreign settlement, yet after ten days of desperate fighting the foreigners had lost a mere few hundred, while no less than twenty thousand Chinese were killed and as many more wounded. "Again, there are no real defences or fortified positions in the Legations at Peking, nor are the foreign Ministers and their Legation staffs trained in the use of arms: nevertheless, Tung Fu-hsiang's hordes have been bombarding them for more than a month, and have lost many thousands of men in the vain attempt to capture the position." Li spoke of the Allied Powers' fleets which were hurrying to bring vast bodies of troops and masses of heavy artillery. Had China the forces to meet them? Would the Emperor and Empress Dowager be able to get away? . . .

"I myself am nearly eighty years of age, and my death cannot be far distant; I have received favours at the hands of four Emperors. If now I hesitate to say the things that are in my mind, how shall I face the spirits of the sacred ancestors of this Dynasty when we meet in the halls of Hades? . . . You should take steps immediately to appoint a high official who shall purge the land of this villainous rabble, and who shall see to it that the foreign Ministers are safely escorted to the headquarters of the Allied Armies. In spite of the great heat, I have hurried northwards from Canton to Shanghai, where Your Majesties' Decrees urging me to come to Peking have duly reached me. Any physical weakness, however serious, would not have deterred me from obeying this summons, but perusal of your Decrees has led me to the conclusion that Your Majesties have not yet adopted a policy of reason, but are still in the hands of traitors, regarding these Boxers as your dutiful subjects. . . ." [Bland and Backhouse, *China* . . . , p. 388.]

"Li Hung Chang looks quite well and seems no weaker than when he called a year ago," wrote Mrs. Conger after the old Viceroy came to call. It was November 16 and he had at last brought himself to travel to Peking, though the court was still hiding out in Sian. He chatted amiably with the American ladies; "He seemed to think eating horse meat during the siege quite a joke and talked and laughed about it. He thought we should forget eating horse meat now." However much resentment the other delivered foreigners retained against the Chinese, Mrs. Conger's attitude was firmly friendly. Throughout the siege she had clung to her Christian Science principles and they did not desert her now. Watching the work that was being done under British direction, of building an extension to the railway through the city wall and up to the front entrance of the Temple of Heaven, Mrs. Conger was distressed to observe that the process led to the digging up of a large number of old graves. She knew how careful the Chinese are of their graves.

"The railroad could have gone a little to the right or left of this large, old cemetery," she reflected. "I have much sympathy for the Chinese, and yet I do not in any way uphold them nor excuse them in their fiendish cruelty. They have given the foreigners the most sorrowful, most degrading, and most revengeful treatment that their fiendish ideas can conceive. But the facts remain the same; China belongs to the Chinese, and she never wanted the foreigner upon her soil. The foreigner would come, force his life upon the Chinese, and here and there break a cog of the wheels that run their Government so systematically. Even if we grant that China's condition has been improved by these invasions, what right has the foreigner to enter this domain unbidden and unwelcome? The foreigner has forced himself, his country, his habits, and his productions upon China, always against a strong protest. It kept getting worse for China, and she recognized the fact. At length, in one last struggle, she rose in her mistaken might to wipe the foreigner and his influence from her land." [Conger, p. 188.]

Later she wrote, "To divide China among the nations would mean wars and a standing army large and strong. The bitterness of the Chinese would grow deeper and more active. . . ." Such a drastic solution to the problem had in fact been discussed among the diplomatic group, and some of the gentlemen favored the course, but most of them felt, with Mrs. Conger, that it would lead to too much trouble. As the days passed, passions cooled, and now here was Li Hung-chang to put the past out of the foreign mind altogether with his gentle jokes and his practiced methods for managing barbarians. The final treaty settlement was very much the mixture as before, though naturally it was even less palatable to Peking. A huge indemnity was to be paid in installments for the next thirty-nine years, out of revenue from the Customs as well as the Salt Gabelle. Two dignitaries, a prince and a vice-president of the Council, were to convey the apologies of the nation to Germany and Japan for the murder of their Ministers. China must promise not to import any foreign weapons for the space of two years, though this promise was abrogated soon after, when the threat of war between Russia and Japan became pressing. But the clause that naturally aroused most personal interest was that which dealt with punishments. In almost any Western country the Empress herself could hardly have got off as completely as she did, but this was China. As we know, Yu-hsien went to his death, and was followed by several other Boxers—among whom Prince Tuan was not included, chiefly owing to the stiff battle that Tzu-hsi put up for him all the way from Sian. There were other important names noticeably lacking in the list as well. Tzu-hsi did her best for her friends. A number of Imperial statements were issued from the court's luxurious exile, directing suicide for this official and decapitation for that, but the foreign powers would not be diverted from their intention of punishing the ringleaders, and kept speaking of Prince Tuan and Duke Lan with what must have been annoying persistency. At last the Empress reluctantly condemned these two to "imprisonment pending decapitation," a phrase which was understood to mean life imprisonment, and later, when passions had cooled, she was able to commute this sentence to life banishment in Turkestan.

Numbered among the smaller fry, the bandit general Tung Fu-hsiung was cashiered but not executed. In a gesture which seems to the Westerner quite remarkably futile but owed itself nevertheless to the demand of the foreign Ministers, the Empress posthumously restored the rank and honors of five officials who had been executed for trying to turn her against the Boxers.

When all this disagreeable business had been attended to, the first of the remarkable "Penitential Decrees" made its appearance from Sian. Dated February 13, 1901, it said in part,

"Last summer the Boxers sowed the seeds of rebellion, which led to our being involved in a war with friendly Powers. Thereafter, our Capital being thrown into a state of great disorder, we escorted the Empress Dowager, our mother, on a progress of inspection throughout the Western Provinces. . . . It having been accorded to us to retrieve our disastrous mistakes, we are in duty bound to promulgate this Penitential Decree, and to let every one of our subjects know how vast and harassing were the perplexities with which the Throne has been beset.

"There are ignorant persons who believe that the recent crisis was partly caused by our government's support of the Boxers; they must have overlooked our reiterated Decrees of the 5th and 6th moons, that the Boxers should be exterminated, and the Christians protected. Unfortunately these rebels and their evil associates placed us in a position from which it was impossible to escape; we exhausted every possible effort of strong remonstrance, appalled at the impending ruin of our Empire. Events moved swiftly until, on the 21st of the 7th moon, our Capital fell; on that day, both her Majesty the Empress Dowager and ourselves decided to commit suicide in the presence of the tutelary deities of our Dynasty and the gods of the soil, thus making atonement and offering propitiation to the spirits of our nine Imperial ancestors. But, at the critical moment of dire lamentation and confusion, we were seized by our Princes and Ministers, and forcibly led away from that place where bullets fell like rain, and where the enemies' guns gathered thick as forest trees. Hastily, and with souls perturbed, we started on our Western tour. Were not all these disasters caused by the Boxers? . . . While the Legations were being besieged, we repeatedly directed our Ministers of the Tsungli Yamen to put a stop to hostilities, and at the same time to keep up communication with the foreign Ministers, assuring them of our kindly and sympathetic regard. This latter order, however, was not carried out because of the continuous artillery and rifle fire between the besiegers and the besieged, and it was impossible for us, under such conditions, to insist upon its execution. Supposing, by some horrible fatality, the Legations had actually fallen, how could China have hoped to preserve her integrity? To the Throne's strenuous efforts is really due the avoidance of such a dreadful catastrophe, and the gifts of wine, fruit and watermelons to the besieged Legations, were an indication of Her Majesty's benevolent intentions. It was but natural and right that the friendly Powers should appreciate these our feelings, and the fact that at such a crisis they have respected the integrity of our Empire as a Sovereign State, goes to prove that the Allies attribute no longer any blame to the Throne. . . ." [Bland and Backhouse, *China* . . . , p. 376.]

The Westerner, reading this farrago, may feel a surge of shock and fury, since in our philosophy it is insulting to be presented with such a lot of barefaced lies. What did the Empress take us for —blithering idiots? A little thought will abate the reaction. In Tzu-hsi's world it was not necessarily an insult to express misstatements of fact. One lied because it was conventional, and to save face, and in general to smooth over the awkward, ugly moment. One lied to spare embarrassment all round. The liar was not foolish enough to suppose he was believed: he was simply following the code. One keeps up appearances, just as one makes fantastically pretty speeches that could not possibly be true. For our part, our compara-tive fidelity to the truth—only comparative; who among us has not signed a letter, "Sincerely yours," when it was not in the least sin-cere?—has often been a source of confusion and mirth to the Chi-nese. It is simply a matter of learning the code. A Westerner knows enough to discount the protestation of another Westerner; a Span-iard, for example, who says "Everything in my house is yours." Lit-tle by little, the foreign diplomats in China were learning. At least, none of them fell dead of apoplexy when the Penitential Decrees appeared.

For a long time the Empress was distinctly nervous about her position. Though Li Hung-chang sent word that she should now return to Peking—bringing with her, of course, the Emperor, that dummy power symbol—she hung back. She even deliberated the advisability of making Sian the permanent capital city rather than undergo what she feared must happen, a shearing away of all her authority. However, when at last she heard the terms of the pro-jected Peace Protocol and knew it was to be signed, and that every-thing as far as she was concerned would be unchanged, she gave the word to her household to pack. Packing was no small task, for she had collected great masses of tribute in Sian. The Protocol was signed in September, and on October 20, 1901, an immensely long Imperial caravan set out on the return journey. They were still on their way, resting for a few days at Kaifeng, when Li Hung-chang died, probably killed from overwork. During his last hours he had named Yuan Shih-k'ai as his successor, and Yuan accordingly slid into the post of Acting Viceroy of Chihli, which carried with it the job of Commissioner for North China Trade. Though it was a very high position for a man of forty-two, Yuan did not leap at it: he had a keen nose for yet more power, and he reflected that even as Viceroy of Chihli he would be outranked by several other officials. Besides, he hated to relinquish control over Shantung. After his two years of governorship that province was in nice shape. Therefore he demurred courteously against the promotion, and not until he had been promised that he could retain authority over Shantung would he accept it.

*　*　*

It was a transformed Empress Dowager who returned to Peking —a woman who had made up her mind to accept the inevitable and be friendly to the Western barbarian. There was a hint of this change in the word she sent ahead of her, that any foreigners who wished to witness the Imperial arrival should be permitted to do so, instead of being requested to stay at home as was the custom in pre-Boxer days. (No doubt they would have taken the liberty in any case. In this manner she drew the sting from the affair.) She also announced her intention of resuming friendly relations with the diplomats' wives. It was noticeable that she took special pains while on the road to wave and smile at any stray foreigner who happened to be about. For the last stages of the journey the party rode in a thirty-carriage train which brought them to the new station on the dot of noon, January 6, 1902—an auspicious date carefully chosen by Her Majesty's soothsayers—and the excitement can be imagined; the pavilions built specially for the reception, lacquer thrones, luxurious decorations, and colored chairs to take the household home. Tzu-hsi watched with the keen eye of an accountant the unloading of her treasure chests, and in the same way summed up the crowd. She said, "Quite a number of foreigners here, I see," in the gratified tones of an actress on tour, and then she bowed to the foreigners and raised her clasped hands to them in courteous gesture. The nobles felt this was overdoing things, but the foreigners loved it. On her way back to the palace in her chair, "by her side ran one of her favourite eunuchs repeatedly calling Her Majesty's attention to objects of interest. Whenever foreigners were in sight he would inform

Her Majesty of the fact, and by one he was heard distinctly to say: 'Look! Old Buddha, look quickly at that foreign devil,' whereupon the Empress smiled and bowed most affably." [Bland and Backhouse, *China* . . . , p. 403.] As soon as she got home she commanded the eunuchs to dig up her cache of treasure. It was untouched, and her reaction was divided between gratification at her luck and scorn of the ham-handed enemy looters who had never found it.

Now that the Empress was back she had to perform many duties. For one thing a decree must be issued in praise of the Pearl Concubine. This interesting document declared that the young woman had committed suicide when she couldn't catch up with the fleeing Court, in reward for which virtuous action she was posthumously promoted to higher rank—another example of smoothing over which must have rendered foreign newcomers speechless with indignation. Then she arranged a reception for six new foreign Ministers, who were permitted for the first time in Chinese history to enter the Forbidden City, and through the front gate, at that. Another reception soon followed to which the whole diplomatic corps was invited, and Tzu-hsi flouted precedent by presiding on the throne. It was there observed that the position of Kuang-hsü was evidently improved since the flight from Peking. He could no longer be called a prisoner. Some foreigners thought they could discern eccentricity in his demeanor, but others did not. It was impossible to say, since he had no direct communication with any of them and was very reserved in their presence. He and the Empress Dowager were scrupulously polite to each other. . . . Mrs. Conger, who with the other ladies and the children of the diplomats was received at the palace soon afterwards, saw nothing odd about the Emperor. "He is rather small, with a young, bright face; his eyes give expression to his smile. He did not impress me as being a frail person," she noted.

Nobody could have been more gracious than Tzu-hsi on this occasion. The presents to the ladies were lavish, the Empress's protestations were practically gushing, and "The Empress Dowager again and again assured me that such troubles as those of the past two years should never be repeated," said Mrs. Conger. [P. 221.] She added, "There were sharp and bitter criticisms of the ladies' acceptance of the Imperial invitation. Individual bitterness still has its poison and would keep the breach open and even widen it if possible; but national wisdom, through peace negotiations, seeks to

close the breach." A few weeks later the Empress invited the whole
lot of females yet again, and though this time she had been requested by the foreign husbands not to give more presents—Westerners and Chinese have never seen eye to eye on this custom—she
smuggled a little jade baby into Mrs. Conger's hand, and said in
dumb show, "Don't tell." Mrs. Conger disobeyed her husband's
wishes, as any lady would have. "I took the dear little thing home,
and I prize it. It showed good will, and I do not intend to let go of
that thought."

Then the Congers invited a number of Court princesses to their
home. The ladies accepted, and so—of course, like a shot—did a select number of American women, and they had a tiffin party. Nearly
five hundred servants swarmed over the premises, giving the Conger
domestics more face than even such haughty officials had ever hoped
for. After that invitations were exchanged between Court and Legation so fast that Mrs. Conger found herself under fire from the great
American republic, for fraternizing with the recent enemy. It is un-
derstandable: the home newspapers had been full, not so long before, of the villainy of the Empress Dowager, and had played up
particularly what would have seemed an unimportant detail to the
lady—her offer of a bounty for every foreign head. But Mrs. Conger
was quite capable of taking on the whole nation when she thought
she had right on her side, as she did in this quarrel. She answered
critical letters with spirited argument. Inevitably, the more she defended the Empress the more genuinely fond of the Empress she
became. Tzu-hsi for her part was attacked vigorously by such of her
compatriots as felt themselves safe in doing so, namely residents in
the treaty ports. "There can be no objection to giving a banquet to
anyone who is likely to be grateful and show some return for hospitality, but what possible good purpose can be served by feasting
those who treat you with suspicion?" demanded an indignant writer
in a Shanghai newspaper. "We Chinese are wont to despise our
ignorant rustics when they display servility to foreigners, but what
is to be said when one in the exalted position of the Empress Dowager demeans herself by being on terms of affectionate intimacy with
the wives of Foreign Ministers, and even with women belonging to
the commercial and lower classes? Nowadays foreign food is served
at the Palace in a dining room decked out in European style: the
guests at these entertainments thank their Imperial hostess on taking leave, and the very next day their Legations will furiously rage

against China at our Foreign Office. Therefore, as for moderating their barbarous ways, her food and her wines are simply wasted. As a matter of fact, these guests of hers do not scruple to compare her banquets of today with the melons and vegetables which she sent to the Legations during the siege, a comparison by no means flattering to Her Majesty. The thing is becoming a scandal. When Russia poured out entertainments in honour of Li Hung-chang she got something for her money; can it be that Her Majesty is looking to similar results in the present case for herself?"

Tzu-hsi gave no sign of hearing these bleats, and went on in the way she chose. She was enjoying herself in all the excitement. Her restless, innovation-loving spirit must have chafed all through the years under the weight of protocol, and here, in the cloak of policy, was an excellent escape. Harry Hussey retails a bit of gossip about her stay in Sian that indicates how very shackled she had been. It seems that Jung-lu made her a present there of a wonderfully embroidered robe of pink satin, set with pearls and jade. Unfortunately the Household Rules stated clearly that Empresses can wear only yellow, blue, and purple. One might suppose that Tzu-hsi of all people would not mind defying this niggling regulation, considering how violently she had broken other Household Rules, for instance that regarding the succession. But in her view this was not a trivial matter. In her entourage was a haughty princess of more aristocratic descent than Tzu-hsi, and Tzu-hsi felt a great awe for her. The princess always knew best, she thought. Even the Empress had moments of insecurity, but if the princess thought she might safely wear the pink dress, all would be well. Accordingly Tzu-hsi, while drinking tea with the princess, began to work around to the question as delicately and indirectly as etiquette demanded, but before she could arrive the unkind aristocrat was there ahead of her, and announced that she had just seen a pink satin robe for sale, embroidered in pearl and jade, which was so lovely that she had been tempted to buy it for Tzu-hsi. She had resisted the temptation, however, because she knew that the Household Rules wouldn't permit the Empress to wear pink. Poor Tzu-hsi got the idea, and the pink robe was never worn. [Hussey, p. 322.] If only she had been given her present a year or two later, who knows what might have happened? Many other petty rules were broken, after she got back to Peking.

She readily accepted Mrs. Conger's suggestion that she have her portrait painted in the Western fashion, and Mrs. Conger excitedly wrote off to arrange matters with an artist in Shanghai, Miss Katharine Carl, whose father, an American, was a Commissioner of Customs. Evidently the Empress was satisfied in advance as to Miss Carl's qualifications for the commission; there is no mention made of showing her samples of the artist's work. It was all quite simple: Miss Carl was presented, and in August 1903, she moved into the Summer Palace and got to work. Later, it goes without saying, she wrote a book about her experiences there. In spite of its gush it gives an interesting picture of palace life and above all of the writer's distinguished sitter, though it is not true, as the American ladies believed, that this was the first time anyone in Tzu-hsi's position had been portrayed by a Western painter. K'ang-hsi's portrait was done by the Jesuit Guiseppe Castiglione, and no doubt the Empress Dowager could have cited his example if she had felt the need for justification.

Though Tzu-hsi's acceptance of Miss Carl had gone easily enough, the work itself did not. The Western woman was accustomed to her world's ways in such matters, where the artist goes about his task according to his own ideas, and his model would not dream of telling him how to do it. It is different in China—the whole attitude toward painting is different. There, the artist is held firmly to certain rules. One paints a vase or a flower just so, and no other way is right. Painting is a sort of variation of calligraphy and depends on complete mastery of brush-handling. The fur of an animal is depicted as faithfully as the artist can do it, with almost every hair in place. A bird's feathers, a lady's jewels, a tree's leaves are all drawn in, and shadow is not represented at all. Miss Carl naturally intended to use light and shade and fuzzy sketch-lines, but Tzu-hsi and the courtiers were having none of that. Firmly if kindly they explained to her exactly what was wanted. There cannot be much in the archives dealing with foreigners in China that surpasses in unconscious humor the unhappy lady's description of how she began her portrait. It had to happen on the exact stroke of eleven in the morning, a lucky hour chosen by the usual soothsayers. Moreover, it had to be done in full view of a number of ladies in waiting, eunuchs and other self-appointed critics. She was expected to produce a luxury version of the "ancestor picture" bought ready-made by Chinese in the market place; a large stock seated figure, male or female, painted in every loving detail save for the face, which is left blank: the features are added when the subject has died. No painter of such pictures ever tried to vary the pattern, and though Miss Carl's effort was presumably to be highly superior to such popular art, the Court's taste was irrevocably shaped by it. When Miss Carl made a timid suggestion as to the disposition of her sitter's hands, she was gently laughed to silence. Tzu-hsi probably thought she didn't know her place, but would learn if she was tactfully treated. Certainly Miss Carl *was* tactfully treated, with the greatest possible hospitality. One of her problems was to get enough time to work, for the Empress argued that she must not tire herself out by toiling away between sittings, and her dictum was enforced by attentive eunuchs who snatched away the painter's colors, brushes, and the portrait itself as soon as a sitting was over.

Tzu-hsi chose her dress and jewels with great care before she sat. Unfortunately she often changed her mind as to what pearls or other pretties she wanted painted, and then she would blithely command Miss Carl to change the portrait accordingly, evidently not realizing that too much rubbing out and painting over cannot be good for a canvas. In the end, despairing, Miss Carl produced quite a good version of an ancestor portrait complete with Tzu-hsi's face and favorite jewels. Tzu-hsi was so pleased with it that she decided to send the thing, ornately framed, to the St. Louis World's Fair and then present it to the American nation, but that was by no means the end of Miss Carl at the palace: she was pressed to stay on and continue painting portraits of Tzu-hsi. She finished three more, but though the Empress would have been happy to keep her there for life's duration, working on portrait after portrait of Tzu-hsi, Miss Carl could not be persuaded to take on a permanency.

Probably the freshest observations in the artist's book [*With the Empress Dowager of China* (London, 1906)] are those on Kuanghsü. This is fitting, since the period she was living in the Imperial household coincides with many of the proofs Tzu-hsi now gave that the dead Reform Party and the Emperor had not been so wrong after all, back in 1898. In decree after decree the Empress made suggestions for reforms, many of them embodying the same ideas that Kuang-hsü's Hundred Day advisers had tried to promulgate, though she took the precaution of explaining in advance that her version was much better. "Ever since the 23rd and 24th years of Kuang-hsu there has been no lack of plans for reform and suggestions of administrative change, but they have all been marked by vagueness and foolish looseness of thought. The crisis which was brought about in 1898 by the archtraitor K'ang Yu-wei was in its possible consequences even more dangerous than the evil which has since been brought about by the unholy arts of the Boxers," she said. [Bland and Backhouse, *China* . . . , p. 423.] With that out of the way she proceeded to imitate K'ang Yu-wei in many particulars and in a fashion calculated to whiten the hair of all the old guard. The examination system was to be abolished, and some bright young men should be sent abroad for their education. In the end, these two reforms turned out to be more important than any of the others in their effect on China's political development. Another edict, though it was much discussed, never came to much; it revoked an old law against intermarriage between Manchus and Chinese, but as things turned out, not many Manchus seemed to wish to marry Chinese after all, or vice versa. Yet another edict, outlawing torture as a means of administering justice, got the Empress what would be called today a good press in foreign lands. Unfortunately Her Majesty's law-enforcing officials did not take it seriously, any more than did the majority of Chinese regarding Tzu-hsi's edict against foot-binding. Manchus had never bound their girls' feet, but until Tzu-hsi's command they had not interfered with the strange desire of the Chinese to do so, and it was to take a revolution and a few years beyond that to accomplish the custom's abolition. As a climax to all this, a mission went to Europe on an observation tour, and when it returned its members recommended that China be given a constitution. The Empress approved this world-shaking notion.

What the Emperor thought about all this is not on record, but it is small wonder that Miss Carl thought she detected a constant, half-hidden smile on his lips. Of course she never chatted with him. She only saw him when he was in attendance on the Empress Dowager, or sitting on his comparatively small, secondary throne next to Tzu-hsi's splendid one. Miss Carl's comments stem purely from her romantic mind, but her unprejudiced opinion is a welcome change from the sneers of his contemporary compatriots, with whom nothing failed so miserably as failure. She noticed that both rulers were often preoccupied with the Russo-Japanese War. At least once she saw Tzu-hsi brush tears from her eyes, and on a day that Miss Carl had spent away from the palace, in Peking, she returned to her apartments—borrowed, during her stay, from the Emperor—to find that he had been there and had left a few papers scattered about, on which he had scribbled with the Vermilion Pencil. He had drawn a rough map of the war area in Manchuria, and a section of the Great Wall nearby. "So the Emperor, notwithstanding his stoical smile, his apparent unconcern, was not indifferent to affairs in Manchuria," wrote Miss Carl. Enforcedly idle, prudently silent, this man appears tantalizingly in the background of events, never again to hold the center of the stage as he had done for a while in the past century. "His tragedy was that he could not escape the control of his foster mother without breaking the conventional rules of filial piety." [Hummel, p. 733.]

National feeling was naturally on Japan's side in the war. Many Chinese and Manchus volunteered to fight side by side with their erstwhile enemies, though without the official sanction of their government. The outcome of the war somewhat surprised the West— the Japanese trounced the Russians—but foreigners who had undergone the Boxer sieges in company with Japanese fighters could have foreseen their triumph. China's pro-Japanese sentiments, however, did not survive the post-war stress of seeing the victors move in and occupy all that portion of Manchuria south of Changchun that the Russians had infiltrated during the Boxer upheaval. Peking had been too weak to claim her own territory from Russia, and things were no better now that the occupiers were Japanese: the latter were just as inflexible and immovable.

The unoccupied part of Manchuria was now divided into three provinces under a common Viceroy, with a Governor for each—all Yuan Shih-k'ai's men. Yuan had been busy since his appointment, strengthening his military forces and keeping the troops up to snuff by holding maneuvers every year. This efficient activity, and the fact that Yuan kept replacing Manchu officials with Chinese, were not lost on the watchful Manchu censors, and they complained bitterly of jumped-up youths, one going so far as to point out that Yuan, who had not performed any outstanding service, had received greater favors from the Throne than either Tseng Kuo-fan or Li Hung-chang. Yuan took note of the opposition's strength and tactfully drew in his horns, handing over a few army posts to Manchu officers again. Under cover, however, he retained his influence over the men. [Ch'en, p. 82.] The Manchus who regained their army posts immediately cancelled some of his reconstructions, but if they had meddled with the new military schools, Yuan would doubtless have resisted, and resisted successfully: his standing with the Empress was as high as ever. Perhaps it was higher, for Jung-lu died in 1903 and left him a clear field. Yuan set up a staff college, a non-commissioned officers' training school, and many similar institutions. He improved the military academy at Paoting, and saw to it that picked men went on to Japan for training. The excellence of Japanese military discipline taught a lesson that had not been lost on Yuan, and in spite of resentment over Manchuria many young Chinese still admired their neighbors and sought to know them better.

One striking effect of all this emphasis on military training was that the social status of the Chinese soldier began to improve. People had always looked down on the army as a catchall for men who were no good for anything else. "Bad iron for nails, bad men for soldiers," was a well-known proverb, and soldiers were deemed even lower than actors. In spite of the generals and warrior princes who were the heroes of traditional plays, the truly estimable man in that Confucian civilization was a scholarly gentleman who avoided unseemly argument. The Manchus had taken on the Chinese prejudice against soldiers, to such an extent that three centuries and a half had transformed those fierce mounted Tartars, tamed them, gentled them, and—corrupted them. Yuan Shih-k'ai's greatest obstacle in his army reforms were those same Manchus, so greedy and shortsighted that they sold commissions and pocketed the funds earmarked for armaments. Nevertheless he made progress, and already government soldiers had risen in public estimation, out of the class of bandits who only happened to be on the right side. In Chekiang a respectable youth named Chiang Kai-shek insisted, against the wishes and advice of all his elders, on going into the army. Of course Yuan Shih-k'ai had never heard of the young man; he is mentioned at this time only as a portent.

*   *   *

Tzu-hsi had every intention of living as long as her sister Empress, Queen Victoria, whom she much admired at a distance. Like other great nobles in her country, she made great play with characters that had auspicious meanings, hanging up large banners bearing them and weaving the lucky ideographs into the patterns of her decorations inside and outside the house. Her favorite character, not surprisingly, was one that means "longevity." Until the year of her death anyone would have supposed that she was well on the way to emulating Queen Victoria and achieving great longevity. Her health and spirits remained excellent, in sharp contrast to those of

Kuang-hsü, who fell ill in the autumn of 1907 and became so weak that he could not perform the traditional sacrifices at the temples which were an Emperor's duty. It was contrary to the Household Laws to select an Emperor's successor before he was known to be dying, but the Court would have been less than human if it had not buzzed with speculation as to Tzu-hsi's next choice. Then, in the summer of 1908, the Empress too had a warning in the form of a slight stroke. She recovered, but for the first time in her life she began to look her age, seventy-three. Until then she might have passed for forty.

Kuang-hsü died on November 14, 1908. That at least is the date given by the officials who announced his death when they finally let the secret out, but the situation was confused by politics and obscured by a number of conflicting versions of what really happened. For some time both he and the Empress Dowager had been ailing, she with dysentery—a common disease in the neighborhood of Peking—and he with something that has never been quite clear, though the usual stories of poisoning were circulated. (As always, they cannot be quite discounted. Possibilities are several as to who would want to do it. Tzu-hsi? Well-meaning friends of Tzu-hsi who feared that he might survive her? There are no answers to these questions.) What we know of the circumstances of his death depends very much on what account is read. They all agree that Tzu-hsi was very ill at the same time, but one narrator says that she managed to visit Kuang-hsü, whereas another declares indignantly that nobody but one faithful eunuch went anywhere near him in the last days, and that his quarters were in wretched repair; he had not even enough bedclothes. This seems hardly credible.

It was not particularly sinister that the news of his death should have been suppressed until a decision was made as to his successor. This was customary procedure. In any case the choice *may* have been made before Kuang-hsü died: it is not certain. Ill as she was, Tzu-hsi got up from her bed and called a special meeting of the Council to discuss the question, always an important one but particularly momentous for her at this time, for she had a long-standing debt to pay to the shade of her son T'ung-chih as well as for the suicide of Wu K'o-tu. She must provide T'ung-chih with an adopted heir; Kuang-hsü had died—or was dying—without issue. The choice hovered between two grown princes and the infant son of Prince Ch'un and Jung-lu's daughter. True to form, the Empress favored the baby boy, Pu-i. She reminded the Councilors that she had long planned to reward Jung-lu for his fidelity by placing his descendant on the throne: that was why she had married his daughter to Prince Ch'un. Now she wanted to name the child Emperor, with his father to serve as regent, and she had her way, as she had always done. The Councilors agreed. Little Pu-i was rushed to the palace, though it is said that his mother and his grandmother battled furiously with Prince Ch'un to save the baby from his fate. Evidently to have a son made Emperor of China was the worst thing conceivable, as long as Tzu-hsi was alive, and the women could not realize how soon that particular state of affairs was to be terminated.

One difficulty remained. T'ung-chih now had his heir, but what of Kuang-hsü? No matter; this too could be arranged, and was, by dividing Pu-i between the two ghosts. The Empress decreed that he should always perform sacrifices to both ancestors at once. It was a full day for a woman who had only one more to live. Yet in the morning of the fifteenth she seemed strong and well, and was able to tie up several loose ends and send out more edicts. She named herself Empress Grand Dowager, leaving her former title to be assumed by her niece, Kuang-hsü's widow. But at noon she fell into a fainting fit, and from then on she gave up. There was still time for one more decree:

"Yesterday I issued an Edict whereby Prince Ch'un was made Regent, and I commanded that the whole business of Government should be in his hands, subject only to my instructions. Being seized of a mortal sickness, and being without hope of recovery, I now order that henceforward the government of the Empire shall be entirely in the hands of the Regent. Nevertheless, should there arise any question of vital importance, in regard to which an expression of the Empress Dowager's opinion is desirable, the Regent shall apply in person to her for instructions, and act accordingly." [Bland and Backhouse, *China* . . . , p. 464.] She died that afternoon, having outlived the hapless Kuang-hsü if only by a day. There could have been no more dramatic proof that she was boss, first, last, and always.

Chapter Seventeen

Though for obvious reasons it suited the Manchus to call the Boxer movement a rebellion, it was not one, for its avowed aim was to strengthen existing authority rather than replace it. Traditionally, genuine Chinese revolutions started in the south, a good long way from Peking, where political control was not so tight and where, for years before the northern coast was open, foreign ideas had been trickling into the countryside, there to be converted by malcontents into a philosophy nearer their needs. Thus, paradoxically, political unrest was imported by Christian missionaries who preached peace and brotherly love. It was not, as some anti-foreigners asserted, that these men deliberately taught treason; they simply handed on Western-style literacy so that their pupils might read the Scriptures. But once a man had learned to read, his thoughts were his own and were apt to roam a long way from the Bible, as witness Hung Hsiu-ch'uan. Hung's example in its turn affected Sun Yat-sen, and Sun changed China to a degree never envisaged even by the Taipings.

He was born in 1866, in the Cantonese village of Choyhung. His parents were peasants, not well off but not desperately poor either. Like many others in the south, they had tenuous connections with the West. Two of Yat-sen's uncles had made family history by getting themselves carried off, as indentured laborers, to California during the days of the gold fever, and his brother Ah-mi, fifteen years older than Yat-sen, had gone to Hawaii and there made good as a farmer with his own property and a general store near a village called Ewa on Oahu. (For some years these Chinese emigrants had been annoying non-Chinese neighbors in the West with their hard-working, thrifty habits.) While Yat-sen was still a small boy, Ah-mi came back to Choyhung to visit his family. He suggested taking the little brother to Ewa on the return journey: the Sun parents decided that Yat-sen was too young, but a few years later, when he was twelve, they shipped him out to Hawaii. Yat-sen—it is simpler to call him by his familiar name throughout this account, though like all Chinese he had several different names—stayed with Ah-mi in the country only a short time before he went off to Honolulu to study at "the Bishop's school," as Iolani College was popularly known because it was founded by Bishop Willis of the Church of England. Though it had been designed for "boys of Hawaiian birth," Ah-mi seems to have got his little China-born brother in without difficulty. Yat-sen learned English at Iolani, for that is the language in which lessons were taught, and though Hawaii was still independent the islands swarmed with British and American missionaries: already English was the *lingua franca*. Besides English the boy picked up something else and thereby incurred Ah-mi's violent disapproval: he became a Christian. It is strange that the older Sun should have been so startled by this acquisition, for after all, Iolani was a mission school, but he was. By the time Yat-sen graduated in 1882 he was deeply Christian by conviction, and only Ah-mi's opposition prevented his being baptized. As it was, he put off the ceremony and went back to work at his brother's store until the end of the year, when the worried Ah-mi sent him home to China.

Yat-sen at sixteen, after so many broadening experiences, was restless and discontented in Choyhung. Fortunately he found a friend of similar temperament to his own, a boy named Lu Hao-tung, who had done a bit of traveling about the country and was as eagerly inquisitive as himself. Lu was better informed on Chinese history than Yat-sen, and he told the other boy about Hung Hsiu-ch'uan and the Taiping rebellion, a story Yat-sen had not heard until then. He was much stirred. One of Hung's youthful exploits, the smashing of his village idols, so much impressed him that he went with Lu and some other boys to the village temple and there, defying the forces of superstition, did a little smashing of his own, deliberately breaking off a finger of the chief image and slightly damaging another idol. There were no repercussions from the supernatural, but plenty from the village councilors when they heard about it. Yat-sen's father had to pay for the repairs in the temple, and was also told to send his son away from Choyhung, a punishment that did not distress the boy at all. He went to Hong Kong, and after a false start or two became a student at Queen's College there. He met and became friendly with a young American medical missionary,

Dr. Hager, who baptized him: Hager and Sun had many conversations about Sun's ambition to become a minister of the Christian church. This was still his intention when, in 1886, he made his second journey to Hawaii, to settle some family business affairs with Ah-mi. Ah-mi's feelings about Christianity were unchanged, and soon Yat-sen was involved in a quarrel with him over the boy's desire to be ordained. Tempers rose so high that Ah-mi declared he would no longer contribute to Yat-sen's support; indeed, he cut off supplies then and there, and Yat-sen was stranded, without enough money to go back to Hong Kong, until some local Chinese Christians heard of his dilemma and passed the hat around, and bought him a ticket. Without any allowance from Ah-mi it was no use hoping to train as a parson. Yat-sen's American friend Hager, though he was full of regret that no mission was able to supply scholarships for aspiring native preachers in Hong Kong, now offered a helpful suggestion for an alternative career. Hager thought Sun should train as a doctor, because he would be able to work his way in the Hong Kong hospital of an old medical missionary named Dr. J. G. Kerr; there was a college connected with it. Sun was willing to try; Hager made arrangements with Kerr, and there it was: Sun Yat-sen became a doctor. His life work, ultimately, was in politics, not medicine, but his training had important side effects nevertheless, not the least of which was his friendship with a British medical missionary, Dr. James Cantlie.

In the nineties a man of Sun's origins and predilections was almost bound to turn to thoughts of reform in national affairs. During the war with France in 1884 his youthful patriotic pride had suffered. The hostilities were not far from his village, and he knew many of the soldiers; in the eyes of the people the Chinese army had fought well, and were badly let down when the Peking Tartars made peace without honor. Later, when Sun had his degree and practiced as a doctor, he saw so much poverty and suffering that he turned against the men in power: he could not have reacted differently. He worked for a while as a clinician in Macao, until he was told that he must either get himself a Portuguese diploma or stop it. In '93 he returned to Choyhung, where his boyish gesture in the temple had been forgotten. There he found Lu Hao-tung and the old friendship revived. The two men made a trip to the north: Sun wanted to apply to Viceroy Li Hung-chang for a medical post in Tientsin, for Li had recently founded a number of educational institutions in that city, and it seemed reasonable to suppose that educated men would be at a premium. It was not only this reason that brought him to Tientsin, however. His mind was churning with ideas for improving the nation, and in preparation for his interview with the Viceroy he had written a "reform memorial"—a long composition, embracing the national situation and putting forth suggestions as to how to solve outstanding problems. Considering the ground that Yat-sen was trying to cover, it is not surprising that he resorted to generalizations: what was remarkable was the scope of his interests. He recommended that the government should set up a department of Agricultural Administration. Mines and the cloth industry needed development. Commerce should be stimulated—but China's most crying need, he said, was for the education of many more people. "The weakness of China is caused not only by a shortage of able people, but by the large number of the ignorant, who try to hinder every new enterprise." These ignorant persons were the principal cause of the illness of Chinese society.

A foreign biographer of Sun points out that since his death he has been deified and embalmed by party adorers beyond recognition. "The making of a lacquered god out of human flesh and blood has probably never been accomplished with such speed and thoroughness as in the case of Sun Yat-sen." [Lyon Sharman, *Sun Yat-Sen, His Life and Its Meaning* (New York, 1934), p. viii.] Moreover, actual events in his career have been rewritten to suit the temper of his followers, whatever that might be at the time of writing. Tsou Lou, an official Kuomintang biographer of the great father figure, gives a version of the reform-memorial anecdote that differs widely from that of other annalists. He says that Sun had an interview with Li Hung-chang and handed him the memorial in person; that the Viceroy, impressed by Sun's ability which was obvious at first sight, promised to underwrite a trip abroad for the young doctor so that he might study foreign methods; but that Sun Yat-sen saw at a glance that the Viceroy was steeped in Manchu weaknesses, so he rejected the offer and struck out on his own. This tale may save a little face for Sun, but it does not make sense. The more likely version is that Li Hung-chang's secretaries never permitted the two young visitors to get anywhere near the Viceroy: they didn't meet him, and Sun carried his memorial back south, thoroughly disgusted with a system that had rejected him.

The following summer was marked by the Sino-Japanese War. By the time it started, Sun had gone again to Honolulu, having left his reform memorial to be published in a Shanghai newspaper—it ran for nearly two months and attracted much admiring attention, but the author had lost all confidence in reform as a cure for China's ills, and was now of the opinion that revolution offered the only answer. With a number of friends he spent much time discussing revolutionary projects. As soon as a Chinese determines on political activity he organizes secret societies, and Sun did not spurn precedent. His first secret group was founded in Hawaii and was called the Hsing Chung Hui, or China Revival Society: it later had a Hong Kong branch. Like all political groups it had a platform, this one with three planks: Drive out the Tartars, revive the Chinese nation, establish a federal government. When the Hui had been organized to satisfy Sun, he made plans to move on to new fields of endeavor in America. By that time, however, the sorry story of the Sino-Japanese War had come to its humiliating end, and the contents of the Treaty of Shimonoseki were known. The Chinese public were boiling with rage and resentment. It seemed to Sun's band of sworn brothers that the time was ripe for constructive action, and one of the most active among them, Charles Jones Soong, wrote to Hawaii advising their leader to return, which he did.

Charles Soong's life had started out rather like Sun Yat-sen's, in that his family had sent him abroad to relatives when he was a boy. His destination, however, was Boston, and his kinsmen there were unwilling to spare his labor merely for the sake of education, so the child ran away from them and became a cabin boy on an Atlantic coastal steamer. An American, Charles Jones, learned of his burning desire to go to school, and made this possible. In gratitude young Soong, who became a Christian in due course, took his benefactor's name. Grown up, he returned to China as a missionary, but he was so shocked by his first impressions of his native land that he felt the quiet duties of a man of God were not enough. It was the most natural thing in the world that he should have gravitated to Sun's club of revolutionaries. He lived in Shanghai, where he published Bibles openly and political tracts secretly: he was Sun's most trusted friend and an ardent collaborator.

After talking things over with Soong, Yat-sen went on to Hong Kong and joined others of the band. There some of them opened a shop to serve as cover for what they were going to do, and others

moved on to Canton city and set up the so-called Scientific Agricultural Association. Secretly both places were centers of sedition,
where new members were enlisted and arms and ammunition were
smuggled into the country. It was tricky work and soon led to disaster. In 1895 a shipment of cement in barrels sent from Hong Kong
to Canton attracted the attention of a Maritime Customs inspector,
who opened one of the barrels and found that it was full of pistols.
The conspirators decamped, but after the shipment had been traced
back to the shop in Hong Kong, which was raided, seventy people
were apprehended, and in the end three ringleaders, including Sun's
old friend Lu Hao-tung, were beheaded. Sun was the man they most
wanted, but he escaped by hiding out in a friend's house in Canton,
then making his way round about the country to Macao. From
Macao he went to Hong Kong and consulted a lawyer, who advised
him to leave the country altogether. He moved on to Kobe and there
assumed a disguise that was to serve him for many years—by cutting
off his queue, letting his hair grow, and cultivating a mustache, he
took on a very Japanese look. A small man with a round, earnest
face and gentle manners, he did not at all resemble the criminal
referred to in Peking as "Brigand Sun Wen," but then he never had.
Six months later, reasonably secure in his Japanese *persona*, he
moved on to Hawaii for a family reunion: his people in Choyhung
after the raid and exposure, rightly fearing that the authorities would
take it out on them, had made their own escape and moved outright to Ah-mi's estate in the islands. Ah-mi had prospered and was
now a property owner in a big way, able and willing to take care
of them all. Family feeling even triumphed over religious differences.
He was ready to resume backing Sun Yat-sen with money and sympathy.

Yat-sen decided to carry out his earlier plans to visit America,
but now he looked beyond it: he would continue on his voyage,
going from the States to England and the Continent so that he
might observe Western government and economics at first hand in
various countries. Arriving in San Francisco in June 1896, he spent
about four months in America, stopping here and there on his way
east to meet Chinese residents in the States: he gave lectures at
their clubs and urged them to support the revolutionary cause, but
on the whole he aroused little enthusiasm. The Chinese in America
were wrapped in their new lives, absorbed in work and the pursuit
of success. They had got away from China, and now they tended to

think of it sentimentally as the home of their fathers and the place where they hoped to be buried, not a viable, modern nation. They saw no reason to stir up trouble in the dear old museum. Nevertheless they were willing to look at Sun Yat-sen and listen to his words, out of curiosity. Every world of exiles has its own grapevine. Sun had entered America in disguise, probably using a faked passport, but one Chinese told another about him, until word of his presence and activities spread all the way across country to the Chinese Legation in Washington. There the minister sprang to the alert and went to great pains to keep track of Brigand Sun Wen. Having learned what ship Sun was taking to England, he sent an advance message to his opposite number in London, with directions to grab the revolutionary as soon as he should arrive, and arrange with the British Foreign Office for his extradition to Peking.

Cheerfully unsuspecting, Sun sailed on schedule in September '96. No avenging government official met him as he disembarked, for the Foreign Office had looked into the Chinese Minister's request and replied that it could not be granted: there was no extradition treaty between Britain and China. However, the Minister did not give up. Detectives watched Sun's arrival, and followed him about London. They saw him call almost immediately on the Cantlies, and they were there when he shifted his luggage from his hotel in the Strand to lodgings in Holborn. They knew that he called on the Cantlies almost every day. In fact, the Legation staff knew all about Sun except what to do next regarding him. Sir Halliday Macartney, a friend of Gordon in the old days, was now serving at the Legation as special adviser for British affairs. He was not a very intelligent man: perhaps it was he who thought of the next gambit. But the Chinese were fully capable of evolving it for themselves.

The Cantlie house, as it happened, was on Devonshire Street near Marylebone Road, just around the corner from the Chinese Legation in Portland Place. Mrs. Cantlie had mentioned this fact to her husband's protégé and jokingly warned him, as a wanted man, not to go near the building. However, London seemed such a long way from Peking that Sun saw no need for caution. For ten days he walked about the city as he wished, exploring it and learning his way to government buildings and libraries, and dropping in at Devonshire Street. On Sunday morning, October 11, he had a date to go to church with the Cantlies. On his way, he was walking by the

Chinese Legation when a young Chinese paused in passing and spoke to him in his own dialect, in friendly fashion. Sun replied. They got on so well that when the stranger—who was, as he truthfully explained, employed by the Chinese Minister as an interpreter—invited his new friend into the Legation for a look around, Sun rashly accepted. He was given a guided tour through all the ground floor rooms, then up on the next floor, and finally to the top— where suddenly he found himself alone, behind a locked door. A bit later this door opened to admit Sir Halliday Macartney, who told him that he was a prisoner.

The next step for the Minister, clearly, was to smuggle his captive out of England, but he had no means of doing it. Ordinary ships were out of the question: Sun would immediately make contact with other passengers or the crew, and as the Foreign Office had already refused extradition, this would be awkward. The only way the Chinese staff—and Macartney—could think of was to charter a private ship for the purpose, but this would be so costly a proceeding that they had to apply to Peking for approval and the necessary funds. Until the answer came they waited, and so did Sun. He tried to keep his mind occupied. He prayed, and now and then wrote a note, wrapped it around a piece of silver, and threw it out the window; none of these missives turned up, at least at the Cantlie house to which they were addressed. Then he hit on a more constructive plan. The Legation was staffed by British servants. One of these men used to clean Sun's room, and the prisoner got into conversation with him. Graphically Sun described what his fate would be if he were to be sent back to Peking. He also gave short lectures on the villainies of the Manchu reign, and explained the object of his revolutionary plans. It did not take long to get the servant on his side, and before the week was out—on Saturday the seventeenth—a note from Yat-sen to Dr. Cantlie was smuggled out of the room in the coal scuttle. That night at eleven-thirty Sun's new friend slid the letter under the Cantlie door, rang the bell, and hurried away before the doctor came down to investigate.

So far so good, but all did not proceed smoothly even now that Dr. Cantlie knew the whereabouts of his young friend. He dressed and went out immediately to appeal to Scotland Yard, but those gentlemen were unmoved, saying it was no affair of theirs. Next day he tried to stir up the Foreign Office, and had just about as much success with them. Hurrying around, Cantlie collected all the people he knew who had any influence, but in spite of their efforts nothing was done until one of them had the bright idea of calling in the press. Immediately the atmosphere up at the Foreign Office changed. Publicity worked such wonders that on October 22 the Chinese Legation had to disgorge Sun Yat-sen, the day before money arrived from Peking to pay for a chartered ship.

Thereafter Sun went on with his program, systematically visiting the capital cities of Europe and reading industriously. Dr. Cantlie said that he turned his attention "ardently" to a variety of studies; "international law, military tactics, naval construction, finance in all its departments, statecraft, and politics in all its bearings . . . he was forever at work, reading books on all subjects which appertained to political, diplomatic, legal, military, and naval matters; mines and mining, agriculture, cattle-rearing, engineering, political economy, etc., occupied his attention and were studied closely and persistently." [Cantlie and Jones, *Sun Yat-sen and the Awakening of China* (New York, 1912), p. 203.]

Sun stayed abroad, consolidating his plans for attack and reconstruction; he was still in Europe during the Hundred Days of the Reformers and their tragic aftermath. He wandered, observed, hammered out his philosophy, and gathered colleagues. Those who criticize him for his later failures—such voices are not heard on the Chinese mainland, however—attribute them to an inevitable ignorance of the Chinese: he spent so little time in China that he lost touch with his own people. On occasion, when he did come back, he had always to slip in in disguise, and his visits were short. In 1904, in America, he organized a new club, the Chih Kung Hui, or Society of Justice, the slogans of which bore something new:— "Get rid of the Tartars, revive China, establish a republic, *distribute land equally.*" Later when he enunciated the Three Principles of the People the last three of this list were repeated in essence—nationalism, democracy, and economic welfare. To achieve these, said Sun, China must have three simultaneous revolutions: national, political, and social. The trouble has always been that his land-distribution principle, or economic welfare, was not accompanied by a blueprint to show his followers how to implement it. How could land ownership be equalized without force? Sun denied that he intended the use of force or violence, but after his death there were people who argued otherwise. Indeed, it was on this ambiguity that the party was to split. Sun had no practical experience on which to base his theories, and Russia's revolution was still in the future.

After America, in 1905, he returned to Tokyo, a city that afforded stimulating society for him, full as it was of Chinese political refugees, including remnants of the Reform Party. As to them, however, Sun was frustrated: he tried to make friends, but their leader K'ang Yu-wei, staunch monarchist that he was, wanted no part of any revolutionary. He refused even to meet Sun Yat-sen, who in his estimation was a common traitor. However, others did not share K'ang's opinions. Not only refugees but more than thirteen hundred Chinese students gave Sun a hero's greeting when he arrived, and when he formed the Alliance Society, or T'ung Meng Hui, young people crowded in to join it. One was named Wang Ching-wei, and a charter member, Chen Chi-mei, who was an ardent revolutionary, introduced another important actor on the stage when he brought in the eighteen-year-old Chiang Kai-shek. Chiang was in Tokyo for a preliminary visit, trying to bypass the military academy at Paoting and get into the Japanese military college direct, for he had no use for North China and like many other young Chinese had been stirred to enthusiasm for Japanese training. In the end his attempt failed and he had to win his passage to Japan the hard way, via examinations and Paotingfu. Nevertheless, thanks to the T'ung Meng Hui, his jaunt to Japan had not been a sheer waste of time. Its aims and hopes were made to order for Chiang. A native of Chekiang, he so resented the tyranny of local petty officials that he had cut off his queue like Sun, and, defying the strong prejudice of his class against army men, left home to follow the flag. When he was forced to come away from Japan in 1905, he was determined to return. Already he had picked up a working knowledge of the language. He was so forceful and single-minded that he had his way; it was not long, as these things go, before Chiang Kai-shek got into Paoting Military College. Two years later he returned to Japan, a properly accredited officer of the army.

❋   ❋   ❋

During the last few years of her life the Empress Dowager brought in a number of changes that scandalized the Old Guard, though it must be admitted that most of the alterations were not radical. Some of them, however, did make a difference, as for instance her decree that Chinese were eligible for the higher posts. Had she not done this, Yuan Shih-k'ai couldn't have been promoted, Irish fashion, to the Grand Councilorship, which carried with it the added post of head of the Ministry of Foreign Affairs. (It was by this title that the Tsungli Yamen was now known.) This change-over took place shortly before the Empress's death, and much against Yuan's will. He preferred his influential Viceroyalty, especially now that it was fairly clear he must soon lose his best friend at Court, Tzu-hsi herself. With Kuang-hsü on the Throne, Yuan knew, he would have been a lot safer away from Peking, protected by his magnificent army. Kuang-hsü would certainly take revenge on the man who had so badly betrayed him.

When the end came for Tzu-hsi, as we know, Kuang-hsü was already out of the way, but his enmity lived on. Yuan as Grand Councilor, during the Empress's meeting with the Council, tried in vain to shake her determination to name the infant Pu-i as heir, for Pu-i's father Prince Ch'un would have to serve as Regent, and Prince Ch'un was Kuang-hsü's brother. Yuan therefore pressed the claims of the other candidate, P'u-lun, but it was no use: Tzu-hsi insisted on Pu-i, and Yuan must have known his career was doomed. Palace gossip had it that the dying Kuang-hsü had written out, in a shaky hand, his last testament:

"We were the second son of Prince Ch'un when the Empress Dowager selected Us for the Throne. She has always hated Us, but for Our misery of the past ten years Yüan Shih-k'ai is responsible, and one other. . . . When the time comes I desire that Yüan be summarily beheaded." [Bland and Backhouse, *China* . . . , p. 460.]

The time had come. Whether or not the Emperor really wrote this document, the spirit was there in Prince Ch'un's heart. For a few weeks after the double Imperial death the blow did not fall; it only hovered in the air. Yuan may have taken comfort in the reflection that Prince Ch'un was not courageous, and that he himself enjoyed an excellent press in the Western countries: the Regent would scarcely dare to have him killed. In fact this was quite true, and the end when it came was not disgrace and death—only an edict at the beginning of 1909, to the effect that the very able Yuan Shih-k'ai was unfortunately suffering from an infection of the foot, had difficulty in walking, and could not work properly. "We command Yuan Shih-k'ai to resign from his office at once, and to return to his native place to treat and to convalesce from the ailment," the edict continued. "It is our resolution to show consideration and compassion."

It was bad, but it was better than decapitation. Yuan retired to his native province Honan, as he had been commanded, and rusticated for the next three years.

* * *

His disappearance was not calculated to help the struggling government. Whatever else can be said about Yuan, he was far more efficient and intelligent than the rest of the Court, and the Regent was floundering without sensible advice. Tzu-hsi had whetted the national appetite for reform and had promised the country a constitution, and the people eagerly waited for Prince Ch'un to pay that outstanding bill. They may not all have had a very good idea of what a constitution was, but they knew Japan had one, and Japan had whipped the Russians, though she was small and Russia was enormous. Russia had no constitution. The inference was plain. The Regent felt compelled to give the country some sort of document; unfortunately for himself he had neither the strength nor the wit to form a reasonable compromise, nor did any of his advisers. He was further bedeviled by Lung-yü, widow of Kuang-hsü, who was also, it will be remembered, Tzu-hsi's niece. Tzu-hsi had given Lung-yü a franchise to make as much a nuisance of herself as she wished, it being clearly stated in the Empress Dowager's testament that the Regent was to be subject, always, to her instructions, for Lung-yü was now Empress Dowager in her turn. She had no political judgment whatever, but set great value by Imperial privilege and stubbornly resisted any suggestion of surrender. As a result of all this bad counsel, Prince Ch'un came out with an effort that made a mockery of the word "constitution" even in the eyes of his unsophisticated subjects. The document provided that the Imperial dynasty should rule in perpetuity and have the power to accept or reject any parliamentary decision. So disgusted a silence greeted it that the Regent was disconcerted. Over in Tokyo, the exiled Reformers who had remained stubbornly monarchist in spite of all now began at last to ask themselves if loyalty might not, in certain circumstances, be overdone. Prince Ch'un realized he would have to try again, and announced that the Empire would get the constitution it wanted in another nine years of suitable preparation. When this benevolent decree still seemed to fall short of expectations, he consented to cut the waiting period down to five years.

The revolutionaries continued busily at their work. Before the final big push they had made ten abortive attempts to overthrow authority, and plotted seven assassinations of high officials. They were aiming at the highest quarry in 1910 when they sent Wang Ching-wei, who had joined the T'ung Meng Hui when Chiang Kai-shek did, to kill Prince Ch'un. Wang failed to carry out his mission and was put into prison, where he had to remain until the revolution. Spurred on by such dangers, the Regent tried to strengthen his armed forces as speedily as he could. He created an Imperial Guard Army and a college for training Manchu officers, of whom there was a grave shortage. He called for thirty-six new infantry divisions as well. He would need funds to meet all these expenses, and he decided to raise them in the time-honored way, borrowing from the Western countries: for security he would pledge China's railways. The railway idea was not original with Prince Ch'un. For years Yuan Shih-k'ai had raised considerable sums on them, but they were still good for more, or would have been if various officials had not got a stranglehold on them, using the national communications revenue to line their own pockets. The Regent would have to nationalize the railways before he could pledge them as state property. This he proceeded to do, but the officials who had been controlling the land involved resisted strenuously, and civil war broke out in Szechuan. It was out of this squabble that the revolutionaries, somewhat to their own surprise, plucked success to their long endeavor. The Governor of Szechuan was caught by the insurgents and beheaded, and at this point the city of Wuchang mixed in. It so happened that Sun's party was particularly strong in Wuchang, where the officers of the Imperial troops had trained in Japan and joined the T'ung Meng Hui. Quietly they had indoctrinated their troops, and were standing ready for the signal. In the Three Cities, the usual secret ammunition had been stashed away here and there; the atmosphere was tense, and when a bomb accidentally exploded in a cellar in the Russian Concession of Hankow, the whole revolution was triggered off. The bomb did its work on October 9, 1911, and next day everybody was fighting, with Wuchang's troops led by Li Yuan-hung, one of the Tokyo officers. The Kuomintang was later to select October 10 for a national holiday, because there was a euphony about that date—the tenth day of the tenth month—which pleased them.

For the first time everything seemed to go well for the revolution. Its champions took Wuchang, and Hankow, and Shanghai, and Hangchow, this last city by troops under the command of Chiang Kai-shek, who hastened back from Japan at first news of the rising, and was given his commission by Chen Chi-mei, managing the Shanghai sector. All over the southern provinces the conspirators rose up and showed their colors. But the international settlements were left undisturbed, and for a time the significance of this particular civil war—"These people are always fighting"—did not dawn on their inhabitants. The attitude was not theirs alone; it took the northern officials, too, some time to realize what had hit them. Soon, however, alarm began to percolate through the capital. One of the first to be disturbed was the Minister of Communications, who had been one of Yuan Shih-k'ai's enemies ever since a quarrel over the railway loot. Swallowing his pride, he telegraphed the ex-Grand Councilor in his Honan retreat, begging him to come to the rescue of law and order. Yuan replied smoothly that he was far too ill to return to public service, but in reality he was keeping a keen eye on developments. His army—the one he had shaped and trained—still considered itself his; the officers, who never failed in their loyalty to him, kept him informed of how things were going. Yuan knew well that in spite of the bad blood between the Imperial clan and himself, he would soon be summoned by the Throne. They would have to call him in. He was their only hope, for no jumped-up Manchu general had his ability, either executive or military. Morever, the foreigners admired him; they called him "the strong man of China," and when he was sent into limbo many Western newspapers had printed laments: Prince Ch'un depended heavily on Western finance and would soon want more funds than ever. For these reasons, when a message arrived from Peking on the fifteenth of October, Yuan was not surprised to see that it came from the palace. In the form of a decree, his services were being called for: he had been appointed Viceroy of Hupei and Honan, it was declared, "in charge of pacification." In reply to this veiled request Yuan said, doubtless with great relish:

"The affection of my foot has not yet been cured." [Ch'en, p. 111.]

The next development was more of a surprise, for it did not come from Peking at all. The rebels of Hupei were making overtures to

Yuan Shih-k'ai, requesting him to join the cause. If he did, they said, after they had won the war they would make him President of the new Republic. Here, indeed, was popularity after his long exile. But Yuan let the revolutionaries wait, just as he did the Regent.

Peking did not leave him in peace: they could not afford to. On October 20 Yuan brought the comedy to an end and replied in earnest to the Regent's latest summons, with a list of demands that must be satisfied, he said, before he would take on the task of fighting. For one thing the insurrectionists must be pardoned, and Prince Ch'un was willing to agree to that, but Yuan's other conditions were much harder to swallow. He wanted to be assured that a National Assembly would be called during the next year, and a responsible government formed. He wanted the promise of a more liberal attitude toward party activities. (It could not well be less liberal; all such activities had been forbidden by Imperial decree.) He, Yuan, must be appointed Generalissimo of all the armed forces, and he would have to have enough money, provisions, and equipment to keep the men supplied: these last items had a way of disappearing before they reached their rightful recipients. Though the Regent was in dire need he could not bring himself to accede to these terms, for they would strip power from the dynasty altogether, and the whole country would find itself in Yuan Shih-k'ai's shadow. However, he grew so alarmed at the progress of revolutionary troops in Hupei that he made a concession and put Yuan in charge of that area, as supreme commander. It was all right as far as it went, but Yuan, as if to show that the war was not yet worth his personal attention, merely gave orders that the rebels were to be pushed back, and he himself stayed at home, waiting for reports. Sure enough, his army regained the territory they had lost. Yuan's name alone was enough, and the lesson was not lost on the Regent. Yuan continued to play a cat-and-mouse game with both sides. He would not brook interference with the simple pattern. Two generals threatened to upset things by plotting to get rid of the Manchus, though they were not revolutionaries of Sun's breed; this meant an offside reform that would not have suited Yuan at all, so he picked them off.

Province after province declared its independence. Most of these capitulations were the result of boring from within, combined with the opportunism that was a familiar characteristic of the Chinese official: shot-and-shell fighting was the exception rather than the rule. Still, it was as disturbing to the dynastic party as if China had been running with blood. They knew what Yuan was doing, but could not handle him. "The Regent," says Ch'en, "was anxious to restore his control by military suppression while Yuan was merely interested in preserving the Manchu Government from disintegrating too rapidly before he could reach a favourable agreement with the revolutionaries. He did not feel obliged to be loyal to the man who had disgraced him; nor was he idealistic enough to join forces with a total stranger, Dr. Sun Yat-sen. He was fully aware that he alone held the balance and was resolved to exploit the situation to the utmost for himself. For the time being, his main concern was how to consolidate the north in order to provide a bargaining counter with the south." [Ch'en, p. 112.]

Within a few weeks the Regent gave in. He ordered the Political Consultative Council, a body that had hitherto been completely ineffectual, to draft a constitution, which they did in short order: on November 7 he appointed Yuan Shih-k'ai to the post of Prime Minister. Yuan had already begun to treat with the revolutionaries; a delegate of his was sent to General Li Yuan-hung of the Wuchang incident to discuss a truce, though Li would not then listen to him. In preparation for the day when a truce *would* be discussed, however, Yuan dug Wang Ching-wei out of prison, where he had languished since his attempt to kill the Regent. Yuan was very kind to Wang, grooming him as a delegate that would soon be needed. At his suggestion Wang became "sworn brother" to Yuan's own son and was adopted into the family.

It was now time to bring the revolutionaries to reason. Yuan gave orders and his troops obediently recaptured Hankow and Hanyang, deliberately refraining from taking Wuchang: fair is fair, and Yuan knew that his opponents must not lose too much face all at once. He waited until they had occupied Nanking, then, satisfied with the balance, he moved his men into Wuchang. Everything was ready for the final act. Though according to the map the revolutionary army had the Imperial troops on the run, Yuan knew that in reality it was not so cut and dried. Many of the provincial declarations of independence were not worth the paper on which they were printed. "The governor of Shantung, for instance, having declared for 'independence,' telegraphed a 'memorial' to the throne to explain his action and promised to withdraw the declaration as soon as the situation became more stable. . . ." wrote Ch'en. [P. 117.] "The governor of Anhwei, Chu Chia-pao, disbanded the revolutionary troops in his province, announced independence and then, three days later, ran away. In Kiangsi, there were three different military governors in a hundred days; in Szechwan, two independent governments; in Kiangsu, thirteen military governors; and in Hunan and Kweichow, confused struggles among local warlords. The revolution was a sham; the independence of the provinces a farce. But Yuan would not destroy them lest he should deprive himself of an opportunity to play them off against the Imperial Court."

✻   ✻   ✻

Sun Yat-sen's name had not appeared in the news, for the good reason that he was not in China at all during hostilities, but in America. When the Hankow bomb went off the "Father of the Revolution" happened to be giving a lecture in Denver, struggling as usual to win friends and funds for the cause, and he had left the city on his way east before he saw headlines about the revolution. It was characteristic of him that he made no effort to rush to the scene and get into the spotlight. Whether or not his sworn brothers made it this time, he knew they would need more money. He continued on his journey, farther and farther from China. In St. Louis he learned—again from the newspapers—that he had been appointed President of a provisional Republic of China, but as he was not so much interested in his personal position in the future as in the Republic's success, he was not excited. Still incognito, he went on to London, for he had an important errand there now that his companions seemed really to have pulled it off at home. The British had been the monarchy's strongest foreign allies, and Sun felt they needed persuasion to change their attitude. He was able to apply the persuasion without too much argument, for the Powers' representatives in China had already come to an agreement to maintain a non-intervention policy in the revolution, holding that Sun's party were respectable dissidents, not to be equated with the Boxers. The Foreign Office agreed to suspend a loan they had been on the verge of sending to Peking, and promised to hold back in future until they saw which way the cat jumped. They also said, when Sun brought up the matter, that they would hold off the Japanese if the latter attempted to extend help to the Throne, and assured Sun that from that time on he would be *persona grata* in British territory, free and undisguised.

Sun could not be expected to feel responsible for the foreigners in the Customs Service, but they were having grievous troubles. Most Superintendents of Customs were Manchus, and many of these officials were murdered, especially at Nanking and other Yangtze ports. Heretofore they had collected the revenues in cash, the foreign Commissioners merely assessing the duty and informing the Chinese Treasury in Peking of the exact sum each Superintendent had to account for. When these Superintendents either fled or were murdered, the Commissioners for the first time had to handle the revenues, and then difficulties began. To whom were the Commissioners to give the money, when various governments each claimed to be the only rightful one?

Sun was still in London when a telegram from his friends at home caught up with him, but there was some delay and confusion before he got it. Inviting him to assume the Presidency, the telegram was addressed simply to "Sun Wen, London," and the post office delivered it straight to the Chinese Legation in Portland Place—a natural if tactless error—before it was redirected to the Cantlies. Sun started back, but he stopped off in Paris to interview Clemenceau, who was as friendly and encouraging as the British. He arrived in Shanghai at Christmas, where he had a celebration with Charles Soong and found that much had happened during his voyage back. All fighting had ceased, and Yuan Shih-k'ai, who was in control in the north, seemed about halfway to a state of mind that would suit the revolutionaries. At least, Prince Ch'un had abdicated, but in the new Prime Minister's statement of policy there remained a worrying sentence: "I submit that the present dynasty and its reigning monarch should be retained in a constitutional monarchy." This did not please Sun Yat-sen, who had made the overthrow of the Ch'ing Dynasty a rallying cry for his followers: still, perhaps things could be arranged even now. Sun had up his sleeve the biggest bribe of all, and he felt that Yuan could be managed.

The rest of the news was interesting. Nanking was to be the capital city for the new republican government. Through the offices of the British Ministry a peace conference had been arranged and was even then in session. Surprisingly, one of Yuan Shih-k'ai's minor delegates was none other than that heroic revolutionary and would-be assassin, Wang Ching-wei, but Sun was not actually as amazed by this circumstance as a Westerner would have been in his place. On these matters the Chinese are broad-minded. The plan was that Sun should first be elected President—a foregone conclusion—and then inaugurated, on New Year's Day. It was at this point that he shook the bribe out of his sleeve, knowing that the ceremony would be meaningless, that his whole government would be meaningless unless he could persuade Yuan Shih-k'ai to deal the final blow to the old Manchu establishment. He sent a telegram to the Prime Minister before his inauguration, declaring that he would relinquish the Presidency to him as soon as peace was restored—if Yuan would support the new Republic. He did not have to be more explicit: everyone knew that Yuan had the vital provinces as well as the monarchy in his pocket. But he did surprise Yuan, who could hardly believe this straightforward offer. Yuan could not fathom Sun. He himself would never have made such a sacrifice, and he decided that Sun was too good to be true. Perhaps he was right.

Chapter Eighteen

Contemporary writers of the Yuan Shih-k'ai period, on whichever side of the struggle their sympathies lie, have little that is good to say of him. All they could admire was his technique, and this they praised wholeheartedly. Foreign observers with less training in the subject found the ins and outs of his manipulations too complex to follow and had to be content with grasping what they could of the main outlines of his method, which could be summed up as playing all ends against the middle and promising more to everyone than he had any intention of granting. But to us, now that a certain time has intervened, the story is clearer and stands out for what it is, a tragedy that should be commemorated in grand opera.

The leader of the Northern peace delegation was an old friend of Yuan's named T'ang Shao-i. Yuan must have regretted giving him the post, as T'ang soon proved himself embarrassingly sincere and really became converted to republicanism. Dr. Wu T'ing-fang, his Southern opposite number, submitted to him a four-point plan, the first two points providing for the abolition of the Manchu Court and the creation of a republican government. The others were merely discussions of details concerning the Emperor's welfare after abdication and that of other Manchus. On the important matters T'ang communicated with Yuan and then put forward an alternative plan to form a National Assembly to decide between republic and monarchy, and also no doubt to make other governmental decisions afterwards. Though Yuan had been the instigator of this suggestion, as soon as it had been made he publicly disowned it and declared T'ang had exceeded his authority in making it. He demanded T'ang's resignation. The aim of these contradictory actions was a reinforcement of Manchu faith in Yuan, which he certainly achieved, though at the cost of revolutionary good will and a certain rift in the lute regarding his relations with T'ang Shao-i. On January 16 Yuan was on his way from the Forbidden City where he had presented what he rightly called "an important memorial." The revolutionaries could not have guessed the contents of that document: Yuan was so tricky that they could not possibly have suspected it was a petition from the Cabinet to the Empress Dowager for the abdication of the little Emperor. It is ironical, therefore, that some revolutionary hotheads should have taken that very outing as a chance to try killing Yuan Shih-k'ai, but they did, and failed. They also gave him a heaven-sent buffer against Imperial displeasure at his having dared to suggest abdication. Instead, though the Empress Dowager and her household were thrown into dismay by the terrible notion of surrender, they could not hold it against a man who was so clearly doing his best for the country and had very nearly died for his principles.

Naturally the petition did not come as a surprise to some of the Imperial family. It had long been discussed under cover, and the Manchus were aligned, most of them against abdication. The leader of this set, Liang-pi, on January 26 was set on and killed in a Peking street, after which arguments against abdication somehow sounded less forceful. Besides, as people pointed out to the Empress Dowager, the little Emperor would not really suffer even if he did stand down. Lavish promises had been made about his future—promises that added to the strangeness of the situation, for he was assured that his title was to be retained for life, even though he abdicated, and that he would be treated by the Republic "with the courtesies which it is customary to accord to foreign monarchs." [Johnston, R. F., *Twilight in the Forbidden City* (London, 1934), p. 96.] There were also promises of a more conventional sort. He was to have a large annual subsidy. The household might continue to live for a time in the Forbidden City, though later they might have to move to the Summer Palace. Temples and mausolea of the Imperial ancestors were to be maintained in perpetuity. All palace employees might be retained, though no eunuchs could be added to the staff. The Emperor's private property would be safeguarded, and so on. Reginald Johnston, an Englishman later employed by the Empress Dowager to act as one of Pu-i's tutors, wrote his account from a partisan viewpoint, as was natural, but his passionate denunciation of Yuan Shih-k'ai for double-dealing was not peculiar to the palace people. He points out that at the time of the abdication the Imperial family was badly misinformed, since all was really far from lost for them. Yuan could have saved the government, and it was pure mendacity to claim that this was impossible. Today we who are less emotionally involved can see that any reprieve for the Emperor would have been a short one at best, but Yuan's perfidy cannot be denied, and nobody has tried to deny it. The Empress Dowager thought that she had no choice but to assent.

It would be a mistake to accept the romantic picture given by jubilant rebels, and assume that the nation rejoiced at the news of the abdication. They were still Chinese, reluctant to accept change, steeped in monarchical tradition, with a history of two hundred and sixty-eight years under the Ch'ing dynastic reign. The vigor and agility of the revolutionaries which had precipitated the fall of the Manchus were far from being characteristic of the majority. Johnston describes the effect of the news on a dinner party of upper-class scholars in Shanghai—Chinese scholars, not Manchu. "The whole company simultaneously rose to their feet and turning their faces towards the north fell on their knees and with weeping and sobbing knocked their heads on the floor." [Johnston, p. 88.] Nor was this opinion and reaction confined to their class. At the time of the abdication Johnston was in Weihaiwei, and there, he says, for weeks the attitude of the Chinese was one of silent incredulity. Sun Yat-sen seems never to have had any illusions that his first revolution was a widely popular rising, though of course for propaganda purposes that was what he had to call it. But he was confident that with education and enlightenment the Chinese nation would come to see things his way and appreciate the Republic he was determined to give them. He firmly believed it was only through ignorance they had submitted through the centuries to their Manchu overlords. They still lacked capacity for resentment.

The ceremony of abdication took place on February 12, 1912, with Yuan Shih-k'ai leading the Cabinet into the great palace hall to join the Emperor's family. It was a moving scene. "Presently the Empress Dowager Lung-yü and the boy Emperor, Pu-i, arrived and ascended their thrones. The Abdication Edict was presented to Her Majesty by a eunuch for her final approval. As she was reading it, tears streamed out of her eyes and all her vassals prostrated themselves on the ground, quite overcome by grief and fear of the verdict of history. Suddenly she stopped, wept bitterly, and handed the Edict to Shih-hsü and Hsü Shih-ch'ang to be sealed with the

Imperial Seal on it. Then the members of the Cabinet signed their names one by one at the end of the document. In silence and with dignity, the last Audience was adjourned; and with it, the curtain fell on another episode in the long history of China." [Ch'en, p. 128.]

The Imperial edict announcing this event said that as there was obviously a desire on the part of the "majority of the people" for a republican form of government, "The universal desire clearly expressed the Will of Heaven, and it is not for us to oppose the desires and incur the disapproval of the millions of people merely for the sake of the privileges and powers of a single House." It continued: Prime Minister Yuan Shih-k'ai, being able to unite the north and south, had full powers to do so and organize a provisional republican government, "conferring therein with the representatives of the Army of the People," that peace might be assured. Yuan was also to see that the integrity of the territories of the five races, Chinese, Manchus, Mongols, Mohammedans, and Tibetans, was maintained.

The message Yuan sent in his own name (he was certainly the moving spirit in the Imperial edict as well) to the provincial governors at the same time is rich in those peculiarly Chinese euphemisms that make such fascinating reading for Westerners. "For three years I had been convalescing from an illness, and the idea of resuming my political career never entered my mind," it began, and went on with a highly colored account of how he was persuaded in spite of all to go back into harness and save the country. Their Majesties were showing their benevolence by declaring a Republic rather than plunge the country back into war, he said. He then telegraphed Sun Yat-sen to report that he had done it; the Emperor was out, and Yuan completely supported republicanism. "Never," he said, "shall we allow monarchical Government in our China." No doubt Sun would recall his promise of the Presidency? Yuan would be happy to come south and listen to Sun's counsels as to how to straighten out all these matters, but he was in a difficult position. . . . The North was in a delicate state. He implied that he could not come to Nanking.

Sun Yat-sen was not at all pleased by the tricky manner in which Yuan had fulfilled the terms of the bargain. He had never expected that the Republic should be bestowed on the nation by Imperial decree; nobody could have expected such an arrangement, which was to say the least original. It took the wind completely out of his party's sails. Besides, the wording of the edict made it sound as if the whole thing was Yuan's conception; Yuan was empowered to form a government, quite as if Sun's government already functioning in Nanking did not exist, and to make matters worse, here was Yuan digging in his heels and refusing to come to Nanking at all, because he felt safer in Peking. However, a bargain was a bargain: Yuan *had* got rid of the monarchy and declared for republicanism, and Sun felt compelled to keep to his side of it. (Besides, he could not have gone to war again.) He immediately resigned from the Presidency, emphasizing in his statement of resignation, however, that the seat of government must remain in Nanking. He also said that he and his Cabinet would carry on with their duties until the new but still Provisional President should have been sworn in, and that the new President must obey the provisional constitution adopted by the Senate, which would remain in force unless or until the Senate itself should revise it.

The dispute over the choice of capital city may seem to foreigners an unnecessary fuss to make for a small matter, but in the minds of the disputants it was important. In China with its shortage of communications, distance was a factor that had to be considered. So was provincial loyalty, and most of the leading men of the Kuomintang, as the revolutionary party was now called—the People's Party—were southerners, just as Yuan was a northerner. Kuomintang objections to Peking, in addition, were strongly emotional: to the revolutionaries Peking represented all that was hateful, corrupt and worn-out, besides always having been the capital of foreign invaders, whereas Nanking had been the city of the last Chinese dynasty, the Mings. Yuan, however, remained unconvinced. He replied that he could not leave northeast China unguarded against the threat of Russia and Japan. It looked like a stalemate until the Kuomintang attempted to force the issue by sending a delegation to Peking to escort Yuan honorably back to what they insisted was to be his new capital city. Yuan knew a trick worth two of that. He was polite and did not proffer any objections, but within four days of the mission's arrival the army in Peking mutinied, and a nocturnal riot in the streets sent the delegates, half-dressed, fleeing for safe cover. Then the unrest spread to Tientsin and other cities. It was always confined somehow to those troops most closely connected to Yuan Shih-k'ai, and the officers never failed to quiet it with a minimum of fuss, but the southern delegates had to confess themselves beaten, for it was clear Yuan could not turn his back on such an unruly city.

A face-saving arrangement was worked out in which Yuan, though remaining in Peking, pledged himself to accept certain conditions. He would take an oath of loyalty to the Republic, and agreed that his Cabinet members' names must be approved by the Senate.

After this unpromising beginning things brightened. The government was taking shape. A National Assembly was formed, composed of a House of Representatives and a Senate, rather like the American system. The Kuomintang accounted for not quite half the senators, who were somewhat outnumbered by the Republican Party's; a few others represented small groups aligned to neither of the big ones. Li Yuan-hung, who was Vice-President, led the Republican Party and Sun Yat-sen, the Kuomintang. T'ang Shao-i was Prime Minister. At the first regular election, held at the end of 1912, the Kuomintang increased its strength and obtained a majority in both chambers, a tendency that did not please Yuan Shih-k'ai. The situation sounded all right and looked most gratifying, but in truth the National Assembly and the whole government were more window dressing than anything else. Power was not really vested in them: whatever was said on paper, civilians did not—could not—govern in China. The power lay in the armies, and Yuan Shih-k'ai, by disseminating the armies, had spread power to many hands that should not have been entrusted with it. He did not deliberately incur such danger, but what he did was shortsighted and arose from expediency. After the abdication he was faced with a grave financial problem: the armies were left without a paymaster, so Yuan simply reallocated the troops to his favored provincial governors. (He also changed the rank of the governors; from that time on they were referred to as "military governors.") At the same time he quietly disbanded the former revolutionary troops of the south, a process to which the Kuomintang could not reasonably object, seeing that they too were short of money for the soldiers' pay and support. These men were rapidly snapped up by northern military governors who could afford them.

Yuan's first preoccupation as President was with funds. He started out as penniless as the Kuomintang, but unlike Sun Yat-sen he was now head of the state and had the means to remedy that situation. The consortium of foreign powers which had in the past advanced funds to the Imperial government was still willing to lend money, though at much harder terms, on the security Yuan managed to scrape up—the Salt Gabelle, railways, a few bits and pieces remaining from customs revenue, and so on. China's credit was poor, but the foreign world still held a high opinion of Yuan's abilities and thought the risk worth taking. The negotiations were lengthy and complicated, and during them the tenuous friendship between Yuan Shih-k'ai and Sun Yat-sen was stretched almost to breaking point. One can see now that the government was doomed before it started, by reason of lack of training. By and large, and quite apart from Yuan's peculiarities of character and his fundamental dislike of republicanism, most Chinese simply did not have the emotional discipline required to take part in such an administration. In the words of today's psychiatrists, they lacked maturity. Li Yuan-hung is a case in point. In Wuchang he had fought well for the revolutionary cause, but afterwards his position as Vice-President seems to have gone to his head, and he was soon embroiled in a quarrel with one General Chang Chen-wu, whom he considered insolent. Chang had been the instigator of Li's tie-up with the rebels, and now felt scorn for Li because he had gone over to Yuan Shih-k'ai. Li smouldered. When he heard that Chang was coming to Peking for consultation on the foreign loans, he appealed to Yuan and asked him to get rid of the general. Yuan obligingly did so; Chang was executed without benefit of trial.

The affair shocked many, and caused a tremendous scandal. If it had happened under those tyrannical Manchus, people said, no one would have been surprised, but it had not; it was murder among republicans, involving the highest officials of the land. The name of the martyred Chang was still reverberating in the air when Sun Yat-sen came to Peking to talk matters over generally with Yuan Shih-k'ai. Again he tried to persuade the President to move to Nanking, and further suggested that he be head of the Kuomintang, but it was no use. Yuan smilingly excused himself. Changing the subject, he appointed Sun Director of Railways. The men parted on what appeared to be cordial terms, but before three weeks were out Yuan passed legislation that was clearly aimed at outlawing the Kuomintang. After that, Sun made no more effort to persuade him to see the light.

The new Director of Railways took his appointment seriously, however, and traveled widely to gather information on the subject. At the same time he kept a worried eye on the progress of the Reorganization Loan negotiations. During the honeymoon the Kuomintang had hoped the loan would go through, but now, with their mistrust of Yuan mounting rapidly, they hoped it would not. With the Western powers solidly behind Yuan and money at the President's disposal, it would be harder than ever to blast him out of his post if and when the time came. Then another scandal burst, even more outrageous than Chang Chen-wu's execution. Sun was in Japan at the time on railway business, and was also trying to promote a loan on his own from the Japanese. In March 1913, an able young Kuomintang member named Sung Chiao-jen, who at thirty-one was chairman of the Party Executive Committee, was assassinated in Shanghai. Subsequent investigations made it practically certain that Yuan Shih-k'ai was behind the killing, for the reason that Sung was a serious threat to him politically.

It was too much, and Sun gave up all pretense of friendship with Yuan. In a strenuous last minute effort to stop the Reorganization Loan he sent cablegrams to all the countries involved, imploring the men responsible not to contribute to it. Nevertheless the arrangement went through. Sun's only comfort, a cold one, was that Woodrow Wilson pulled America out at the last minute, saying that the loan would endanger China's independence, and even he offered a loan on easier terms, which Yuan found it wise not to accept for fear of incurring Consortium disapproval. Until the last minute the Kuomintang fought the agreement and tried to postpone the signing of the documents, arguing that such an important decision should go through the National Assembly, but it was settled without Assembly approval on April 27, 1913.

Sun was speaking openly of war, and the provincial military governors accordingly sorted themselves out and decided which man to support when the break came. Most of them, probably correctly, saw more future for their kind under Yuan Shih-k'ai, and all but six chose him, but out of those six only one, the Governor of Kiangsi, openly aligned himself with Sun and the Kuomintang. There was scurrying among the lower echelons as well. Many members deserted the Kuomintang because they were afraid, and others because Yuan bribed them. The President did not wait for events to overtake him; on his orders, Li Yuan-hung began to harry the Governor of Kiangsi, hijacking at Kiukiang a consignment of rifles the governor had ordered. In retaliation the governor declared the borders of Kiangsi closed to northern troops, whereupon Yuan said he was discharged from his post, and appointed Li Yuan-hung "Acting Military Governor" of the province. Hostilities commenced on July

12, at Hukou in Kiangsi. The displaced governor's troops were quickly pushed back, and the attackers soon occupied the capital, Nanchang, as well. Elsewhere Sun's troops, scanty and ill-armed as they were, fared no better. Nanking itself was sacked. By the middle of September the Second Revolution was over. Sun Yat-sen fled once again to Japan, accompanied by a number of friends and officers. In the party were Charles Soong with his wife and children, also Chiang Kai-shek. They were to live in the wilderness for the next three years. In China the Kuomintang was declared dissolved. The National Assembly was given a few months more to live only because Yuan still needed it.

He had to be elected President, and he wanted this done before the mystic date of October 10. The difficulty was that the permanent constitution was supposed to be ready before the election, and clearly it was not going to be; both Houses talked and wrangled without ever settling their differences. Losing patience, Yuan made them pass a special law that permitted his election regardless, and he got his wish, being elected on October 6 and installed on the tenth. General Li Yuan-hung's Vice-Presidency was also confirmed. The volatile Li was one of Yuan's problems, and the President kept him close at hand so that he should not be got at by Kuomintang sympathizers and cast in his lot all over again with the forces of revolution, but that was only a detail in Yuan's crowded life. He had his troubles at the other extreme as well, and the chief of these was a general named Chang Hsün, who had helped him to quell Sun in the Second Revolution. The President fully realized that Chang Hsün was not so much pro-Yuan as passionately monarchist in his loyalties. This meant that he would have to be handled very delicately during the next phase of Yuan's plans to found a new Imperial dynasty—for such indeed was the dream that possessed Yuan, and had perhaps been with him ever since the First Revolution. Yuan wanted to be Emperor, with all that it entailed. In preparation for this move he had earlier requested the Imperial household to leave the Forbidden City and take up residence in the Summer Palace, in accordance with the articles agreed upon at the time of abdication: he wanted to live in the Forbidden City palace himself. But the suggestion had brought such a loud protest from the Empress Dowager, and the household made such heavy weather of their preparations, that Yuan found it wiser not to be too precipitate. He was not ready as yet to broadcast his plans, and he wanted to avoid publicity on the score. Slowly, carefully, he stalked his prey. He took another step when, in 1914, he made the Council of State change the law and prolong the President's term of office from five years to ten. There was no limit to the number of times he could be re-elected, but in any case the whole formality of election could be dispensed with if the Council "deemed it justified." However, presuming the President did submit himself for re-election, he was to name three and only three candidates for the post of succeeding him, and these were to be the only men eligible for candidature. What this rigmarole amounted to was that Yuan was President for life and could so arrange it that anyone he liked would succeed him. It was fairly obvious that this heir would be his eldest son K'e-ting, sworn brother to Wang Ching-wei.

Some of the officials close to Yuan were not easy in their minds about the life Presidency, and ventured to question him closely. Yuan gave them no hint that he was making plans for even greater aggrandizement. He soothed them and vowed that it was not his intention to make a sort of crown prince of K'e-ting. The whole arrangement was for the good of the country, he said; for himself he had outgrown ambition and wanted only to retire as soon as things were running in proper order.

*   *   *

A glance at China's international relations just before the outbreak of World War I shows how staggeringly swift and comprehensive had been the change since 1900. A country that had moved, when it moved at all, at a stately pace through the centuries, had been transformed in the space of little more than a decade. China's isolation lay in tatters, and her President did not mourn it. The West, against whose invasion Emperors and people had fiercely struggled, now had the whole great country tamed and in leading strings, but the West's loans were essential to her economy, and Yuan Shih-k'ai sought more and more eagerly to tie himself to the people his ancestors had called barbarians. The West was everywhere. Only a few years before it had been exceptional for the authorities to accept foreign colleagues in the Maritime Customs, and Sir Robert Hart was constantly exercising his tact so that the situation might continue, and the foreigners remain in control. Now Hart was gone—he died in England in 1911—but no such difficulties harassed his successor, Francis Arthur Aglen. The emphasis now was all on revenue for the money-hungry President, and because the customs revenues were not enough after indemnity payments were subtracted, Yuan had turned to other sources, the railways and the Salt Gabelle. In the past the Gabelle had been a state monopoly jealously guarded by the Chinese: now it was supervised by the British Sir Richard Dane. After all, the British had paid a good deal for their entrance ticket. The Reorganization Loan was followed by others, all heavily weighted on the foreign side. Much borrowed money vanished in merely priming the pump, so that after each loan China was soon left with nothing to show for it but one more crisis weathered and a heavy debt stretching on out of sight into the future. There were now a number of foreign experts living in Peking. Some of them were responsible for a monetary reform that was vitally necessary to China, and did much good. In the last analysis, however, all these developments stemmed from the personal ambition of Yuan Shih-k'ai, who was undermining his own position with every Westward step he took. The would-be Emperor was creating a world receptive to outside influences, a world that would never again countenance an Emperor. He did not realize it.

The outbreak of the war in Europe seemed at first merely a temporary setback to Yuan, in that it put a stop to foreign loans, but soon it made itself felt in a calamitous way, through Japan. From the time Yuan's supremacy in Chinese politics was confirmed the Japanese had been rather out of the picture. The President's early career in Korea had taken the edge off his appetite for closer relations with Japan. As we have seen, one of his most cogent reasons for staying in Peking, as he pointed out to Sun Yat-sen, was that he had to keep an eye on the national borders in the northeast for fear of Japan and Russia. Though he had declared that China was neutral in the war, Japan was a member of the Allies, and now, by special agreement with Britain, she announced her intention of taking over German-occupied territory in China. She said that all German vessels in the vicinity of either country must withdraw, and Germany was to cede Kiaochow to her; Japan would restore it to China—eventually. The benevolent tinge of this vague promise did not prevail in further exchanges between Japan and China, for there were more and more demands. Japan declared that the exigencies of the war were such that she must—temporarily—patrol the Tsingtao-Tsinan railway, which necessitated possession of a strip of land, or "zone," running alongside the track the whole way. There was not much if anything that Peking could do about it, and the Japanese troops moved in without incident on August 4, 1914, noticeably spreading out over a good deal more of the area than they had said they would occupy. Yuan did not mind too much; he felt the game was worth the candle, because he wanted Japanese support when the time came for his enthronement. Ignoring the invasion, therefore, he made friendly overtures to Tokyo. He had a reward of sorts when the Japanese replied enthusiastically in January '15, with a note embodying the notorious Twenty-one Demands.

Even Yuan Shih-k'ai was shocked out of his obsession, at least for a while. Japan set it all down in a list. She wanted no objections from China when she took over the German privileges of Shantung: China was to cede no coastal territory of the province to any third power: Japan would build more railways: Japan's leases in China were to be extended ninety-nine years: Japanese were to be free to live, travel, trade, and manufacture in South Manchuria and Eastern Inner Mongolia: they would work mines in Manchuria: they were to share in China's biggest coal and steel works: no harbor, bay, or island along the China coast was to be ceded or leased to any third power. In a special additional paper were embodied the worst demands of all, known as Group V, as follows: The Chinese Government must employ Japanese advisers in political, financial, and military affairs, and Japanese must be "employed" in the police departments of all important Chinese cities. Japan must have first refusal of the privilege to lend money to China, and must give her consent to any third-power investment or loan in the country: China must buy at least 50 per cent of her arms from Japan: Japanese hospitals, churches, and schools in China could own their land: Japanese missionaries must be permitted to live and work in China.

It was a blueprint for enslaving the nation. After he had caught his breath Yuan rightly saw that he could not afford to let this document appear in public. When the secret slipped out in the form of harmful rumor he had to divulge some of it, but he was careful to tone down the worst of the clauses, even then. He may have expected the West to come to China's aid, but if so he was disappointed: the European nations were too deeply involved in their own troubles to spare a thought for his. Even the British, who had most to lose, refused to worry and said that it would not amount to much in the end. The United States had not yet been caught up in the war, and her government could afford to face the facts; in an attempt to do something her Minister tried to round up some of the Western countries for a conference, but that was unsuccessful. In the end it was left to the Chinese alone to cope with the Japanese. For four months they parleyed. The Chinese delegates, having been instructed by Yuan on no account to give in to the demands of Group V, understood that if the worst came to the worst they might relinquish their objections to the other sixteen. They fought hard, however, and argued every word, until the Japanese lost patience, or pretended to, and presented an ultimatum on May 7 saying that if an end was not made to all this in two more days, force would have to be used. At the same time they sent out general mobilization orders to their settlers in Manchuria, and ostentatiously advised all Japanese then in China to hurry home. This seemed to settle things, especially as the British Minister in Peking advised Yuan to accept the ultimatum. Yuan did so, with the proviso that the controversial clauses of Group V should be further negotiated, to which Japan acceded.

Such a miserable crumb of comfort was not sufficient for the pride of a nation which—perhaps for the first time *as* a nation—was genuinely aroused. The humiliation of the Twenty-one Demands was felt by Chinese who had remained unmoved by both recent revolutions, and paid little heed to the dissolution of the National Assembly. For some reason this was much worse. No doubt the old Chinese attitude toward Japan of scorn for the little fellow, which had prevailed up until the Russo-Japanese War, still lurked in their hearts and made the Demands so bitter a pill. In any case, men asked themselves who had let them down. They would not soothe themselves with the reflection that China, as the British Minister pointed out to Yuan, was not equipped to fight a strong country like Japan. Nineteen of Yuan's generals, who of course knew this, made defiant speeches nevertheless, urging that China fight a war of resistance. Chinese in the treaty ports held mass meetings and rioted against Japanese residents. Inevitably as Yuan Shih-k'ai lost favor, the missing Kuomintang gained in popularity, and Sun Yat-sen worked hard to keep the fire burning. With his fellows he had kept up a steady undercover pressure in the south, much as he had done in old pre-revolution days. Sometimes one of the exiles would slip over to China and foment rebellion. But it is safe to say that nothing they did had the nuisance value for Yuan that was offered

by the generals he considered his own men. He was losing touch
with his warriors. The nearer he drew to the consummation he so
longed for, the less attention he could spare for duties that had
formerly called forth his best talents, the organization and maintenance of military efficiency. Since he had become President, Yuan
had delegated such tasks to underlings. Inevitably the officers, especially those who deputized for him, developed delusions of
grandeur, and quarreled with each other, and would have got rid
of Yuan himself if it had been in their power. The military governors
were an especially sore trial, and Yuan perceived that he had made
a bad tactical error in encouraging them to manage their own armies. He had raised up a whole regiment of potential enemies in
these war lords. When, belatedly, he tried to take away their power,
he merely failed and turned them against him that much the sooner.

Even so, Yuan was so much in the grip of ambition that he spent
little time pondering these threats. In 1915 one of his agents founded
a "Society for Peace Planning," the object of which was to prepare
the people for Yuan's transformation into something Imperial. Surprisingly, he had acquired an ally in the Imperial family—Prince
P'u-lun, whose claim to the throne he had supported back in 1908
when Kuang-hsü died. P'u-lun had always been grateful for Yuan's
advocacy, though it came to nothing, and now he was a great help.
He advised Yuan as the President searched the records of the former
Board of Rites, now called the Department of Ceremonies, to learn
how ceremonies had been conducted in the palace in the good old
days. He was able to give Yuan many pointers on ancient rules of
etiquette. At one point he even kowtowed to Yuan, an act which
his horrified relatives considered atrocious as well as blasphemous.
Yuan Shih-k'ai had a wonderful time getting ready his dress and
ornaments for the great ceremonial he had settled on as his first
public appearance in the guise of Emperor, to sacrifice at the Temple
of Heaven. After much research he bestowed various titles on his
followers—resounding names which they had never expected to hear
again—and commanded the minting of coins with his face on them.
He caused his name, or rather the reign-title Hung-hsien which
he had selected, to be impressed on the choice porcelain and pieces
of pottery being made at the time, as Emperors had done in centuries
past. He gave one or two interviews which he called audiences, to
people he addressed as subjects. Most farfetched of all his projects
was a double one he set in motion to dig out of history the heroic

if shadowy figure of one Yuan Ch'ung-huan, a seventeenth-century general—quite possibly Yuan Shih-k'ai's ancestor—who fell in battle against the Manchu invaders. The idea was to deify this man and provide the new Emperor with a suitably well-connected background, since all genuine Emperors had gods in their lineage.

At last he deemed that the goal was in sight. Late in 1915, at what he decided was the psychological moment, his advisers spread orders to people in all parts of the country to send petitions—the wording of which was dictated to them—imploring Yuan Shih-k'ai to restore the monarchy to China by ascending the throne. By post and telegraph these messages fluttered in in their thousands. Yuan then called together, in lieu of the extinct National Assembly, a crowd he described as an assembly of popular deputies. These voted him into the head post of a "constitutional monarchy." Yuan was amazed, Yuan was shocked, Yuan refused. This was all right and proper: the rules of etiquette demanded that he refuse three times. At the fourth try, with a great show of lingering reluctance, he accepted, just in time to make the traditional sacrifice at the Temple of Heaven, which took place at the winter solstice. He had carefully chosen this occasion as a trial flight, as it were, for only an Emperor could sacrifice to God at that time, at that place. The thing was not done exactly as the Manchu Emperors had done it; certain regrettable solecisms were thought advisable—changes, as the Home Minister said, appropriate to republicanism. For one thing the Emperor rode to the Temple, outside the city walls, in an armored car, and did not change over into a vermilion coach until he had arrived at the Temple's south gate. He was wearing a field marshal's uniform until he got to the top of the stairs, when he was helped to change into a royal purple—not yellow—robe decorated with dragons, and a headdress of antique style. Otherwise the old ceremony was unchanged.

The formal accession had yet to take place. No thunderbolt had killed Yuan at the Temple of Heaven, and he must have thought he was out of the wood. But in the medley of congratulations there was a sour note from Japan, though Yuan had expected sympathy from that nation once they got their way with most of the Twenty-one Demands. It is true that in the early stages of Yuan's transformation Tokyo had not objected, but in the autumn her Cabinet was changed, and suddenly a breeze from the outer world began to blow cold on Yuan. The new Japanese Foreign Minister thought that the proposed monarchy would "disturb the peace in the Far East." In the recently assumed national role of governess to China, the Japanese imparted this opinion to the Western powers and asked them to join Tokyo in condemning the idea. After some havering, Britain, Russia, France, and Italy brought their wandering thoughts to bear on the question and consented to Japan's suggestion. Sunk in his dream, Yuan refused to let foreign attitudes affect him at this stage of the game, and his supporters urged him to hurry up with the accession, the date of which had not yet been fixed. In Peking everyone was so sure it would go through that generals began to quarrel over the identity of the *next* Emperor after Yuan Shih-k'ai. There seemed small doubt that Yuan had already chosen his son K'e-ting, but there was no law against hoping however wildly.

Japan's was not the only dissenting voice in the East. Others, which had been drowned earlier in the manufactured chorus of acclaim, grew stronger and more insistent as the great day approached. They were important voices, belonging to some of the leading military governors—or generals—or war lords—in the country; most of these men had been uneasy long before Yuan disclosed his ultimate object, though one had started out in favor of the monarchy and was only later overtaken by second thoughts. The capital was buzzing so loudly with Yuan's friends that the dissidents could make no headway, so they got out of the dilemma by means of an age-old Chinese method: they fell ill, one by one, and got permission to leave Peking. Safe outside the city they quickly recovered their health and got together at a predetermined place: Kunming, the capital of Yunnan, which is at a judicious distance from Peking. On December 23, the same day that Yuan sacrificed at the Temple of Heaven, they sent a telegram deliberately addressed to the President, not the Emperor, demanding that he cancel all his arrangements forthwith, give up the idea of the monarchy, and execute the men who had urged him most ardently on his course. This set of demands was put in the form of an ultimatum expiring in twenty-four hours. Yuan did not reply. Possibly the sacrificial ceremony had filled his brain with fumes of incense, and he really did not take in the significance of the warning. When the twenty-four hours had expired, Yunnan declared independence—on Christmas Day. The French more or less recognized it by raising the status of their Consul General in Yunnanfu to that of "Minister Designate."

Yuan had to take action after that, and he cashiered the generals. They retorted by marching into Szechuan province, at the same time sending out a call for other discontented officials to join them. They captured one ally immediately, the Governor of Kweichow, and there were fair prospects of taking in the two Kwangs—Kwangtung and Kwangsi—as well, though their governors hesitated for a time. Ultimately they came down on Yunnan's side. This was the signal for the Kuomintang to show signs of life, and party members hastened to start excitement in Changsha and Nanchang. Everyone outside Yuan's immediate circle took the cue and began hammering at him. The Japanese, angry at having been ignored, threatened to move in to "restore order." For what it was worth, K'ang Yu-wei in Japan, all his pro-monarchist sensibilities in a state of outrage, sent Yuan a remarkably unpleasant cable in which he called him a usurper from the Manchu Imperial house's point of view, and a traitor from the Republic's.

Even a man possessed by an idea as Yuan was could not hold out against this barrage. By March 17, 1916, he had no more fight in him, and announced that he would give up the monarchy. Yuan was as ready as the next Chinese official to assassinate his rivals and lie to people who trusted him, but he had his feelings, and perhaps at that point one can admit that he was pathetic. There could be nothing worse in his society than to lose face, and here was a face-loss of truly staggering proportions. Like a man who has been hit on the head, he went through the proper gestures. He abolished the Hung-hsien Empire by decree. It was not his fault, any of it, he implied: he had retired years before from public life, and had returned to it only because of popular demand. However, he had brought trouble and strife to the nation and he blamed himself. As President it was his duty to keep the peace.

As for the Presidency, Yuan did make a feeble effort to resign from that as well, but he was prevailed on by K'e-ting and others to stay in office. This decision angered his enemies among the generals, who insisted that he should retire altogether. His estranged friend T'ang Shao-i also took exception to it and said so in a telegram addressed to "Mr. Yuan." He said that people would consider Yuan's remaining in office as "the most shameless action, unprecedented in the history of China and of every other country." [Ch'en, p. 228.] The people began splitting into groups, each headed by some war lord who wanted to be President in Yuan's stead. At last one of Yuan's closest generals, Feng Kuo-chang, spoke up openly and advised the President to resign before he was forced out. Still Yuan hung on. Another month passed before he received the blow that smashed the last vestige of his resistance—a declaration of independence from the war lord of Szechuan, Ch'en Huan, who had always been his most trusted adherent. When he read Ch'en's telegram Yuan had a stroke from which he never completely recovered. He died June 6, 1916, when he was fifty-six years old, not much of an age for a man who had done so much harm.

Chapter Nineteen

Yuan's death left China almost completely disintegrated, broken into bits each of which was under the rule of a war lord. Yet, though he had debased the representative government by using it as a tool for his ends, a form of it remained which saved Peking from immediate civil war when the Vice-President, Li Yuan-hung, slipped into the Presidency in accordance with the rules. The war lords paused to take stock of the situation, and stayed their hands not because they expected the weak Li to put up any resistance, but for fear of each other. In the pause President Li reconvened parliament.

The Sun Yat-sen contingent found it possible to return from Japan, though it was still necessary to stay out of Peking's reach. Canton was their only safe foothold apart from Shanghai, where Sun had a house in the French Concession, and it was in Canton that they made plans to start once more on the long-delayed task of unification. During the long exile two men in Sun's coterie had risen to the top as his most trusted lieutenants, Chiang Kai-shek and Wang Ching-wei, though at the time Yuan died Wang was under a temporary cloud and had gone off to France to meditate on his sins. As for Sun's old friend Charles Soong, their relationship had suffered change and strain over a delicate family affair. Soong's three daughters had spent most of their childhood and adolescence at school in America. The two elder girls, Eling and Chingling, were now back in the East, though Meiling remained at Wellesley to finish her university course. In Japan Eling, the eldest, worked as Sun's secretary for a time before she married Kung Hsiang-hsi, scion of a rich Shansi family. The Kungs claim descent from Confucius, but Kung Hsiang-hsi was a Christian and had cast in his lot with republicanism. The young couple returned to Shansi, leaving Sun without a secretary until Chingling stepped into her sister's place.

In the strange concoction of legend that has grown up around Sun's memory, the Chinese moral code is heavily covered over with a puritan pall, nearly smothered by the same attitude that characterizes society in Russia today. Yet Sun was no puritan as far as women were concerned. He had been married in the Chinese way, as a youth, to a girl he had never met until the wedding day. She was a good wife, but he didn't see very much of her. Sometimes on his wanderings she accompanied him, but there were children, and it was simpler for Sun to leave her with them in some friendly place where they might grow up in approximate security. One of these places was Penang. Mrs. Sun spent a good deal of time in Penang. Sun found the Federated Malay States the most useful of all his points of visit abroad, for it was full of overseas Chinese who adored him. They were not as rich as the Chinese in America; most of them were poor working people, but they would always contribute to the cause. They also took care of Mrs. Sun and the children, who stayed in Penang year after year.

"He had a concubine there as well," a Chinese from Malaya told the writer. "She was the daughter of an important man in the community, and I believe he practically forced her on Sun. When Sun finally took the family away and stayed in China the concubine remained in Penang and never married anybody else. She was held in great esteem. Oh yes, they adored Sun Yat-sen, and of course there was no blame attached to his connection with the girl. After all, he *was* Chinese."

Charles Soong did not take so philosophical a point of view, nor did his wife, when they found that their old friend and their second daughter intended to marry. What about his first wife? What of the Christian tenets they all professed to have embraced? Their protests did not avail, and Chingling, enamored of Sun and the cause, became the wife of a man more than twice her age.

*　　*　　*

Li Yuan-hung had not long been President when, in February 1917, he received a message from the West. President Woodrow Wilson was making an attempt to end the war in Europe, and he summoned China, along with the other uninvolved nations, to come in with America on the side of the Allies. The suggestion did not meet with favor with the majority of the Chinese parliament, where national affairs seemed much more pressing than the problems of the West, but this reaction was not unanimous, and there were stormy scenes in the Congress. In Canton, Sun's government voted against participation—not that this had any effect on most of the country. While the northern capital was preoccupied with this question a strange little plot grew up, with few to witness, around the person of Chang Hsün. Chang was the monarchist who had aided Yuan Shih-k'ai against the revolutionary army. He occupied Hsü-chou, between Peking and Tientsin—a spot with good nuisance value. He was so passionately attached to the Ch'ing Dynasty that he refused to follow the example of practically all other Chinese, who cut off their pigtails after the success of the revolution. He still wore his, and so did his troops, for which reason they were generally known as the pigtailed general and the pigtailed army. For months he had been conspiring with men who shared his sympathies to restore the eleven-year-old Emperor, Pu-i, to the throne. K'ang Yu-wei, home at last from his years of exile, was one of his stoutest adherents, but there were others, including the war lord of Manchuria, Chang Tso-lin. Chang Hsün got his chance when Li Yuan-hung invited him to Peking to help mediate in the World War parliamentary dispute. The pigtailed general accepted with the greatest alacrity. Overconfident in the strength of his conspiracy, he left the main body of his army in Hsüchou, and in June 1917 brought only a small force to the capital. Even so he was able to awe the President, and made him dissolve the parliament, after which he simply brushed aside Li Yuan-hung, summoned his allies, marched into the Forbidden City, and proclaimed that Pu-i was once again an active Emperor with all that that entails. He put out a manifesto by telegram, which said in part,

"On this day (July 1) we have jointly memorialized His Imperial Majesty to again ascend the throne in order to establish the foundation of the country and to consolidate the minds of the people." Chang Hsün was to be Regent and also appointed himself Viceroy of Chihli, but he did not occupy these exalted posts very long, nor was the Emperor to retain his power. There was a war lord in Tientsin named Tuan Ch'i-jui who had long wished to get rid of President Li Yuan-hung. He had no particular objection to the monarchy, but he resented the pigtailed general's leadership and his bullying manners. Now he moved in. His army defeated Chang's on the road to Peking, and he introduced a novel method of warfare by sending an airplane over the capital, which dropped bombs on the Forbidden City. They were not large bombs nor were there many of them, but they chased away the monarchists, and Li Yuan-hung vacated the Presidency, to which he was succeeded by General Feng Kuo-chang. (It is hardly necessary to follow all the chopping and changing that went on at this time in the Presidency.) As for Pu-i, he was put back under wraps after reigning something less than a fortnight, and none of the affair could have meant much to a child of his age. Johnston repeats a story, possibly apocryphal:

"A few days before the restoration, Chang Hsün had a secret audience with Hsüan-T'ung (i.e., Pu-i) in the palace. Chang knelt and informed the emperor what he proposed to do. Hsüan-T'ung shook his head and refused to agree to the restoration. 'May I invite Your Sacred Majesty to tell your old servant your reasons for refusal?' 'My tutor Ch'en Pao-shen,' replied the emperor, 'keeps telling me all day long about how the Classic of Poetry says this and Confucius says that. There is never an end to it. How can I possibly find time to attend to anything more than my endless lessons?' 'If Your Sacred Majesty,' said Chang, 'will only ascend the throne again, you will have important affairs of state to attend to and you need not spend any more time at lessons.' Hsüan-T'ung brightened up. 'Do you really mean,' he said, 'that if only I become emperor again I may give up all my lessons?' 'History tells us,' replied Chang, 'that the Son of Heaven has always been a horseman. No one ever heard of a *Tu-shu T'ien Tzu*—a Book-reading Son of Heaven.' 'In that case,' exclaimed Hsüan-T'ung joyfully, 'let it be as you wish. I will do whatever you want me to do.'" [Johnston, p. 143.]

The question of participation in the World War was settled at nearly the last possible moment, and during the interim the Presidency was kicked back and forth between war lords like a football. China's part in the war consisted almost entirely in the sending overseas of coolies who worked as carriers and general heavy laborers for the Allied troops. No Chinese soldiers actually fought in Europe, but China *had* joined the Allies nevertheless, and at the end, after the armistice, this fact carried weight when she demanded the return by Japan of Kiaochow and the Shantung territory the Japanese had wrested from the Germans. The Japanese had to accede to the demand, but they probably told themselves it would not be for long.

As the West recovered from the war, her traders turned again to China. Once more the treaty ports flourished, and the foreigners there thought of the struggling government and the squabbling generals in the light of their own interests. A generation of Westerners was growing up that knew China only as a nation constantly racked by little local wars, a nation whose stability existed exclusively and paradoxically under foreign extraterritorial law. Everyone knew that Chinese politicos, whenever fortune went against them, scuttled straight to the nearest treaty port for sanctuary. Westerners who ventured into the interior were considered rather in the light of daredevils, though the dangers of the hinterland, like other aspects of Chinese life, seemed faintly comic. The Christian missions were so firmly entrenched that some missionary families were almost dynasties in themselves. Their members could boast of parents and grandparents who had labored in the same vineyard.

The struggle of the Kuomintang in those days to spread their influence from Canton probably looked like more of the same mixture that prevailed in the North—a series of battles between war lords. In fact it was quite dissimilar. Sun was no bandit chief or military governor: he never showed any particle of self-seeking, or desire for power in itself. But he had learned the hard way that he could not introduce democratic government without force nor maintain it without strength. The focal point of Canton acted like a magnet when the Peking parliament was dissolved: a number of members recalled their old faith in the Kuomintang and came to join Sun. He declared that he was reconvening the parliament, which he claimed represented the true will of the people, but his immediate need was not so much a popular assembly as a good modern fighting force, and he was glad to accept the proffered alliance of a local war lord named Chen Chiung-ming. Incidentally, it should be pointed out that Sun was as arrant a bargainer and salesman as any northern war lord. He won much of his support by making promises to men who could help him—promises of posts, business advantages, anything they wanted—and when they helped him it was usually because they thought him a good investment. When they turned against him it was because they gave up hope of ever realizing on the investment. At that time, Chen Chiung-ming thought Sun and the Kuomintang a good risk, and Sun named him commander in chief of the Kwangtung army, of which he himself was generalissimo. It was not, as things turned out, a happy arrangement, for

Chiang Kai-shek could not get along with Chen Chiung-ming. In fact, all the generals set to quarreling, until Sun lost patience and retired to Shanghai, declaring that he was through. The mood, of course, did not last, and soon he was back on speaking terms with his staff. He needed a good deal of patience to deal with Chiang Kai-shek, who was hardheaded and short-tempered, but Sun knew he was also a good knowledgeable officer, and bore with him. At one point Chiang in turn flounced off to Shanghai, and stayed there for a time, working in the stock market. This was at the end of 1919. Not until 1921 did Sun persuade him to return to Canton, and even then peace was not long maintained. By this time Sun had made Chen Chiung-ming Governor of Kwangtung, and Chiang's jealous nature could not brook the appointment: soon he retired again to his family village in Chekiang, south of Shanghai.

Through the months and years Sun's chief study had been the rapidly fluctuating situation in Peking, which now seemed to be settling down to a protracted struggle between two strong figures, Wu Pei-fu of Loyang and Chang Tso-lin, the "Old Marshal" of Manchuria. Though competitors, they joined together to rid the Presidency of its then incumbent, Hsü Shih-ch'ang, one of Yuan's men. Various extraneous elements entered into their plots. For a time they thought of using the unfortunate Pu-i once again as a pawn. Chang Tso-lin's connection with Manchuria gave him a proprietary feeling about the young Manchu; he was also a relative of Chang Hsün and felt sympathy for the rugged old monarchist. However, this idea was dropped, probably because the Old Marshal became friendly with Russia—not Czarist Russia, of course, but the new Soviet state under Lenin, which had no use for emperors, Manchu or any other sort. In time Hsü Shih-ch'ang tired of his dangerous position and resigned from the Presidency. That was the moment Sun thought he might grasp: he sensed a vacuum, and determined to fill it. It was 1922 when he set out on his Northern Punitive Expedition.

From Chekiang, the watchful Chiang Kai-shek pelted his chief with telegrams of warning. Governor Chen was dragging his feet, declared Chiang; he was sabotaging the war effort; he was committing treason. Sun felt that it ill behooved Chiang to express any opinions at all on the subject, since he had kept aloof from the affair altogether, and one of his officers replied smartly to this effect, also by telegram. It must have been very irritating to the expedition when Chiang was proved right, as shortly happened. Chen Chiung-ming, having decided that his investment was not going to pay off after all, waited only until the dust of the expedition had died down in Canton before starting to bring all his army inside the city walls. Sun had just reached the Kwangtung border when he heard the news, and with his customary courage turned around and came back, leaving the expeditionary army to continue on its way under deputy command. He was confident that he could persuade Chen to change his mind again, but he reckoned without a number of other important Cantonese, who were thoroughly tired of the Kuomintang. They had a point, for the Kuomintang had been encouraging the new trade union movement and had played an important part in fomenting a big seaman's strike in Canton. The rich Cantonese had begun to ask themselves why they were supporting a government that aimed at destroying their cherished property rights. Thus whether or not Sun could spellbind Chen Chiung-ming, their minds were made up: he had to go. They attacked—or rather their troops did—and Sun made a narrow escape to a Chinese gunboat on the river, which lay at anchor among the usual cluster of foreign craft near the Custom House. He was in plain view of his enemies, but they did not dare fire at the boat for fear of hitting some Western vessel and bringing down reprisals. The expeditionary army more or less evaporated when the news arrived at the front. Those Kuomintang members who could do so got away from Canton, and those who did not simply changed their politics for the time being. Chiang Kai-shek showed up best: he hurried to Canton, all grievance forgotten—for had he not been justified?—and joined Sun aboard the gunboat, tending and guarding his chief for nearly two months, until it was obviously useless to stay in the vicinity any longer. Then they both slipped away in the dark to Shanghai.

There they had a clear view of an interesting new development in Peking: the Russian influence. Relations between China and Russia were an old story, so old that Russia had never been classed with the other foreign nations, but stood alone as something almost Eastern. The threat of Russian encroachment on Mongolia and Manchuria was an integral part of Chinese history. Now, since the Russian revolution, things were different. Chicherin, Commissar for Foreign Affairs—whom Sun had met, long ago, in Paris—had renounced on behalf of his nation all previous Russian treaties relating to China or dealing direct with her, which had been formed to advantage Russia at China's expense. The Karakhan Manifesto of 1919 repeated this renunciation and enlarged on it. Treaties "by which the Czar's government, . . . through force and corruption, enslaved the peoples of the Orient, and especially the Chinese nation," were abrogated. Close on the heels of this statement came Soviet missions to visit Peking and make friends. This was not because they deliberately chose the Peking government as opposed to Sun's in Canton, but because nobody in Russia knew much as yet about the Kuomintang. They thought of Peking as the center of authority. Besides, they had a foothold there: a Chinese Communist Party (the CCP) already existed.

Marxism had first struck roots at Peking National University, where the librarian Li Ta-chiao and Ch'en Tu-hsiu, dean of the Department of Literature, happened on the works of the prophet and were captured by his theories. Li's assistant in the library, a youth named Mao Tse-tung, was equally fascinated; in fact, since he came of peasant stock in Hunan and had to work his way through college, he was more strongly attracted by Marx than his elders would be, for they belonged to a privileged class. With these three as a nucleus the CCP was founded in 1920. By that time they were in touch with Moscow. A genuine Russian Communist made a special trip for the event. Sun Yat-sen, however, was something new to the ever-alert Russians, and in 1921 they sent a man whose working name was Maring to Canton, to find out more about him. Now, a year later, Maring went to see Sun in Shanghai. He found him depressed by the Nine-Power Treaty that had just been signed in Washington. Sun had always thought of the Western democracies as models for his country, but recent events had shaken his faith in their sense of justice, and the Nine-Power Treaty was the greatest disappointment of all; though it canceled out a good deal of the Japanese threat it did little to lessen exploitation by other nations. Worse, in his opinion it substituted Britain and America for Japan in the role of exploiter. Maring could see that Sun was in a receptive state of mind, and when he returned to Moscow he advised his associates to concentrate on the Kuomintang rather than Peking. His advice was taken. The Russians did not drop Peking, and continued to behave as if the northern capital was the proper place for their formally sworn-in Ambassador. They even signed a Sino-Soviet Treaty in Peking, but their main interest in China thereafter was with Sun and the Kuomintang. While the Ambassador dealt with Peking, the Comintern concentrated on Sun's party.

Sun's next visitor from Moscow was Adolph Joffe, who offered help in practical matters. When Sun showed a natural caution about accepting favors that might have strings tied to them, Joffe assured him that the question of handing over the nation to Soviet rule simply did not arise: Communism, he said, would not suit China. With a clear conscience, then, Sun accepted whatever help Joffe's people were willing to give, and to soothe the nervous anxieties of conservative Chinese and foreigners, he made a statement conjointly with Joffe, declaring that they had no intention of establishing Communism in China, because the conditions were not right. It was a statement that was to be repeated many times in the following years. Their aim, they said, was for national union and national independence. There can be no doubt that Sun at least meant every word of it. Joffe promised that Russia would help Sun to achieve his goal, and that promise was kept.

He suggested that one of Sun's lieutenants should go to Russia for training in one of the new projects, a military academy for the Kuomintang, and Sun elected Chiang and sent him off. By February 1923, Chen Chiung-ming had been vanquished by another war lord who still saw a future in Sun and invited him back to Canton. Everything seemed to be coming right at last for the Kuomintang. A stream of supplies and money—and advisers—kept arriving in Canton from Russia. Most important of the advisers was Michael Borodin, who came to join Sun in October. He was an expert in organizing revolutions; under his guidance the Party was vastly strengthened. The Kuomintang had done a certain amount in the way of labor organizing, but it was Borodin who showed them how to appeal to the people of the city by promising relief in concrete form, instead of talking in generalities. If the Kuomintang came into power, the officials now declared to the public, rents would be reduced 25 per cent and laws introduced to improve labor conditions. The effect was amazing. Next time Chen Chiung-ming tried to root his old friend out of Canton he got a horrid surprise; not only was the army much stronger, but ordinary civilians fought along with the soldiers, completely routing Chen's troops in a show of discipline never before witnessed in all Canton's sorry history of trainbands, Taiping riots, and the rest. Sun must have felt as if he had arrived in Paradise. As advice, armaments, and cordial friendship flowed in from Moscow, he looked back wonderingly at the barren years when he had tried so unrewardingly to get official help from America and Europe. Yet he was no fool, and he realized the danger that one day his Party might be filched from under his nose. He showed suitable gratitude when Moscow commanded the CCP to co-operate in every way with the Kuomintang, even to join it, but he made membership conditional. He declared that no Communist who became a member of the Kuomintang could put the CCP above the Party, or keep two equal allegiances. The Kuomintang must come first. It must be admitted that he failed to understand the true nature of a faithful Communist, since clearly he believed it possible that a man could or would sacrifice the very essence of his faith on command.

The CCP for its part was not at all happy with the Kremlin directive, for it looked as if they were being told to merge their identity in a rival group. The word "co-operate" instead of "merge" did not reassure them. They felt it was a shabby reward for what they had accomplished all on their own, as pioneers in the field of labor organization and dissemination of propaganda. They submitted and obeyed, but there was much grumbling in the ranks. As a result Chiang found himself viewed by the Chinese he met in Moscow with aggravated hostility. There were many of these compatriots, all members of the CCP, who at the best of times would not have cared for an unenlightened running dog of the *bourgeoisie* like Chiang. At that particular time their resentment was so strong it filled Moscow's air like fog. Chiang's lifetime attitude toward Communism may very well have grown in part from this experience. If he had been welcomed, cosseted and cozened like so many other visitors, he might have accepted the dogma with a whole heart. On the other hand, he was no green youth to be dazzled, but a man of thirty-six, tough-minded, and already committed to another master. On one occasion in Moscow he was invited to give a lecture to a Chinese audience. They heckled him savagely, but he gave back as good as he got. They made no bones about attacking Sun Yat-sen for his ideology—criminally imperfect, of course, from their point of view—and Chiang found them exceedingly offensive, all the more so because they were Chinese who had pledged allegiance to a non-Chinese cause. He stayed on guard through the four months he spent in Russia, though his relations with his sponsors were perfectly correct and he learned much that was useful regarding military academies.

He returned to Canton to find Sun in the middle of a fight with the Western powers over the question of customs revenue. In Canton this amounted to an important sum, and Sun had long protested against the foreigners' dictum that he must send such money to Peking. He argued that his government, not Peking's, was in control of Canton: by virtue of Kuomintang law and order, not Peking's, the Canton customs duties were collected. The money should stay in Canton and be applied to Cantonese expenses. He now declared that he would no longer remit the revenue; instead, he would seize the Custom House itself. The Western reply to this threat was prompt. The ministers involved quickly whipped round the coast and collected all available naval vessels of any sort, as long as they flew foreign flags. On December 7 seventeen ships of great variety, flying the flags of six nations—American, Japanese, British, French, Italian, and Portuguese—steamed up the river and assembled outside the Custom House. There was no need to show more strength: there they sat at anchor, a silent warning that Sun dared not ignore. He did not seize the Custom House. Later the British, who still held control of the Customs Service, climbed down somewhat and arranged to split the money between Canton and Peking, but as far as Sun was concerned the concession came too late. His last, lingering ties of emotion with the West, where he had first studied and admired enlightened forms of government—the West of Dr. James Cantlie and all his other teachers, the West that had given Ah-mi his chance—were broken. On the other side of the scales were Western support of the corrupt Peking regime, Western admiration in the past of Yuan Shih-k'ai, Western opposition to Kuomintang reforms such as unions, that might make China strong and independent and thus cut down their profits. The West had refused him help when he asked for it. Very well, he would take help where it was offered. Not four weeks after the affair of the "Custom House," on December 31, 1923, Sun made a speech at the Canton Y.M.C.A., saying,

"We no longer look to the Western powers. Our faces are turned toward Russia."

Surely this was not a pledge to hand over the Kuomintang to Communism, as the CCP was later to claim, but the statement of a man who saw himself as an independent leader making a free choice of friends. How he could have considered such freedom possible in the circumstances is another matter. The question is often asked: how clearheaded at this stage was Sun Yat-sen? Nobody was then aware that he had cancer of the liver, but he showed signs of ill-health, and though he was not an old man he tired easily. It is likely that his intelligence, too, was losing its vigor. Chiang Kai-shek was younger than Sun by more than twenty years and could not be called, like the older man, a seasoned veteran in revolution, nor had he traveled widely. Yet he saw reason to be suspicious of the Russians where Sun evidently did not.

The Whampoa Military Academy was soon under way, with Chiang Kai-shek its President and a faculty liberally sprinkled with Russian professors. Here again the CCP found cause for resentment —no Chinese Communist was asked to work at Whampoa. The course was a crash program that turned out its first class in four months. For all the brevity of their training, when the cadets were called on to put down a local rising they gave a good accounting of themselves. But the administration of the Academy did not run smoothly. Chiang complained that the Russian teachers ordered him around. (Oddly enough the same complaint against Russians was heard in other quarters, from CCP members.) As time went on, Chiang was not the only Party member who thought there was far too much Communism about. In July 1924 three Kuomintang members "impeached" Communists who had joined the Party for failing to keep their promise to Sun of putting aside their loyalty to Communism. The plaintiffs declared that these people had formed a party within a party. Wearily Sun smoothed over the quarrel. He could not afford a break with his advisers, at least not until he had united North and South.

*　　*　　*

In Peking, where the official Russian government kept its official Ambassador, some readjustment of the Karakhan Manifesto had been found necessary. One of the secret treaties repudiated en bloc by Soviet Russia had formerly given the Czar control over the Chinese Eastern railway. Now, somewhat to her embarrassment, Russia found it necessary to ask for the railway back again, repudiation or no repudiation, restoration or no restoration. At the time the request was made, Wu Pei-fu held Peking, and he made no trouble at all, readily agreeing to give it back. However, as Chang Tso-lin was quick to point out, the railway did in fact run through *his* territory in Manchuria, and was not Wu's to give. To keep the Old Marshal happy, Moscow therefore made a separate treaty with him, in which his claim to be lord of Manchuria was officially recognized.

Wu Pei-fu had made an alliance with a picturesque ruffian, General Feng Yü-hsiang, well-known to Westerners as the Christian General. When in 1922 Chang Tso-lin made a serious attempt to occupy Peking and push out Wu Pei-fu, Wu and Feng threw him back and forced him to retire to Mukden. Two years later, in 1924, Chang tried again, this time having taken certain measures in advance. The Christian General by prearrangement tricked his ally Wu Pei-fu. Both generals started out in different directions to engage the enemy, but Feng doubled back to Peking, came in by the back door as it were, and opened up the city to the Old Marshal. He expected to be given a high position in payment for this feat, but the partners fell out, very likely over Feng's action respecting the Emperor. Pu-i, now eighteen, was still living in the Forbidden City, somewhat precariously since the allowance that had been promised in the famous Articles providing for his abdication was hardly ever paid in full nowadays, and often never turned up at all. Chang Tso-lin had not yet arrived in the city and Feng Yü-hsiang had just taken control, when suddenly the Emperor was ordered out of the palace. For a time he was permitted to live in his father's house, but he was kept under surveillance, threatened and insulted, until some pro-Manchu gentlemen, aided by Reginald Johnston, the tutor, succeeded in smuggling the unfortunate youth into the Legation Quarter. There they appealed to the Japanese Minister, who readily took him in. According to Johnston, who met Chang Tso-lin when the matter had gone this far, the Old Marshal was furious with Feng for having persecuted Pu-i. Whatever the basic cause, Feng left Peking angry and disappointed.

Chang Tso-lin now turned his attention to the South, and sent a message to Sun that was reminiscent of an earlier overture. Was it not time to patch up their differences? He invited Sun to come to Peking and talk it over, and Sun thought favorably of the idea. After all, the Old Marshal was not of the same kidney as the other war lords, who had been closely connected with Yuan Shih-k'ai. Sun had never disliked the Old Marshal. He asked Borodin what he thought, and Borodin was of the opinion that he ought to go. Sun did go, taking with him Wang Ching-wei among others. Chiang's duties at the Academy kept him in Canton. It was the end of 1924. Just as the party arrived in Tientsin Sun collapsed, and was hurried into the Peking Union Medical College. An exploratory operation revealed the hopeless truth—cancer, terminal phase. Sun spent the last days of his life in the beautiful old house of Dr. Wellington Koo. He was strong enough much of the time to hold conferences at his bedside, and it is possible, just possible, that he himself composed and dictated the document, now occupying the place of honor in the Sun hagiography, known as his Will. Wang Ching-wei always claimed that Sun wrote it, and that he also named Wang as his successor, but Wang's word is not particularly dependable. Sun Yat-sen died on March 12, 1925.

The death put an end to the project of a peaceful, sensible union between Peking and Canton, though there was soon a common cause that should have brought them together if anything could. The movement toward trade-unionism had met with considerable response in industrial Shanghai. It flared up in gang warfare between Chinese and Japanese millworkers a few weeks after Sun died, then turned into anti-foreign riots that led to attacks on the International Settlement. Inevitably, Chinese students threw themselves into the affair. A number of them were demonstrating outside a police station to which some of the rioters had been taken; a large number of rioters were trying to break into the police station to seize the arms there and the police fired into the crowd. Thirteen students were killed as a result of this fusillade. Of course this violence touched off more of the same. Strike after strike led, like a train of powder, to more serious riots in Canton which culminated in another shooting incident, known as the Shakee Massacre, when police of the British and French communities of Shameen fired into a large mob of demonstrators and killed many of them. For a while it looked as if Chinese all over the country would forget their regional disputes and combine in an all-out effort to get rid of the Western imperialists. Certainly the Russians did their best to maintain the fervor of Chinese indignation, but the crisis passed without more big shootings.

It was July, and a new National Government had been formed in Canton, streamlined and built on the Russian pattern. Hu Hanmin was Foreign Minister; he had been one of the Japan exiles, and his politics slanted toward the right. Wang Ching-wei was Chairman of the State Council and the Military Council. Hsu Ching-chih was Chiang's commander in chief. With Borodin at their elbows these officials and Chiang Kai-shek busied themselves planning the expedition that was to unite the country at last. The troops would march through Kiangsu, Honan, and Shantung; already propagandists had been sent out to soften up the people in those regions. Everything was going well until on August 20 a man named Liao Chung-kai, a good friend of Chiang but openly sympathetic to the Russians, was assassinated just after he had been appointed to a high place on the Military Council. The identity of his murderers was not a very well-kept secret, and Chiang knew that one of them was a brother of Hu Han-min the Foreign Minister. Chiang acted quickly: he sent a party of his Whampoa cadets to search the house and office of every government official in the city. Soon afterwards Hu Han-min was quietly sent off to Russia for a while, and Chiang also got rid of his commander in chief Hsu Ching-chih, who did not see eye to eye with him on that ever-vexatious question of Chen Chiung-ming. Hsu was connected in a farfetched way with the murder of Liao, so he bowed out. Then there were two: Chiang and Wang Ching-wei.

With the twofold aim of settling Chen Chiung-ming and testing the troops, Chiang, now invested with full military powers by the Central Executive Committee (CEC), led the army on the East River Expedition, and chased Chen as far as Swatow. The army fought as no Chinese army had ever fought before, and propaganda had clearly worked wonders with the countrypeople, who came out to meet them with food and pleasant greetings instead of running for cover, as they had always done before. He would have been ready now, at the end of 1925, to start for Peking if it had not been for another quarrel that threatened to break up the United Front and disturb his plans. In the Western Hills near Peking, at Sun's tomb, some anti-Communists in the Kuomintang held a secret meeting at which they resolved that all Communists must be expelled from the Party, and the Russians told to go back to Moscow. Though Chiang had every sympathy with these sentiments he did not want them to prevail, not yet. He still needed Russian help, and most especially he needed Borodin. Unfortunately, Borodin when he heard of the Western Hills meeting seemed anxious to resign and get out, so that Chiang found himself in the strange position of arguing against his own convictions, apologizing to Borodin and assuring him that the majority of the Party did not subscribe to Western Hills ideas. Borodin did go, but not out of China; he went to visit the Christian General in Honan. His place in Canton was taken by two other Russians who hadn't his touch. Chiang hated them both. He disputed with them over the Northern Expedition plans, and with Wang over the Russians. On March 20 he staged another one of his lightning raids, ordering the arrest of a number of people he had long suspected, including his Russian advisers. This was startling—no Russian had been arrested before in Canton —and, though he merely ordered them out of the country, Wang Ching-wei took him to task. Chiang retorted by making public an interesting fact: Wang, he said, had recently tried to frighten Chiang himself out of Canton. The result of the exchange was that it was Wang who left, bound for another long holiday in France. With this accomplished, Chiang's temper improved and he made propitiatory gestures toward Moscow. Moscow did not seem to hold a grudge. In May Borodin came back from Honan and the two men resumed their relationship where it had left off, on an amicable footing. Even when Chiang conducted a purge of high-placed Communists in army and civilian posts, Borodin did not object. The purge removed, without fanfare, the head of the Propaganda Department among others, Mao Tse-tung. It left undisturbed Sun Yat-sen's widow Chingling, who had signified her desire to go on working for the cause and now had a place in the same Department. Before he left Canton Chiang was appointed to three posts: Chairman of the CEC, Chairman of the Military Council, and commander in chief of the army.

* * *

Chang Tso-lin held Peking, and Wu Pei-fu reigned in Central China. Feng Yü-hsiang was an unknown quantity. He might team up with either of the other two war lords, he might hold aloof, or he might join Chiang. He liked none of these men personally and none of them liked him, but that had nothing to do with the struggle for power. Whatever could be done in the way of persuasion and propaganda had been done already.

The National Army, numbering fifty thousand, was divided into three prongs. Chiang joined the middle one, his own command, on

August 10 in Hengchow, Hunan. Their journey to that point had been unobstructed, and peasants had cheered them on their way. Chiang took the troops on to Changsha, the provincial capital. It was garrisoned by Wu's men, but the Nationalists occupied it without difficulty. The two smaller armies were making equally good progress, one through Kiangsi, the other in Fukien. Wu Pei-fu was slow in getting under way with his more formidable troops, and he arrived at the Three Cities only just before Chiang did. On the first of September the Nationalists tried to take Wuchang, and found themselves held up: the walls were strong and the officer in charge would not surrender. In the old days the attacking army would have sat down and composed themselves for a siege of months, but this was 1926 and China was changing. After several tries came to nothing, Chiang simply bypassed Wuchang and made for Hanyang, which his troops entered within the week. They were now too near Hankow for Wu's comfort. He retreated and the Nationalists moved in, taking Wuchang later without fuss. Thereafter, however, their first swift push died down. For the next two months they were stalled at Nanchang in Kiangsi, but the subsidiary armies were moving ahead.

All these changes had an unsettling effect on the populace. Possibly it was true, as Chiang later alleged, that the Communists deliberately fomented unrest in Hankow: possibly their counterallegation that it was one of Chiang's own officers who made an incendiary speech against foreign imperialists and stirred up the mob is the real explanation. In any case, a mob rushed the British Concession, so that the foreign residents were forced to take to their gunboats in the river. The British felt they had had enough of Hankow. Later an agreement was signed between the Kuomintang Foreign Minister Eugene Chen and the British representative O'Malley, in which Britain relinquished her concessions both in Hankow and nearby Kiukiang.

February 1927 saw the occupation by Nationalist troops of Chekiang province, Chiang's own. The army entered Shanghai on March 22, bringing uneasiness to the foreigners of the International Settlement and the French Concession, though their ships were alerted and standing by. The foreigners were pleasantly surprised when nothing like the Hankow riots took place. All was peaceful, all was orderly; nobody needed the ships. But it was a different story two days later in Nanking. There, as the troops marched in everything seemed to go to pieces. The townspeople and the soldiers joined in looting, rioting, and burning of foreign property. It happened so quickly that the crews aboard the foreign gunboats lying in the river did not realize what was wrong until much harm had been done. As soon as they began to shoot the rioters rushed for cover, but many foreigners had been hurt, six were dead, and some women had been raped. When it happened Chiang was traveling down-river from Kiukiang, and he did not learn of it until everything was over and the foreigners had been evacuated to Shanghai. Already in a cold fury over news from Hankow, he plunged immediately into an inquiry as to how the disaster had come about. His troops put all the blame on the Northern army which, they said, committed the crimes as they fled, but many witnesses declared that they had heard rioters speaking the Cantonese dialect. Chiang's dilemma was more complicated than any of the other officers realized. He had been repudiated and disowned by the CEC.

It came about in Hankow. After his army had taken the city, the government in Canton packed up and moved up to Hankow, where they settled in as before, with Borodin keeping an eye on all departments. Incidentally, Soong Chingling was now given a place on the CEC. It is hard to make out just why they chose that moment to get rid of Chiang. Certainly he had many enemies in the government, friends of Wang and Hu Han-min, and Soong Chingling herself who had always hated him: the Communists were well aware of his feelings for them as well. But Stalin had cautioned Borodin to avoid precipitating a split. Just as Chiang had been playing along with Borodin because he needed him, so Borodin had played along with him for the same reason. Stalin had said, "At present we need the Right." The Right had capable people who were needed to defeat the capitalists. Chiang Kai-shek, though he had no sympathy with the revolution, would win the war for the Communists, or might even manage to bring Chang Tso-lin over to the Communist side without striking a blow. The Right had connections with rich merchants and could get money for the Communists. "Use the Right to the end," was Stalin's advice, "squeeze it like a lemon, then throw it away." This being so it seems strange that the CEC, at a special meeting in Hankow, should have voted Chiang out of all his posts and elected Wang Ching-wei—who was enroute from France—in his stead as Chairman of the CEC. Perhaps Borodin did not expect Chiang to resent the demotion so violently:

Borodin, used to the harsh discipline of Communism in Russia, may have assumed that Chiang would accept his punishment without protest. In fact, he must have assumed it, as otherwise he would have been on his guard against Chiang's vengeance.

A fierce sense of wrong possessed Chiang as he came to Nanking to be greeted by news of the outrages against foreigners. He thought they were due to Communist incitement, like those of Hankow; the Russians were probably trying to get rid of him this way too, by discrediting him in Western eyes. He thought of offering this theory to the foreign Ministers, but he rejected the notion: he did not wish to alarm the Communists quite yet. Instead, he apologized to the countries whose nationals had suffered, and promised to track down the offenders and punish them. He declared that from that time on he would hold himself personally responsible for the safety of every foreigner in the territory his army controlled. When Eugene Chen argued with the intermediaries and tried to minimize foreign grievances, claiming that more Chinese than foreigners had been hurt, Chiang told him in the presence of the others that this was simply not so. His attitude pleased the Westerners. Panic subsided, and Chiang was left to carry out his plans against the Communists.

Giving out that he was pursuing to Shanghai certain of the Nanking culprits, he went to that city and talked at length with Chinese bankers and businessmen, friends he had made in the past during his stock market days. They approved of his intentions, and collected the funds he said he would need to take the place of Russian money, after the debacle. He then made contact with the leaders of two secret societies he had joined in the past.

In April Wang Ching-wei came back to China, and went to Hankow to assume his new post. Immediately a statement appeared, signed by him and one of the Russians, to the effect that there was no truth in the rumor of a split between the CCP and the Kuomintang. A few days later, on April 12, Chiang gave the signal to his secret societies and the "white purge" was on.

No one had suspected it because he had been careful not to use his regular soldiers. It was a brutal business. In Shanghai mainly, but also in other cities where Chiang's part of the army were in occupation, the executioners went about their task of digging out Communists. Not only regular party members were to suffer: suspects, sympathizers, trade-union leaders, members of labor organizations, agitators were all the quarry as well. The men who did the work wandered through the streets tracking down houses and names, and sometimes killed then and there, without pretending that a trial was necessary. Many innocents must have disappeared without trace while the terror reigned; people who had never heard of Communism. Certainly the CCP was extirpated for some time to come.

When it was over, Chiang sent commands to Hankow, ignoring the fact that he had been removed from his posts. He said Communist propaganda must cease, that political agents with the army should have no authority any more, and that Nationalist soldiers should be answerable thereafter only to their regular officers—a list of directions that gives an interesting picture of the conditions under which he had been fighting until then. In reply the CEC denounced Chiang and all his works, cast him from his posts all over again, and read him out of the Kuomintang. They still had their third of the army, and it looked very much as if they would soon set up a Soviet state in Hankow. Chiang started an entirely new government in Nanking.

But as the summer wore on, the Hankow government began to feel misgivings. Their army met with defeats. An Indian Communist, M. N. Roy, was sent from Moscow to see how Borodin was getting on, and the two experts disagreed on strategy: Roy favored consolidating their position in the South, whereas Borodin wanted to make for Peking. The most pressing problem, however, was that of the Kuomintang's divided aims. By no means all of the Party wanted to be part of a Soviet. The richer members were opposed to being communized, and the rest of the Party hung back from antagonizing their financial supporters. This dichotomy was dramatically illustrated when the Autumn Crop Uprising which was to take place at Changsha, when thousands of peasants under the leadership of Mao Tse-tung marched on the city, fizzled out because of last-minute orders from the CEC, who feared their rich men. The Russians did not press these points, because Stalin continued to send word that the time was not yet, that they must not break with the Kuomintang, and that the agrarian movement must be curbed. However, some Russians kept reporting to Moscow that the time *was* ripe; the agrarian reform was going ahead and could not be stopped; when the split came they were sure most people would come over to their side. Suddenly, embarrassingly, Stalin reversed his policy and sent a directive by telegram. Let the agrarians go ahead and discard members of the Kuomintang who hung back. Recruit new leaders from the peasants and the proletariat. Liquidate unreliable generals. Mobilize twenty thousand Communists; mobilize fifty thousand workers and peasants. Bring before a tribunal any officer maintaining contact with Chiang Kai-shek, and when it came to the general sharing-out, spare the possessions of Kuomintang officers and men.

The effect of this telegram on most of the Chinese in the government was disastrous. Even Wang Ching-wei, on whom Roy was banking, drew back and said it was hopeless; the Party would never consent, and Sun Yat-sen's son, Sun Fo, agreed. In fact, the time had come when the Russians must leave, they said. Eugene Chen and Soong Chingling took the other side of the argument. With them it was all or nothing: if the Soviet was not to be, then there was no future for any of them in China, and they would go to Moscow with Borodin. This they did, while the soldiers who had accepted Communism remained behind, determined to fight on as guerrillas.

Chapter Twenty

Chang Tso-lin had accepted a loan from the Japanese. For this reason and because of certain plans of their own, they were determined to protect him. The end of the World War had loosened their grip on China; the Treaty of Versailles and the Nine-Power Treaty had cancelled their Twenty-one Demands. Nevertheless the Japanese were still in Tsingtao, and their presence in other areas of the North, while not exactly covered by written documents, was not disputed as long as the Old Marshal remained on friendly terms with them. This presence was one barrier against Chiang's making a rapid finish to his Northern Expedition, and there were two more—the Hankow forces, whose general had pulled them together and was now advancing on Nanking from the west, and the defection of that arch-defector Feng Yü-hsiang, who had promised to attack Chang Tso-lin but later changed his mind.

The Nationalists had entered Shantung and were on the last push to Peking when, as Chiang was about to lead them into Tsinan near Tsingtao, he found the way blocked by Japanese troops. He did not feel ready to take them on, and the army fell back on Hsuchao; in a short time the Northern forces had pushed it back nearly to Nanking. This reverse alarmed and angered lesser generals, and Chiang's leadership, which had survived much strain during the violent interruptions of the summer, now began to totter. The generals quarreled with him. Chiang, veteran of many such resistances, realized that the time had come to stage one of his withdrawals. He resigned from the army as he had so many times in the past, and retired to his native hills. To newspapermen who followed him he made several statements: It had been said that he sought Russia's friendship and advocated co-operation with the Communists until the break. He wished to refute this. He had always been of the same consistent opinion regarding Communism. In Russia he had seen "essential differences" between Chinese and Russian policies. He had been unable to persuade Sun Yat-sen to accept his views, but he was well aware of Sun's, who had said to him more than once that Communism and the Kuomintang could never co-exist in China. Chiang insisted that Sun had admitted the Communists to the Party in order to convert them, with the Three Principles serving as a "melting pot." "But Russia has now betrayed us," said Chiang, "and we must look to America as our only real friend among the nations."

Though Chiang had never been to the United States, this statement—as neat a contradiction of Sun's famous speech in the Canton Y.M.C.A. as anyone could wish—had a reasonable basis: on several occasions America had taken a sympathetic stand. She had not joined in the battle of the concessions, and there had been that time when Wilson opposed a consortium loan to Yuan Shih-k'ai because he thought it would stand in the way of China's independence. Whatever the self-interest that may have prompted these attitudes, on the record a good case could be made for America, and no doubt Chiang was influenced as well from a personal source—the American-educated Soong Meiling. For some months he had been paying court to her. Now he had time on his hands to pursue this campaign, at least, to the end. Leaving Fenghua after several weeks he went to Japan where Meiling and her mother were on holiday. There Chiang asked Mrs. Soong for her daughter's hand in marriage.

The subject had long been a topic of family discussion. Chingling had strongly opposed the match, but now that she had gone over to Communism, a faith not shared by the rest of the family, her opinion carried no weight. Chiang had still to satisfy his prospective mother-in-law that he was properly divorced from the wife he had been married to, sight unseen, at an early age: he armed himself beforehand with documents to prove it. He promised her as well to study the Christian religion, with a view to accepting it if he became convinced it was the right thing to do. (He did become a Christian some time later, and was baptized in the Methodist Church.) Chiang and Soong Meiling were married December 1, 1927, and lived in Shanghai for a time.

During the first days of his absence the Northern Expedition carried on fairly well. The substitute commanders soon relieved the threat to Nanking. Furthermore, the general who had been leading the Eastern Expedition from Hankow fell out with his comrades and came over to their side. As he brought a large number of his troops with him he left the Hankow government stranded, and they had to scatter, most of them to Canton. The Nationalists occupied Hankow. Beyond these two points, however, they could not seem to go, and with their lines extended to Hankow they offered a target to the Communist forces that were gathering once more near Canton. Cantonese war lords, as soon as they felt control relaxing, began fighting each other again. Clearly the Kuomintang needed Chiang to set all in order. The CEC considered the matter, decided to put pride in pocket, and sent their chairman, Wang Ching-wei, to Shanghai to invite him back. This was an unpleasant errand for Wang, especially as it meant that he must cede to his old rival his own proud position on the CEC. However, he did it because he had to, and afterwards set out on the old well-traveled route to France. The Kuomintang was itself again, with Chiang as its leader, and his first action was to break off diplomatic relations with Russia, sending home all Russians still in China.

As we shall see in greater detail later, the CCP was at this time getting orders from Moscow to take advantage of the "wave of revolution" which the Comintern was confident it could detect in China. A rising to form the "Canton Commune" had been planned, and a German Communist, Heinz Neumann, went to the city to lead it. "Victor Serge and Souvarine have charged that the uprising was ordered directly from the Kremlin by Stalin, who urgently needed a victory in China to vindicate his theory of the rising revolutionary wave in China, at the Fifteenth Congress of the Communist Party of the Soviet Union. Further strength is added to this claim by Li Ang, who claims to have been the corresponding secretary of the party at this time. 'The Comintern,' he says, 'sent telegrams daily urging the Chinese Communist Party to bring about uprisings in Canton and other large cities. These telegrams were all extremely emphatic in tone and allowed no room for argument.'" [Schwartz, Benjamin I., *Chinese Communism and the Rise of Mao* (Cambridge, Massachusetts, 1951), p. 105.] In fact it was an ill-planned operation, moved forward in a hurry from a later date because word had just been received that Wang had gone to see Chiang. For three days, from December 11 to the thirteenth inclusive, the fighting continued, but the expected rush of workers to join the Communist side never materialized. When the Kuomintang turned its "avenging executioners" loose on the city at the end of the fighting there were horrible scenes of torture and slaughter. Heinz Neumann escaped, but five Russians were killed among what was estimated as 5700 dead.

At the beginning of 1928 Chiang was formally reinstated as Chairman of the CEC and commander in chief of the Nationalist forces, at the CEC's Fourth Plenary Session. He was granted dictatorial powers for the duration of the Northern Expedition, which he pledged to bring to a victorious end by August of that year, and he also promised to call a National People's Convention immediately afterward. He declared that the Party would follow the program Sun had laid down: a phase of military supervision first, then a period of political tutelage, and finally a constitutional government. Then, for the second time, he set out for Peking at the head of the army, on April 7.

Again the forces were divided into three parts. The changeable Feng Yü-hsiang led one, Yen Hsi-shan another, and Chiang was head of the main portion, who followed the Tientsin-Pukow railway. As before, he came to Tsinan and found himself faced by grim Japanese guards; they had taken the added precaution this time of guarding the railway lines as well as the road into the city. Apparently they were quite ready to go to war with the Nationalists if necessary. When one of Chiang's officers tried to go inside the walls he set off a violent reaction: for several days the Japanese garrison fired all their weapons wildly. Chiang had a difficult task restraining some of his young hotheads who wanted to reply in kind, but restrain them he did. He had no desire to be seduced from his goal. The Japanese problem was a serious one and later it must be settled, but for the moment it had to wait. Chiang sent word to Yen Hsi-shan to carry on from where he was and make for Peking, out of reach of the Tsingtao garrison.

It is not hard to understand why the Japanese had become so touchy. Their erstwhile accomplice and friend, the Old Marshal, had lately shown disturbing signs of veering toward the Nationalist cause. He had long chafed under the indignity of lacking control over railways he considered his own. He disliked the fact that in his own particular area, Manchuria, the Russians controlled the northern section of the main railway, the Chinese Eastern; the southern from Changchun to Dairen, the South Manchuria railway, was run by the Japanese; while the Peking-Mukden line was British. He determined to effect a change. Moreover, he could see how steadily the Nationalists were approaching. He began to wonder if it might not be better to retire peacefully to Manchuria, where he could hatch out plans to free the railways without the necessity of fighting Chiang. In fact, before Chiang arrived at Tsinan the Old Marshal had sent a telegram to all three commanders, offering to negotiate his withdrawal from Peking. If he thought that this was not known to the Japanese, he was mistaken. Thanks to their excellent espionage they knew all about his plots, both regarding the railways and retreating from Peking. Their demonstration at Tsinan was aimed as much at Chang Tso-lin as at Chiang Kai-shek, and for a while it convinced the Old Marshal that his best course would be to behave as they wanted him to, since they seemed able to hold off the Nationalists. He was on the point of repudiating his offer to treat with the enemy, when he discovered that Feng and Yen, unlike the commander in chief, had not been stopped in their tracks but were quite close to Peking's walls. The Old Marshal waited no longer. With his son Chang Hsueh-liang, the "Young Marshal," he hurried out of the city and took a train on one of the South Manchurian spur lines, across the border into his own terrain. The train was running under a bridge outside Mukden when it hit a land mine and exploded, killing the Old Marshal on the spot. Nobody doubted that the Japanese had planted the mine. On July 5, a few days later, Yen Hsi-shan led the first Nationalist forces into Peking, and Generalissimo Chiang, having made a wide circle around Tsinan, followed close on his heels. North and South were united under one government at last, with several weeks to spare before August. The pledge had been redeemed.

＊　　＊　　＊

After the CCP was founded in 1920, cells had been organized here and there throughout China, and many of the charter members later became leaders in the movement. Some, like the librarian Li Ta-chiao, had died for it. Li was in Peking at the time of Chiang's purge, when the Old Marshal seized the opportunity to copy what he considered a good idea and sent his men out to scoop up what Communists they could find. They found Li among others, and executed him. However, the greater part of his companions remained, toiling in the wilderness but always in touch with Russia.

In 1961 it became not only fashionable but obligatory in Russia to decry Stalin. Stalin's corpse has been removed from its place of honor next to Lenin's in the memorial chamber, and his picture has disappeared from Russian walls, but in Peking it is quite different: there Stalin is honored still. This is especially paradoxical in the light of what happened to the CCP for painful months after the Shanghai purge. It was Stalin and the Comintern who were the cause of wrecking the CCP program. Stalin's struggle with Trotsky made him cling stubbornly to his own theories and stretch all facts on his particular Procrustean bed. The Comintern insisted that a grand revolutionary upsurge was just on the verge of happening to China. It would be based on the proletariat in the big cities. It simply had to be based on the proletariat, because that was how Marx had said it would happen. The peasants might help—in fact, they would have to help— but their part would be subordinate, because the Peasant, qua peasant, has bourgeois aims at the bottom of his heart, whereas the Urban Worker is rootless, a born revolutionary.

At the time of Chiang's breakaway the other co-founder of the CCP, Ch'en Tu-hsiu, dean of its literature, stood high in Comintern estimation, and when the Russians had to get out he was left as leader of the party operations. Soon, however, Moscow grew impatient with him because China never seemed to arrive at the famous upsurge. "Stalin needed victories in China," [Schwartz, p. 92] and the Comintern began to reproach Ch'en for not being a true revolutionary, tainted as he was by his intellectual origins. At length he was removed in favor of another man named Ch'ü Ch'iu-pai. It was Ch'ü who put Mao Tse-tung in charge of fomenting peasant unrest in Hunan, his native province. Ch'ü did not at the time think of this as much of a post. Like most of the other Communists he was wedded to the theory of the importance of the proletariat. However, it was because of this appointment that Mao learned technique that was later to prove invaluable. He gathered together peasants, miners, and a few ex-Kuomintang troops. He taught them and trained them, and finally led them on the first of their forays of rebellion, the "Autumn Harvest uprisings." These were planned by Mao's superiors as one part of the upsurge, at a time when the Communists believed the urban workers would be most likely to down their tools and join in. But though the peasants did their part, surrounding city walls and clamoring for the day of liberation, the proletarians inside the walls did not. The worst case was that of Changsha, when hundreds of peasants were slaughtered at the walls. Because of these failures Mao fell from grace and was dismissed from the Politburo. This was late in 1927. That winter he retired with the remnants of his troops, who were to form the nucleus of the Red Army, to the Chingkanshan range between Hunan and Kiangsi, and quietly continued with his program. The chief leaders of the CCP, considering him of no importance, paid little attention.

It was inevitable that he should begin to wonder if the faulty synchronization of workers with peasants was not perhaps peculiar to China, where 80 per cent of the population was connected with rural life. The fact was, Comintern theory at the time simply did not fit the concrete facts. Possibly, however, Mao's doubts did not rise so much from these statistics as from the position he was in vis-à-vis the peasants. He saw with his own eyes how they reacted to the revolutionary ideal.

The theory changed slightly during the next phase of the CCP, but not very much. When the Canton Commune failed so drastically, Ch'ü Ch'iu-pai was rebuked and removed from his position in his turn, and replaced by Li Li-san, who with Chou En-lai had organized the first CCP cell in Paris, where they were both students. The Comintern now admitted that peasants had their place in the revolutionary scheme, but they still clung tenaciously to the idea that the working class must be leaders. If the workers didn't lead, well, they must be taught to do so; they must be recaptured, and cease fearing (as they did) the vengeance of the Kuomintang, which had murdered many of the trade-union leaders and agitators. The Russians grew quite testy about the obtrusive peasants. At the Sixth Congress it was stated that "In certain sectors of the agrarian struggle an inclination has arisen to treat lightly the leadership of the urban proletariat. All such deviations within the party must be strictly opposed." [Schwartz, p. 125.] Yet they kept happening, for the Communist method worked like magic with the poor tenant farmers. "When the army marched into an area, the provincial representatives or Nanking appointees were killed or forced to flee; the large landholders, industrialists, bankers, and money lenders were terrorized or executed and their property confiscated. The downtrodden peasant and exploited laborer suddenly found himself emancipated, rid of debt, and usually in possession of land fairly adequate to yield a livelihood. Workers took over the management of factories and mills and trade unions were organized. After an area had been politically consolidated and military control established, it was incorporated into the ever-expanding soviet system." [Eckel, Paul E., *The Far East Since 1500* (London, 1948), p. 487.] Of course the former have-nots wanted more of the same, though the outnumbered workers were too chastened to take steps.

All in all, Li Li-san found his task hard going, especially as the great upsurge somehow never quite precipitated. The Chinese proletariat didn't have enough dynamism. Such union leaders as had not been executed by Chiang's strong-arm men felt they had learned their lesson, and found it safer, if not as profitable, to stick to their Kuomintang masters than to cast in their lot with dangerous Communists. Besides, Li must have been puzzled by the "slippery directives" he got from the Comintern, muddled as they were and contradictory: "Comintern leaders addressed to the Central Committee of the Chinese Communist Party a series of directive letters preparatory to insurrection: the upsurge was imminent, but not yet in sight; the Communists must take the lead, but not rush ahead; the peasants were important, but not a central force. Reading these contradictory analyses, prognostications, and programs for action, one does not wonder that Li Li-san's leadership was confused." [Robert C. North, *Moscow and Chinese Communists* (Stanford, 1953), p. 129.] The people in Moscow were apt to interpret events in China too hopefully, to say the least—the war-lord rebellions against Chiang which followed on his success meant what they had always meant, someone else's desire to get on top, but the Comintern thought they heralded the beginning of the break-up and of course they misconstrued the success of peasant guerrilla warfare as showing that peasants were subordinate to the urban proletariat. The "allegedly imminent and violent upsurge among the masses" never happened, but Li was as firmly wedded as any Moscow armchair expert to the theory that the proletarians must and would touch it off, inside the cities. "All talk of 'encircling the city with the country' or of relying on the Red Army to take the cities is sheer nonsense, and so much hollow bluff," he wrote stoutly. [North, p. 134.]

* * *

For Chiang there was never any question of staying in Peking and directing affairs from there. The Kuomintang prejudice against the northern capital had been heightened by the bitter story of

Yuan Shih-k'ai. Nanking was to be the capital of China, and one of the things done by the provisional government, while the city underwent vigorous reconstruction, was to build a magnificent mausoleum for Sun Yat-sen in the Purple Hills, overlooking Nanking, and move his body there from the North.

The first problem to be faced was a familiar one that had dogged Sun Yat-sen, Yuan Shih-k'ai, and many others—financing. According to T. V. Soong, Chiang's brother-in-law and able Finance Minister, they must shuffle more than half the wartime army of two million men off the payroll, to start with. It was a painful process, leading to much bad blood between administration and generals. Chiang, now appointed President of the country—though later he resigned this post to Lin Sen—planned that the provisional government should remain in office during the period of political tutelage from 1930 to 1935, by which time, presumably, the people would be ready to vote and a permanent constitution would have been written. The temporary body was made up of five committees ("yuans"), the Legislative, Executive, Control, Judicial, and Examination. Yen Hsi-shan and Feng Yü-hsiang were among the ministers of the Cabinet, but only for a while. They had other ideas.

The Young Marshal of Manchuria, Chang Hsueh-liang, had stepped into his father's shoes, but unlike the Old Marshal he evinced from the beginning a desire to belong to Chiang's projected Republic, and he flew the Kuomintang flag. He had, however, inherited unchanged the Old Marshal's desire to throw off Russian control of the Chinese Eastern railway: Chang Hsueh-liang was virtually certain that the interlopers, not content with running the railway, were conspiring to oust him. Too hastily he sent his police swooping down on the Soviet consulates, where they unearthed documentary proof—at least so the Young Marshal claimed—of plans for fomenting rebellion. In Harbin he took more than forty Russians prisoner, and seized the railway. Moscow immediately threatened to cut off relations with China *in toto* and send home all the Chinese in Russia. Russian troops crossed the border from Siberia and easily defeated the Chinese in Manchouli, until Chang Hsueh-liang submitted and allowed the Russians to come back to the railway, with a stronger position than before. All this was observed by the Japanese and filed for future reference, for they themselves had designs of long standing on the territory. In the meantime, however, immigrants were encouraged by the Young Marshal to come from

China and settle on Manchurian land, and he took to building railways which he ran for his own profit, contrary to treaty. This too the Japanese took note of.

Inevitably the Chinese generals began quarreling among themselves, suggesting that Chiang's inheritance of war lords was a doubtful blessing. It was all very well to talk of a voting public, but the war lords in the government were not—to put it as mildly as possible—of a republican mentality. Sooner or later they were bound to feel dissatisfied and revert to their old ways, scrambling by force, intrigue, or a combination of both toward the top. Yet the first voice to protest was not a war lord's; it was Wang Ching-wei's. Moping in his French wilderness he saw no signs of forgiveness on Chiang's part. He had forsaken the Communists, yet it seemed as if the Kuomintang had forsaken him: the erstwhile leader of the Party Left had been caught in the middle, then dropped. He published a manifesto attacking Chiang as a hidebound reactionary, and the complaint set off, in chain reaction, more of the same. Feng Yü-hsiang chimed in to express his unhappiness, which was deep. After his spirited, variegated career the Christian General was faintly astonished to find himself occupying the respectable berth of Minister of War. Looking back on the exploits of yesterday was not enough, though indeed they made an interesting picture. In the past he had visited Russia and tasted the sweets of favor in Moscow, petted and bribed by the Soviet. Later in China, intoxicated by leadership, he forgot the brotherhood of man. He had juggled the destiny of emperors, and hobnobbed with great war lords, and been a fairly great war lord himself. He had betrayed and been betrayed a dozen times over, and had had a wonderful time. When he gave his so-called allegiance to Chiang Kai-shek he had expected a reward commensurate with his service, possibly the gift of Shantung as soon as the Japanese should have gone. But though the Japanese were gone, Chiang did not give him Shantung. Life in Nanking was slow and the pickings poor, and Feng wanted to get out. After echoing Wang Ching-wei's complaint, with a few other similarly disgruntled officials he packed up and left, going to his old stamping ground in Honan. Nationalist troops followed him and long-drawn-out hostilities ensued. The "war lord period" was under way.

Two other discontented generals were Pai Chung-hsi and Li Tsung-jen. In the first flush of victory Chiang wanted to centralize all authority in Nanking, abolishing among others the administrative bodies, or subcouncils, of Canton and Hankow. Pai and Li had been heading these and they objected to Chiang's proposal: they refused to close down. For a time they went on as before, managing the provinces of Kwangtung and Hupei and collecting taxes, but soon they decided that this revenue was not enough; they wanted Hunan as well. The Governor of Hunan would not acknowledge their right to his province's tax revenue, and continued to turn it over to Nanking, so Pai and Li drove him out. In reply Chiang drove *them* out of Hankow. They retreated to Canton and there holed up. Occasionally their troops made forays into the countryside, but they were always stopped and beaten by Nationalists.

The Christian General turned his remarkable powers of persuasion on the Governor of Shansi, Yen Hsi-shan. Yen was unusual for a war lord. He managed his province well if autocratically, and really earned his nickname, "the Model Governor," but he too had been feeling the pinch of authority and was not averse to allying with Feng Yü-hsiang in an effort to kick over the traces. Their combined forces went under the name of "The People's Army." Yen and Feng summoned Wang Ching-wei to lend a modern gloss of politics to what was in truth merely another old-fashioned buccaneering venture. Wang was as pleased as a hermit crab that finds a ready-made shell to slip into; with alacrity he joined the others.

Chiang was caught between fires: if he fought the Southern war lords for Canton he would have to neglect the Northwest, and vice versa. He sent a lot of telegrams to no avail. In March 1930 the Model Governor moved with his army and allies into Peking, easily defeating the Kuomintang troops he found there: Wang was given the post of political leader and Feng was deputy commander. Chiang moved slowly, doing nothing at all until August when he dislodged the outer ring of The People's Army in Shantung. Then he made a move calculated to draw out the Young Marshal, who until now had been silent and presumably neutral. Chiang named him deputy commander in chief of the Nanking troops, and Yen hastily followed up with the offer to Chang Hsueh-liang of a place on his Peking "State Council." Hsueh-liang at last plumped for Nanking. He suggested a cease-fire and talks in which Nanking should be the final arbiter, and then he sent Manchurian troops to Peking. The war lords gave way. By the end of 1930 China's unity, though precarious, seemed on the way to being re-established. Canton had still to be wiped up, however, and there were two other even more important

bits of unfinished business—the Communist guerrillas and the growing strength of Japanese militaristic ambitions. Besides these two
challenges to stability, local disturbances were to shrink to insig-
nificance. Japan and the CCP had nothing in common but their
final aim to possess China. Unwittingly they aided each other. Each
in turn was to attain the objective, Japan in part, the Communists
wholly.

*   *   *

The Reds could not afford to be in a hurry. The light of Moscow's
interested approval had faded for a bit after the Canton Commune
fiasco, but now Stalin's interest, reawakened, bid fair to overpower
the CCP, or at least its leader, Li Li-san. In August, at the time
Chiang was occupied by his troubles in Shantung and Peking, Mao
Tse-tung, with Chu Teh and some others, led the peasant army in
an attempt to take Nanchang. They failed, but after that they went
for Changsha, and to everyone's surprise actually captured and occupied it. For a few days, while in possession, the leaders made
happy plans to spread out and conquer the Three Cities, but it all
came to an end when foreign gunboats steamed upriver, while at
the same time a Nationalist army moved toward Changsha's walls.
The Red Army had to get out.

Voices criticizing Li Li-san were loud among the group known
as the Returned Students. These young people were of the same
sort as those who had so irritated Chiang Kai-shek in Moscow, seven
years earlier. Fresh from Sun Yat-sen University in that city they
now came to China under the wing of a Communist, Pavel Mif, who
was known as a Chinese expert, to move into positions of authority,
and they made the CCP veterans quite as angry as Chiang had been,
though for different reasons. It seemed violently unfair to the old-
timers that such whippersnappers, whom they bitterly called "the
Twenty-eight Bolsheviks," who knew nothing at firsthand about
China or the situation, should be placed over themselves. "These
fellows were all young students who, needless to say, had made no
contribution whatsoever to the revolution. While we were carrying
on the revolution they were still suckling at their mothers' breasts.
. . . These men who were infants in terms of the revolutionary
background were now sent back to be the leaders of the Chinese
Revolution!" [Li Ang, quoted by Schwartz, p. 149.]

Mif and his unpopular party immediately set to work to tear down Li Li-san, but for a time it looked as if they could not do it. Chou En-lai had a genius for scenting out the winning side, and he wrote a report in defense of Li's work. He cleverly managed to get around one very sharp corner when he explained away the disconcerting success of the peasants in capturing Changsha; complicated as it may seem at first glance, the Comintern did not at all approve of this victory, since it had proved Moscow wrong in that it was not proletarian but peasant. Chou En-lai explained all that and pointed out that the capture had logically followed Stalin's line. Stalin had hailed the Depression of 1929 as the harbinger of a new revolutionary upsurge: Capitalism was crumbling just as the prophet Marx had said it would. Stalin had declared that the crisis would spread all over the world, even to the most obscure corners of the backward agrarian countries. The taking of Changsha had been one manifestation of the breakdown, that was all, and Li Li-san had not diverged from Stalin's policy save in a few unimportant details.

"The Central Committee had perhaps underestimated the 'unevenness' of the development of the revolutionary situation in China but its contention that an initial success in one or several provinces could not be realized without the presence of a general revolutionary situation throughout the country was entirely in accord with the analysis of the Sixth Congress. As for the attack on Changsha, it might have been ill-timed but the fact that the Red Army was able to take and hold the city demonstrated its strength and pointed to better things in the future." [Schwartz, p. 153.] Chou ended his report by saying as if in passing that the Central Committee had believed, as Comintern directives stated, that a Soviet could not be established until the party had occupied large cities, but this had been proved erroneous, and the Committee would now proceed with the setting-up of a soviet government without waiting for such occupation.

For the moment Li Li-san was saved and remained in power, and Mif with his Students' clique had to bide their time. But one fact still stuck in the craw of the Comintern: the Chinese revolution was *not* proceeding well. Between them the Returned Students got Li out at last, citing an imposing number of his misdeeds. Li cited them himself in his recantation: "I maintained that the victory of the bourgeois democratic revolution directly passes over into a socialist revolution. This point of view is semi-Trotskyist." [Schwartz,

p. 161.] It was not by any means the full extent of his crimes. He had been guilty of petty bourgeois chauvinism, adventurism, and opportunist passivity: he had harbored rightist inclinations. The list was long. By the end of 1930 Li was out, and after another struggle with resentful veterans the Returned Students were in, under the leadership of one of their number, Wang Ming.

Li Li-san disappeared into Moscow until 1945, when he turned up with the Russians who occupied Manchuria, but Chou En-lai managed to stick and wriggle to the top. He always did.

* * *

With the Northern war settled and the Southern war lords at least quiescent, Chiang felt able to announce on the Double Tenth celebration of 1930 that constitutional government was within sight, and the first People's Congress would meet on May 5, 1931. At a plenary session of the CEC he made more announcements. He was ready after all to permit some degree of autonomy to provinces. He mentioned the three divisions he had sent to Kiangsi and Hunan to fight the Red Army, and said he could probably completely eradicate "Communism and banditry" before six months were out. The Committee accepted this promise with a grain of salt, for reports from the Kuomintang troops were always the same—the Reds were on the run and it would not be long now—yet the government army never seemed to change position. In fact, the Red Army's guerrilla tactics outmaneuvered the Nationalists every time. The Communists would strike, dissipate their numbers, run away, and re-form at a safe distance. The cost of the campaign was weighing heavily on the exchequer, and there was no real end to be seen.

Foreign relations, however, gave a brighter picture. The government had been trying for a long time to abolish extraterritoriality, and British and American replies hinted that these nations might possibly consider giving way. As for foreign concessions, equally offensive to the Chinese, the British had followed up their relinquishment of Hankow and Kiukiang territory by giving up their land in Chinkiang and Amoy. In Shanghai, the Municipal Council had long controlled the International Settlement under the eye of the various Consuls General, especially the American and British. The Japanese had been given seats on the Council. Now for the first time five Chinese representatives were admitted.

Shortly before the Congress there was a spot of trouble in the capital. Hu Han-min had made up his differences with Chiang in 1927, and became President of the Executive Yuan, but the two men never got on really well, and now they quarreled over the provisional constitution. Hu resigned from the Yuan: Chiang counterattacked by putting him under house arrest. There was a loud outcry and the term "dictator" was bandied about freely. Suddenly Wang Ching-wei popped up again in his best jack-in-the-box manner, this time in Canton, where with Eugene Chen (last heard of in foreign exile) he had made an alliance with Pai Chung-hsi and Li Tsung-jen. Wang "impeached" Chiang Kai-shek, and his three companions helped to sign the document. Had it not been for Chiang's cavalier treatment of Hu Han-min—though the house captive was unhurt, and soon set free—a large number of officials would have rallied round him, but as it was the response was half-hearted. Several Kuomintang members even slipped off to Canton. The opening of the People's Congress was all but lost in the general shuffle. On May 25 the Canton group, much strengthened by new support, sent an ultimatum to Chiang demanding that he resign. Chiang disdained it and did not reply, so they declared a new national government in Canton. For the following eight weeks parleys were held in Shanghai, but no compromise seemed possible. As an anchor to windward, the Canton group sent word to Japan asking for support—a move that did not meet with favor in the rank and file—and Pai Chung-hsi led an army out of the city and started toward Nanking. He got about halfway, and Nanking prepared for the attack. Then on September 18 the Japanese moved swiftly and smoothly into Manchuria.

Chapter Twenty-one

The leaders of the militarist party that dominated the island empire were committed to expansion. Their lack of control over Manchuria had long exasperated them, particularly after Chang Hsueh-liang's new railways began to take revenue away from the main South Manchurian line, and the Young Marshal evaded their attempts to discuss the matter. That summer a fight took place between a few Chinese and Korean farmers in Manchuria; exaggerated reports of the affair resulted in an anti-Chinese riot in Korea in which many Chinese were killed. In August a Japanese army captain, Nakamura, was traveling in Manchuria mysteriously disguised as a teacher, on a Chinese passport. He was carrying, if the Chinese were to be believed, heroin with which he intended to buy information. He was assassinated, and the two countries were still arguing about the incident on the decisive date of September 18, but the explosive spark was a row over a length of railway track near Mukden. The Japanese later claimed that Chinese soldiers were ripping it up and their men tried to prevent it. Whatever the truth might be, the fight gave them the chance they had long wanted; Japanese troops now moved in on the pretext that their nationals must be protected. They arrived with such efficiency that the Young Marshal, ill in bed at the time, was slow to round up his troops and resist. Though after they got started his men fought well, Japan had control of the country before the middle of February. Throughout the hostilities the Japanese maintained the fiction that Manchuria was seeking independence and they were helping her. Each time a region was occupied, they set up a so-called independence committee of puppets, and on March 1 they proclaimed the new state of "Manchukuo," which is Chinese for "Manchuland." As a finishing touch Japan presented to Manchuria as their chief executive none other than our old friend Pu-i, whom they had been saving up ever since 1924, when he found sanctuary in their Peking Legation, for just this occasion. After all, it was logical. He was hereditary King of Manchuria.

Within three days of the first invasion China appealed to the League of Nations. At that early stage the Council tended to accept the Japanese representative's assurance that it was all a great fuss over nothing. He said that Japanese forces would withdraw from the country as soon as the safety of their nationals was assured. It soon became obvious, however, that this was not true, and the Council had to reconsider the matter. Though the United States was not a member of the League, she was asked to take a seat on the Council, and the offer was accepted. The Council ordered Japan to withdraw from Manchuria. Japan did not. If the Leaguers had been determined about it the next stage would have been to apply sanctions against recalcitrant Japan, or even, if necessary, to use force, but they were not determined. Britain and France had invested heavily in the Far East and had much to lose if the peace was upset there, whereas America had far less at stake and carried little authority. All the nations, in any case, were beset by the great Depression and did not want to involve themselves in such a struggle. The League appointed a Commission of Inquiry, which could safely be trusted to take a good long time: in the event, by the time its report was ready everything was over. The Americans tried to do something more: Secretary of State Stimson wrote a warning note to Japan and sent the American fleet to the Pacific, but that was as far as things went. The Japanese were irked by Stimson, but did not alter their course. On January 18, 1932, they were given the chance to go into Shanghai, when a mob there killed a Japanese. The Japanese navy moved swiftly in and landed marines, who fought the Chinese for some weeks, until the Chinese forces retreated on March 1. The Americans organized talks between the combatants in the International Settlement, and the Japanese finally agreed to withdraw; a demilitarized zone was created around the city after they had done so. In October the League Commission's report appeared. It condemned Japan's actions in Manchuria, declared that the Manchurians had not at all wished to be liberated, and advised all nations to refuse to recognize Manchukuo. The Japanese were well aware that the British and French had subscribed to the report for appearances' sake, for they had been told so, privately. For the sake of appearances on their own part, however, they put on a show of hurt indignation and walked out of the League. Manchukuo was declared an empire, and Pu-i mounted the throne March 1, 1934.

* * *

In Nanking the first reaction to Japan's invasion of Manchuria was violent. The younger men, especially the students, wanted to go straight to war with Japan. There were riots, but Chiang, knowing he could not fight the Communists and Japan at the same time, insisted that the nation wait to see what the League was going to do about it. Pai Chung-hsi's threatened assault withered away in the face of the new crisis. The leaders of the Canton group got together with Nanking officials to compound their differences, but could not come to terms. There was much criticism of Chiang, until he was angered and in the middle of December handed in his resignation, retiring as usual to Chekiang with his wife. At this point the bankers of Shanghai, who for financial reasons were able to call the tune in Nanking, spoke sharply to those concerned. Apologies were made and Chiang returned to a city chastened and ready to listen to his reasons for refusing to make war on Japan. The country was not strong enough, he said. Until they had stamped out Communism, they could not take the risk of turning their backs on it. His audience grumbled, but held their peace.

The Manchuria affair displeased Moscow almost as deeply as it had Nanking. Russia had always looked on the northern territory as a future colony of her own. Now, unless she wished to risk war with Japan—and she did not—she would even have to give up her share of the Chinese Eastern railway, for Japan had made an offer for it and was clearly not going to take a refusal. Moscow had to accept; ultimately the railway was rechristened the North Manchurian, and incorporated into a national system organized by the Japanese. Russia was now out of Manchuria altogether, and it became increasingly apparent that the time had come for Moscow to patch up her differences with Nanking on the diplomatic level. Chiang was receptive to tentative advances to this end. He too could play the ambiguous game: Russian diplomats reappearing at the capital had no effect on his campaign against the CCP. For that matter, Moscow and the CCP were not particularly close at the time, especially as communications were difficult owing to Nationalist pressure, but the bonds were to tighten again in due course. The Chinese Communists now took their cue and stimulated more outcry against Chiang for wasting his time pursuing war against his own people—i.e., the Chinese Communists—instead of attacking the real enemy, the outsider, Japan. The disgruntled young, who had been snubbed for saying the same thing, took up the refrain more eagerly than ever, and were echoed by politicos of many colors, but Chiang ignored them all and intensified his anti-Red campaign. He too resented the Japanese encroachment: all the more reason to hurry and extirpate the threat nearer home.

At the beginning of 1933 the Japanese struck again and occupied Jehol, between Manchuria and China. One would think that this was hardly a tactful time for old-fashioned war-lord tantrums, but some of the generals were incorrigible and began making threatening noises. This time they were surprised. When in the autumn there were rumbles of revolt in the South, Chiang suppressed them ruthlessly; he had improved the training of his troops and acquired some modern armaments. As soon as all was quiet he turned again to the anti-Red campaign.

It has often been pointed out that the CCP and the Kuomintang organizations had much in common, and it is true, since they had their roots in the same source. Borodin trained them all. Chiang knew more about Communist methods than was, perhaps, good for the enemy, since he had gone to their school, and he applied their own tactics now to the problem of defeating them. If the Communists could use propaganda, so could he. He too could perfect an intelligence service. It was borrowing a leaf from their book when he instituted the "New Life Movement," which was framed to supply rules of hygiene and a code of morals to people demoralized by years of change and insecurity. Chiang sent with his forces earnest, dedicated young men who were better educated than ordinary soldiers. They went ahead of the troops to exhort the villagers and win them over. He utilized planes to find out where the Reds were hiding. Among the foreign advisers in Nanking were several German soldiers. One of these, General von Seeckt, planned an important offensive against the Communists, and the year of 1933–34 marked a change in the story of Chiang and the Red Army.

The autumn of 1931 had seen not only the Japanese invasion, but a shift in the Chinese Communist hierarchy. Mao Tse-tung had risen by slow, careful stages to the top at last. How he pushed out the Returned Students clique is an obscure story: some of their disgruntled friends alleged that he deliberately sent several of them on projects bound to be disastrous, but his most telling blow was against the Secretariat, which had until then operated as Chinese conspirators usually did, from the safe purlieus of Shanghai. On November 7, 1931, Mao took an important step and proclaimed the "Chinese Soviet Republic" in Juichin, a village at the southern border of Kiangsi near Fukien. It was the nearest thing to a stable capital that the Communists had yet known. Mao sent word to Shanghai that the Secretariat, which was headed by Wang Ming, should now leave the city's underground and join them in Juichin. It was a reasonable suggestion; the Secretariat was under pressure from the authorities and could scarcely function there at all. However, they were reluctant to go and would not move until, according to the story, Mao simply stopped sending them any money. Cut off from their work and livelihood, they had no choice but to obey. Wang Ming went back to Moscow as delegate to the Comintern, and the smaller fry went to Juichin. The Comintern had to accept the situation. "In the apt phrase of Li Ang, 'Moscow itself had to buy "face" through Mao Tse-tung.'" [Schwartz, p. 188.] Mao was acknowledged leader of the CCP, and Chou En-lai became Commissar of Military Affairs.

The Soviet Republic endured at Juichin for three years, until 1934 when von Seeckt's offensive made things too hot for them. Driven in to the center by the German's encircling tactics, the guerrilla groups were pinned down and could no longer use the hit-and-run methods that gave them so much advantage. Toward the end of the summer they faced the necessity of pulling up stakes altogether. With some difficulty they managed to refer the question to Moscow, and received the reply that they must evacuate the territory and make for the northwest, possibly the Russian-occupied Outer Mongolia. On October 15, between one hundred twenty and one hundred thirty thousand troops set out on the Long March from Juichin, with the object of meeting two other smaller processions in the west. The extraordinary feat of the March has been celebrated ever since in Communist annals, but the epic seldom includes certain details that have to do with Mao Tse-tung's career. To begin with, his predecessor Ch'ü Ch'iu-pai, who had been with him in Juichin, was left behind because he was tubercular and Mao declared him unable to make the trip. He was captured and executed by the Nationalists.

For a week the army marched at night, until they had gone through the enemy lines, and after that they went at a forced pace for three days more, until the Nationalists were safely behind. For the first lap the column drove straight west, across south Hunan, to Kweichow. They took their first long rest in January. It was in Tsun-yu, Kweichow, while they were unable to communicate with Moscow, that Mao began pressing charges against some Returned Students who still challenged his supremacy. When the marchers had almost reached the western border of the province they turned north, marching across part of Yunnan and crossing the Yangtze into Sikang. From there they turned back into western Szechuan where, by prearrangement, they joined the other columns of minor soviets. There was disagreement as to where they should make for now. Mao and Chou opted for Shensi, the others for Sinkiang. By this time they were again in touch with Moscow, so the dispute was referred to headquarters and the arbiters told them to go to Sinkiang. On the way, however, the marchers ran into harrowing difficulties in the swampy Grasslands. They were also set upon by Kuomintang forces, and in the end had to go to Shensi after all, coming to rest in Pao An. There Mao managed to settle the last of the trouble-making Students.

"The Westerner cannot refrain from noting how Mao Tse-tung appears to have risen in spite of—rather than because of—Joseph Stalin and other Communist leaders in Moscow. Once the Chinese leader had achieved control, however, the same Communist hierarchy which formerly had subjected him to discipline lost no time in bestowing its approval." [North, p. 167.]

Another important move had been made during the Long March. Halfway, during the pause in Szechuan, the Reds on August 1, 1935, made a public gesture toward Chiang that might almost be called conciliatory. They called on him with all their fellow countrymen to join together in fighting Japan, and promised that if Chiang would halt the war against them—"his own people"—they would co-operate with him in the struggle. Three weeks later they made another public announcement to the effect that they wished to form a United All-Chinese People's Government of National Defense with the USSR government and the anti-Japanese partisans of Manchuria. Chiang ignored these appeals, believing them to be no more than tricks. Other Kuomintang officials, however, thought he should consider the proposition. The Southern generals had made another attempt in June to force his hand; they telegraphed him demanding immediate action against Japan, and prepared to send troops from Kwangtung and Kwangsi. Public opinion was strong against them, and the entire air force of Kwangtung flew their planes to Nanking, where they handed them over to the Kuomintang. Chiang profited from this event. Though Pai and Li remained defiant and unregenerate in Kwangsi, the war lord of Kwangtung joined forces with Nanking, obviating at least half the nuisance.

Chiang's next problem was Chang Hsueh-liang. At first the dispossessed Manchurian troops had been left on duty just south of the Wall, but it was too near their old homes for flesh and blood to stand. So many incidents arose that they were moved, with the Young Marshal in command, to the ancient city of Sian in Shensi, south of the Yellow River. The Young Marshal's orders were to assist the local general, Yang Hu-cheng, in suppressing Communists, who by this time were close neighbors in the province, but his heart wasn't in the work. Chang more than any of the other generals wanted revenge on Japan, and he had reason: they had stolen his country and murdered his father. He couldn't see why Chiang Kaishek should waste his time on a few Chinese rebels when the real enemy was sitting up there in his Manchuria, which they'd had the cheek to re-christen Manchukuo. And Chang had more troubles than that: he had lost face over Italy. A few years before, Mussolini's son-in-law Ciano served a tour of diplomatic duty in Shanghai, and the Young Marshal became friendly with him and his wife, the vivacious Edda. The Cianos returned to Italy in due course. A little later, Chang, who had undergone a cure for morphine addiction, was advised by his doctor to take a long sea voyage, and he went to Europe and saw the Cianos again. Chiang Kai-shek had entrusted him with a commission; he was to buy planes. It seemed perfectly natural, things being as they were, that the Young Marshal should have chosen Rome as the place to buy them, and Ciano as the go-between to help him in his purchase. Unfortunately the Italian planes proved to be so much rubbish. Chang Hsueh-liang had been cheated, and his fondness for Mussolini's daughter was mocked. As if that were not bad enough, Italy had now joined in the Tripartite Pact with Germany and Japan; she agreed to recognize Manchukuo in return for Japan's recognition of her recently snatched possession, Abyssinia. The Young Marshal, full of chagrin, told Chiang Kai-shek that he could not be expected to keep his mind on Communist suppression when all he wanted was to fight Japan. What was more, he said, General Yang Hu-cheng was of the same mind.

Chang sounded so agitated that Chiang Kai-shek went up to see him in October at Sian, and talked things over. It annoyed him that both Chang and Yang were fascinated by the Communists' latest appeal for a united front against Japan. He scolded both generals and assured them that the suggestion was worthless. He then gave a lecture to the cadets at the Sian Military Academy and scolded them too, because a few angry young men talked back to him. Finally he left Shensi, feeling more or less confident that he had convinced everybody: he was mistaken. At the end of the month he had to fly part of the way back to Loyang, there to meet Chang with Yen Hsi-shan the "Model Governor" and other generals, Chang having written desperately to say he could no longer control his troops. Again Chiang rallied his reluctant officers and returned to Nanking. But it seemed hopeless. Fighting against the Communists in Shensi grew more and more desultory. In December they were able to leave Pao An and move into the important city of Yenan, and this in spite of the fact that Chiang Kai-shek had sent a crack division to Yang and Chang, in order to stiffen their backbones. He decided to go yet again to blow them up. There was no doubt Shensi was difficult. He had heard that in an unofficial vote they had balloted overwhelmingly to drop the anti-Red campaign in order to fight Japan.

Chiang of course flew up; he used planes on all his long journeys. A number of men accompanied him as usual, but they were billeted several miles from his quarters, which were at a hot springs resort outside town. The first day's conversations were mere repetitions of the earlier arguments. On the early morning of December 12 his hosts mutinied against Chiang: troops came after him, and he injured his back trying to scale the hotel wall. He was then locked up. The incident has been described as a kidnaping, which is somewhat inaccurate: in fact Chiang was held right there in Sian with his staff. In Nanking the alarm went out and the country mobilized for war, but before hostilities could begin Madame Chiang and an Australian friend were able to get into contact with the Young Marshal: they went to Sian and fetched Chiang back. After everything had been sorted out, General Yang Hu-cheng took the customary trip to Europe, and Chang Hsueh-liang, who gave himself up like a gentleman, was sentenced to ten years' imprisonment. Exactly what really went on during Chiang's days as a captive is a moot question, and his version has never been accepted as the full story, but it soon became clear that a bargain had been arranged between the Kuomintang and the Communists. The venture may have been planned by the Reds, or by Yang and Chang on their own, in which case the Reds hurried to take part as soon as they knew what was going on. Certainly Chou En-lai rushed down from Yenan, and was much in evidence during the aftermath of the mutiny. However it came about or who motivated it, the bargain is what matters; the fact that Chiang consented at last to a temporary alliance with the CCP. What was called a united front was soon arranged. The Nationalists were to stop chasing the Communists and the Communists said they would cease being communist "for the present," with all that such a vacation entailed: no more soviets to be set up, no more landlords victimized. For the present.

At the same time Sino-Russian relations suddenly took a turn for the better. Nanking had noted with resentment the USSR's abnegation of influence in Manchukuo and increased pressure in Outer Mongolia, but now Russia promised not to indulge in antagonistic activity against the Chiang government. In August that year an agreement was signed between Moscow and Nanking, by which China and Russia promised not to fight each other nor lend aid, "direct or indirect," to any third power showing aggression to either signator. Russia also lent credit, though not very much, and began to send a certain amount of ammunition and some war planes, as well as the inevitable advisers, to Nanking.

If the Japanese had not already believed it this alliance would have convinced them that it was time to subdue China altogether. In Nanking most officials expected some reaction from Tokyo, but could not be sure where it would be. "Incidents" involving Japanese were already a dime a dozen, and big trouble could have flared up over any one of them. It happened that the particular quarrel that touched off hostilities was at Lukuochiao, Marco Polo Bridge, at Wanping near Peking on the night of July 7, 1937. Chinese guards at the bridge later claimed that Japanese had fired on them for no reason, while the Japanese said they were simply on maneuvers and had been opposed by the Chinese, though they were going about their rightful business. As Chiang pointed out, Japanese troops had no right to be holding maneuvers anywhere near Wanping, but the arguments scarcely mattered and were soon lost in the noise of what followed. After not quite three weeks of talk Japanese soldiers from Japan itself began to pour into Manchuria, then across the border into China. With them came great numbers of bombers. The Nationalists evacuated Peking before the city could be smashed up, and the Japanese occupied the province. Then they turned to Shanghai, landing their main force of marines on August 11.

It was the Japanese aim to control the Yangtze Valley, the heart of China, and they lavished men and munitions on Shanghai, but the Chinese put up a resistance that surprised the world. For three months they stood their ground, during which time an extraordinary situation prevailed in the foreign concessions, with people going about their daily business as if the air were not resounding with gunfire on the other side of the magic boundary. Now and then a housewife had to duck a bullet, or a rider in the countryside was enraged by a Japanese plane swooping down so that its crew could shoot a machine gun in the general direction of his horse. The proper diplomatic authorities kept sending proper diplomatic protests; it was not yet apparent that Japan was almost ready to dispense with foreign friendships.

"The war will take at least three years," said Chiang, though the Japanese insisted that the incident was not a war at all, officially speaking. Nobody had declared war. It was an Incident.

There was still unfinished business between the Nationalists and the Communists, which was tidied up at a National Salvation Conference. In August the Communists issued a statement of "Ten Great Policies" for anti-Japanese resistance and national salvation, and followed it on September 22 with a manifesto on interparty co-operation. This document declared the CCP's sincerity regarding the cause of national emancipation, referred to Sun's Three Principles, and offered formally to abandon its policy of overthrowing the Kuomintang. It would relinquish the soviet form of government in favor of democracy and reorganize the Red Army into the Nationalists' National Revolutionary Army. But, Mao added, this arrangement was not to be permanent. [North, p. 179.] All this was done, ostensibly, and the Red Army reorganized itself under the name of the Eighth Route Army. In actual fact it did not work out that way—not that Chiang, at least, had ever expected it would—for the Communists continued to fight only for themselves and lived for the day when they could turn openly against the Nationalists. The Nationalist soldiers were all too aware of this. Lack of co-operation by the Communists amounted at times to outright sabotage. Propaganda did its work, however, and allegations filled the air: people who until the truce had said, "The Nationalists won't fight a real enemy but have plenty of ammunition to use against their own countrymen," now complained, "The Nationalists don't do anything effective against the Japanese. Only the Reds really resist."

"To what extent were the Communists acting in good faith? . . . Mao believed that Communist troops should remain autonomous throughout the war, engaging in campaigns that would advance the Communist position—and in no others. The chief Communist objective, Mao believed, was to achieve power—regardless of the fate of the Nationalists." [North, p. 180.]

To Western eyes it seemed an old-fashioned war. Most Chinese arms were passé. But there was nothing old-fashioned about Japanese equipment or the mass bombing to which the countryside and cities were subjected. Cruisers and destroyers supported the landing of Japanese forces and shelled the ports. Chiang's army was at last forced from Shanghai on November 9. The Japanese followed by river and railway, arriving at Nanking within the next month: the Chinese had again evacuated, and their pursuers thought the war was practically over. After all, they now had Tientsin, Peking, Shanghai, Hangchow, Nanking: North China was being consolidated: there was a puppet government in Mongolia as well as Manchuria: all that remained to Chiang, surely, was to negotiate the best peace terms he could get? It may have been the elation of this belief that led the Japanese in Nanking to indulge in behavior against the civilians that was exceptionally brutal even by their standards. Protests rained in on Tokyo from all over the Western world. Even then, to Japan's surprise, in spite of the mass bombings and widespread pillage, the Chinese would not acknowledge themselves beaten. Instead the Nationalists fell back on Hankow. From north, east, and southeast the Japanese attacked the Three Cities, and to hold them back the Chinese destroyed their ancient dikes and flooded the plains. This held up the invaders, but within the year, near the end of October 1938, the Japanese occupied Canton. The Chinese had not expected them to go so near the British crown colony, and it was a severe blow. Chiang's forces left Hankow, now that it was untenable, and moved to Chungking, capital of Szechuan, set among rocky hills. Following, the Japanese took Nanchang and tried to capture that veteran city of many sieges, Changsha, but there at last they came to a stop and even suffered a reverse: the Nationalists encircled them at the walls and routed them. Deserting the Changsha project, the enemy now devoted his attention to the conquest of the two Kwangs. Kwangtung was captured, but Kwangsi, which had in the past proved a nut too hard for the Nationalists to crack, held out against the Japanese, and by the end of February 1940 they had been chased out of the province almost completely. Now they concentrated on the direct approach to Chungking—Ichang, which guarded the river's gateway to the mountain area and the Nationalist stronghold. It was hard for the Japanese to get Ichang. Even after capturing it in June they were at a standstill, with overextended supply lines. Frequently they were attacked by Chinese from the rear. For some months they remained at Ichang, mass-bombing Chungking almost daily in a vain attempt to break down this last resistance.

It did not really matter, Tokyo declared. Their intention was not to conquer China mile by mile, merely to persuade her to "co-operate." If only she would give up her anti-Japanese sentiments and enter on a partnership with the empire, all would be well. In the occupied territories this persuasion found a few willing Chinese ears, and under Japanese guidance the quislings—not that the word was yet in currency—set up governments, one in Peking and the other in Nanking as it had been in the old days. They quarreled as well, just as Peking and Nanking had quarreled before, until in 1940 the Japanese reorganized them and centralized the puppet government in Nanking, under that ace of apostates, Wang Ching-wei. His was to be the only outstanding name they ever acquired for their purposes.

The Chinese withdrawal to Chungking took place at a time when the United States was the only major Western power to take full note of Chiang's plight. Britain contributed something and Roosevelt appealed for, and got, a million dollars to aid Chinese civilians who were victimized by the bombings, but Europe in general was distracted by Hitler's activities and the extraordinary gyrations of Stalin. The Russian pact with Germany, signed in August 1939, had preceded the declaration of war in Europe by only three days, and it is not surprising that few Europeans gave much thought to China. Britain cast an anxious eye now and then at Hong Kong and Singapore, but these colonies, like the British communities in China's treaty ports, seemed not much worse off now they were surrounded by Japanese than they had been before the start of the China Incident. It was thought that Russia's new friendship with Germany might cancel, or at least dilute, the Chinese Communists' hostility to Germany's treaty partner Japan, but it did not, for Russia's long-term planning included Manchuria. Technically, however, Russia's relations with Japan were unlike those of the Chinese Communists, being amicable.

Chinese had found that guerrilla hit-and-run raids were the best strategy against the Japanese who were now spread widely over the country, since the Japanese were better armed and could always beat the Chinese down in open fight. The Communists, practised in guerrilla warfare, managed better than the Nationalists to hold their own in this way. By arrangement with Chiang the Eighth Route Army was based on an area of the northern border region comprising parts of Shensi, Kansu, and Ninghsia. With Kuomintang knowledge and consent it enlarged its sphere a little later and set up a soviet state in the Shansi-Chahar-Hopei border region. The former area surrounds Yenan and the latter is near Peking, well behind the enemy lines. The Reds also operated, officially, in a third large area in Kiangsu, Chekiang, and Anhui provinces near Hangchow and Shanghai. All this was possible because the Japanese could not occupy the land between their patrols and supply lines. Though the Eighth Route Army was supposed to stay in touch with Yen Hsi-shan's Nationalist troops, much of the time it operated on its own, and though Chu Teh was appointed deputy commander under a Nationalist superior, and the Army drew pay and ammunition from Nationalist centers, Chu Teh to all intents and purposes was their only commander and they never looked on the Nationalists as allies.

Both armies ranged the land where Japanese were thin on the ground, but Yen's men and the other Nationalists continued to fight in formation, as they had been trained to do. Thus they suffered heavy losses whereas the Reds kept winning their battles. None of them, of course, aimed to capture and keep territory, which would have been no good to them at that phase. Their aim was to harass the enemy, and also, as far as the Communists were concerned, to make friends with and influence the peasants. Many peasants were indoctrinated at that time and taught to look upon the Nationalists as well as the Japanese as their enemies. Secret soviets were created, in spite of Mao's promise to stop such activity. The Reds kept themselves equipped with weapons from two sources—vanquished Japanese, and vanquished Nationalists as well. They operated as a third force, not as allies.

Their methods were so successful that before a year had elapsed under their new name, the Communists began to take in more area for operations than had been allotted to them. Chance meetings with Nationalists when they were thus out of bounds led to quarrels between the so-called allies. In January 1941 a big clash of the sort occurred when a Communist group called the New Fourth Army, whose official field of operations was bounded on one side by the Yangtze, crossed the river and came up against Nationalists who questioned their right to spread out in this manner. For eight days a battle raged between these parties, and many on both sides lost their lives. Certainly the Kuomintang-Communist relationship could have been called an alliance by only the most cynical observer.

"Chiang continued to fear the Communists more than he feared the Japanese," said Harold Isaacs. [*The Tragedy of the Chinese Revolution* (Stanford, 1951), p. 306.] "He feared social reforms more than he feared military defeats." It all depends, one would think, upon what constitutes social reforms. China had known them in her brief spell—from 1927 to 1937—of comparative peace under the Kuomintang, when the labor movement, agricultural conditions, and education all made considerable headway even when reactionary opposition and backsliding are discounted. There can be no doubt, however, that the Communist type of reform, short and sharp and effective, was much appreciated by some sections of the population. "Among the major achievements of the border governments was the development of effective bases for guerrilla attacks on the rear and flank of the enemy. These governments, with their wartime interpretation of democracy, extended every possible benefit to the peasants and workers so that food and supplies might be forthcoming for the fighters. There was a 25 to 50 per cent reduction in land rents; miscellaneous taxes were abolished and replaced by a single income tax; land of absentee landlords and traitors was confiscated and put to productive use; co-operatives were encouraged; and a three-year moratorium was announced on all debts." Landlords' opinions were not solicited.

※　　　※　　　※

In April 1941 the USSR signed a "Neutrality Pact" with Japan which was rather like the treaty already signed with China. Each signator promised to respect the other's territorial integrity, with special reference to Outer Mongolia and Manchukuo. Each country also pledged itself to remain neutral in case the other was attacked by a third power. The pact affected China on two levels, since a Russia friendly with Japan presumably meant a Russia inimical to China, and Communist solidarity might affect the Chinese Reds in their attitude to Japan. This latter alteration in sentiment was never openly expressed, but the former rightabout hit the Nationalists immediately, when Russia announced that she was cutting off supplies to Chungking forthwith. Less than two months later Japan's stronger partner in the Tripartite Pact, Germany, marched into Russia, and Moscow's interest in Far Eastern questions suffered a temporary eclipse. Indeed, for the time being Stalin probably forgot the CCP itself.

The year wore on. In his mountain city where buildings and streets were bashed and fire-blanched from air raid upon air raid, Chiang anxiously watched the reports from Washington, where an argument with Tokyo was going on. He knew Japan was trying to persuade the United States to bring pressure to bear on him and settle the Incident so that Japan might remain in control of everything she had taken. If Roosevelt should refuse, Chiang like most other observers presumed that Japan would react violently, but the Pearl Harbor attack outdid all expectations. It was a nasty shock to the States, but to Chiang it was a heaven-sent diversion and lifeline. America was at war with the Axis countries, and so—at last, officially, after four years of the real thing disguised—was China.

Chapter Twenty-two

At the time China so suddenly became one of the Allies there was almost a stalemate between three combatants, Japan, the Nationalists, and the Communists. The struggle between the two latter was particularly complicated and under the surface. A foreign visitor might well wonder why Chou En-lai should be in Chungking, apparently in a diplomatic capacity and in good standing with the Nationalists. Soong Chingling too was a Chungking resident. Yet the Communist headquarters of Yenan and Red-controlled territory were marked off from the rest of China either by Japanese or determined Nationalists who spent their time making sure the Reds did not cross the line. The Japanese, as a matter of fact, were for a time after Pearl Harbor almost a negligible factor in western China. They had bigger fish to fry elsewhere.

Foreign allies were very much of two minds about China's value to them. It is necessary to remember the contrasting backgrounds of the two chief powers, Britain and America, in relation to China. Like many of his compatriots, Churchill could not take the Chinese seriously. He looked upon them as "natives," funny, exasperating, childish creatures, inhabitants of a country that had never in the past given Britain any genuine grown-up opposition at war. The only reason Japan did not occupy the same category was that she had just administered a shock, and was in fact—he had to face it—being a definite problem in Hong Kong and Singapore. But Roosevelt was an American with all his country's prejudices and traditions, and he started out on China's side. He had clearcut notions about imperialism and exploitation. Americans—who, it is true, depended on other traffic than overseas trade for their livelihood—had sent missionaries rather than salesmen to the East. Without going too far into the generalities of popular psychology it is probably a fact that Roosevelt, as America, did not have Churchill's—Britain's —guilt complex regarding China. Whatever the difference in their opinions, however, the two nations had now to deal with a common problem in Japan. It was touch and go for the Allies, the more so because Russia had just reminded them that *she* was not at war with Japan, and by the terms of her treaty with Japan could not permit the others to use Siberia for air bases in the Pacific war. Stalin held out hope that when Germany had been beaten he would reconsider this matter, but for the present the other Allies had to think of alternative bases from which to fight back. Hong Kong, Singapore, the Philippines—all were likely soon to be lost. The Dutch East Indies? They too might go. If India was to be saved, Burma must be shored up. There were many other difficult and sensitive areas as well. For example, if the Japanese should entrench themselves in Australia. . . . Roosevelt thought Chungking would be a good center, and looked with favor on Chiang's suggestion of a joint general staff there. He pointed out to Churchill, who was opposed to the idea, that the Burma Road still gave access to Chungking, and that an air lift was already operating over "the Hump," with planes piloted for the Chinese by foreign mercenaries under the direction of the American Colonel Claire Chennault. (These Flying Tigers were soon to be incorporated with the American air force.) Churchill was not convinced, holding that Chiang was a weak reed. He preferred a center in Burma. Finally the Allies made Wavell supreme commander of their forces in the Southwest Pacific theater, while Chiang, as Roosevelt told him, would be Wavell's opposite number commanding the China theater including Siam and Indo-China. He was to have an American chief of staff, and this officer, General J. W. Stilwell, arrived in Chungking in February 1942. By this time Hong Kong and Singapore had been taken by the Japanese.

The Western Allies decided they must take care of Germany first, containing Japan as best they might in the meantime. They would bomb Japanese centers in China however, and send in supplies to Chungking over the Burma Road, stockpiling them for the future decisive battle. British and Dutch ships would guard Australia, Burma, India, and Ceylon from sea attacks, and all the Allies except Russia would provide land forces, which would be predominantly American. The Chinese were not happy at being put at the end of the schedule. Chiang reminded his allies at every opportunity that his country had already been engaged in war with Japan for many years, and could not be expected to hold out longer without plenty of help. The Allies replied that one kind of help at least would soon be arriving—a stream of supplies over the Burma Road and in the air lift—but as things worked out, the stream was seriously interrupted. As one crisis after another overtook the Allied troops to the south, supplies were diverted all the way along the line. There was always good reason for this official hijacking: British and Dutch needs were pressing. But so, said Chiang, were China's.

The arrangement was never a happy one. Stilwell hated Chiang and did not care for the British either: Mountbatten always annoyed him. The British snubbed the Chinese and treated them like poor relations. At the beginning they haughtily refused Chiang's offer of troops, though as to that, times were to change—there would come a time when they wanted more men than Chiang was willing to provide. The squabble over supplies became an endless tug of war. The foreigners blamed Chiang for being interested only in his local defenses, which was largely true. Chiang blamed them for caring only for their individual interests, and this too was largely true. It is the way military alliances do work out.

The expansion of Nationalist China's importance in world affairs left Mao Tse-tung where he preferred to be at that period, out of the limelight. He stayed on his side of the line, most of the time in Yenan. What with all the coming and going of European VIPs in Chungking it was not the time for action against the Nationalists. Instead, he used the leisure to introduce to the community the "Cheng Feng," or "Ideological Remolding Movement" which the world nowadays knows as brainwashing. His methods were not unlike those meetings in certain Western societies at which the sinner is urged to testify to his sins in public. Mao put a limited number of his disciples through the course first and then sent them out to train others. He said that the aim of the exercise was to correct what he called certain unorthodox tendencies that had crept into the community. The method was to teach people to search their own souls and those of their companions, rooting out the three sins of subjectivism, sectarianism, and party formalism. Each person would confess to whatever isms he had committed, then join with zest in catching out the others. "Once the movement was well launched and once the guiding documents had been published, it was painfully evident that the movement was intended to cut much deeper than the political level of human thought and behavior. The design of the

Cheng Feng movement was to probe the very depths of the human psyche, to remold the individual party member, and to destroy traditional morality in order to set up a new order of ethics and behavior." [North, p. 196.] Thirty thousand leading spirits in the party went out to wash the brains of the lower echelons; these people in turn trained lesser lights. In village and country the Communists attended evening classes, after their day's work, and the method spread quickly. "The psychological effect of public confession as an organizational device in Communist Parties is difficult to understand in the West, but it should not be underestimated. It was a major tool of the Cheng Feng reform." [Boyd Compton, quoted by North, p. 198.]

When Stilwell was in Chungking he snarled and complained, hating the Chinese in general and Chiang in particular. Outside, on active duty, he was in a slightly better mood, even when Burma fell to the Japanese and he led a ragged force into India, but the British continued to get on his nerves, and the loss of the Burma Road boosted Chennault's importance because everything now depended on the air lift, and Stilwell did not like Chennault. Once he sighed wistfully for an army of Russians. He had never been to Russia, but they sounded like fellows who knew how to behave: "tough physique; unity of purpose; pride in their accomplishments; determination to win," he wrote in his journal. ". . . Compare it with the Chinese cesspool." If some informants could be believed, there was even hope for China; not all of the country was like this capital city. Up in the Northwest were men of a different sort, sturdy and honest and self-sacrificing as the Russians. At their head was an admirable character named Mao Tse-tung who had led them heroically out of bondage. These Communists must be fine people. They were not at all self-seeking: all they wanted was social reform. They wanted to help the people, who were being ground into dust by the despicable Kuomintang. They wanted to defeat the Japanese, and they were the boys who could do it—the only ones in China who could do it. And what did the Kuomintang do about these paragons? Just what you would expect—they mewed them up in the Northwest and wasted much of their own manpower in placing guards on the Communists to make sure they wouldn't break out and institute reforms. Once Stilwell suggested to Chiang that they utilize these splendid warriors, but Chiang was angry, so angry that he asked Washington to recall the general. The affair blew over, but Stilwell did not forget the Communists. Nobody did; nobody was allowed to. In the summer of 1943 they felt ready to begin a publicity campaign, and the Russians helped.

That summer Chou En-lai and Chiang held several discussions, in which Chiang reminded Chou of the terms of the agreement signed in 1937. If the Communists would live up to that agreement, he said, submerge their army in the Nationalist army, and relinquish their separate government, they could be accepted as a political party like any other, with representatives in Chungking and all the rest. Chou said it could not be done, since if it were the CCP would lose its identity. Again Chiang reminded him of the agreement, and said he would want a definite reply by September. Chou complained to various listeners that Chiang was not acting in good faith, since at the same time he reinforced his guard in the Northwest. The Russian Ambassador mentioned the matter to the American envoy and asked what attitude America was going to take if there should be civil war in China: would she go on helping Chiang? All this coincided with a quiet, industrious push on the part of the Communists, a bid for the sympathy of visiting American writers and journalists. These newcomers found it pleasant and titivating to be permitted a glimpse of a mysterious, romantic minority group. Each was given the impression that he alone of all foreigners really understood the situation and could see into the hearts of the hitherto inscrutable Chinese. Soon magazines and newspapers in the United States were printing articles referring to the Chinese Communists as stout fellows of uncommon virtue, who could save China if only they could get out from under the wraps kept on them by a corrupt, swollen bureaucracy. Americans read that these Communists were the only Chinese who were really fighting the Japanese, since the Nationalists spent their energy and ammunition—ammunition, let it not be forgotten, given to them by American taxpayers—fighting the Reds. A few missionaries chimed in to corroborate the story, until people began to wonder.

That August there came a meeting between Roosevelt and Churchill in Quebec to discuss, among other matters, postwar settlements. Chiang was not asked to come, nor was Stalin. During the discussions Stalin sent a message definitely committing himself to fight Japan when his European enemy was beaten. This was good news for everyone except Chiang Kai-shek. If she became an ally in the Pacific war, Russia would have a voice in Pacific affairs as soon as the war was won by the Allies, which meant a clash between her interests and China's. Roosevelt decided not to let Chiang know about the message. The following November, when he met Chiang in Cairo, Roosevelt still maintained silence on this subject, but he was very agreeable in other ways. Despite the presence of Churchill, bland but impatient, like a busy uncle sparing a few minutes for the nursery—he and Roosevelt were en route to Teheran to meet Stalin—they came to several constructive if tentative agreements. Chiang wanted the campaign to recover Burma started immediately so that it might be over and out of the way: the program had been more or less decided on, with Britain supplying an amphibious force in the Bay of Bengal and Chinese troops, now training with Stilwell in India, combined with the Chinese "Yoke Force" standing ready in Yunnan. What he wanted more than this was added help for Chungking itself: more supplies, more money to counter the rapidly increasing inflation, and assurance of protection against the Japanese: at any moment, he reminded his hearers, they might step up their pressure on Szechuan. Provisionally he was given word that these affairs would go as he wished, and he was pleased by a promise that after the war Manchuria, Formosa, and the Pescadores would be returned to the Republic of China. That last agreement was the only one that stood unchanged, however, when his allies met Stalin in Teheran. The tentative plans for the Burma campaign were shelved. Chiang learned that the whole East must wait on Operation Overlord in Europe. However, the promise of the lost territory still stood, and Chiang was not ill-pleased.

He would have been disturbed if he had realized with how much favor Roosevelt had begun to regard the Yenan group. Roosevelt made remarks to his son Elliott that show he was determined to force Chiang into changing his domestic policy regarding the Communists: "He wanted very badly to get our support against the British moving into Hong Kong and Shanghai and Canton with the same old extraterritorial rights they enjoyed before the war," he said, and when Elliott asked if America *would* support Chiang in this matter, he replied that he wouldn't do it for nothing, at any rate. "Before it came up, I'd been registering a complaint about the character of Chiang's government. I'd told him it was hardly the modern democracy that ideally it should be. I'd told him he would have to form a uniting government, while the war was still being fought, with the Communists in Yenan."

As a matter of fact the question of extraterritorial rights had been settled on the Double Tenth of 1942, when Britain and America formally promised to relinquish them; later they had signed a treaty to this effect. But Hong Kong was not included in the promise. Strictly speaking, the Crown Colony was not a case of extraterritoriality, and Roosevelt seems to have shown some confusion of thought in mentioning it with the others. No doubt, however, Chiang had brought it into the discussion deliberately: he wanted to reclaim Hong Kong to soothe his ardent Nationalists, and Roosevelt may have sympathized with this desire.

✿　✿　✿

The foreigners in China who admired Mao and the CCP pointed with relief and triumph to the much-advertised dissolution of the Comintern. If anything would, they said, it should prove to the most hidebound reactionary that Chinese Communists were not really Communists at all, just as they had always claimed, but agrarian reformers who clearly had no political ties with Moscow. All the Reds wanted was a voice in the government, a democracy in which social reform would be possible. They talked in this fashion though Mao spoke bluntly and frankly enough to those who would listen, making no attempt to disguise his intention of leading the country, ultimately, to Communism. Some did listen, and observed signs— "continued, though carefully camouflaged and probably somewhat loosened, ties between Russian and Chinese Communists; a systematic Communist campaign for expansion at Kuomintang expense; Nationalist retaliation and the emergence of a 'war within a war'; the rapid growth of Communist military and political power, and Mao's foreshadowing, through his statements on 'coalition government,' of what co-operation with Communist forces really meant. From these and other circumstances a few observers foresaw that the historical power structure in Asia was about to be overturned, that the USSR would soon emerge as the greatest single Asian land power, and that the United States was now an increasingly important factor in Soviet relations with China—entirely apart from whether or not it so chose." [North, p. 201.]

In August 1943, the same month as the Quebec Conference, a Tass correspondent named Rogov published an article attacking unnamed elements in the Kuomintang who resisted Chiang's program to reorganize his army. These anti-democratic forces, he alleged, wanted to weaken China by deepening her internal conflicts, then make an "honorable peace" with Japan: "Discontent with the Kuomintang's policies is widespread throughout China." Rogov and the voices that promptly joined in to echo his held off from Chiang himself at first, but the inevitable soon followed. "Unfortunately—all aside from Rogov's doctrinaire charges—the integrity and efficiency of Chiang Kai-shek's government were open to a measure of legitimate criticism," said North [P. 202]. "In facing the Japanese invasion Kuomintang leaders had resorted to a series of special measures —the expansion of the New Life Movement devoted to a regeneration of Confucian teachings, the formation of the rigidly disciplined San Min Chu I Youth Corps, the granting of extraordinary powers to Chiang, the arbitrary designation (rather than election) of a portion of National Congress membership, the reintroduction of party cells, and the further development of party purging facilities through the party supervisor's net . . . all of them features which impressed many Westerners as essentially nondemocratic and potentially authoritarian in spirit."

Chiang chose—or circumstances forced the choice on him—this most unfortunate moment to make renewed demands on the United States, reminding Roosevelt that the Japanese were most likely to attack Chungking with fresh vigor as soon as Overlord was under way. He had already borrowed half a billion dollars from Washington, which melted away in inflation almost as soon as it arrived, but now he asked for a billion more, as well as the usual supplies, which still were not coming in fast enough for his needs. The reply was that money would not settle Chungking's economic problems. Only material goods would help, and the supply of these could not be stepped up until some overland route again existed through Burma. A new one called the Ledo Road was under construction but could not yet be used. Washington added that more men were needed outside China, but Chiang was reluctant to lend more manpower, claiming that he needed those he had left for home defense. He reminded Roosevelt of the broken Cairo promises, upon which the President, backing down a little, agreed to train and outfit thirty more Chinese divisions. Resentfully and jealously the British watched this gesture, which to their mind meant deprivation of supplies *they* needed. Soon they were involved in a direct squabble with Chungking over the division of Lend-Lease. Chiang pointed out that this division had to date been inequitable, with Britain getting the lion's share, and Mountbatten said angrily that he didn't see why the Allies should continue to supply Chiang with munitions if they were to be used "solely for internal purposes." Why not forget Chiang altogether and drop the Ledo Road? Events replied in short order. In March 1944 the Japanese attacked the British at Imphal and threatened to cut off Assam. There was no more talk of forgetting China: Britain and America now pressed Chiang urgently to send his men to reinforce the British. He held off for some days, but finally assented, and the Yoke Force started out from Yunnan.

*   *   *

Washington grew more and more uneasy about Chiang versus Mao. It was not that public opinion was swinging more and more toward the Communists, though it was, but that Chiang was now complaining about Russia, alleging that the USSR was helping Mao to build up his forces in preparation for a take-over of Sian in Shensi. Besides, Chiang said, Japanese forces were moving in great numbers across the Manchurian border into China, and Russia did nothing to hold them in place; on the contrary she had recently signed a fishing-rights agreement with Japan. Furthermore, Russian planes had attacked Chinese troops just across the border, in Outer Mongolia, where they had a perfect right to be. Though the State Department did not agree with Chiang that any of these allegations were convincing proof of Russian perfidy, they felt that the whole situation was overdue for investigation. That spring of 1944 Roosevelt sent Vice-President Henry Wallace to see how things stood in Chungking. Wallace went out via Siberia and stopped in Moscow on the way, where he had a pleasant, enlightening visit. By the time he arrived in Chungking he felt he already had a fairly good idea of what was going on.

Chiang talked a good deal with Wallace. He insisted that the Chinese Communists were not merely agrarian reformers, but were internationalists in their outlook rather than Chinese—in other words, they were committed to the Russian kind of Communism. The American people did not understand. The Reds *wanted* Chinese resistance against Japan to break down, as this would make it easier for them to take control. . . . At this point, according to the report that went back to Washington, Mr. Wallace expressed amazement.

He assured Chiang that in America Communists were very patriotic. "President Chiang said that the difference in the attitude of the American and Chinese Communists might be explained by the fact that there was no possibility of the American Communists seizing power, whereas the Chinese Communists definitely desired to do so." Chiang repeated several times that a coalition would not work: alliance with Chinese Communists simply would not be beneficial to the war effort. Why, he asked, did America always talk of his government coming to terms with the Communists? Why should not the Communists come to terms with his government? Wallace was able to persuade him to agree on only one point, that China must not come up against Russia if she could possibly help it.

Harriman, American Ambassador in Moscow, asked Stalin what he thought of Chiang. Shouldn't Chiang make it up with the Communists? Genially Stalin agreed that he should, but added that Chiang wasn't so bad; it was the men around him—"crooks and traitors." He added, "The Chinese Communists are not real Communists. They are 'margarine' Communists. Nevertheless, they are real patriots and they want to fight Japan."

This exchange took place in June, and shortly afterwards the Japanese launched the attacks for which they had obviously been preparing. Stilwell was called back from Burma to Chungking, and Chiang, bracing himself for more unpleasantness, reminded Roosevelt of his earlier request for another American official trained in politics as well as military matters, to act as Chiang's "personal representative"—actually to be a buffer between himself and Stilwell. To fill this post, Major General Patrick Hurley came out in August, stopping off enroute for the customary visit in Moscow, where he had a talk with Molotov, then Foreign Minister. Molotov said that the USSR was unjustly blamed for much that had happened in China: many of the so-called Chinese Communists were simply desperately poor people who had banded together and were fighting as a group for their livelihood.

In Chungking, Hurley's presence was not enough to avert a head-on collision between Chiang and Stilwell. In accordance with Washington's urgent advice Stilwell had been appointed by the reluctant Chiang to the post of commander in chief of Chinese forces. "What they ought to do," wrote the new commander in chief as soon as he returned, "is shoot the G-mo and Ho and the rest of the gang." Now he came up against Chiang's reluctance to send more men to

Burma, where the Yoke Force was retreating before the Japanese: Stilwell was also demanding authority to reorganize the entire Chinese forces, and Chiang would not consent. Hurley suggested that Chiang send to Burma the troops he was keeping in the Northwest, as well as the Communists. He assured Chiang that America would willingly equip the Reds and give them all necessary arms. Chiang refused peremptorily. He would never have consented in any case, but he was shorter in temper than he would ordinarily have been because he suspected that the whole crisis had been engineered by Stilwell with this end in view. It happened that the news of his refusal reached Roosevelt just as the latter had succeeded, with the help of General Marshall and after a lot of trouble, in persuading the British to permit the Burma operation at that time, before the Allies should plunge into their big attack on Japan, planned for 1945. Losing his temper, Roosevelt sent word to Chiang on September 19 that he *must* send reinforcements and *must* put Stilwell in unrestricted command of the forces, or face the consequences. The circumstances in which the message was delivered to Chiang—by Stilwell's own hand—could not have been more humiliating. Stilwell gloated openly: Chiang closed up like a clam: Hurley could only hover remorsefully. Chiang delayed his reply for six days, during which time the President of the United States began to regret his action. By the time the Chinese replied, Roosevelt was ready to give in to his demand, incorporated in the message, that Stilwell be recalled. On other points Chiang was ready to compromise. Stilwell therefore went home, loudly championed by friendly, indignant American newspapermen—Chiang couldn't *do* that to one of our generals!—and General Wedemeyer came out in his place. Wedemeyer had no chip on his shoulder.

For nearly seven months while Hurley was there on his first mission, he tried to mediate between the CCP and the Nationalist government, and thought he was getting more forward than in fact he was. He reported that he had convinced Chiang that Russia was not supporting the Chinese Communists, did not want dissensions or civil war in China, and desired more harmonious relations with that country. Hurley was sure Chiang was now hopeful of agreement with the CCP and would willingly unite with them against Japan: the danger of civil war, he said happily, was over. Yet somehow, as the days went by, in spite of negotiations that went on and on, perfect trust and friendship were not achieved. The Communists refused to hand over their troops to Nationalist command unless the Nationalist government should abolish their "one-party rule" in favor of a coalition: the government retorted that what the Communists wanted was not a coalition but their own one-party rule.

Early in 1945 Hurley, going back to Washington to talk things over, stopped again in Moscow and saw Molotov and Stalin. He checked up with Molotov just to be sure he had understood what he said in the first interview correctly—that the Chinese Communists were not really Communists at all, that they aimed merely for necessary and just reforms in China, that the USSR was not supporting the Chinese Communists, and so on: Molotov said yes, that was right. Hurley told Stalin that America and Britain believed it was absolutely necessary to support Chiang for a "united, free and democratic China," and Stalin replied—at least Hurley was later to insist that Stalin had replied—that he agreed absolutely and the USSR would support this policy. He said, too, that Chiang was a selfless patriot. All this Hurley put into his report, but the American chargé d'affaires in Moscow, George Kennan, warned the State Department that Stalin's words should not be taken at face value. "Russian words mean different things to them (Russians) than they do to us," he said.

There were other Americans as well who did not share Hurley's optimism, among them the Ambassador to China, Clarence Gauss, who declared that to ask China to meet Communist demands was equivalent to asking her unconditional surrender to a party known to be under a foreign power's influence. Brigadier General P. E. Peabody, chief of U. S. Military Intelligence, made several strong statements in his report of July 1945. He said flatly that the "democracy" of the Chinese Communists was Soviet democracy; the Chinese Communist movement was part of the international Communist movement sponsored and guided by Moscow: Soviet Russia in all probability planned to create Russian-dominated areas in Manchuria, Korea, and perhaps North China: the Chinese Communist movement was "represented by what is a state in all but name, possessing territory (the combined area of which is about the size of France, or one-fifth of China proper), a population of more than 70,000,000 people, armies, law and money of its own. The Chinese Communist state is economically primitive but (on a primitive level) fairly self-sufficient. . . . In October 1944 the strength of the Chinese Communist regular forces was reliably reported at 475,-

000 men." [North, p. 212.] He warned the government that when Japan was defeated there would be a serious problem regarding Russia.

The Peabody analysis came too late to affect what went on at the Yalta Conference, for that had taken place in February. Roosevelt, Churchill, and Stalin met at the Black Sea port to discuss the question of Stalin's entry into the Pacific war when Germany had been beaten. The time was coming and Stalin himself had reminded them of his promise. The Allies wished to keep this secret, and there were many leaks, as the gentlemen agreed, in Chungking: it seemed better, therefore, not to let Chiang know anything about this phase of the meeting. Stalin presented his conditions. His proposed agreement stated that within two or three months after Germany's surrender the Soviet Union should enter the war against Japan on condition that the status quo in Outer Mongolia (the Mongolian People's Republic) should be preserved. (When the other Allies signed this, they unwittingly gave Stalin entry into Outer Mongolia.) The former rights of Russia violated by Japan's attack should be restored—that is, the southern part of Sakhalin and the adjacent islands should be returned to the USSR, Dairen should be internationalized and the lease of Port Arthur restored, and the Chinese Eastern and South Manchurian railroads should be jointly operated by a Soviet-Chinese company with China retaining full sovereignty in Manchuria. (In approving this, the other Allies were handing back to Soviet Russia her Czarist empire in the East). The Kurile Islands should be handed over to the Soviet Union. As a postscript it was stated that those parts of the agreement concerning Outer Mongolia, the ports, and the railways would require Chiang's concurrence, and there was another paragraph: "For its part, the Soviet Union expresses its readiness to conclude with the National Government of China a pact of friendship and alliance between the USSR and China in order to render assistance to China with its armed forces for the purpose of liberating China from the Japanese yoke."

The Pacific aspect of the war, or rather of the peace following it, was outside Churchill's range of expert knowledge. Roosevelt when he signed the agreement was a dying man; moreover, his judgment was based on faulty intelligence. The Allies were predicating a formidable concentration of Japanese troops still waiting in Manchuria, where in truth many men had been taken away for battle areas in the southwest. Japan was weakening fast. It was learned later that she might well have surrendered by the end of 1945 even if the atom bomb had not been used: certainly, as things turned out, Russia's entry into the war did not affect her.

In June, on the fourteenth, T. V. Soong, China's Foreign Minister, was told in Washington about the Yalta Agreement, and Chiang heard of it next day from Hurley, who was now Ambassador to China. Soong said that he was delighted, but that certain ambiguities would have to be ironed out. Chiang said he was disappointed, but it was observed that he did not really show much reaction at all, no doubt because the news had leaked to him long since. On July 15 Soong met Stalin and Molotov in Moscow to work out their own agreement, and difficulties immediately made themselves evident. From that time on everything happened rapidly.

While Soong and the Russians were still wrangling, the Allies presented their ultimatum to Japan. That was July 26. The bomb was dropped on Hiroshima August 6. On the eighth, Stalin declared war on Japan. On the ninth, before the negotiations with Soong were concluded, Stalin sent his troops into Manchuria. By the time a "Treaty of Friendship and Alliance between the Soviet Union and the Chinese Republic" was signed on the fourteenth, Russian troops were a long way north of the Manchurian border and fanning out. A few hours after the signing, the Emperor of Japan announced by broadcast that his nation had surrendered.

Other agreements between China and Russia were signed at the same time as the Treaty of Alliance. Some, dealing with waging war against Japan "to the point of final victory," were out of date before the ink dried, but others presumably still had a certain bearing on the future. For example, each country was to refrain from concluding any alliance or taking part in any coalition directed against the other. They were to work in close co-operation, to respect each other's sovereignty and territorial integrity, and each was to refrain from interfering in the internal affairs of the other.

Two days before the Japanese Emperor made his announcement, Chu Teh at Yenan broadcast that all Japanese and their puppets were to surrender to the Communists and that Communists were to occupy all towns and other centers formerly held by Japanese. Communists, he said, were to go north to meet the Outer Mongolian armies; Communists were to seize the Tatung-Pukow railway. Chiang quickly denounced the broadcast and issued orders that the Communists were to stay where they were, to which Chu Teh retorted that Chiang was a Fascist. Then Chu wrote to the American, British, and Soviet governments declaring that it was the Communists, not the Nationalists, who had won the war. His own forces had liberated most of nineteen provinces. The Nationalists had done nothing: the Reds really represented the people of China. Wedemeyer sent warning to Washington that a civil war was boiling up. The three powers replied to Chu Teh that Chiang was the country's leader, and Hurley began again trying to persuade the Communists and Chiang to arrange a coalition.

Later Stalin was to say that he and Mao were at odds at this point; that he thought there was as yet no chance for the CCP to get the upper hand in China, and he told them that they ought to join Chiang Kai-shek's government until things looked brighter. He said the Chinese Communists agreed with him, but went back to China and "acted otherwise," and that he had to admit they were justified by the results. It may be so, but whatever their differences of opinion the two Communist parties worked well together from then on. The Nationalists had more men and more arms, but the Communists were better placed to get control quickly of territories occupied by the ex-enemy. Nationalists and Communists raced to beat each other into these areas, and if it had not been for American help the Communists would have won in most cases. As it was, Nationalist armies were carried by American planes and ships to distant localities, and U. S. Marines moved into North China to hold railroads and coal mines for Chiang's forces. There were many battles, but by the end of the year the Nationalists were in control of Peking and Tientsin. Manchuria was occupied by Russian troops, who, according to the treaty Soong signed with Stalin, would be withdrawn in an operation beginning three weeks after Japan's surrender and completed within three months.

Japan's formal surrender took place September 2. By the end of September Chinese Communists were busily moving into Manchuria, meeting the Russians they met there on the most friendly terms. Moscow announced then that her troops would all be out by the end of November, and the other Allies faced an awkward question they had not envisaged until then: how were the Nationalists to get into Manchuria? American ships carried some of them, but when they arrived at the ports of disembarkation, expecting to be greeted by Russians, time after time they were faced, instead, by Chinese Communists. If the Nationalists landed they were immediately involved in fierce fighting. "In other parts of China the Communists, refusing to obey Nationalist orders concerning the capitulation of Japanese and Chinese puppet troops, were manipulating every surrender possible according to their own designs, seizing enemy materiel, and occupying enemy territory." [North, p. 224.]

At the middle of November Wedemeyer, taking a long view of the situation, advised Chiang to give up the idea of occupying Manchuria for the time being and concentrate on establishing control south of the Wall. He recommended that Chiang turn to the task of social reform and try to eliminate official corruption "immediately," as well as make a satisfactory settlement with the Russians and the Chinese Communists, without which, said the general, he could not occupy Manchuria for years to come—though as Wedemeyer himself added, the chances of such a settlement were slim. Equally unlikely to succeed was his suggestion that America, Britain, and Russia establish a trusteeship over Manchuria until the Nationalist government was strong enough to take over. But Chiang could not face the prospect, after his long struggle, of giving up Manchuria, especially with victory just won over Japan.

Though it was obvious that the USSR was helping the Chinese Communists in every way possible to gain control of Manchuria, diplomatic forms were observed within certain limits. The world during the next few months was presented with the confusing sight of Russian troops, at the direct request of the Nationalist government, remaining in many parts of Manchuria far longer than they were supposed to: some of them did not leave until May. As it turned out this was convenient for Russia, who, basing her actions (when in time they were detected and criticized) on the Yalta Agreement, was busy the whole time dismantling Manchurian factories, mines and other industrial enterprises, and taking back to her own country as much plant as could be carried. When necessary the Russians changed their defense and said that Japanese enterprises in Manchuria, having assisted the Japanese army, were fair booty. Millions of dollars' worth of machinery and rolling stock were taken out on this pretext.

Then, in spite of Wedemeyer's gloomy prophecies, things in Manchuria began to look up for the Nationalists. Large numbers of troops finally managed to get there. They found the factories gutted and everything of value gone, but they were there, and the Chinese Communists who had got in ahead of them did not seem able to stand up to their attacks. The Nationalists captured large tracts of territory, and Chiang picked up hope.

Washington was getting very tired of the civil war in China. The American public was clamoring to get the boys back home, and could not see why, even if those Chinese didn't know how to behave themselves, America need go on wet-nursing them. The State Department took a less personal view of the situation. As Peabody's report had pointed out, there were grave possibilities of a Communist-dominated Asia. It was therefore decided once more, in the face of what must be described as a bitterly unpromising prospect, to try to coax the Communists and the Nationalists into a coalition, and form, in Truman's words, a unified, democratic, and peaceful nation. Ambassador Hurley, however, refused to try again. He was tired and he felt beaten, so he handed in his resignation. Truman thought of appointing Wedemeyer to the post, but Chou En-lai would have none of that. Another man became ambassador—Dr. Leighton Stuart of Yenching University in Peking—but it was thought that the task of getting the two parties together needed the superman touch, so General Marshall, who had just retired from his post as chief of staff, went out to Chungking. Marshall had been a patron of Stilwell's and expected, perhaps, to find the Communists as splendid as Stilwell thought them. If so, he was soon to be disappointed, but the situation looked fairly hopeful at first. His mission was twofold: he was to talk the combatants into making a truce and then unifying, and he was also to give a hand to Chiang in transporting troops and supplies to North China and Manchuria.

Marshall arrived in the middle of December. He found all official Chungking busy packing to move back to Nanking, but Chiang was willing to try another bout of negotiation, and so, it seemed, were the Communists. A cease-fire was arranged surprisingly quickly, and conferences began. They too seemed to go well. Between them, Reds and Nationalists worked out a Political Consultative Council of thirty-eight members, with eight from the Kuomintang, seven Communists, and the rest representing minority parties. Among them a resolution was passed for a national assembly convened on May 5 to draft a constitution. By February 15 conditions were even better: an agreement to integrate Red and Nationalist armies had been signed. Marshall, much encouraged, left Chungking on March 13 to make an interim report to Washington—and on April 15, as the last Russians withdrew from Changchun in Manchuria, Chinese

Communists seized the city. They continued to do as they liked in Manchuria until Marshall came back to China, then once again there was mediation and more talking. This time, however, nobody stuck to the cease-fire, and war went on in the North. The Communists were growing much stronger and were better armed. They had the use of plenty of weapons left behind by the Japanese: these had been turned over to the Reds by the departing Russians. Chiang's troops in Manchuria, moreover, were a long way from home, and were wedded to the standfast and shoot school of warfare. The Communist guerrillas were able to dance rings round them.

The government duly moved to Nanking, where everything was supposed to be all right and people could live happily ever after. It did not work out like that. Inflation was worse than ever, and brought much suffering. Officials who had held authority through the war years had grown chronically overbearing. Financial corruption spread rapidly. The trouble with Chiang was that he was not a man of wide vision. He was single-minded and had great powers of concentration, but these qualities, though they are virtues, can also be drawbacks in a place like China after 1945. The dishonest plundered, the humble suffered, the bullies swaggered, and the ordinary people, who had waited so long for freedom from the Japanese, found it all a great disillusionment. More and more Chinese, especially the poorest, began to listen to the Communists.

The negotiations were so frustrating that Marshall gave up his mission before a year was over. In Washington he explained his action in a report, saying in part, "Between this dominant reactionary group in the Government and the irreconcilable Communists who, I must state, did not seem so last February, lies the problem of how peace and well-being are to be brought to the long-suffering and presently inarticulate mass of the people of China. The reactionaries in the Government have evidently counted on substantial American support regardless of their actions. The Communists by their unwillingness to compromise in the national interest are evidently counting on an economic collapse to bring about the fall of the Government accelerated by extensive guerrilla action against the long lines of rail communications—regardless of the cost in suffering to the Chinese people." [North, p. 237.]

When Marshall returned to Washington in January 1947, the plight of the Nationalists did not seem at all desperate. They held plenty of territory in Manchuria, and could depend on America for aid: money still came in. In reality, however, they were doomed, and the Communists were only holding back, as they had done many times before, until they could deal one smashing blow: guerrilla tactics applied to the whole area, as it were. Suddenly they attacked all along the line. The Nationalist defense in Manchuria crumbled. Disintegration went on so rapidly that in July Truman sent Wedemeyer out to see for himself what was happening. Wedemeyer did not come in the spirit of friendliness he had felt in the past for Chiang's China, for the scandal of Formosa had intervened. Formosa, or Taiwan, which is its Chinese name, had been restored to China when the Japanese surrendered, according to the Cairo agreement. All the inhabitants except for one tribe of aboriginals are of Chinese stock, but in the many years they were ruled by the Japanese they had become like their rulers in habits and loyalties. A number of them had served in the Japanese forces in China, and earned a bad name there for brutality. At the time of the restoration a governor and some officials were hastily selected and sent over from China, with businessmen in their wake. The Taiwanese were hostile and the Chinese were at least equally so. The governor was oppressive, his lieutenants were worse, and the men who came in for business reasons were carpetbaggers of the worst sort. At last the Taiwanese broke out and rioted. The ugly story was told in America, to a public already conditioned by Communist propaganda. Though Chiang investigated, punished the governor, and cleaned up Taiwan's administration, the mischief had been done.

Grimly Wedemeyer surveyed the Chinese scene: his report agreed in most respects with Marshall's. The Kuomintang's reactionary leadership, corruption, and repression had led to a loss of popular faith in the government. The Communists were bound to the Soviet Union and aimed "admittedly" at a Communist state in China. The unfortunate moderates were caught between them and could not make their influence felt because of the repression of the government. However, said Wedemeyer, "Notwithstanding all the corruption and incompetence one notes in China, it is a certainty that the bulk of the people are not disposed to a Communist political and economic structure. Some have become affiliated with Communism in an indignant protest against oppressive police measures, corrupt practices and mal-administration of National Government officials. Some have lost all hope for China under existing leadership and turn to the Communists in despair. Some accept a new leadership by mere inertia." He advised Chiang to initiate drastic reforms, saying that it would be no use for America to prop up a government as unpopular as his. The war must be stopped in Manchuria and a guardianship of five nations, China, Russia, America, Britain, and France, set over it, or if this did not work, a trusteeship the UN General Assembly might set up.

It was no use. Chiang did not, or could not, start cleaning house at that stage of the game, and the swift decline continued, gathering momentum. In Manchuria the Communists won one battle after another. During the last four months of 1948 the Nationalists lost a million men, mostly by desertion, and half a million rifles. In October Mukden gave way, and North China soon followed; Tientsin and Peking went in January of 1949, Shanghai in May, Canton in October. Mao Tse-tung proclaimed the People's Republic of China on October 1. Chiang had sent his government to Taiwan before that, and now he went to join it, on the tenth of December.

Pu-i was caught by the Communists in Manchuria and made to work as a gardener and path sweeper. Serve him right, they reasoned, for having been an Emperor.

GLOSSARY

Chinese and Manchu names are confusing to foreigners until they are accustomed to them, and at first all seem much alike. It is well to remember that the Chinese place what we know as the surname first. Thus General Chiang Kai-shek is General Chiang, whose "Christian" name is Kai-shek. Chinese also have a custom that makes things all the more difficult for us, of using more than one "Christian" name in the course of a life. The bearer discards his childhood or "milk" name in favor of an adult one, or may be known by a nickname. Emperors' nomenclature is even worse for the unfortunate foreigner. A man succeeding to the throne acquired a reign-title, which strictly speaking was not a name at all. The Emperor commonly called "Kuang-hsü," for example, was in fact the Kuang-hsü Emperor. He also had a temple-name. To avoid being cumbersome, the writer has not been too meticulous about observing the niceties of reign-titles, and like other non-Chinese writers sometimes uses them as names.

Word comes from the East that the new regime in China is scrapping the Wade system of romanized spelling for Chinese characters, and writes —for one instance—"run" for the character meaning "man" instead, as in the Wade system, of "jen." It is actually pronounced "run," after all, and is a common-sense reform long overdue. But the change has not yet spread to these parts, and the writer, therefore, has cravenly continued to abide more or less by Wade, a standard of more or less being all one can ever claim to achieve. That is part of the trouble with Wade.

The following list is of people in the book with names that might give the reader trouble.

Aluteh. The Empress, wife of Emperor T'ung-chih and daughter-in-law of Tzu-hsi.

An Te-hai. One of Tzu-hsi's favorite eunuchs.

Chang Hsueh-liang. The "Young Marshal" of Manchuria, son of the "Old Marshal."

Chang Hsün. The "pigtailed general" of monarchist sympathies, who defended Pu-i and fought Sun Yat-sen's army.

Chang Tso-lin. The "Old Marshal," war lord of Manchuria.

Eugene Chen. West Indies born; the Kuomintang Foreign Minister, who broke with Chiang Kai-shek in 1927 and stayed on Russia's side.

Chen Chi-mei. One of the early Sun Yat-sen revolutionaries.

Chen Chiung-ming. War lord in Canton, sometime supporter of Sun Yat-sen.

Ch'en-huan. The title of Hung Hsiu-ch'uan's most trusted prince at the Taiping "Imperial Court."

Ch'en Tu-hsiu. Dean of the Department of Literature, Peking National University, and co-founder of the Chinese Communist Party.

Chiang Kai-shek. Sun Yat-sen's successor as leader of China.

Ch'i-erh-hang-a. Manchu general.

Ch'i-ying (Kiying). Manchu official sent to Canton to manage foreigners, at which he was considered peculiarly adept.

Chou En-lai. Runner-up for leadership of Chinese Communist Party.

Chu. Pretender to Ming Imperial title, adopted by Taipings as temporary figurehead.

Chu Teh. Communist general.

Chunghow. Manchu official who carried to France Peking's apology for Tientsin massacre, and went to Russia to draw up Treaty of Livadia.

Feng Yü-hsiang. The "Christian General," war lord and opportunist.

Ho Kuei-ch'ing. Governor General of the two Kiangs, later Imperial Commissioner.

Hsiao-ch'en, or *Tzu-an,* 1837–81. Empress, senior consort to Emperor Hsien-feng and later co-Regent with Tzu-hsi.

Hsien-feng, reign-title of *I-chu,* son of Tao-kuang. 1831–61, reigned 1851–62.

Hsü Kuang-chin. Imperial Commissioner for foreign affairs, succeeding Ch'i-ying; Governor General of the Kwangs.

Hsü Shih-ch'ang. Follower of Yuan Shih-k'ai.

Hsüeh Huan. Taotai of Shanghai in 1857, later Imperial Commissioner and Minister in Tsungli Yamen.

Hu Han-min. Official of Kuomintang.

Huang Tsung-han. Imperial Commissioner for barbarian affairs in 1858 and successor to Yeh Ming-ch'en as Governor General of the Kwangs.

Hua-sha-na. Mongol, one of commissioners negotiating with foreigners at Taku, 1858.

Hung Hsiu-ch'uan. Visionary, leader of Taiping Rebellion and self-made "Emperor."

I-liang. Manchu official who worked with Lin Tse-hsü and later with Ch'i-ying.

Jung-lu. Manchu official; maternal grandfather of Pu-i, last Ch'ing Emperor.

K'ang Yu-wei. Leader of Reformers group under Emperor Kuang-hsü.

Kuang-hsü, reign-title of *Tsai-t'ien,* 1871–1908. Reigned 1875–1909. Nephew of Hsien-feng, second son of Prince Ch'un (the first Prince Ch'un).

Kuei-liang. Manchu official. Treated with foreign invaders in 1854 at Taku, as also in 1858. Later Grand Councilor.

Kung Hsiang-hsi. Minister of Finance in Chiang's government, married to Soong Eling.

Li Chen-kuo. Colonel in charge of troops at Burma border.

Li Hung-chang. China's leading statesman before the revolution of 1911.

Li Li-san. Communist leader, founded cell in Paris with Chou En-lai.

Li Lien-ying. Another of Tzu-hsi's favorite eunuchs.

Li Ta-chiao. Librarian at Peking National University, co-founder of Chinese Communist Party.

Li Tsung-jen. War lord.

Li Yuan-hung. Revolutionary general, later Vice-President under Yuan Shih-k'ai.

Liang Ch'i-ch'ao. One of Reform group under Emperor Kuang-hsü.

Lin Tse-hsü. Imperial Commissioner sent to Canton in 1839 to stamp out opium trade.

Mao Tse-tung. Leader of Communist China.

Marquis Tseng. Son of Tseng Kuo-fan. First Chinese Minister in England and France.

Pai Chung-hsi. War lord.

Po-kuei. Manchu official, Governor of Kwangtung after Yeh Ming-ch'en's capture.

Prince Ch'ing. I-kuang, President of Grand Council until removed because of anti-Boxer sentiments.

Prince Ch'un (the first), 1840–91. *I-huan,* brother of Hsien-feng and paternal grandfather of Pu-i.

Prince Kung. I-hsin, brother of Hsien-feng.

Pu-i, last Ch'ing Emperor, 1906– . Son of second Prince Ch'un, Tsai-feng, and daughter of Jung-lu. After forced abdication of Chinese throne installed by Japanese as ruler of Manchukuo. Removed from that throne by Communists in 1948.

Seng-ko-lin-chin. Mongol prince.

Soong, Charles Jones. Friend and supporter of Sun Yat-sen and father of Mmes. Sun, Chiang, and Kung.

Soong Chingling. Second wife of Sun Yat-sen.

Soong Eling. Sister of Soong Chingling and Soong Meiling and wife of Kung Hsiang-hsi.

Soong Meiling. Wife of Chiang Kai-shek.

Sun Fo. Son of Sun Yat-sen.

Sun Yat-sen, 1866–1925. Leader of the revolution that overthrew the Ch'ing Dynasty in 1911.

Su-shun. Manchu of high degree who conspired against Empresses after death of Hsien-feng, and was executed.

T'an Ssu-t'ung. Philosopher and member of Reform group under Emperor Kuang-hsü. Martyred.

T'an T'ing-hsiang. Governor General of Chihli during British and French invasion.

T'ang Shao-i. Statesman who broke with Yuan Shih-k'ai over projected plan to make Yuan Emperor.

Tao-kuang, reign-title of *Min-ning,* 1782–1850; reigned 1821–51.

Tseng Kuo-fan, 1811–72. Organized resistance to Taipings, later Viceroy of Chihli.

Tso Tsung-t'ang. Military leader best known for able work in Northwest.

T'ung-chih, reign-title of *Tsai-chun,* son of Hsien-feng and Tzu-hsi, 1856–75, reigned 1862–75.

Wang Ching-wei. Follower of Sun Yat-sen who went over to the Japanese during their occupation.

Wang Ming. Leader of "Returned Students" group in Communist Party.

Wen-hsiang. Manchu official, one of first members of Tsungli Yamen.

Weng T'ung-ho. Tutor to Emperor Kuang-hsü who encouraged liberal ideas.

Wu Chien-chang. Merchant and official; Taotai in Shanghai when Imperial Maritime Customs Service was founded.

Wu K'o-tu. Official who committed suicide as gesture of protest against Tzu-hsi's behavior.

Wu Pei-fu. War lord.

Wu T'ing-fang. Revolutionary and Kuomintang official.

Yeh Ming-ch'en. Successor to Hsü Kuang-chin as Governor General of the Kwangs: captured by British.

Yehonala, or *Tzu-hsi,* or *Hsiao-ch'in Hsien Huang-ho,* or *Lao Fu-yeh,* etc. Best known to Westerners as "The Empress Dowager." 1835–1908. During the greater part of her widowhood, virtual ruler of China.

Yen Hsi-shan. Governor of Shansi, "Model Province."

Yu-hsien. Manchu official, Governor of Shantung and champion of Boxer Movement, later as Governor of Shansi commanded massacre of Christians.

Yuan K'e-ting. Son of Yuan Shih-k'ai.

Yuan Shih-k'ai, 1859–1916. Military leader who became President of new Republic of China and tried to make himself Emperor.

Bibliography

Anderson, Flavia. *The Rebel Emperor* (The story of Hung Hsiu-ch'uan, Taiping leader). London, 1958.

Appleton, W. W. *A Cycle of Cathay.* New York, 1951.

Ball, J. Dyer. *Things Chinese,* edited by E. Chalmers Werner. Shanghai, 1925.

Bland, J. O. P., and Backhouse, E. *Annals and Memoirs of the Court of Peking.* London, 1913.

——. *China Under the Empress Dowager.* London, 1910.

Bonner-Smith, D. and Lumby, E. W. R. *The Second China War, 1856–1860.* Navy Records Society, London, 1954.

Boxer, C. R. "Jesuits at the Court of Peking, 1601–1775", from *History Today,* September, 1957.

Bridgman and Williams (editors). *A Chinese Repository,* (a quarterly), Canton, 1833–51.

Cantlie, Sir James. *Sun Yat-Sen.* London, 1912.

Cantlie, Sir James, and Jones, C. S. *Sun Yat-Sen and the Awakening of China.* New York, 1912.

Carl, Katharine A. *With the Empress Dowager of China.* London, 1906.

Ch'en, Jerome. *Yuan Shih-k'ai.* Stanford, 1961.

Collis, Maurice. *Foreign Mud.* London, 1946.

Conger, Sarah Pike. *Letters from China.* London, 1909.

Der Ling, Princess. *Old Buddha.* London, 1929.

Doolittle, Reverend J. *Social Life of the Chinese.* London, 1866.

Duyvendak, J. J. L. "The Last Dutch Embassy to the Chinese Court, 1794–1795", from *T'oung Pao,* Vol. XXXIV. Leiden, 1938.

Eckel, Paul. *The Far East Since 1500.* London, 1948.

Elgin. *Letters and Journals of James, Eighth Earl of Elgin,* edited by Theodore Walrond. London, 1872.

Fairbank, John K. *Trade and Diplomacy on the China Coast, 1842–1854.* Harvard, 1953.

Fairbank, John K. and Teng Ssu-yo. *China's Response to the West.* London, 1954.

Fleming, Peter. *The Siege at Peking.* London, 1959.

Forbes, Lieutenant F. E., R. N. *Five Years in China*. London, 1848.

French, Edward Gerald. *Gordon Pasha of the Sudan*. Glasgow, 1958.

Giles, Herbert A. *A Chinese Biographical Dictionary*. London and Shanghai, 1898.

Gray, John Henry. *China*. London, 1878.

Grousset, René. *The Rise and Splendour of the Chinese Empire*. London, 1952.

Hahn, Emily. *Chiang Kai-shek*. New York, 1955.

Hamberg, T. *Visions of Hung Siu-Tshuen*. London, 1935.

Hickey, William. *Memoirs of William Hickey*. London, 1925.

Hudson, G. F. *Europe and China*. London, 1931.

———. *Questions of East and West*. London, 1953.

Hummel, Arthur W. *Eminent Chinese of the Ch'ing Period, 1644–1912*. U. S. Government Printing Office, 1943.

Hunter, William C. *Bits of Old China*. Shanghai, 1911.

———. *The 'Fan Kwae' at Canton*. Shanghai, 1911.

Hussey, Harry. *Venerable Ancestor*. New York, 1949.

Hyde Lay, A. C. *Four Generations in China, Japan and Korea*. Edinburgh and London, 1952.

Isaacs, Harold Robert. *The Tragedy of the Chinese Revolution*. Stanford, 1951.

Johnston, Reginald F. *Twilight in the Forbidden City*. London, 1934.

Jones, C. S. See Sir James Cantlie.

Kirby, E. Stuart. *Introduction to the Economic History of China*. London, 1954.

Kulp, Daniel Harrison, II. *Country Life in South China*. New York, 1925.

Kuo Ping-chia. *China: New Age and New Outlook*. New York, 1956.

Latourette, Kenneth Scott. *A History of Christian Missions in China*. London, 1929.

———. *A History of Modern China*. Yale, 1954.

Laurie, B. M. *Shanghai, the Model Settlement*. Shanghai, 1866.

Lindley, A. F. (Lin-le) *Ti-Ping Tien-Kwoh; The History of the Ti-Ping Revolution*. London, 1866.

Loch, Henry Brougham. *Personal Narrative of Occurrences During Lord Elgin's Second Embassy to China, 1860*. London, 1869.

Lumby, E. W. R. See Bonner-Smith.

Mayers, William Frederick. *The Chinese Government*. Shanghai, 1897.

Michie, Alexander. *The Englishman in China*. London, 1900.

Montalto de Jesus, C. A. *Historic Shanghai*. Shanghai, 1909.

Morrison, G. E. *An Australian in China*. London, 1902.

Morse, Hosea Ballou. *In the Days of the Taipings*. Salem, Massachusetts, 1927.

———. *The Gilds of China*. Shanghai, 1932.

——. *The International Relations of the Chinese Empire.* London, New York, Bombay, Calcutta, 1918.

Moule, A. C. *Christians in China Before the Year 1550.* New York and Toronto, 1930.

North, Robert C. *Moscow and Chinese Communists.* Stanford, 1953.

Oliphant, Laurence. *Narrative of the Earl of Elgin's Mission to China and Japan.* London, 1859.

Palmer, Norman D. See Shao Chuan Leng.

Playfair, G. M. H. *The Cities and Towns of China.* Shanghai, 1910.

Pritchard, Earl H. *Anglo-Chinese Relations During the Seventeenth and Eighteenth Centuries.* Urbana, Illinois, 1930.

——. *The Crucial Years of Early Anglo-Chinese Relations, 1750–1800.* Pullman, Washington, 1936.

Putnam Weale, B. L. *Indiscreet Letters from Peking.* London, 1906.

Richard, L. *Comprehensive Geography of the Chinese Empire,* translated by M. Kennelly, S. J. Shanghai, 1908.

Robbins, Helen H. *Our First Ambassador to China* (Lord Macartney). London, 1908.

Romanus, Charles F., with Sunderland, Riley. *Stilwell's Mission to China.* Washington, D. C., 1953.

Schwartz, Benjamin I. *Chinese Communism and the Rise of Mao.* Cambridge, Massachusetts, 1951.

Serge, Victor. *From Lenin to Stalin.* London, 1937.

Shao Chuan Leng and Palmer, Norman D. *Sun Yat-sen and Communism.* London, 1961.

Sharman, Lyon. *Sun Yat-Sen, His Life and Its Meaning.* New York, 1934.

Siren, Osvald. *The Imperial Palaces of Peking.* Paris and Brussels, 1924.

Smith, Arthur H. *Village Life in China.* New York, Chicago, London, Edinburgh, 1899.

Stilwell, Joseph Warren. *The Stilwell Papers.* New York, 1949.

Swinhoe, Robert. *Narrative of the North China Campaign of 1860.* London, 1861.

Swisher, Earl. *China's Management of the American Barbarians.* New Haven, 1951.

Tong, Hollington K. *Chiang Kai-shek: Soldier and Statesman.* London, 1938.

Waley, Arthur. *The Opium War Through Chinese Eyes.* London, 1958.

Wittfogel, Karl A. *Oriental Despotism.* New Haven and London, 1957.

Wright, Stanley Fowler. *Hart and the Chinese Customs.* Belfast, 1950.

Wu Yung. *Flight of an Empress.* London, 1937.

Index

E10

951   Ha
Hahn

China only yesterday

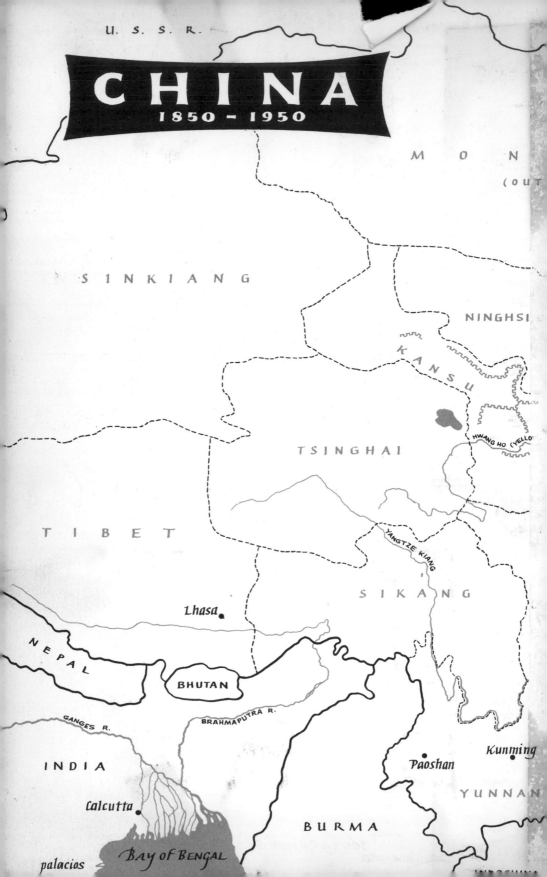

U. S. S. R.

CHINA
1850 - 1950

M O N
(OUT

S I N K I A N G

NINGHSI

K A N S U

HWANG HO (YELLO

T S I N G H A I

T I B E T

Y A N G T Z E K I A N G

S I K A N G

Lhasa

NEPAL

BHUTAN

GANGES R.

BRAHMAPUTRA R.

Paoshan

Kunming

INDIA

Calcutta

YUNNAN

palacios

BURMA

Bay of Bengal